GET TO THE HEART

GET TO THE HEART

MY STORY

BARBARA MANDRELL
WITH GEORGE VECSEY

BANTAM BOOKS
NEW YORK · TORONTO · LONDON · SYDNEY · AUCKLAND

GET TO THE HEART

A Bantam Book / October 1990

Book design by Glen M. Edelstein.

Library of Congress Cataloging-in-Publication Data

Mandrell, Barbara.
    Get to the heart : my story / Barbara Mandrell with George Vecsey.
      p. cm.
    ISBN 0-553-05799-5
    1. Mandrell, Barbara. 2. Country musicians—United States—
Biography. I. Vecsey, George. II. Title.
ML420.M219A3 1990
782.42'164'092—dc20
[B]   90-37575
                                             CIP
                                           MN

Published simultaneously in the United States and Canada

Bantam Books are published by Bantam Books, a division of Bantam Doubleday Dell Publishing Group, Inc. Its trademark, consisting of the words "Bantam Books" and the portrayal of a rooster, is Registered in U.S. Patent and Trademark Office and in other countries. Marca Registrada. Bantam Books, 666 Fifth Avenue, New York, New York 10103.

PRINTED IN THE UNITED STATES OF AMERICA

DH 0

This book is dedicated
to
my precious Daddy,
whom I dearly love and respect.
All the aspects of my life, Christianity,
family, and music were given to me by him.

Acknowledgments

So MANY PEOPLE have been important, but this list can only acknowledge those who were involved in preparing this book. Even then, I'm afraid we'll leave some people out. Still, here goes:

Ken Dudney, for reading and remembering, for being patient with yet another intrusion in our lives, for the trips to the airport and the helicopter ride for our writer and our editor, and mostly for loving me and taking care of me.

Mom and Dad, for being there whenever I needed them, as they have always been.

Louise and Irlene, who shared their memories and feelings, for forming an equal-sided triangle, the strongest unit of all.

Matthew and Jaime, for being willing to go back over the wreck one more time, and Nathaniel, for being himself.

JoAnn Berry, for being a close friend even more than the best agent a performer could have.

Alan Siegel, for persuading me it was time to do this book, and for being right, as always, and for Charlotte Siegel, for the mezuzah by the door.

Kathy Brown Shannon, for giving us ten years, starting as a hired assistant, becoming family.

Dr. Newton Lovvorn, Dr. David Jones, and Aubrey Harwell, for going over all the details I didn't remember.

Scott Salmon, for his memories of the television show. Tom Collins and Jim Foglesong, for all the good years.

My band members, for making George feel like one of the gang.

Jeannie Ghent, Kathy Gebhart, Kathy Nan McGee, Marcia Hestle, in the offices in Nashville, for putting aside all the other important things and making sure this book got done.

Ric Boyer, Bobbe Joy, and Earl Cox, for their skill and patience on that long photo session that produced a cover that makes me more than proud.

All the nice hotel people in Las Vegas and Atlantic City, who made it comfortable to work on the book on the road.

Marion Payne, Glenda Duke, and Phil Hobdy, who keep the house going, who always make my guests feel at home, and Jill Stowe, for stepping in so gracefully.

All my friends, like Minnie Pearl, Janice Lovvorn, and Tim and Cathy Bucek, for encouraging me about this book.

All my fans, for always asking for more, for making me want to keep going, both on stage and in writing this book. And all the good people at the museum in Nashville, for making it feel like an outpost of my home.

And finally, for the people at Bantam Books, who told me there was a book waiting to be done, and for Barbara Alpert, not only for her editing skill but for her enthusiasm. Now I understand how she ran the marathon!

Prologue

I'M DIFFERENT NOW

SOMETIMES MY HANDS SHAKE when I try to put on makeup for the show. Sometimes I try to recall old song lyrics, or put a name together with a face, and it all goes blank. Sometimes when I think about appearing in public, I get that queasy feeling in the pit of my stomach.

Until the wreck, the only time I had ever been nervous was the day I was married. I was eighteen years old and in love, standing in the side room with Daddy, getting ready to marry my dashing Navy pilot, and I started to quiver like a seismograph.

The great performers I had met when I was a little kid— Patsy Cline, Johnny Cash, George Jones—used to talk about stage fright. I never believed them.

"So, this is what it's like," I said on my wedding day.

I never again felt fear for nearly twenty years. Not even performing in Vietnam at the height of the war. Not even when Irlene and Louise and I were doing the television show. Not even when I won some of the top awards a musician can win. Not when I played the Las Vegas strip. Married life with Ken? Childbirth?

Piece of cake. Hi, I'm Barbara Mandrell. Let's do it. *One* magazine called me Snow White because I seemed untouchable.

Then came the wreck, September 11, 1984. A young man died in the other car, and my life has not been the same since.

Hardly anybody knew how bad it was. We kept it a secret, a family matter. For a long time I was a recluse, unwilling to see anybody except my immediate family and a few of my closest friends.

I had mood swings like a runaway tornado. One moment I could gush praise at my children, the next moment I could be screaming at them. I have apologized a thousand times to Ken for treating him like dirt. I don't know what would have happened if God had not given us a child—a gift, a miracle—in the middle of my pain, to bring me back to reality.

Now I'm back working. It just about kills me to get on the bus and leave my family, but I have a job to do.

"She's ninety-nine percent back," Daddy says.

To me, that sounds like the most gigantic one percent in history.

A while ago, somebody suggested I write my life story.

"You've got to be kidding," I said. "I don't even read anymore. How am I going to write?"

I used to curl up in bed with a Louis L'Amour western, but since the wreck I couldn't concentrate on the printed word.

"Nobody knows what you went through," one of my closest friends said. "You ought to tell your story."

Everybody knows Snow White doesn't do things halfway. When we were doing the television show out in Hollywood, I had to be coaxed into dancing, but within two weeks I was giving orders to Scott Salmon, one of the finest choreographers in the business.

It had to be that way with my book, too. I got together with George Vecsey, who had done books with Martina Navratilova, the tennis player, and Bob Welch, the baseball pitcher who is an alcoholic, and my friend Loretta Lynn, the Coal Miner's Daughter. He said he only did books with people whose lives might read like a novel.

We started talking about my parents, with their roots in the hard times back in the thirties, how their humble family band turned into a popular television show for their three daughters.

We talked about the twists of fate that put me on a highway when another car crossed two lanes and struck my car head-on. We talked about the painful steps back, the fragile balance between surviving and going under. And we talked about accepting the differences that could never be changed.

Now we have a book, although not the story I might have imagined a few years ago, the cheery tale of Snow White and her family. This became a story about tragedy, about a blow to the head, about changes. I'm different now.

1

THE SCARE

THE POLICE OFFICER TOLD us the only things in the man's car were tools, the kind of tools you might use for breaking in. He said the man had no belongings at the motel—no suitcases, no toiletries, no clothes, just grocery sacks scattered around the room.

The stranger showed up in front of our house one night around eleven, early in September of 1984. We were used to fans driving in front of the house, slowing down, stopping, getting out, waving, taking pictures. Coming home from an awards show, I was always thrilled to see a small knot of fans waiting outside the gate, bearing flowers, holding up signs that said, "We Love You, Barbara."

This man was different, lurking at the top of the driveway at that late hour. We have plenty of security to protect me and the children, but this man put us on guard, particularly with Ken out of town. As soon as I started to worry, I called the person most like me in the whole world, the man with the stare that I call "the Mandrell Look."

I can see that look in my wedding pictures, when my father brought me down the aisle, and I can still see that look when Daddy visits the house—his head tilting back slightly, his eyes peering slightly sideways at the rest of the world, as if to say, "This is who I am."

I've seen that same look in my father's family in photographs in my museum in Nashville—generations of Mandrells, movers, doers, trailblazers, settlers, all with the same steely cast in their eyes. Somebody might call it a touch of arrogance. I call it confidence.

Irby Mandrell was a police officer for five years back in Texas. I remember how handsome he was in his uniform, his boots, and his helmet, how strong and confident he always seemed, driving his own motorcycle, putting me over the gas tank with Momma riding behind him.

That night in Tennessee, I was a scared housewife alone with two children, wishing my husband were home. But I felt better as soon as Daddy said he would rush over. He did not stop protecting people when he left the police force back in the Fifties. And there had been an incident in 1981 that showed me Daddy could still handle himself as well as any officer.

It happened while we were living in California, working on our television show, *Barbara Mandrell and the Mandrell Sisters.* One night we had a business meeting with executives who were trying to talk me into things like bad language, lower necklines, risqué skits, things I just won't do. There were also business details I wanted to handle, but eventually I had to go home to sleep and I let Daddy and the executives argue—or should I say negotiate?

As soon as I pulled into the driveway, Kathy Brown, my assistant, came running out of the house, looking frightened.

"Barbara, call your mother," she said. "Your father has shot a man."

I hate to admit it, but my first reaction was, "Good heavens, he couldn't have shot that man over a business disagreement."

I ran into the house to call Momma, who told me what had happened:

After the meeting, my father drove home in his white Jaguar. He was well into his fifties by then, always in a business suit, with gray hair and glasses. He got out near his apartment complex and saw four young men sitting in a car. He had never seen them before, and his old police instincts took over.

Daddy says you never look directly at people you don't know, on the theory that if you just mind your own business, you won't make them suspicious that you're keeping an eye on them. Out of the corner of his eye, he saw two of them get out of their car and stand several feet apart. He kept walking, but as an old police officer, he put his briefcase in his left hand because he's right-handed.

All of a sudden, one of them pulled a pistol on Daddy when he was about six feet away, and said, "Give me your wallet." The other one stood at an angle.

Daddy acted as if he was hard of hearing. He said, "Huh?"

In his wallet, Daddy had a deputy's badge. They were mean-looking men who just might have reacted badly if they found out he was an officer.

"Give us your wallet," one man repeated.

"Huh?" Daddy said, still walking.

"I'm going to kill you," the man said.

Daddy believed him. He had one split second to decide what he was going to do. He remembered the FBI training he had been given, the drill where you hit the ground and draw your gun as you roll sideways. You see them do it on television all the time.

This man who had had two heart bypass operations threw himself on the sidewalk, rolled over, drew his gun from under his jacket, and shot the man with the gun, twice. Both men ran away.

"Fantastic!" I said when Momma finished the story. "I bet those two guys thought they had an old dude they could rob and kill. I bet he really surprised them."

Within the next few days, the police found the man who had been shot. He was in a hospital giving some story about how he got the two bullet wounds at a party. The police also found the two men had ties to a gang in the area. Daddy, of course, was not charged with anything.

The police officers who investigated the incident asked Daddy how he got off two shots while rolling on the ground. Daddy told them about his FBI training thirty years earlier. The officers looked at each other, and one of them said, "Yeah, that stuff's supposed to work. But you never know."

I told Daddy: "Roy Rogers has been my biggest hero, but you know what? I bet even Roy Rogers couldn't have done what you did."

I'm a law-and-order person. A hawk. There's a strong side to me that I'm only still discovering, the kind of business and military instincts we call "masculine" for lack of a better word. I've asked questions about my business with a hardheadedness some people might call "masculine." I stood up and entertained the troops in Vietnam with a war going on.

But I am also a blonde female singer, and glad of it. If I'd come along in a different time, who knows, I might have been a police officer like my daddy or a Navy pilot like Ken Dudney, my husband.

Guns don't bother me, as long as the good guys have 'em, too. I know a lot of city people are not comfortable being around guns, or even hearing a country person like me talk about them, but I grew up around guns, and feel comfortable with them, and I can argue my right to own them. Our fore-fathers gave us the right to bear arms, and I resent anybody trying to take that right away from us.

Daddy taught me to shoot, and then he taught my children, Matthew and Jaime. Lately he's been saying that he won't even compete with Matt in the range we built into our house because Matt is so good. But I think Daddy could still show us a thing or two.

On that scary night in Tennessee, I didn't think Roy Rog-ers was available, and besides, I had Daddy. He called some dep-uties and then he rushed over to our house on Old Hickory Lake. The man was gone by then, but they checked out the li-cense plate number and traced the man to a motel not far from us. They caught up to the man and asked him what he had been doing walking in front of my house at eleven o'clock at night.

"I'm going to get her," he said, which the officers said did not exactly constitute a death threat. I've had worse. Anybody in the public eye does. The officers could not just throw him in the slammer for a while, although I would have voted for it. Instead, the officers suggested that fall was coming on and maybe he would like to take off for a more hospitable climate.

He said, "Okay, I'll go to New York." Guess where my first stop was on my next tour. Daddy said he thought he'd go back on the road with me for a little while, like in the old days, when he was manager, agent, bus driver, mechanic, guitar player, paymaster, and father.

As soon as I heard Daddy was coming along, I felt better. That man could have been dangerous to my family. At the very least, he seemed like a dark cloud, a premonition. And the way things turned out, I guess he was.

2

IRBY

WHEN I WAS SIX, back in Corpus Christi, I always loved to
see the police car parked in front of our house. That meant Daddy
was home safe from his shift. It also gave me an edge on my
playmates.

If things were not going my way in a game or an argument,
I would say, "If you don't do what I want, my daddy's a policeman
and he'll put his handcuffs on you and take you to jail."

Unfortunately, one of my friends told her mother, who
promptly told Daddy. We are from a law-and-order family, and
Daddy promptly applied some law-and-order to me. He did not
have to read the Miranda warning to me because that Supreme
Court ruling had not come down yet. Momma and Daddy were
the Supreme Court in our household, and when I messed up they
took out the switch, and for that I thank them.

When he was finished applying the law-and-order, Daddy told
me that the last thing you want is for a child to be afraid of a
police officer. Suppose a child was in trouble but was afraid the
police officer would make it worse? So he took all the neighbor-

hood kids for a ride in the police car, showing them how the lights and the siren and the radio worked, letting them know that police officers are our friends.

I never tried to take advantage of Daddy's job again. I also never stopped thinking he was the most wonderful man in the world.

Even today, I sometimes think I'm too close to my father and my mother. I can't imagine losing them. Just the thought of it makes me tremble, and that goes back before the wreck, too. I'm not stupid. I know we're only here on the earth for a short time. Everything is in God's hands. But I don't want to think about what life would be like without my father and my mother. Perhaps I depend on them too much. I would not have had a career without them, but there is so much more than that. I still rely on them for advice.

Just recently I called my mother to say, "I want to apologize for all the trouble I caused you when I was a kid."

"You were no trouble," she said.

"Now that I have kids of my own, I just want to say this to you," I added.

Then I asked my parents for some advice. I was having a terrible time adjusting when Matthew went away to college. I missed him so much, even though we had been butting heads sometimes since the accident. The house just felt so empty without him.

I said to Daddy, "Momma has told me that in the past it was hard for you to let go of me and let me marry Ken. I never realized, but I sure realize now with Matthew going to college."

Then I added, "Even if it wasn't difficult, tell me it was."

Daddy answered: "Come on, you should be so happy. Here's your son going to college and you've never had any problems. What if he were a drug addict? Here he is, embarking on something, and he loves you so much, and you can afford to pay for his college." He kept pointing out all the positive, all the good, and it helped me. I don't care. When I'm a grandparent, I'm still going to call them and ask their advice.

I don't remember who said, "The older I get, the more intelligent my parents get." Well, I have always relied on my parents, even when they were making me do something I did not want to do.

I've learned a lot watching Daddy get involved in show business. He could have been an executive, a leader, if he'd had an easier start back in Arkansas. He might have become a police chief in Texas if he had stayed in law enforcement, but he had always been a musician, and so he wound up running a music store and having a family band on the side.

Some people will call him a stage father, which is often a derogatory term the way people use it. He wasn't a stage father. He was a father who raised his children to succeed. Our business just happened to be music.

He's a conservative man, a southerner, a police officer, a product of the Depression, a man's man. He and Momma wound up having three daughters, and if it ever bothered him not to have a son, we never felt it. He treated us like little ladies, but he also taught us there was nothing we could not do. "You can't be a brain surgeon if you don't go to medical school," I've heard him say. "But once you've qualified yourself, don't let anybody say you can't do it because you're a girl."

He has always known how to motivate me. I was a pretty good athlete back in junior high school, even though I was always short for my age group. One time a very tall girl beat me at the standing broad jump. Daddy walked over to me and whispered, "Old daddy long legs beat you by half an inch." That was his way of letting me know that I came close—and maybe could have found a way to win the doggone event.

There have been many times when I thought other people might be better singers or better musicians or prettier than me, but then I would hear Daddy's voice telling me to never say never, and I would find a way to squeeze an extra inch or two out of what God had given me.

When the feminist movement began in the Sixties, I was shocked to find it was such a big issue. I couldn't understand what women were talking about. I listened to women on television talking about being stereotyped, I heard about organizations for women, and I was stunned. My father and mother had raised their daughters to believe there was no difference between men and women.

I guess that's one of the reasons Daddy and I are so much alike. You do not have to be of the same gender to be a chip off the old block. I'm so much like him that we argue. Two hardheads.

We just turn sideways and give each other the Mandrell Look. A dead standoff. Me saying "Yes, sir!" and him saying "No, ma'am!" Both just as firm as you can be.

When we started to play instruments, Daddy said, "Don't ever let anybody say, 'You pick good for a girl.'" As far as I knew, there was only one woman in country music who played steel guitar, Marion Hall, and the saxophone always had a reputation as kind of a man's instrument, but those were the two instruments I played when I went to Las Vegas at the age of eleven. Later I picked up the Dobro and the banjo, two other instruments very few women played.

I don't think I'm the best singer or the best musician in country music, but I am very proud of being so versatile. When I run around the stage, going from instrument to instrument, what you see is Daddy's confidence in me.

I really don't know where Daddy got the idea that women could do anything men could do. Maybe it was just solid pragmatism, or maybe it was watching Momma accomplish anything she tried, or maybe it came from having three daughters and putting all his pride into them.

There were no women on the force when Daddy was a cop, but I've heard Daddy say, "I would have no objection to a woman riding with me as long as I felt comfortable that she wouldn't hesitate to pull the trigger or use the night stick if necessary." Daddy once tried to break up a fight in a bar in Corpus Christi and turned around to look for his partner. Later he found him sitting in the car. The man said, "Well, I thought I'd stay close to the radio so if we needed help I could get it." And Daddy also had a partner who saved him from a guy pulling an ice pick out of his sleeve. So you can see why Daddy would be a little particular about his partner, but he thinks women can be police officers.

It was the same thing with business details. Daddy would never say, "Now don't you worry your pretty little head about this." He didn't just call a shot, he would explain to me. I would sit near him while he was driving the bus, and he would talk to me about his theories about show business.

I know I would not have been nearly as good in business had it not been for my father. There's a family legend about the time I was around nine or ten and my parents got a note from my teacher. I was an A student except for arithmetic, so Daddy went over to see the teacher, who said, "What's interfering with her arithmetic is that she's in the glee club, then she goes to band during arithmetic period, and she also goes to all-district band during arithmetic."

"Let me ask you a question," Daddy said. "Is she doing well in music?" The teacher said I was doing just terrific.

"Well, is she learning enough arithmetic to be able to count money and figure percentages?" Daddy continued.

The teacher said I was.

"Well, that's great," Daddy said, "because all I ever expect her to do is play music, count money, and figure percentages."

The teacher must have thought Daddy was nuts. I'm sure Daddy would have pushed me if I was failing arithmetic. But he knew what I would need to know. You hear about female performers getting ripped off by their husbands or managers, but that could never happen to me because Daddy and Ken and I discuss every move we make.

I've often thought about where this stubborn independence— the Mandrell Look—comes from. I didn't just show up on stage one day, some pampered little princess, taught how to play an instrument and smile at the camera. I'm the product of a lot of strong men and women.

In my museum, Barbara Mandrell Country, on Music Row in Nashville, there's a photo of a strong-looking man on a horse, my father's father. Grandpa Mandrell left Sumner County, Tennessee, early in the twentieth century to help build the Cotton Belt railroad out of Little Rock. He was a rip.

Grandpa Mandrell used to supervise a whole crew of workers, and he wasn't afraid to use his fists. There is a family story about the time Grandpa saw a worker using a loaded whip on a horse, and Grandpa just knocked him down, no questions asked. You wonder where Daddy and I get it?

My father lived in Arkansas, Texas, and California, and I never set foot in the state of Tennessee until I was nineteen. But the first time I went there, it was like going to some ancestral home, retracing my family roots.

Some people think my name is one of those stage names, a lot of musical M's and N's and L's, like the Marvells and the Shondells, but it's my real name, an old Tennessee name going back a century.

We used to wonder where the name came from. Then Ken looked it up in the New York Public Library and discovered some evidence that the name was German, from the area that borders France. There was also reason to believe the name was originally Jewish, according to Dad. It could be. My father's family was Christian as far back as anybody can remember, but his brother had an old family name, Ira, which is often a Jewish name. So how do you know? My mother is Mary McGill, going back to Ireland, so that makes me a true multi-breed, an all-American.

We were always a little mystified why forty million people would watch me and Louise and Irlene cavorting around the television screen on a Saturday night. I mean, Irlene is funny, and both of them are beautiful, and the three of us can play a bit, but there was more than that. I think people liked us—and not just hillbillies, my people, but folks in New York and Los Angeles and Chicago—because we really were what we said we were. We were part of a family.

You saw us up on the stage, but you knew there were generations behind us, Mandrells and McGills, who cared for each other, who stuck together. It wasn't just the Mandrell sisters. It was the whole family. America pays great respect to the family, family values, even when the divorce statistics and the census takers show that more people are living alone, more families are separated. Whatever else people might think about us, we came from somewhere. We knew who we were. We were Mandrells.

I just barely remember my father's parents putting a leash around me so I wouldn't run off. I had so much energy, I was always a good prospect to take off down the street. I remember my grandfather walking me through huge stalks of bananas, as if we were in a tropical jungle in Africa, but my parents tell me, no, it was just an outdoor grocery in Little Rock.

I only got to know my grandfather when he was old. My grandmother had tuberculosis and sugar diabetes and was in the hospital in Little Rock. The only way she ever got to see me was if they held me up outside the hospital, and she looked out the third-floor window and down at us. My grandfather bought a little trailer and lived near the hospital so he could be near Grandma until she passed away. Then we brought him down to Little Rock near us and put him in a trailer park. One night there was an explosion from the butane stove. My grandfather didn't die of the burns but from a heart attack, three days after the explosion.

That's an awful way to remember an old man. I'd rather remember him the way he looks in the photograph in the museum, a tough young cuss on a horse, looking kind of sideways at you, the Mandrell Look.

The Mandrells were proud, hard-working people who did what they had to do to survive. My father's brother, John Ira, was a preacher, but preachers don't make much money unless they go on television, and that was not Uncle Ira's style. He supported his family by being a barber. The family tradition is that he always gave the boys their first haircut. He cut Matthew's hair for the first time, and Nathaniel's hair for the first time, just before Uncle Ira passed away.

Daddy's sister Thelma means so much to me. She's my aunt, my sister, my mom, my grandmom, my girlfriend. She's in her seventies, a nurse retired from the Arkansas State Hospital. When I was a kid, it was always a joy to visit Thelma and her husband, Eddie Sullivan. I just liked to listen to her talk. She's all the things I admire—strong-minded, independent, good sense of humor, good brain.

When I was just a little girl in Texas, no more than four or five, I used to pretend I was Loretta Young. Remember the way Loretta Young made her entrance on the television show, so graceful and glamorous and controlled? I would make poor Aunt Thelma sit and watch me do my big entrance. I'd find one of Momma's dresses and I'd put on a show and sing. And Aunt Thelma would sit patiently through it.

Somebody said that I talk about my family as if they were legends, which is true. Daddy and Momma are heroes to me. I would give anything for my three children to feel about me the way I feel about my parents, but I don't know if they do.

The wreck changed things with our two oldest children, put a wedge between us on a lot of things. They saw me hurt and vulnerable and acting angry toward Ken and toward them, and they could never quite see me as being totally in control after that. But at least they know I'm human. I'd like Nicole and Vanessa, my two nieces, to feel about me the way I felt about Aunt

Thelma. I want them to think of me as good meals and kind words, the security of my home. If they just thought of me as Barbara Mandrell, I would be disappointed. Aunt Barbara? Now you're talking.

I know this. My three children will always know what they've got as grandparents. Through the whole time since the wreck, my parents have been rocks for me. It's the way my parents were raised. They are from the old school. You do everything you can. Then you do some more.

Times were hard when Daddy was a kid. He had to work to support his family and never had the chance to finish his formal education, but he did find time to play in a band with a buddy of his named Clinton Johns, until Clinton joined the Civilian Conservation Corps. When World War II broke out, Daddy joined the Navy's medical corps, and was assigned to the *Sommelsdyk,* a Dutch ship carrying troops toward an amphibious landing in the Pacific.

One night—Daddy thinks it was Thanksgiving night—the *Sommelsdyk* was hit by two torpedoes, forcing everybody to evacuate ship. Daddy got into a huge life raft and there they were floating around in the Pacific, and he looked around at the sailors in the raft and spotted his high-school buddy Clinton in the very same raft. Clinton was a sailor assigned to the *Sommelsdyk.* What are the odds on a couple of buddies from Little Rock finding each other in the same life raft in the middle of the Pacific Ocean?

Later, Daddy worked in the oil fields, working like a dog for twelve to sixteen hours a day. And he worked even harder when he had a family to support. Daddy was a conscientious police officer. The only time I ever heard about him having any flexibility was when he and his partner spotted a string of speeders.

"Whoever is setting this pace, I'm going to spring a ticket on him," Daddy said. He barreled around the speeders and finally saw the lead car—a Hudson Hornet. Daddy decided to let that speeder go. With a salary of $267 a month, Daddy was not going to give his wife a ticket.

Money is always tight for police officers. I remember the Christmas when I turned five, I got it into my mind that I wanted a bicycle so badly. That was not so easy on a police officer's salary, but he signed on to be a security officer for two full weeks, working all but three hours a day.

He was still working that hard when Louise came along. One time he crawled home from his two jobs and he lay down on the floor and Momma didn't know whether to feed him or just let him sleep. He put his handcuffs alongside him on the floor and baby Louise came by and picked them up and whopped him over the head with them. He woke up bleeding, hurt worse by his baby daughter than he ever was on the job.

He also got me the bike, which I promptly dented by trying the old "Look, Dad, no hands" trick to impress him. Another Christmas he worked two jobs just to buy gorgeous red velvet dresses for me and my sisters.

He's had two heart bypass operations, but he still works hard. In the early days of the band, I used to sit behind him on the bus, putting cold towels on his neck to try to make him comfortable and to keep him awake and alert.

You always hear little girls say, "I want to marry my Daddy." Of course, little boys are just as possessive. A year ago, Kathy Brown, who has been a second mother to our three children for more than a decade, broke the news to my little boy Nathaniel that she was getting married to Bob Shannon, a wonderful guy. Nathaniel wouldn't give his permission because he wanted to get married, too. He spotted my wedding ring and asked if I would marry him. I said, "Nathaniel, I love you, but I'm married to your Daddy." Nathaniel was only three, but I think he understood. It was the same way with us. My Daddy was the greatest and I'm sure I wanted to marry him, what with the police uniform and the motorcycle and the squad car. I think that's a good healthy feeling, and it stands to reason that I wound up marrying a strong man, a military man, a good man.

With a police officer for a father and a Navy pilot for a husband, it figures that I am the corniest, flag-waving, patriotic person you ever saw. I just love police officers, firemen, military people who lay it on the line for us yet are underpaid and unappreciated. Teachers. We put our children in their hands. Nurses. They keep us alive when the doctors are not there. Those are very giving people, and yet performers and athletes get paid so much more. There's a lot of injustice as far as I'm concerned.

Wherever we traveled, I felt safe as long as Daddy was around. When we were doing the television show in California, I had to sleep on my bus on Wednesday night so I could get an extra hour of sleep between prerecording at night and taping the next morning. Daddy always left me his .38 pistol if he couldn't be there himself. I'm supposed to be a big girl now, but when there's a problem, I feel better just knowing I can call on the man with the Mandrell Look.

3

THE HOMESICK BLUES

WE NEVER HEARD FROM our evening visitor again. I felt secure as we played our dates in New York and New England, protected by Daddy and Gordon Terry, a burly fiddler and singer who had given me my first break in Nashville. Gordon didn't fiddle on this trip. He was there to help with security and deal the cards and crack some jokes about being my insurance policy.

But even having Daddy and Gordon along did not protect me from another visitor—the homesick blues.

I woke up one morning missing my kids even worse than usual—the emptiness a parent feels, the ache to hold them, to hear them, to feel them, to smell them. "Sleeping Single in a Double Bed" may have been one of my hit songs, but this wasn't a song on a jukebox. This was the real thing.

Ken was still off in Washington State fixing up a log home

for his grandmother. I was in a motel room in Cohasset, Massachusetts. Matt and Jaime were back home in Gallatin, Tennessee.

When they were little, they used to travel with me all the time, three hundred days a year, snuggling in the bunks of our tour bus, eating home-cooked meals, singing and laughing and playing. I loved playing those one-nighters. The time went fast, and it was just like the Willie Nelson song, "On the Road Again."

We've been lots of places, from Vietnam to high-school gyms, playing for forty million people on television or a few hundred convicts in a prison.

The prisons get to me more than almost anything. There is nothing quite like driving through those heavy-security gates, having the guards inspect the underside of the bus to make sure no guns or explosives are taped underneath, having the guard dogs sniff out your bus for drugs and weapons, and then hearing those gates clank behind you.

No audience loves you quite the way prisoners do. In Missouri one time, the men carved a monument from a big piece of stone from the old prison wall. They gave up their cigarette and gum money to have the stone polished with a plaque in my honor.

You know the prisoners have done something wrong, or they wouldn't be there. You forget their humanity until you stand in front of them. You think you're just "doing the show," until you're reminded what your songs might mean to these men. At one prison, a guard handed me a note from one convict asking me to sing my hit, "Years," which is all about the passing of time. I started to think about this man, how long he'd been away from his wife, and what time had meant to them. I sang the song, but it was not easy, what with the lump in my throat.

Later, I gave the guards a fit by walking down in the audience and saying hello to the men. I knew I had given my heart to the prisoners, and I was not afraid. The prisoners made us sandwiches and gave me a prisoner's shirt with my name on it. I hope I gave them as much in return as the love they gave me.

I have also played for Presidents of the United States.

The first President I met was Mr. Jimmy Carter, a truly religious man, kind and gracious when you saw him up close. I sang for him in Washington while the Country Music Association was celebrating its twenty-fifth anniversary. We didn't have enough notice for Bill Hargate, my designer, to come up with a new gown, so I called home and had one of my old gowns rushed to me. However, when I went to put it on, I discovered to my horror it was too big for me because I had been sick and had lost some weight.

Whenever I lose weight, I lose it in the bust rather than the waist. Ain't that the way it goes? When I put on that dress, I snapped down the built-in bra, and it just stayed pushed in because there wasn't enough of me to fill it out.

I had this sudden horror of bumping into the microphone and feeling that bra go *boing,* and me standing there with a sunken chest in front of the President. What was I going to do?

We were standing around the dressing room, about eight of us from Nashville—Dolly, Lynn Anderson, others. I put on this dress and asked Bobbe Joy, my dear friend and makeup artist, what I was going to do.

"Well, I have these powder puffs," she said.

"Give 'em to me."

She wasn't talking about the tiny puffs you might use when you're in junior high school and trying to make your sweater look like senior high school. These were large professional facial powder puffs. I stuffed 'em in there, and I looked great.

One of the girls said, "What if you take a bow and one of them falls out?"

"I'll powder my nose and toss it to the President."

I went out and did the show without any problems. A few years later, after Mr. Carter had left office, we were playing at Pennsylvania State University and Mr. Carter attended my concert. Not only that, but he wanted to say hello backstage afterward, which was great. The reception room was fairly crowded, so I sat on the floor next to the former President and we began to visit.

I had never dreamed of meeting great people like that, and I found it so comfortable chatting with him that I told him the story about my gown and the powder puffs. He thought it was the funniest thing.

Momma did not think it was funny. When I got home, I told her about meeting Mr. Carter, and she said, "Well, leave it to one of my daughters to say something like that to the President of the United States."

Hey, I just say whatever pops into my head.

Now it was September of 1984. Matt and Jaime were too big to trundle on the road anymore, and they had Kathy Brown, their "mini-mother," caring for them at home.

They grow up so fast. They didn't seem to miss me that much. I would call home and talk to Jaime and sense that I had interrupted her reading a book or watching a television show. Was my life getting away from me?

I wanted to be in my own house, drinking a cup of coffee, watching the kids get ready for school, doing some work on Music Row during the day, picking them up after school, listening to the babble of homework and television and kids squabbling with each other.

This morning in Massachusetts, I was desperate to see my children. I began plotting a way to get home. A few hours would be worth it.

"Let me see the itinerary," I told JoAnn Berry, my agent and my close friend.

The itinerary showed that we went by bus from Massachusetts to the Kansas State Fair in Hutchinson. I followed the road map with my fingernail—since I always wanted to be a jet pilot, the least I could do was read maps—and discovered something very interesting.

"We're passing ninety miles north of home," I told JoAnn. "Is there any reason we couldn't go home?"

"You'd only have about thirty hours there," JoAnn said.

"Sounds good to me," I said.

I remembered being eleven and twelve years old, the Sweetheart of the Steel Guitar as I was called in Las Vegas. I remembered how Momma and Daddy used to come with me on all my trips so I would not feel homesick. And I remembered how Momma managed to play in our first family band but still filled our lives with hot meals and birthday presents and kind words. I wanted to be there for my children the way Momma had been there for us.

4

MOMMA

WHEN I WAS IN high school, I used to be so embarrassed at the way my mother and father behaved. Momma would get in the car and sit next to my father like they were teenagers on their first date, or you'd see them walking down the street holding hands. Sometimes when I'd bring a date home, Momma and Daddy would be curled up on the couch, watching TV, and when the commercial came on, Daddy would say, "Commercial time," and he'd give her a hug or a kiss, and Mom in her cute way would say, "Oh, Irby."

Looking back, I probably said, "Oh, Mother," or "Oh, Daddy," but I thought it was nice they were so affectionate with each other. I know I feel that way about Ken. We have a family tradition called the three-way kiss where Ken and I just smooch with one of the children. We don't do it with Matthew and Jaime so much anymore because they're so sophisticated, but Nathaniel thinks it's great. And so do I.

Everybody thought my mom was cute. We lived in a trailer park when I was about seven, and I had a crush on a boy my age.

My mother used to ride my bike every day for exercise. She's such a health freak. When we were traveling with the family band, she would take a suitcase full of heavy things and lift it and lower it like a barbell because that helped keep her muscles toned. She never could sit still, which is where I get a lot of my energy.

Anyway, she would ride my bike, and one day a little note and a bunch of wildflowers arrived on our doorstep. I was so thrilled—until I read the note. It was for Barbara's big sister. Guess what. I ain't got a big sister. The boys kept asking Daddy if his daughter could go outside and play. And they did not mean me.

Jealous? Me? When we first started to travel to Asia with our family band, I was the seventeen-year-old blonde, but guys fussed after her. I thought she was so ancient. She must have been all of thirty-five, the age I was when I had the wreck, when I was just getting to the age where people were saying I looked sultry and sexy, and I kind of liked that.

You could see why Daddy fell in love with Momma, but don't let that shy little-girl smile fool you. This is a very talented lady who can learn anything she wants. I don't know how she does it. I can't teach myself things like that. I had a talent for music, so my teachers and I worked with it. Momma has a theory she can learn anything, as long as it's written down.

She did it with computers. Just started studying them until she could run the whole business using them. I hate computers. They are just foreign to me. I can hear a tune once and play it on half a dozen instruments, but I couldn't learn a computer if my life depended on it—which it might someday, the way things are going. But Momma just read a few books and she had it down pat.

Ken is Mr. Brain. He can program computers to do whatever he wants. Whenever he and Momma get together and start talking computers, Daddy and I look at each other and roll our eyes and start talking about something else. Momma's got our whole business locked up inside a computer. Where's Louise gonna be next month? Click. Momma's computer says West Palm Beach.

Momma comes from Fairfield, in southern Illinois, where there must be more than two hundred people all related to each other. Grandpa McGill died when I was ten, but I have great memories of him quoting from Scripture. Grandma McGill lived long enough to see our television show. She was a great old lady, mother of ten children, two of whom died early. But the others had such big families that Grandma wound up with almost two hundred grandchildren and great-grandchildren. Ada McGill was forty-five when she gave birth to Momma. Grandma got sick, so Momma's sister Leda, who also had a baby at the same time, breast-fed Momma for a couple of months. My momma was an aunt many times already when she was born.

I've been blessed in having a strong sense of family and place. Whenever I went to visit Grandpa and Grandma McGill, I used to think they had a huge backyard, but when I was grown up, I looked around and said, "This is not a big yard and this is not a big house." But from the perspective of a child, it was. I loved Grandma McGill so much. She always made me feel so special. She grew her hair all the way down to the back of her knees, so long and pretty, and she would let me brush it for her, over and over again.

Momma was just a little girl in high school when she met Daddy at the church in Fairfield, Illinois, where her brother, Ralph McGill, was the preacher. Uncle Ralph and Daddy's brother, Ira, had become friends somewhere along the way, and they kept in touch. When Uncle Ralph was having a revival at his church in southern Illinois, Uncle Ira and his wife, Marjorie, and Daddy formed a gospel trio and traveled up from Arkansas to perform.

Somebody told Momma there was a nineteen-year-old boy who might need some attention, so she was appointed his official hostess. She liked him because he was a cutup. They double-dated with my mom's nephew James and Imogene, who became his wife. Daddy would stop his car at night in the center of this sleepy little town and he would turn up the car radio and want to dance on the sidewalk. He was a live wire. Later, Momma found out he was twenty-three, but it was too late then. He had already proposed. He courted her for two weeks but then he had to go back on the road again, promising to come back for her. Six weeks later he returned with an engagement ring.

Momma had just turned sixteen, and was on the honor roll at the high school. A lot of her teachers tried to talk her out of getting married because there was a rule that no married students could stay in school. To this day, she doesn't know if it was legal, or just local custom, but she quit school to get married on November 15, 1947.

Daddy had promised that he would stick close to Fairfield, but after a few months he took a job as foreman of a painting crew in Houston, and took Momma away from home.

She was still a little girl when she became pregnant. And she was a long way from home when she went into labor on Christmas Eve of 1948.

Daddy rushed her to the hospital, but her labor seemed to slow down after she arrived, and she could not deliver. The hours stretched on, and Momma grew more and more tired, and it became a serious business. I was stuck there, head first, in no position for a cesarean section, not even close to a normal delivery. This was a Roman Catholic hospital, and some of the nurses and nuns went to the chapel, lighting candles, praying for the mother and the baby who might not make it.

Daddy was pacing out in the hall when he spotted a doctor.

"Don't I know you from somewhere?" the doctor asked.

"I was thinking the same thing myself," Daddy said.

They compared notes, and it turned out they had both served in the same unit in the Pacific. They got to talking, and the doctor said it was time to do something about Momma. He thought they could take the baby and save Momma's life, but that the baby might be lost in the process. The doctor said Daddy would have to sign a paper saying he gave them permission to use strong measures to take the baby.

At that point, Daddy wanted to save the life of his slender young wife, the woman he loved, so of course he signed the papers. They had to grab my head with their forceps and pull me out. I had been lodged in there so long that my head was totally flattened on the top—"almost as if it had been cut with a knife," Momma said later. But the nurses massaged my head with their hands for as long as Momma was in the hospital, and the flatness went away, along with the marks from the forceps.

Several hours later, Daddy was told that his wife was out of danger and that he had a healthy little girl. It was now Christmas afternoon. Daddy could have lost his wife or his baby or both of them on that day, but instead we were a family, a gift from God. Without that gift, perhaps there would have been no Louise, no Irlene, no Mandrell family as we know it.

I have always thought it was the greatest honor to be born

on my Saviour's birthday. Even as a child, we separated those two days. First came Jesus. We would thank God for the gift of Jesus, and we would bake a birthday cake for Him and blow out the candles. Only later, at three o'clock in the afternoon, would we celebrate my birthday with another cake and more candles. And we still do that in my family. My children bake two cakes, one for Jesus and one for me. Without Him, there would be no me.

After that long and grueling Christmas in 1948, the nurses came in and asked Momma what my name was going to be.

"I have to ask my husband," she said.

"He's leaving it up to you," the nurses said.

Momma had been wanting to call me Barbara Ann, after a high-school friend, Barbara Ann Holmes, now Thompson, who got good grades so easily and was always friendly and talented. Momma wanted me to be just like her. Now that Momma and the baby were safe, Daddy would not quibble over names.

Daddy still maintains he had another name for me, but he can't remember it anymore. Grandma McGill and my parents called me Bobbie as a term of endearment, but when I was in trouble I was Barbara Ann. In grade school, the kids called me Barbed Wire. Only two persons call me that now: Roy Acuff, the most important man in the history of the Grand Ole Opry, and his Dobro player, named Brother Oswald. Because I was always short for my age, the kids in school used to call me Shorty.

I didn't always like my name, but I guess all kids go through that. The only time I had another name for myself was when we lived in a mobile home when I was seven or eight. There was a crawl space under the house, and I would hide under there and play paper dolls. My favorite dolls, my alter egos, would always be named Lyneta, after a cousin of mine whose name is Lynn Pollard Stevens today. Even though she is four or five years older than I am, whenever her family was visiting from Phoenix, she would play with me. She was beautiful, a homecoming queen, and I loved her name, but I only appropriated it when I was playing paper dolls. Lyneta Mandrell? Lyneta Dudney? Hmmm.

I must have inherited some of Momma's energy. She says I walked at the age of six months—stood up, held on to a chair, reached out for another chair, took a couple of steps and then just kept walking. This was in Grandma McGill's house in Illinois.

Grandma said, "Look!" and I was walking. Momma was so stunned to see me walk so early that she was afraid to tell people, for fear they would think she was making it up.

Momma said I never wanted to be held, that after a few months I just wanted down, wanted to do something all the time. When I was about a year old, we were staying in our house trailer, and I started throwing a fit. Momma tried to hold me to quiet me down, but I screamed even louder. Then she tried giving me a bottle, to see if that would quiet me down, but I screamed and screamed until Momma laid me down, and she went outside so people wouldn't think she was beating up on me.

Momma had great instincts for being a parent. I wouldn't say I was particularly sassy, but I had a confidence that sometimes got me in trouble.

When I was on the Johnny Carson show one time, they got me talking about what a little stinker I was. I said I didn't get anywhere near as many spankings as I deserved—only we didn't call them spankings, we called them whippings. You violated a house rule, you got a whipping.

One time my mother was getting ready to whip me and I said to her, "You can whip me if you want to, but it ain't gonna do me any good." Well, she took me into the bedroom and started whipping me, and after the third lick I started yelling, "It's doing me some good, it's doing me some good."

After I told that story on the Carson show, you could not believe the mail we got from people saying how horrible it is to spank children. But I meant what I said. I've heard all the arguments against spanking, and I can appreciate what people are saying, but I feel spanking is a form of loving and training your child. I wrap my arms around my kids and kiss them after I spank them. I used to think my parents were lying to me when they said, "This hurts me more than it hurts you." But it does.

Some people say that spanking is a form of psychological or emotional abuse. The Bible says, "Spare the rod and spoil the child." I'm against abuse of children, but I think it's mental abuse to not love your children enough to discipline them. I think I would be cheating my children. Excuse me, but I think there are two extremes—no discipline at all, and child abuse. One's probably as bad as the other.

I don't think there's any greater compliment you can give

your parents than to say you want to be like them. I have always tried to pattern myself after my father and my mother. It is their image that keeps me hurtling home to be with my family.

After Momma got married, she continued to study shorthand, typing, and bookkeeping. Once I was born, she went to business college, but the people told her, "You don't belong here. You already know this stuff, so just go down to the unemployment office and they'll put you to work." She did, and her first job at seventeen was as secretary to the manager of the division of forestry and parks in Little Rock. When we moved to Texas, she took the civil service test. She finished at the top of two hundred women applying for the same position, and she got it, working at the naval base. She loved to work, and she would leave me with Aunt Thelma or whoever else was around.

Later, when we moved to California, Daddy took a job at Standel Amplifiers, and Momma worked as secretary to the president. And when Daddy decided to open his music store in Oceanside, Standel offered her a better job—with her own secretary— but she turned it down. They were going to have a band, and Momma was going to play in it.

Momma does not have natural music ability, but when she was about thirteen, she began studying books and teaching herself music on the piano in her home.

After she married a musician, Momma learned how to play guitar from him, and with the help of more books, taught herself to read music and understand music theory. After a while, she knew as much as a college music student did. She knew enough to teach somebody else the basics. I was one of her first pupils.

5
BACK IN THE BUS

THE BUS STARTED ROLLING as soon as I signed the last autograph. My theory was that if the fans cared enough to come to
my concerts, the least I could do was sign an autograph. It used
to drive my band members a little wild to see me signing when
we could have been rolling down the highway, but I owe my
entire career to the fans, so I stayed.

While the bus headed south, we sat up front and told stories. It's hard for me to wind down after a show. I cannot eat
my main meal until after I work, and then I catch my second
burst of energy and sometimes stay up until three or four in the
morning. Show business hours.

The bus is probably the most important instrument in
country music. A lot of people say we could get along easier
without our guitars or our hair dryers. Sometimes we fly, of
course, but the bus is usually the easiest way to transport the
show from place to place. Just stick the gear in the compart-
ments under the bus, the boss sleeps in the bedroom in her
bus, and the band sleeps in the bunks on the aisle in theirs.

When I was the opening act for the Statler Brothers in the late Seventies, they would invite me and Daddy on their bus to watch old western movies. They had a whole library and we'd sit up late at night, as if we were in our own living room. They'd bring popcorn from the concert just to make it feel like the movies.

We eat better on the bus than we do in hotels, too: fresh salads and fruit and meat from our refrigerator. We've got a microwave, a stove, and even a charcoal grill for barbecues.

You see our buses crossing the country on the interstates, me and Bill Anderson and Loretta and Conway Twitty and the rest—ships that pass in the night. A lot of good songs have been written in the late hours out on an interstate. A lot of lies have been told, too. In my bus, of course, we only tell true stories.

"Remember when you almost introduced me to Elvis?" I asked Gordon Terry.

We know all the stories by heart. I was a little kid playing on Gordon's show in Las Vegas, and Gordon was driving me around the parking lot of the hotel when all of a sudden he said, "There's Elvis."

There he was all right—pompadour hair and sultry eyes—heading straight at us, closing speed probably fifty miles an hour. These old buddies were playing chicken in a hotel parking lot. One of them swerved at the very last minute to avoid a collision. They were crazy and having fun with each other.

I always figured I'd get to meet Elvis somewhere along the line, but unfortunately that never happened. I feel a kinship with his macho southern blues, and I can always say I almost met him—head on. At the time I thought it was funny. I'm not too high on playing games in cars anymore.

In between the stories on our way home from Massachusetts, we played poker—nickel, dime, even a quarter sometimes. I once won a whole twenty-dollar pot.

Another bus where you just might find a card game belongs to Tom T. Hall, that great storyteller. When my Matthew was as little as my Nathaniel is now, Tom "adopted" him. Now that Matthew's in college, one subject he does well in is math. He should. He learned to count playing poker with Uncle Tom T.

When Matthew was about six, we were playing a show on

the ultimate rainy night in Georgia. Matthew was all excited to see Uncle Tom T. again, so he knocked on the bus door and found Billy Carter over there, playing poker. I didn't find all this out until later, but when Tom T. had to go play his part of the show, he looked at Matthew and said, "Matt, I've got to change clothes. Would you sit in for me?"

Billy Carter looked at Tom T. and Matt like they were crazy, but Matthew sat in, and here come the cards. I mean, they were playing for real money. Can I get them arrested by telling this? I guess not. Poor Billy Carter is gone, and Tom T. would have a perfectly logical explanation for letting a minor play poker. Anyway, Billy kept raising, and Matthew kept calling, and other people kept folding. Then Matthew raised and, as I remember the story, Billy Carter said, "I've got three of a kind," and Matthew said, "Well, I've got four threes," and he won the big pot.

Oh, yeah. After the show, Uncle Tom T. came back and gave Matthew a one-dollar bill for winning the pot, which must have been a couple of hundred dollars. Or maybe it was a two-dollar bill. Somewhere, Matt's got it autographed from Billy Carter and Tom T. Hall.

That same night, Miss Lillian, the mother of the President, visited me backstage. She found out my mother was traveling on my bus, and said she wanted to meet her. I said, "I'll be happy to get her," but she said she wouldn't think of making my mother get out of the bus on a rainy night, so she hiked over in the mud to meet my mother. That's the way that lady was, going out in the rain to welcome my mother to Georgia. Sooner or later, the real life in country music takes place on the bus.

On this night in 1984, there were only a few nickels and dimes riding as we rolled from Massachusetts toward Tennessee. The cards were really just a way of staying awake until all the stories had been told.

Kathy Brown went to sleep in the back. By the time she woke up again, it was already light out—and we were still playing cards. I took that as a sign it was time to get some sleep, so I went to my room with the full-size bed, which was a far cry from our first dinky bus that used to break down all the time. Old bus, new bus, I was still on the road—after nearly twenty-five years in the business.

6
MUSIC

THEY CALLED US PEW jumpers. Holy rollers. We went to Pentecostal-style churches where people believe in celebrating the Lord in music. My earliest memories of church are Sunday mornings with some inspired believer slamming away at the piano and sometimes the drums, picking the guitar and a bass, and people singing hymns.

On Sunday afternoon we'd have people over to the house and we'd sing some more—friends from our church plus friends who were Catholic. They'd break out the guitar and the banjo and the accordion and whatever else anybody had, and people from both sides of the fence would be playing and singing away—old-time standard gospel music like "Lord, Build Me a Cabin in the Corner of Glory Land" and "Amazing Grace" and "Precious Memories" and "I've Got a Mansion Just Over the Hilltop."

Just recently, I was in the recording studio, doing an album of old gospel favorites. I've always considered myself something of a lyric freak, but I suddenly realized I had not listened to the full meaning of the words in a while. I was singing "Sweet Hour of Prayer," a song that goes all the way back with me, and I suddenly got goose bumps right in the studio. The song talks about praying for a full hour, and I remembered that I had prayed for a full hour only once in my life, when Daddy had his first bypass operation.

So right in the middle of the recording session, I found myself trying to stay with the lyrics while promising myself to put aside more time for prayer. The Lord has given me so much and I have given Him so little back.

I believe this is the power of prayer, but it is also the power of music. If people love my music, if they buy my happy songs and my blue songs and, yes, even my cheating songs, which are all part of the secular world, then they should know where my music began.

To me, there is no better music than what people play and sing on their own in church. I am extremely proud that my Grammy Awards have come for gospel music (although I wouldn't have minded a Grammy in any other area, too). It's one thing Elvis and I have in common. His only Grammys were for gospel, too.

But my gospel is nothing compared to black gospel. That is the best. If I could hear only one more song before I die, it would be black gospel. On our car radio, a couple of buttons are always tuned to the black rhythm and blues stations in Nashville. Visit my dressing room before a show and, wherever I am, I will have found the local R&B station.

How does blonde Barbara Mandrell, sometimes known as Snow White, occasionally accused by critics of performing white-bread country music, warm up her voice for her shows? R&B, honey.

Don't take my word for it. Ask the girl at the Sam Goody store in Las Vegas. She was still shaking her head from my flying visit not too long ago. After I left, she told somebody with surprise in her voice, "Barbara bought Aretha Franklin and Teddy Prendergast and George Benson. She didn't buy a single country album."

Don't get me wrong. I love country music. It's my life. But everybody wants to be somebody else. The athlete wants to be a comedian. The politician wants to be a tennis player. The journalist wants to be President. We've all got our fantasies. God did not bless me with an instrument that could sing R&B. That's a fact of life.

I like listening to a symphony orchestra in person. It gives me the chills. I love all music styles, if played well. Dixieland, mariachi. Rap music. I'm for it. But in my eternal life, it's like I told a couple of my black girlfriends: "You may sing like that now, but when I go to heaven, I'm going to be a Navy fighter pilot singing black gospel music." They just laughed.

I understand that some of the strong feeling of the black church has to do with suffering and injustice. That has only made some of the blacks deeper Christians, brought that feeling into their music. I've seen prejudice, and I am against it. Scripture tells us to love one another. It doesn't say, "Love your brother or sister if they're white or black or red." It just says, "Love."

A couple of times I've visited the local black church where I live outside Nashville. The feeling and the music remind me of the little white churches back in Texas and Arkansas and Illinois and California, when I was a kid.

After church, of course, there was also country music. Daddy had a record player, and records by Merle Travis, Hank Thompson, Webb Pierce, Kitty Wells, and Bob Wills. Texas swing, all the old stuff. I used to love the bands, with the steel guitar and the horns and the tricky arrangements.

Sometimes the men would work on our house on the weekend and bring the record player outside. One time Daddy and Al Long and Charles Ott were building a brick wall, and the record player was going on this hot afternoon. All of a sudden I heard one of them yelling. The sun had moved until it was glaring down on those old vinyl records, melting them, warping them, giving them a scalloped edge like a seashell. The sun must have ruined a dozen records. But there was more music where that came from.

Daddy played guitar and bass in a police band in Corpus Christi. Once, to raise money for a police emergency fund, Daddy organized a country benefit show, and he brought in Johnny Horton, who recorded "The Battle of New Orleans" and a few other hits before dying a few years later in a car wreck while heading on up to Nashville.

When you think of it, there's been a lot of musicians who died too young—Buddy Holly, Hank Williams, Patsy Cline, Jim Croce, Otis Redding, Sam Cooke, Marvin Gaye, and but for the margin of God's grace and a seat belt, yours truly. Did you buckle up today?

Johnny Horton was known as The Singing Fisherman. Daddy still tells the story about going out fishing with Johnny Horton after the show, out on the intercoastal canal. Daddy caught two fish and Johnny Horton caught twenty-seven. Guess that's why they called him The Singing Fisherman.

We had country music on in the house all the time. Daddy's brother Al had a band, and he played drums in it. There were always musicians around the house, and Daddy was one of them, but he was too busy working as a police officer and at his outside security jobs to teach me to play.

The first person ever to notice my music ability was not my father or my mother but Grandma Ada McGill back in Illinois. Grandma, who lived to be nearly a hundred, always remembered your name and recognized something about you, when somebody else might have needed a doggone scorecard to sort out all the children.

Grandma had a player piano in her house, and she respected that old instrument so much that she would never let her grandkids beat away on it. Momma and Daddy were good disciplinarians, not like some parents you see today who sit back and watch their kids tear up the place and say, "Oh, what are we going to do?" They knew exactly what to do. They said, "Barbara, no!" But one day when I was three, I went and put my hands on the piano, and when Momma and Daddy tried to stop me, Grandma said, "Let her alone, she's musically inclined." I wasn't playing anything that vaguely resembled a song, but Grandma heard something.

When I was five, Momma taught me the accordion, the bass, and how to read music. She just put this accordion in my hands, placed my fingers where the notes were, and told me to squeeze. I don't want to brag, but music came as naturally to me as painting does to some people, or writing, or mathematics. I could just *do* it. In a few days, I was playing "Gospel Boogie," an instrumental with a kind of Pentecostal hymn feeling to it. I was pretty confident about my new skill, but in fact I still hadn't gotten all the notes perfectly.

We were visiting my mother's family in Illinois again that summer. On Sundays we would attend service at the Holiness Pentecostal Church, where Uncle Ralph McGill was the preacher.

My parents thought I was safely tucked away at Sunday school, so they settled into a pew for a morning of prayer and preaching and music. They did not know I had volunteered to play during the service.

To their great surprise, I suddenly materialized in the middle of the service, carrying an accordion about as big as I was, and proceeded to play "Gospel Boogie." The people seemed to like it, so I played it again. The ham in me was totally unleashed. It has never been tamed since.

Not long after that, Daddy became disillusioned with the new police chief in Corpus Christi and decided to leave the force. He heard there was security work at military bases in California, so we packed up our belongings and moved out to Lancaster, a hot, dusty town in the desert.

Daddy started to build up his music contacts. As soon as he arrived, he got in touch with his old buddy, Clinton Johns, who had played in the band with him back in Hot Springs and with whom he had been reunited on that life raft in the middle of the Pacific. Clinton was living down near San Diego, and he would come out on weekends sometimes and play the guitar and the harmonica, and he would encourage me to play. Another friend, Larry Barker, also played Sunday gospel music on the steel guitar and I would listen to him.

One of our weekend visitors was a man named Carmen Botticello, who worked at Edwards Air Force Base. I was intrigued by the way he played the steel guitar in a pop style, songs like "Indian Love Call," and he began teaching me to play.

At about the same time, Daddy became friendly with Norman Hamlet, a steel guitar player who was booked into a local club on weekends. Norman had been paying for a motel, so Daddy invited him to stay with us whenever he had to be there overnight. It was inevitable that Norman would practice his steel guitar in the house, and you-know-who would place her chin on the steel, and observe from up close.

I thought Norman could play pretty good. My judgment must have been all right, because he's been Merle Haggard's steel man and band leader for more than twenty years. In turn, Norman thought I showed some promise, too. He would show me how to play the country pedal steel for three and four hours at a time.

Norman was a marvelous teacher. He played so fine, but he

could also explain things so it all made sense. I could hear a lick of Norman's and imitate it, maybe not as good, but you knew who I was copying. It was like somebody throwing you a ball for the first time and you just put your hand out and catch it. And you say to yourself, "Oh, yeah, I can do that." It was just that natural.

One time Norman took me to a little homemade studio with his friends who were all professional musicians, and they let me sit in with them. I think I had been playing about four months. They were impressed with me, and they recorded our session, which was special to me. I look back and I know now how difficult this stuff is, and I think, "How did I play that? How could they let me play with them?" Daddy still has a copy of that tape. I listen to it, and I cannot believe it.

Momma says in retrospect that I was probably a child prodigy, but we didn't think in those terms. I was just a kid who could play music easily. Sometimes Norman would get mad because he thought I wasn't listening, but when he asked me to play it back, I could repeat it, note for note.

Momma still tells the story about Norman bringing his band to the house to work with me. When they were leaving, one of the band members told her, "Norman kept telling us how great she was, but the minute I saw her, I didn't have to hear her play, I knew she could do it." To me, that's kind of scary, to think a ten-year-old kid could affect a grownup professional musician that way. But you look at what people like Mozart could do when they were children, or mathematical geniuses at the age of ten. It was a gift from God. The hard part was using it the right way.

To my mind, I am really a steel player, more than a singer, more than a jack-of-all-trades. I used to be a million times better than I am now. I don't think the steel gets the credit it deserves. People think of it as a novelty item on Hawaiian records or something, but no one's ever reached the potential of the instrument. I bet if you had asked Mr. Segovia if he had ever mastered the classical guitar, he would have said that it was impossible, that you could never fully know that instrument.

Well, people like Norman Hamlet, Doug Jernigan, Julian Thorpe have expanded the potential of the steel guitar, made it a great instrument. Curley Chalker, a guy I met when I was a kid, would watch Ella Fitzgerald in the jazz clubs, listen to her scats, and try to duplicate her notes on his steel guitar. So please don't tell me it's just a novelty instrument.

I think I love the steel because it's so versatile, so mysterious. No matter what I learned, there was more. All these guys played with such different styles, they got so much out of it. There seemed to be no boundaries to the steel guitar, and I was hungry to play it.

My dad is a great coach. He couldn't pick a lick on steel, but he could teach. More mellow. More staccato. He would sing a song and tell me what key, tell me to use my ear and start picking. Practicing would have been very boring if Daddy had not been there with me.

Two weeks after I started the steel guitar, my school began offering band lessons. Daddy drove up to Los Angeles to buy me an old silver alto sax that had been overhauled. Momma's lessons really helped, because it's hard enough to learn how to hold the saxophone and not make the reed squeak all the time without having to think, "What is that—a C or a D?"

My first solo was "Milk Cow Blues," an old Bob Wills song. I didn't know the tune, so Daddy hummed it for me. Then he did the same thing with "Twelfth Street Rag," "Hey, Good-Lookin'," and "Goodie Goodie."

Daddy knew I hated the school band harmonies because I wanted to be a soloist, and my part was not even a recognizable melody. But he would take a clothes hanger and beat out the tempo on the music stand until I had my part right.

His attitude was, "Do your job." Momma's was, "Study it until you get it right." I still hear those voices as I follow my professional career. They are not the voices of stage-struck, get-rich-quick parents. They are the voices of honest workers, paid to do a job. I am fortunate enough to carry a Gucci bag, but to me it's the same thing as a lunch pail.

7

A Shopping Expedition

W<small>E GOT HOME ON</small> a Monday evening, just as it was getting dark. I rushed into the house to greet Matthew and Jaime, I was so glad to see them.

Kathy was outside, helping to unload the bus. I called to her, "I want you to go shopping with me tomorrow." I had some errands to run out in Hendersonville, and I wanted some company. She didn't look thrilled about it, so I said, "Never mind. Take the day off. Somebody else will go with me."

Even with Ken away, it felt great to be home, to be stealing a full day from the road. The next morning, the kids went off to school, busy with their own lives. Louise couldn't go shopping with me because she had a cold, and my friend Gail Cook couldn't make it, either, but I didn't mind. I felt great, puttering around the house, feeling as if my real life had begun again, even if for only a few hours.

I was wearing mauve silk pants and a beige blouse. Somewhere around the house, I've still got those pants, all blood-stained and jagged from where the doctors cut them off me.

In the afternoon, I drove my beautiful Jaguar across town to pick up the children to go shopping. I was not wearing a seat belt. Didn't believe in them.

This shopping trip was to furnish Grandma Esther Johnson's log home that Ken was building out in Washington State. Being perfectionists, Ken and I couldn't just build a log home; we had to fill it with antiques and completely prepare it for Grandma.

I knew a shop in Madison, near my house, where they had all the good stuff—bellows, irons, shaving equipment, an old oxen yoke, a saw, great wall decorations for this contemporary log home.

I picked up Matt and Jaime at their Christian school. One of the children from the neighborhood was supposed to ride home with us that day, but we told him we were going shopping, so he made other plans.

We stopped first at the bank window at the Rivergate Mall to get cash and then we went to the antique place on Gallatin Road. Jaime had homework to do, and I could tell she was getting fidgety. She's a reader. If you can't find her at home, she's probably in her room, reading a book. When she says she has to do her homework, it's no act.

We spotted a pretty log dollhouse in the store. I bought it for Jaime, and then finished my shopping. The woman said she could pack the things in large wooden crates and ship them out to Washington. I thanked her and got back into the car with only the dollhouse.

It was around six o'clock, still plenty of daylight as we headed home along Gallatin Road, where Grandpa Mandrell used to ride his horse early in the century. We were riding in my 1982 silver XJ6 Jaguar. Matthew was in the front seat and Jaime was in the back reading the Bible. Her homework that night was to memorize the names of the books of the Old Testament, and she was reciting them out loud as we drove along.

The Bible reminded me of something. I was saddened because Loretta Lynn's oldest boy, Jack Benny, had died in an accident in July. I remember asking Loretta if she read her Bible on the road, and she said it was difficult to focus with the bus being so bumpy. I had meant to buy her a Bible with large print, but I had not done it yet.

Maybe thinking about Loretta's tragedy put me in a different frame of mind. I'll never know. I cannot remember this, but the children tell me that as I passed a cemetery, I said, "Now that's where I would like to be buried when I die." Jaime said she thought it was "sort of weird" for me to be talking about that, but children don't like to hear grownups talk about death. I guess we all start off thinking we're immortal.

The strange thing is that I had never given any thought to where I would want to be buried, and I doubt that I would have chosen that particular cemetery. But both children say I said it.

A lot of details have been blown out of my memory, but I do remember stopping at a red light on Gallatin Road. A station wagon was in front of us with the tailgate down and a few children frolicking in the back, inches from the edge. If the driver had to slam on the brakes or turn suddenly, those little kids could have been thrown out into the roadway, under the tires of oncoming cars.

"Look at that, Momma," Jaime said.

The foolishness of the driver made me want to lean out the window and say, "Hey, your tailgate is down." But the moment passed, and the wagon was gone, with the little kids wriggling around, inches from death.

"That's insane," I blurted. "I think we should put on our seat belts."

That was not my position on seat belts. Up until that moment, I never used the dad-gum things. I truly believed seat belts were the device of liberal politicians to further take away our civil rights. Honest. I had every excuse ever made not to use them:

Seat belts were uncomfortable. They were designed for men. They cut across you at the wrong angle. They mussed up your hair. They wrinkled your clothes. If there's a wreck, I want to be able to get out in case of a fire. I don't want to be strapped in my seat. Federal bureaucrats are always trying to tell us how to live our lives. It's a plot. Freedom is what America is all about.

I had used every one of those reasons at one time or another.

But it wasn't my voice I was hearing at that moment, out on Gallatin Road.

I was hearing Louise's voice.

On our old television show, Louise is The Beautiful One. Irlene is The Funny One. I am The Bossy One. Those were the roles assigned to us by the people who conceived our television show. We're much more complicated than all that, but there is a lot of truth to the stereotypes.

Louise is like Momma—our certified health freak. Doesn't smoke. Eats healthy foods. Exercises. Louise is also one pretty tough cookie. She loves playing Las Vegas with her group because they can play outdoors so much. She'll be up early the next day after doing a couple of shows and organize a water volleyball game in the hotel pool.

Or maybe a softball game. I could tell you about the time Louise was playing catcher for her softball team and her very own husband, R. C. Bannon, came barreling home trying to score a run, and they collided at home plate, but she held the ball with blood dripping down her chin.

"You're out!" she shouted. "Now take me to the hospital."

She did the show that night with stitches in her chin. Tough.

Louise also loves traveling because she can organize a shopping expedition at the drop of a credit card. That girl was born to shop. And we are talking Neiman-Marcus. She is very generous, always giving people gifts she buys on afternoon forays through the nearest mall.

One other thing Louise dispenses with regularity is advice. And one of her biggest causes is the use of seat belts.

You cannot get in the car with Louise without putting on your seat belt. Being the oldest sister had some perks on the television show. I got to be the boss. In Louise's car, she was the boss. You wanted a ride, you put on a seat belt.

Not only that, she would lecture you: "If you have to stop short, that seat belt will keep your head from cracking like a hard-boiled egg on the dashboard or the window. It could save your life."

And I would yawn and say, "Sure, Louise." And she would

dangle the car keys in her hand until I buckled the doggone thing. It was a Communist plot, and Louise had gone over to the enemy.

So when we saw those little kids hanging out the back of the station wagon that afternoon on Gallatin Road, God was with me and my family. But the way He protected me was through the prim, proper, infringe-on-your-liberties voice of Louise Mandrell.

"Buckle up," I said.

The kids looked at me as if I had gone nuts. This was not the Momma they knew. They rustled around in their seats, thinking it would pass.

"Buckle up. I mean it."

They buckled up. We headed east, just a few minutes from home.

Doggone Louise.

8

SISTERS

AFTER FIVE YEARS OF being an only child, I had gotten to like it. I wasn't pampered, but I had loads of relatives and friends fussing over me.

For nearly nine months, Momma and Daddy talked up the notion of how nice it was going to be to have a new baby. I was going to be a Big Sister, with all the benefits and responsibilities that entailed. People had cared for me, and now when my turn came, I was to care for others. But my parents were not convinced I was seeing it that way.

The baby was born on July 13, 1954, and this time Momma had an easier time with childbirth. A few days later, Daddy brought Momma and the baby home. With me watching, he stormed into the house, shouting: "They gave me the wrong baby. Look at all this black hair. This is not my baby."

With that, Daddy rushed into the bathroom, closed the door, and announced he was going to flush her away. The next sound I heard was the rushing of a couple of gallons of water.

I didn't really believe he would do such a thing, but just in case, I opened the door, and there was the baby, resting in the bathtub. Daddy had just been teasing me. It sounds kind of crude and cruel the way we tell it, but it had the desired effect. From that moment on, she was my baby, too.

Years later, I asked him why he did it, and he said, "Oh, I knew what I was going to do. I had it figured out when I got out of the car." There isn't much that Daddy doesn't plan out in advance.

From that moment, Daddy knew that I was part of the team. I was fiercely protective of my sisters, the way my parents had been of me.

They named her Thelma Louise, the first name for the aunt who had suffered through my Loretta Young imitations, and the second name for a cousin on the McGill side.

We called her by her middle name right away, but to me she was always Sissy. Still is. She was part tomboy and part mystic, a middle child with her own secrets, a woman whose beauty sometimes obscures her music and her feelings.

She was such a pretty baby, with that thick dark hair. It might have given most big sisters a complex, but not me. I did not mind that I thought I was a homely little girl with a Buster Brown haircut and very red hair (which eventually turned blond). Even though Louise had this beautiful black hair, blue eyes, pretty features.

I'm not trying to be Miss Modest. If we're sitting around washing our hair and getting ready for a show or something, I can't help noticing that Irlene's hairline is pretty while mine is not. Even with four or five inches of makeup, I still cannot match Louise's eyes and eyebrows.

And short? I was always short for my age, and the truth is, I never minded. I've always made jokes about being short, and I've enjoyed people poking fun at me. I wouldn't change it. I like having my clothes custom-made by Winnie-the-Pooh. I particularly like the pajamas with the little feet at the bottom.

I don't mind that God made my middle sister The Statuesque One. I always tell people, "Well, we didn't have much money, so Momma gave Louise all the vitamins." As for me, I've always wanted to catch a chest cold. I just never had a place to put it. Do I have a complex? Not me.

I claimed Louise as my responsibility. While Momma was making dinner, I had to watch Louise like a hawk or else she would grab a cube of butter off the table and eat it like a hunk of candy.

On January 29, 1956, Ellen Irlene was born. Daddy likes to tell her that he was going to call her Irbalene if she was a girl— sounds like a shampoo to me—or Irbus if she was a boy. To me she was always Ene or Enie. Still is.

We almost lost Irlene when she was less than a year old. We had moved to California, and Daddy was working in security at Edwards Air Force Base. Not long after we got there, Daddy had to swerve his little Volkswagen Beetle to avoid an oncoming truck. Daddy was thrown clear, Momma was knocked unconscious, but Irlene was pinned under the front hood. She was trapped under the car, which rolled over six times, and when the car stopped in a ditch, it was upside down.

Daddy raised the front end by himself and pulled Irlene out. They rushed her to the hospital, where it was discovered she had a brain concussion and a broken leg.

This was the first time my parents had ever left me alone with Louise because they were just going on this short trip home from work. I didn't worry when they didn't come back right away. I made a salad, set the table, and thought it was fun. Then I saw Momma and Daddy getting a ride home, with Daddy's uniform all dirty, and I found out they'd had a car wreck.

Fortunately, Irlene recovered. She was just starting to crawl, so they set a cast for her to scoot around the house. Later, they set the cast so she could hold onto a chair and try to walk with it. We used to reassure her that at least the *leg* healed properly— meaning that one of Irlene's roles is The Naive One. But since my wreck, I don't make jokes about head injuries.

That was just the start of what the family came to call "The Perils of Irlene," after the Saturday-afternoon movie serial thriller *The Perils of Pauline.* She had so many accidents that I used to complain she was only doing it so she could get a present.

"I'm going to jump off the stairs," I would threaten, just so I could get some sympathy too. My two sisters would laugh and say, "You could fall down a mountain and only get a scratch." Those were our roles. I was the formidable one, the leader. They looked up to me. I was rarely hurt. I was indestructible. I never felt any responsibility or pressure to be the leader, I just was. I was the oldest.

The three of us were The Mandrell Sisters as soon as my

parents had the good sense to get us all assembled. Our stage was in a trailer or in a series of small houses out in California. We had pets, we put on shows, we played with dolls, all the normal things. We put on Christmas shows and Easter shows and Halloween shows. We wore costumes, sang songs, danced, clowned, did dopey things. Like Judy Garland and Mickey Rooney used to say in all those movies—"Hey, let's do the show right here in the garage." We were doing them in the living room.

Usually with me giving the orders. I loved being a big sister so much that I took charge automatically. I went to their classes, I organized the shows in our living room, I fussed over their clothing and their hair. I included them in whatever I was doing, not to be bossy, I liked to think, but because that was what big sisters do. My parents never treated one of us as special, never tried to divide us.

But I was definitely the leader of the pack. I would give the marching orders to Louise and Irlene whatever was going on. If we were making a dinky little home movie, I'd say, "What can we get Irlene to do?" and maybe suggest that she skip around and look busy. I would organize carol-singing expeditions at Christmastime.

After Momma and Daddy bought us a two-foot-deep swimming pool, I'd make up a whole elaborate scenario about us being frogmen, or frogwomen, or frogpersons, or whatever we were, and say, "Don't make any waves," while we made believe we were sneaking onto an enemy ship. Or I'd decide we should climb a tree and pick green apricots.

When we lived in Vista, we had an old dead avocado tree with a tree house already built in the branches. We'd climb up there and, keeping our voices down, we'd whisper, "Better not tell Daddy. If he sees us up here, he'll make us get down." That added to the danger of it.

We liked to live dangerously sometimes. One time I made strawberry shortcake and put whipped cream on everybody's except Daddy's, which had shaving cream. Daddy is a hearty eater when he likes something, so he scooped up a great big bite of this shortcake and then spat it out all over the table. We thought it was funny, but he was not real amused.

We were always active outdoors, getting into things. One time Irlene was just skipping on the grass when she fell down and broke her arm. The break was so close to the growth control center that they didn't know for forty-eight hours if her arm would grow anymore from the elbow down. They didn't set it, and the arm is still slightly crooked, although nobody can tell except Irlene, and it certainly did not hamper her drumming.

From the moment we were put together on this earth, we became a unit. The Mandrell Sisters. We might quarrel over a game or an item of clothing, but we never had any natural pairings, any two-against-one stuff. I think if Daddy and Momma had caught us taking sides, they would have busted all three of us. Sisters stick together. People would say, "Barbara and the little girls," but that was only because I was older.

Our childhood was a happy blur of homemade cookies and pretty dresses, church and company, little shows we would improvise in the living room, animals all over the place, bandages and bruises, games and music. I can tell you our childhood was not very different from what we did on television for two seasons. The writers of the show just had to know us for a few weeks and they could fill in the blanks. Or one of us would say, "Hey, remember the time . . ." Whether it happened in Lancaster or Palmdale or El Monte or Oceanside, it worked on television.

Holidays were played out like a ritual supplied by a script writer. We all had our roles. Daddy has always been terrible about having to know what you have bought for him. He cannot wait. One Christmas, I bought him an engraved gold lighter, and I hid it in a shoebox, and wrapped it, and put it in a grocery bag, and put it in a bigger box, which drove him nuts.

Now, I never should have been this stupid, but one day I picked up the phone and a high-pitched voice said, "Hi, what'd you get your daddy for Christmas?" and I said, "A gold lighter," and the voice dropped a few octaves and said, "Thank you very much." Nowadays, whenever he wants to tease me, Daddy will say, "What'd you get your daddy for Christmas?"

Mealtimes were for getting together, chattering about what we were doing. Our parents were interested in us no matter how busy they were. Momma was a good cook. I'd come home and smell potatoes frying, and couldn't wait for dinner, so she'd give me a slice of raw potato, which I still love with a little salt on it.

She would fry doughnuts, which were so good, and her absolute all-time treat was tomato soup with lots of pepper in it. I am always after Momma to make a batch of tomato soup for me to take on the bus, but she says it's only good if you eat it right on the spot. I guess there are some things about childhood you cannot recapture, and one of them is all of us sitting around the table eating homemade tomato soup.

Also at dinnertime, when Momma or Daddy was not looking, one of us would take food from our plates and feed it to the latest puppy. Momma said I favored our puppies so much that I didn't eat enough.

One time we found a bird shivering and fluttering in the backyard and we took it inside to our own little veterinary office. I wrapped it up, and cuddled it while I was watching television, but after I got up to change the channel, I sat down on the bird and I did not notice it until too late.

I was in hysterics, crying and running out the front door, screaming for Daddy, "Save it! Save it!" but the poor bird died in my hands.

"Murderer!" Louise and Irlene called me. "You killed the bird!"

Now it sounds almost funny, but we were devastated. I'm sure the girls meant it at the time.

From playing with our menagerie, we kind of blundered into the facts of life. There was a rabbit farm down the street. We got one and named it Sammy. Later, we changed the name to Tammy when we found out it was a girl. One day I went to check on the rabbit and I saw all these little creatures swarming all over her. I ran back in and screamed, "These mice are attacking the rabbit!" Surprise. Tammy had been pregnant and we hadn't even known it.

Well, some of us learned the facts of life. After I moved away, the rest of the family moved to Newbern, Tennessee. Irlene would go off into the fields almost every day, carrying a beat-up blue hairbrush.

"Bessie likes me to brush her," Irlene would say.

I thought, "Maybe brushing feels good to the cow." One day when I visited the family, we took a walk into the fields to see Bessie. Irlene was draped over Bessie's back, just brushing away, unperturbed by the large, pointed horns on Bessie's head. Bessie, need it be said, was a bull. You think we made up this stuff about Irlene?

There was always something going on at our house. One Halloween at Oceanside, Daddy and Momma set up a party in our enclosed patio. We had a record of chains clanking and ghosts howling and the wind blowing. We put the speakers inside the patio, and when kids rang the doorbell, one of us would pull a string, real slowly, and open the door with these eerie sounds coming through. We took turns making frightening sounds into a microphone, and after we had scared people, we would give them candy.

All the kids in the neighborhood started coming around, saying, "We've already been here, but we brought our friends over just to hear this." Irlene and Louise were out trick-or-treating, but they said everybody they met talked about the Mandrell house, so they figured they better come back.

That was how our home was. Other kids were welcome there. I'm not saying we were perfect. We had our squabbles and got our spankings, but there was a feeling that the five of us were a family.

Sometimes I find it impossible to explain to people how close we three girls always have been. I always had this idealistic, fairy-tale belief that all brothers and sisters are so close, and all parents and children are so close.

Yes, in a way the focus was on me, because I had been around the longest. Both girls will say they always thought of me as a big sister who was protective and talented. I was singing in church, and when they were just starting in grade school I was performing in Las Vegas and around California. And even in our home town, I was chosen Miss Oceanside when I was a sophomore in high school. In most families, jealousy and resentment would be natural, but I didn't feel any of that.

Irlene has said, "I was never jealous. I was always proud. But maybe I was envious. I always thought enviousness was when you were glad somebody had something but you wanted the same thing." I've heard Irlene say it hurt her more than it hurt me if I didn't win one of the major awards from the Country Music Association that year.

Both my sisters have been loyal and supportive to me. They

never complained about my first career as a child performer. In fact, they practiced their instruments so they could join me, first chance they got. And they have loved and helped raise Matthew and Jaime when I was busy working.

To this day, I depend on my sisters for love and guidance. I talk with Irlene almost every day when I am home in Nashville, and Louise and I share messages on yellow legal pads. We both rely on each other to criticize our shows. If we don't help each other, who will?

The last time I dropped in to watch Louise perform in Las Vegas, her assistant, Kelly, handed me a yellow pad with "Barbara, hope you enjoy the show—Sissy" scrawled across the top, with a pen attached. She beat me to the punch. So when Louise dropped by to watch my show, JoAnn Berry handed her the legal pad with my note: "Sissy, if you love me, you'll do it for me—Bobbie."

Although I am older, both my sisters were tested in this life before I was. I, who was Big Sister, watched with open admiration while they survived crises that probably would have broken me.

Louise—this beautiful, interesting woman, with so much to give—had two marriages break up, with a lot of pain and rejection. I know if something like that ever happened to me, I would be devastated, and I'm sure Louise was. But she bounced back. She prayed and she struggled and she worked. Louise is very thoughtful and disciplined, always taking classes to improve her stage skills. She's also a professional decorator, and loves creating a new home. Eventually, she married the talented and handsome R. C. Bannon, and she deserved it.

On our television show, Irlene played the family role of the flighty younger sister, naive and bewildered, but in real life she has shown more strength than I ever believed I could have. The first time she was pregnant, she began having difficulties at six months. When the doctor told her the baby had died, Irlene could not understand why she had to go through a delivery, but the doctor said it was the only way. She wound up going through eleven hours of labor for a child she knew was dead. None of us will ever show the wisdom and courage that Irlene did.

I stayed in that labor room with her. You could see her heart was broken, but she was so strong. We would talk, and I would hold her hand every time she had a contraction. I was there, smiling and acting as if I was fine, but when she would go to sleep for a few minutes, I would start weeping. And I just prayed and prayed.

As a woman and wife, I had been through nine and a half hours of labor and two cesarean operations by then, but I could not imagine what she was going through. When it was over, I remember thinking, "If something happens to Irlene or Louise or Mom or Dad . . ." I felt weak and frightened. I knew I couldn't take it the way Irlene had. I had to keep going, to be strong, to be successful, to be untouchable.

I always thought it was something natural and easy, being the officer among the three girls. I liked being the leader. It was the way I was raised: Big Sister would bluster ahead, making life easier for everybody else, running the show for Louise and Irlene. One day that all changed.

2
THE WRECK

JAIME SAYS I WENT "Uh!" just before the two cars hit. I don't remember. The last thing I can recall is those children playing on the tailgate of that station wagon, and my telling my own children to buckle up.

If I saw the other car, if I had time even to go "Uh!," I have no way of knowing. The next two weeks will always be a gap in my life, filled with tragedy and suffering for so many people.

The police say the other car had crossed through the turning lane and was heading into oncoming traffic on Route 31. The pickup truck in front of me barely had time to swerve out of the way, and my car was suddenly exposed, an innocent, anonymous, unlucky target. We were hit head-on.

The 1981 Subaru was driven by Mark P. White, a nineteen-year-old college student from Lebanon, not too far from Gallatin. He was dead before anybody could do a thing, so we will never know why he was on the wrong side of the road that evening. The police say there was no suggestion of alcohol or drugs being involved, and they have no theory why he was in the wrong place at the wrong time.

Everything I have heard about Mark White since that time is that he was a fine young man. Our lives will always be intertwined in tragedy. I cannot imagine the horror of a parent losing a child. My heart and my prayers have gone out to his family since the moment I learned of his death.

All I know is that God and the seat belts saved my life, and Matt's life, and Jaime's life. Without those seat belts, we would have been tossed and broken like cheap toys.

The front of my silver Jaguar was crumpled in, the hood mashed straight into the windshield. The tire and door on my side were crushed. If you looked at it, you would say there was no room left under the dashboard for my body from the waist down, but somehow I survived. I had a broken thigh bone, broken ribs, broken ankle, broken toes, cuts on my knees and my left arm, bruises on my face and cuts inside my mouth from hitting the steering wheel. Also a concussion, worse than anybody knew.

Everything I know about the wreck, I know from other people. For a long time, I hurt so badly that I could not even talk about it, could not muster up the curiosity to ask many questions. The intrusion into my being was so severe that I could not cope with it.

The scars remain to this day. Four years after the accident, I still could not drive a car in traffic. If I saw another car coming, I felt a stab of fear, knowing that something beyond my control could hurt me, could change my life. I had never felt that way before that moment.

The moment my life changed will always be a blank. This was Jaime's version from the backseat:

"I felt one collision, or maybe two. I was sitting there for a minute and I leaned over. It felt like somebody had hit me really hard. I knew my neck was hurting real bad and I could hear Mom moaning. I didn't see any blood except for on the backseat.

"Matt turned around and looked at me and asked if I was okay," Jaime remembers. "At first, I didn't say anything because his face looked like razors had scratched across it. There was blood all over him. He knew what had happened, but he didn't know he was bleeding. He just asked, 'Are you okay?' and I said I was.

" 'What happened to us?' I asked, and Matt said we were in a wreck. He said he was fine but he said, 'I think Momma's hurt.' She was lying over the steering wheel. I undid my seat belt and got out of the car. I noticed there was a really big red scrape on my neck.

"Then people started running, shouting, 'Are you okay?' and 'Who are you?' and 'What's your name?' I didn't say anything because I was shaking so bad. I was still feeling the hit. I went down—I remember lying down on the grass.

"The ambulance finally came and they got Matt out. They brought him over by me, and we were lying on the grass and discussing what was going on. There were some ladies around us, doing things like putting water on our faces.

"I remember a man coming up to Matt and giving him all this money. We had been shopping and we had a lot of money left over. He said, 'This is your mom's, keep it.' A little boy and his mom were bringing the dollhouse out, and I heard the boy say, 'Mommy, I wish I had a dollhouse.'

"I remember a man coming by and saying, 'She's dead.' I thought for sure it was Mom. I got scared then. These people were yelling, 'It's Barbara Mandrell.' That's when it really hit me."

Jaime recalls that she and Matt were lying on the side, holding hands. She seems to remember hearing me yelling, but she isn't sure. Then people came up to her and asked, "Can you move? Can you sit up?"

"No," Jaime said, and they got all nervous.

"Don't move her, she might have a broken neck," somebody said.

Jaime tried to move her head, but it didn't go very far. They all started to fumble around, afraid of what that might mean.

"I can't get up because I'm sitting on my ponytail," Jaime said.

She raised her shoulder, lifted her long hair, and then she was able to move her head. They put on a neck brace anyway, just to make sure.

By that time, Jaime was getting the feeling she might be all right. But she was not reassured by what she heard about me. A fellow we know, whose nickname is Papa John, showed up at the scene of the wreck and was trying to comfort Matt and Jaime. Suddenly, a man came running over and said, "Hi, Papa John. That's Barbara Mandrell up there in the car, isn't it?"

"Yes," Papa John said.

"I think she's dead," the man said, right in front of the kids.

Despite his own injuries, Matthew tried to scramble to his feet.

"I've got to see my mom," he kept saying.

"No, she's not dead, Matt," Papa John reassured him. "She's fine."

That was nice of John to say, but nobody could be sure it was true. The two children would go for anxious hours and days worrying because they had heard their mother was dead. And it was more than a private apprehension, a family matter, because whenever they put on the radio or the television, they would be reminded of the accident. I wasn't just their mother. I was public property.

10

A LITTLE KID PLAYS VEGAS

MY PRIVATE LIFE ENDED when I was ten. One of my first public appearances was with Cousin Herb Henson in Bakersfield. We drove up for his noon live radio show, and I played the steel and the sax. Nobody would believe I was only ten until we did his television show that night. But it seemed like no big deal to me because we jammed back into the car right after the show. Had to be in class the next day, homework done.

About the same time, Daddy left his security job and went to work for the Standel Amplifier Company. A man named Bob Crooks had created a custom-made amplifier for Merle Travis, the man who wrote "Sixteen Tons," and other people were starting to request them. You could even say business was booming. Uncle Merle used one of the Standels when he played for Hank Thompson, so naturally Hank had to have five. One went to Joe Maphis, a musician who played the Vegas-California circuit, another to

Speedy West, one of the great steel players in country music. And I believe the next one went to Chet Atkins.

Daddy used to take me down to the factory, and Bob Crooks let me try his different amps. But mostly I was a little kid tagging along with her daddy. Mr. Crooks used to keep a magnifying glass in his office, and when I started getting bored, I'd go find some dead flies and look at them. Then I'd tell Mr. Crooks all about it, and he would be nice and make a big show of interest in my scientific discoveries.

Daddy's job was to chat up the giants of country music, get them interested in Standel amplifiers. In the summer of 1960, there was a trade show coming up at the Palmer House in Chicago. Daddy decided he would bring along a gimmick—an eleven-year-old steel guitar player, twanging away into a Standel amplifier.

It sounded good to me. I was on summer vacation, looking for something different to do. I never thought of it as an audition, or a chance to break into show business. I was a little kid who had learned to play the steel guitar and I was going to help Daddy on a business trip. We left Louise and Irlene with Momma's family in downstate Illinois, and stayed at the Palmer House, right in the middle of town, in the Loop.

All the companies were assigned rooms in the convention center at the hotel. There was a front door from the hallway, and a side door connecting each room, which made it easy for buyers to wander around and listen to the merchandise. Daddy would play guitar and I would twang away on the steel guitar.

The first day, Daddy was standing near the wall, but the side door kept butting up against him. The man in the next room was sticking his head in to listen. It was Joe Maphis, a guitar player from California who was demonstrating an echo chamber for his own client. In between numbers, Joe would pop his head in the door. Joe knew Daddy from visiting the Standel factory. He knew all about the amplifiers. What he did not know about was me.

Other big names kept dropping in: Daniel Webster, who was probably the first person ever to play the touch system on guitar; Julian Thorpe, one of the well-known steel players in the country; and Speedy West, another fine musician.

Daddy still recalls that after Speedy listened to me for a while, he took his guitar picks and his bar out of his pocket and put them on the steel and he said, "Well, I think I'll just give up." Then he thought better of it and retracted the bar and picks, saying, "No, I'd better take this with me because I've got to make a living."

Daddy was proud that his daughter was attracting attention— mostly because it helped him sell a few more Standel amplifiers. He was not expecting what happened next.

On the final day of the trade show, Joe Maphis took Daddy aside and said he had been listening to me every day.

"I just wanted to make sure I didn't have the big eye," Joe said, meaning he didn't want to overreact. "But when I saw all the other musicians flipping out on her too, then I knew I was right."

He asked if he could use me on a show he was putting together in Las Vegas the following week. I had been performing in church and in school, at home and now at the trade convention, without ever showing any fear of the stage. I was a ham. I was too young or too stupid—or both—to be afraid. Daddy and Momma asked me if I wanted to play on Joe Maphis's show and I said, Sure.

As soon as the amplifiers were all packed up, we drove out to Las Vegas to the Showboat Hotel and Casino. I was to appear on the same show with Joe and Rose Maphis, Tex Ritter, Cowboy Copas, Hank Morton and Les Anderson in a show that ran from 5:00 P.M. to 5:00 A.M. I was one of the supporting acts—billed as "The Sweetheart of Steel."

It was no different from getting up in front of the little church back in Fairfield, Illinois. They called my name and I came out and played.

Well, there was one difference. At church, they passed around the plate and I put some money in. At the Showboat Hotel and Casino, they paid me.

At the end of the first week, I was paid two hundred and fifty dollars—my first paycheck. All it looked like to me was a piece of paper. I had observed that the common denominator of the casino was chips and coins. That looked more like money to me.

"Could I have the first hundred in silver dollars?" I asked.

When you're a performer, you can make a few requests. It was one of my first lessons. So they put a hundred silver dollars in a bag and I carried it up to our room and dumped it on the bed and started to count—one, two, three. When I was finished, I started counting all over again. Pretty soon, my parents said, "Come on, Barbara, let's go eat dinner." And I said, "No. Eighty. Eighty-one." Do you think Wayne Newton started this way?

Back in 1959, Las Vegas was not as much a part of the public consciousness as it is now. It seemed very foreign to an eleven-year-old girl from a small town. You have to be twenty-one to gamble, so I was always escorted through the casinos to get to the stage area, and we never dallied. I was either in the coffee shop or the dressing rooms or on stage.

But I could see the guards dumping coins from the slot machines into large metal trash cans, and I thought, "How can these people gamble like that?" You'd see these trash cans full of money, and you knew that somebody had worked hard on the night shift at a factory, or standing up in front of a bunch of little kids teaching the third grade, and then gone to Las Vegas and lost it. Chung. Just like that.

Gambling was not for us. I remember seeing Daddy twice put one quarter in the slot machine, but we didn't hold anything against the drinking or the gambling. I know it's a pretty wild lifestyle in Las Vegas, but I try not to worry about other people's business or judge them. As a Christian, I have never felt out of place performing in Las Vegas, and I don't get any pressure from religious people. In fact, if you took a poll, I bet you'd find a lot of people from religious homes bellying up to the craps table.

The way I see it, Las Vegas has become another of the most typical American places, like New York and L.A., Opryland and Disney World, the national parks. It's who we are. And I have noticed that a lot of people I meet in Las Vegas—mostly room service people, security people, the maids, the executives—are as varied as the rest of the country. It's no den of evil to me.

Many years later, when I was playing my Las Vegas show with Bobby Jones and New Life, that wonderful gospel group, they were singing a great gospel song, "Call Him Up." Somebody turned to me and said, "Wow, you've brought gospel music to Las Vegas." So there's a question as to who's affecting whom.

In my show, I make a joke about Ken losing five hundred dollars at the craps table, and then getting mad at me because I lost forty-five dollars playing blackjack. The punch line is Ken saying, "Yeah, but I know how to gamble." It's a joke about men and women, not really about us. I can't go out there and play the machines because people might come over and ask for autographs and disrupt the people who are gambling. So I don't gamble more out of practicality than morality. But I have nothing against it. Las

Vegas feels like home. I've been going there since I was eleven.

That first July in Las Vegas seemed like an extended vacation to me. I had fun up onstage, but I was just as interested in eating in the coffee shop or going swimming in the pool. I'd see Uncle Joe Maphis by the pool and make him go swimming with me. I can appreciate now how he probably wanted to say, "No, thank you, I just want to relax," but he went swimming instead.

I was just a little kid having a good time. But I wasn't a bundle of laughs to some of the musicians. There is an old show-business adage about not trying to follow a child's act—and it makes sense. I can see why W. C. Fields got a sneer on his face whenever a child walked into view. I'd like to think I wasn't malicious. I had been taught to say "Yes, sir" and "No, ma'am" to everybody. Just by being there, I think I was a pain in the neck to some of the musicians, particularly a steel player named Noel Boggs.

Mr. Boggs had a good reputation in Las Vegas, and like most performers, he enjoyed feeling that he was special. Apparently, Uncle Joe had promised Mr. Boggs that he would not bring in another steel player on the same card, but there I was. And when I finished my short solo act, I'd back up Uncle Joe, which was tricky.

Uncle Joe was a great musician who played the music for the movie *Thunder Road* and improvised great solos, but he did not believe in practicing. He would play for a while and all of a sudden he would say, "Take it, Barbara," which, when you think about it, is quite a tribute to an eleven-year-old squirt. And I would just twang away on the steel guitar, working with the same general chords and themes that Uncle Joe was using, and he would wander around, sip a soda, wipe his forehead, whatever he felt like, and after a minute or two, he would get back in the act again.

Uncle Joe's trust in me was giving me a lot of confidence. The audience was also getting to like me. Fine for me. Not so great for Mr. Boggs.

The next act on was Noel Boggs. He was a great player, but you know how audiences can get after a beer or two. While the poor man was playing, some of the people started shouting, "Bring that little girl back, let her play." Just what he needed.

There was a little balcony where the entertainers could sit and watch the other acts. The fans knew I was up there, and Mr. Boggs didn't have much choice but to ask me to come down.

Daddy admitted later that he was afraid the little kid would steal the show. He and Momma had tried to teach me how to do the right things, but Daddy thought, What's she going to do under these circumstances?

I got down to the stage, where Mr. Boggs was trying to perform. You did not have to be very smart to know he was in a tough spot. He was so sweet and nice, and he asked me to play something. Without thinking about it, I said, "Mr. Boggs, you're one of the greatest steel players in the world and I would consider it a privilege just to stand by you and watch while you play."

The crowd kept shouting, "Let the little girl play," so I played something, but by being polite to him, I had defused the crowd. I did not need to steal the scene. At eleven, life seemed pretty easy.

11

THE AMBULANCE

So MANY KIND HANDS, so many caring hearts, but I knew none of it. Emergency workers pulled me from the wreckage and rushed me in an ambulance to Hendersonville Hospital, where they began treating me for trauma. Meanwhile, the word was spreading all over Nashville. My Daddy has filled me in on what happened next:

"We were at the marina down at Old Hickory Lake, and we left to go home around seven o'clock. As I drove back, I got to a certain street and saw the blue lights of a police blockade. We drove around and came out on the other side of the wreck, only about eight blocks away, and went on home.

"As we came through the front door, the phone was ringing. Tony Smith, the marina manager, said somebody had called the marina to say Barbara was involved in a wreck. He started to tell me where it was, and I said, 'I know exactly where it is.' So we hopped in the car, turned right back around, and headed there.

"Coming from that direction, they were letting them pass

the wreck in one lane, but I took the center lane, a turning lane. Of course, the police knew my car and they motioned me on up there. The officer, a sergeant or a lieutenant, told me the other fella was dead, and he said Barbara was pretty seriously hurt, but he thought the kids were okay.

"I took a look at that Jaguar, the front all bashed in, and remembering my days as a police officer, I got in the car and said, 'Mary, prepare yourself for the worst. I don't see how she could have possibly lived through this.'

"The officer told me the new Hendersonville bypass wasn't officially open yet, but he knew it was completed all the way to the hospital. With no traffic on the bypass, I just kind of lowered the boom and got there in a hurry.

"They had just gotten through the door with Barbara when I pulled up. She was still on the stretcher—and she was out. Mary took her hand, but she just had a blank stare. She was saying things, but she had no idea what she was saying. I tried to talk to her and tell her the kids were okay. I figured that would be uppermost on her mind, and if she could hear anything, she might respond. But there was no sign of recognition.

"When we reached the emergency room, the doctor was trying to hold her femur bone stationary. They couldn't give her anything because of her head injury, so she was feeling the pain.

"Every time the doctor would move her leg, she would just scream. I'll never forget it. First she reached up to the doctor and patted him on the cheek. But every time he hurt her by moving her leg, she whammed him one in the face.

"I asked another doctor to draw her blood and send it to the lab to check for any narcotics or alcohol. A police lieutenant said, 'Well, Mr. Mandrell, everybody knows Barbara doesn't drink or take drugs,' but I said, 'I'm an ex-policeman and I know that someplace down the road, this may come up. I want a record of it.'

"Next I called her doctor in Nashville, Dr. Newton Lovvorn, and said we wanted to bring her to Baptist Hospital downtown, which is a bigger hospital and better equipped to handle something like this. I asked Newt about getting a Medivac helicopter, but he said by the time they warmed it up, we'd be better off bringing her to town by ambulance.

"Louise rode with Barbara in the ambulance to Baptist Hospital while Mary and I stayed at Hendersonville to check on the children. Matthew had some internal injuries, and his cheekbone was broken and his face was cut, and Jaime was released to spend the night with our friend Gail Cook.

"Another thing I want to mention—the story went like wildfire around Nashville. Before Barbara ever left Hendersonville, people like Johnny Cash, just about the entire country-music industry, heard about it one way or another. They were calling Hendersonville, asking if we needed blood, or if there was anything else they could do.

"After making sure the kids were all right, and that our friend Ron Cook was with Matthew at the hospital in Hendersonville, Mary and I headed downtown to Baptist. We were still worried. I've seen a few wrecks in my time, and I know that people can suddenly pass away from shock. I said, 'Mary, this could be bad.' "

12
SHOW BIZ

WHEN MY FIRST LAS Vegas engagement ended in July, Uncle Joe Maphis invited me back for a show he was putting on in December. At different times, he and Aunt Rose and Jimmy Dickens and Tex Ritter all suggested I learn to sing. I wasn't sure anybody wanted to hear my girlish eleven-year-old voice, but I started working on it as soon as I got home. I knew I could sing because Momma and Daddy had always told me I could do anything I wanted.

My father would give me lessons in our living room. At first, I thought it sounded so pretty to sing in a soft voice, but Daddy told me to project it, so I could be heard across the street.

"Don't sing to me," Daddy would say. "Don't sing to the chair. Sing to Monica across the street." He would say, "Sing," and he would accompany me with the rhythm guitar.

Because of his own job, he did not have the time to work with me as much as he thought I needed, so he arranged for me to have voice lessons. But he stopped them after about six sessions because the person teaching me believed in the firm pear-shaped tones of an opera singer. He didn't think that would go over so well singing "Your Cheatin' Heart," so I dropped the voice lessons.

The classical voice training didn't carry to Las Vegas, but my schoolwork did. When I went back to Las Vegas in the wintertime, I discovered something that very few performers probably know: the city has a public library. You thought it was all casinos and lounges and swimming pools? My teachers back in El Monte made sure I had enough homework to keep me in the library to do reports on rock formations or flags of the world. I was such a regular in the Las Vegas Public Library that the librarians knew my name. I even had my own library card.

Meanwhile, I was still a scene-stealer onstage. I loved showing off for the audience, and sometimes I just couldn't help being a little pain in the neck to the people I liked best.

After that visit to Las Vegas, I was invited to join a package tour put together by Johnny Cash, who was becoming a national legend, The Man in Black. It was an all-star cast—Gordon Terry, master fiddler and singer; Don Gibson, singer; Patsy Cline, at the peak of her career; George Jones, the one and only; and June Carter, from the fabulous Carter family of southwest Virginia.

June Carter, so smart and beautiful, was along as a singer and comedienne. There was nothing between her and Johnny at that time, and she was more like a family friend, a cousin or a sister, sighing and clucking while John did his thing. I have to smile now, every time I see them billing and cooing as an old married couple.

My job, as a specialist act, was to open with a couple of songs, one on the steel guitar, one on the saxophone, trying out my voice on a couple of choruses. The crowd would scream and yell and call for an encore, which I didn't mind a bit. I was a novelty, just turned thirteen, too young to be in awe.

The very next person on was George Jones, the greatest of all country voices. George has had his bad times, but when he would get up there and start lamenting, strong men would start weeping and strong women would start fluttering.

George was not fazed in the least by the Miss Goody Two-Shoes who had preceded him. The band had no steel guitar, and I knew that every George Jones song has a steel guitar. So after the first night, George came up to me backstage and said, "Would it be all right, when you come off, if I come out and do one song and then call you back out to play the steel guitar for me?"

What do you say when George Jones asks you to play for him? You say, "Yes, sir," that's what you say. But you also say, "But Mr. Jones, I also need a list of the songs, and what key they're in." I would play a little intro, and then back up his voice. Playing for George Jones at the age of thirteen, I had hit the top, right there.

Johnny Cash was the leader of the tour. He was already famous for songs like "I Walk the Line," with that big, deep voice, slipping and grabbing like a twelve-wheeler trying to get into gear going up a hill, and just as powerful. He is a giant of a man, much bigger than his pictures or his image on television, looming over everyone, those dark eyes glaring out at the world.

He's calmed down a lot over the years, become a statesman of country music. When he's backstage at the Opry, or visiting with friends, he is the center of attention, not because he wants to be but because he is Johnny Cash. He walks into a room and heads turn. He is the focus of what people are saying and doing. People tell me that Ted Williams, the great baseball hitter, is easily the focus of a roomful of Hall of Fame players because of his size and his charisma. Maybe it was the same with John Wayne, whom I never met, much to my regret. I know it's that way with Johnny Cash. When Louise and Irlene and I were doing our television show, he was our guest. I could feel his presence on the set before I even saw him. Johnny Cash. You knew he was there.

Back when I was thirteen, he was much more nervous, his hands and eyes always fidgeting. One time we went into a truck stop and sat in one of those Naugahyde booths. The material was slightly ripped, but Johnny kept picking at it during the meal until he had torn it completely apart. When he paid the check, Johnny also paid for the damage he had done to the booth. Actually, the place was better off because the thing was ripped to begin with, so they got paid to reupholster it.

In his book, Johnny talked about those wild days, tearing up motel rooms, running around, the booze and pills. He's got no secrets. My parents and I saw what was going on, but we didn't make faces and say, "Bad boys." Any destructive thing he did, he paid for, as far as I could see.

Maybe it was because Johnny had kids of his own, but he was very sweet with me. A real gentleman. No drinking, no cussing, no wild talk, as long as I was in sight. That was his code. My parents trusted him to take care of their daughter on the road, and he always did, but I must have been a trial to him. At least, that's what he says.

He is always telling the story about our first airplane flight on that trip. He made sure I sat next to him so he could keep an eye on me. This was my first jet-plane ride, so I was all excited. You've got to hear Johnny's rumbling voice trying to imitate my goody-goody thirteen-year-old voice, but he says I never stopped chattering.

"Oh, look at that, Mr. Cash, did you see those cars down there, just like postage stamps."

"Yes, Barbara."

"Oooh, look, Mr. Cash, the higher we get, those cars look like fleas down there."

"Uh-huh, Barbara."

"Mr. Cash, did they bring you something to drink? Look at this, they brought me a Coke and some peanuts."

"Mm-hmmm, Barbara."

He says he was trying hard to sleep, and I would say, "Oooh, look at those clouds, Mr. Cash," and he never did get any sleep.

To his everlasting credit, he never barked at me, or tried to ditch me with somebody else. And he always made sure I was safe before the boys went out for a sarsaparilla.

Luther Perkins, his guitar player, who has passed away, used to mother me. He'd say, "Did you eat?," and he'd accompany me to the coffee shop in many a motel. Back home my classmates were taking social studies, while I was on the road with George Jones and Johnny Cash.

Men dominated the world of country music, but I looked around and discovered there were more women than you might have thought. Marion Hall was an inspiration, playing the steel guitar. Rose Maphis could keep pace with Uncle Joe onstage. Of course, on the Grand Ole Opry, there was the immortal Minnie Pearl, who would later become a great girlfriend of mine: a comedienne with a price tag dangling from her straw hat, and the mind and manners of a diplomat.

Out on the western circuit, I became aware of Martha Carson, a gospel singer on the *Town Hall Party* television show who had great showmanship and energy. And there was Rose Maddox from the group called The Maddox Brothers and Rose. I learned a lot from watching her on television and in person. She wasn't just a woman sitting up there sweet and pretty. She took charge.

Obviously, there was Kitty Wells, who was the best-selling female singer of the time, representing the women's point of view with songs like, "It Wasn't God Who Made Honky-Tonk Angels," with that sharp mountain voice of hers. And even before Kitty Wells there was Patsy Montana, who had the first million-selling hit by a female country singer, a record called "I Want to Be a Cowboy's Sweetheart," complete with yodeling. Patsy had done it back in the Thirties. God bless her, she comes to my fan club breakfast sometimes. She was even on the David Letterman show not too long ago, and they treated her with such respect. I became a huge fan of Paul Shaffer after I saw him play the fiddle on the synthesizer for Patsy.

With role models like Minnie Pearl and Patsy Montana at a distance, I got the feeling that a woman could be a star, just like a man. And my beliefs were strengthened when I took a two-week trip with a woman who was then at the top in country music—a good old Virginia girl named Patsy Cline.

Patsy Cline was a true professional, a big woman with a voice like an angel's trumpet and agile dancer's feet. They made a movie about her life, *Sweet Dreams,* a few years back, that concentrated mostly on her stormy marriage to Charlie Dick. I don't know much about that. I never met him. I only knew Patsy Cline as a star who was nice to me. She was a country girl, but she had the poise and the brassy voice and the diction of a café singer, too. No guitar. No western yoked outfits. She was a model of a country singer who could cross over toward pop music, touch anybody.

We were introduced as the two-week tour began. We checked into our separate motel rooms and went out for a bite. Then she insisted, absolutely insisted, that I room with her. She would not hear of me staying alone in my room.

Her room had only one bed, so she showed me which side was mine, and we went to sleep. I am not a kicker today, but as a kid, with growing pains while you sleep, you turn a lot and you kick a lot. In the middle of the night, she kept calling my name until I finally woke up.

"Barbara, could you please move back to your side?" she asked.

I was sprawled horizontally, right across the top of her.

After that, we'd get twin beds, but I was officially her roommate for the rest of the trip. Not only her roommate, but her hairdresser. I had been doing Momma's hair for years, so when Patsy complained about the chop job done to her in a beauty parlor, I said, "Would you like me to try to comb it for you?"

She loved it so much she insisted I comb her hair every night before the show. After we moved to Nashville, many years later, I visited the Country Music Hall of Fame (now directly across the street from my museum, I might add). I was looking at the exhibits in the Hall, and I came upon one of the wigs she used. The sight of it brought tears to my eyes because it made me remember how wonderful she was to me. She was so much fun.

She had a great way of introducing her newest hit. She would tell the audience: "I recorded a song called 'I Fall to Pieces,' and I was in a car wreck. Now I'm really worried because I have a brand-new record and it's called 'Crazy.' "

For all her bluster and sense of humor, there was a fragile side to her. I remember when the tour reached Des Moines, Iowa, in the dead of winter, and there was ice on the pavement of the parking lot. She was so graceful onstage, still with that dancer's grace from when she was younger, but on that slippery pavement she clutched my hand, putting a lot of weight on me—and she was a big woman.

I realize now why she was so nervous about falling. Patsy had been badly hurt in a car crash on June 14, 1961, and had spent a lot of time in traction in the hospital, being put back together again. Her accident had happened in East Nashville while she was driving out to the general store to buy hamburger rolls. There had been two cars coming at her in the opposite lane. One car had tried to pass the other, but couldn't get through, and they hit head-on. One passenger was killed in the other car, and Patsy had nearly died, too. She had head injuries as well as leg injuries, but she fought back to perform again.

This was barely six months later, and you couldn't tell Patsy had been injured, if you didn't know. But I remember feeling the tension in her hand as she leaned her big frame against me on that icy sidewalk in Des Moines. She was looking after me on that trip, but in a way, she needed me to look after her, too. She was a grown woman, in the prime of life, and she was fearful. That seemed so foreign to me then.

13

BAPTIST HOSPITAL WAS READY

NEWT WAS PLAYING TENNIS when the call came. He has reminded me of this on more than one occasion, and I apologize. Tuesday is the day off for Newton Lovvorn, our family doctor, my gynecologist, my friend, Jaime's godfather, and the man who has delivered all three of our children.

He has been my doctor since I settled in Nashville. I delayed getting a doctor as long as possible because gynecologists tend to make me nervous, which I guess is a normal thing for women. I did not know many people in Nashville, so I did what any bright twenty-year-old would do: I went to the Yellow Pages.

I opened the book to the L's, probably just by chance, and noticed there was one with an office in Madison, where I was living at the time. I made an appointment, and walked in feeling very nervous to find a handsome, charming young doctor, which did not help my nerves very much.

He was just starting out, having gone through college and medical school and internship and residency, and he thought he was pretty hot stuff starting out with his own office. He told me later it was a little distracting to have completed all this education and now having to wait for the phone to ring with new patients. I wasn't exactly his first patient, but he was still glad to see another one come through the door.

"How did you happen to hear of me?" he casually asked, hoping, I guess, that I had been referred by a doctor with a large practice.

"I picked your name out of the phone book," I said, without thinking I might be hurting his feelings.

"Oh," he said.

We got to be good friends right away. He had never heard of me—hardly anybody in Nashville had at the time—but he dearly loved country music, and in fact he played guitar. He had been in the Air Force, and of course Ken was a Navy pilot, so we were able to talk easily.

We'd been through a lot of good times and bad times together. Newt had gotten us started on skiing, and I had returned the favor by coming up with autographed albums by Willie Nelson and Waylon Jennings for him.

He loves to tell what happened when I went into the hospital to have Jaime on February 23, 1976: The radio was playing George Jones while I was getting my spinal injection, and when Jaime was delivered by C-section, the radio was playing my current hit, "Can't Help But Wonder."

The disc jockey said, "Here's Barbara Mandrell," but Dr. Lovvorn looked down at me and said, "No, here's Barbara Mandrell."

You never think life will get worse than a 103-degree fever in the middle of the night. Dr. Lovvorn was always there for those things, looking after our children and Ken and me, obviously not just a gynecologist but our family doctor. You like to think your doctor will be there for you. We never had any doubts about Newt.

His wife, Janice, called him at the club where he was playing tennis, and told him I was at Hendersonville Hospital. He immediately talked to Louise's husband, R.C., who told him as much as he could, that it looked like I had a broken leg and

that Jaime and Matthew were banged up. Dr. Lovvorn has always stressed that I would have gotten good care at Hendersonville, but because he was my doctor, he wanted me at Baptist
Hospital. As Daddy has told me, a helicopter was not practical,
so they put me into the ambulance while Newt got ready to
head downtown.

I had no way of knowing it, but I had loving company on
the ambulance ride. Louise had gotten to Hendersonville Hospital and she was not about to leave me now. When the ambulance arrived at Baptist, she noticed that the press had gathered
outside the emergency room. She jumped out and stood in
front of the photographers and asked them not to take any pictures, saying, "Please, Barbara has always been there for you,
please do this for her." Some of them backed off, but others
did take pictures of me being trundled into the hospital. Television and the next day's papers would have pictures of me
strapped onto the gurney. As always, Sissy was fierce in protecting somebody in her family, but we never took it personally
that they photographed me anyway. They had a job to do in
covering the news. I had just never made this kind of news before.

Since he was more "there" than I was, I'll let Dr. Lovvorn
tell the next part:

"I took a shower and got to the hospital before the ambulance did. It must have been fifteen or twenty minutes before
she arrived. Then I began to realize how serious it was. She was
awake, but she was talking out of her head. Her leg had temporary little casts, plastic binders, on it, and it was just awful. We
looked at the X rays, and I found out there was a fatality involved. I asked more about Jaime and Matthew and people assured me they [their injuries] were not quite so serious.
Matthew would be observed at Hendersonville, which is a good
hospital, and I knew he'd be safe."

Two other doctors were also waiting for me at Baptist:
David Jones, an orthopedic surgeon, and Art Bond, a neurolo-
gist. In the small world of Nashville, it happened that I had met
Dr. Jones before, because he is quite a good musician and also
a fraternity brother of Tom Collins, who was my record producer. I was not exactly in shape to discuss the Tennessee Vols
when Dr. Jones met me this time.

Dr. Jones has said that "it looked real bad" at first. He added: "The fracture almost came through the skin. We noticed a compound injury to the knee, with two penetrations and scuffed-up cartilage. When I saw the abrasions all over the arms, I knew we would need a plastic surgeon, so we called Dr. Ruben Bueno."

I have since learned that there was leather and plastic from the inside of the Jaguar embedded in my left arm and other places, probably from the steering wheel.

"It was a real rough scene," Dr. Jones continued. "We did a spinal tap and discovered some blood in there, which is not a good sign. We also discovered that because there was some blood in there, the anesthesia didn't work very well. We weren't sure about Barbara's brain status, but we did tests right away and discovered there was plenty of Barbara left. She seemed to respond appropriately to some things, and we had to wonder if she was play-acting at other times, but with head injuries, you never know."

Dr. Lovvorn has added:

"Cursing? Absolutely. Everybody gets a little violent when there's an injury. We had a prominent patient from country music who came in with a heart problem not too long ago, and it leaked out that he had been a difficult patient. Well, everybody is different. Barbara didn't know what she was saying under those circumstances.

"Later, she gave Ken a difficult time, but Ken was a prince. He understood. It was hard on him, but he understood she was significantly injured. I don't know that much about the connection with head injuries and language, but I've heard a lot of wives in labor cursing their husbands right there on the delivery table. Pain does something to you. I can't explain it," he finished.

Let me interject something here. I've been told I was a model patient in my three childbirths, but maybe some other women are cussing their husbands for putting them in the delivery room, or maybe some of them are suggesting the husbands handle it next time, equal rights and all that. But I'd love to know where my foul language came from in that emergency room.

It's not that I'm such a Goody Two-Shoes. The people

closest to me know the truth about me, that I have a terrible temper. Ken sees it. My father sees it. It's my father's fault because I'm a chip off the old block. My children see it. My sisters see it. JoAnn Berry sees it. Kathy sees it. My immediate people. But that's okay. The beautiful thing about family, whether it be blood family or people you take into your family and you love, you can be yourself with them.

So I blow my top once in a while in private, more now since the wreck. But I pride myself on always keeping some control. My language is something I believe I can control, as a Christian, as an adult. But you always fear loss of control. We hate to think of ourselves getting old, losing control of one thing or the other. What's the thing your mother tells you when you're a kid—"Make sure you wear clean underwear in case you get hit by a bus." Well, I did get hit. And it was my language that was foul.

I still haven't gotten over the fact that I was cussing in front of Dr. Lovvorn and everybody else in that room, as well as my parents and Louise. Newt tells me I used nearly every curse word you'd hear from a drunken sailor—but I did not take the Lord's name in vain. I'm proud of that.

I cannot tell the following story without using the word I used then. It is not a word I use under normal circumstances, but it's part of the story. Newt says the doctors were more nervous than usual when they assembled in the emergency room. I mean, doctors are always professional, but sometimes they hide it under a façade of casualness, which I can recognize from being around musicians. I understand athletes are much the same. They start chattering and joking just before going into the arena or onto the stage.

This time, though, the doctors were nervous. Maybe it was because they were about to operate on a so-called celebrity. Or maybe it was because they knew it was a close friend of Dr. Lovvorn. Or maybe it was because I was alternately smacking them and stroking them, jabbering away, out of my head.

Anyway, when one of the doctors or the nurses touched me, I screamed at the top of my lungs: "Shit!" A couple of people jumped back, but Newt made a nonsense comment like, "Well, gentlemen, as you can see, Barbara is a downhill snow skier." I know it doesn't make much sense, but Dr. Lovvorn said that loosened them up as they prepared to operate on me. I also hate to admit this, but my doctors say that if I used that word once, I used it a thousand times.

Dr. Jones has since filled me in on the rest of that evening:

"I knew we had to put the femur in traction that night. I washed out the knee and left the skin to the plastic surgeon. Then I had to drill a hole across the thigh, to insert a threaded pin called the Steinman pin. It's a barbaric-looking thing that looks like a knitting needle, and you feel like something evil while you're drilling through the leg, knowing this is a blonde lady entertainer, but you have to do it.

"We got her in traction, with ropes going up to pulleys—you can picture it—and balanced with weights. Barbara was thrashing around, and every so often she would get it out of kilter.

"The next thing we had to do was decide where to put her," Dr. Jones has said. "We didn't want to treat her like a celebrity, because it's a known fact that celebrities don't get as good a treatment as other people because you're bending over backwards to be nice to them. Still, we wanted to put her in the most private place, which we decided was the cardiac-care unit, away from other people. The room was a little cramped, but it worked out fine. I remember the security people surrounding her around midnight as we took her to the recovery room, and then we brought her to the cardiac-care unit."

Dr. Lovvorn has added: "I was still concerned about a concussion. The other surgery had to be done, but the concussion was more severe than anybody thought at the time."

I was surrounded by the best doctors in a great medical town, and my family was doing what it could.

However, there was one part of me missing, somebody so strong and kind that he would absorb much of the anger and the tension in the days and months to come. That night, I was too far out of it to miss him. But I could not have lived without Ken.

14
KEN

SOMETIMES IT SEEMS KEN has been there forever—a big, gentle man standing in the wings, holding one of the children, talking to some of the fans, dealing with the business people, being there for me. In my worst moments, it was his touch, his voice, his presence, that reached me the most.

But I have to remember that it didn't start off with him being there for me. I have to remember this is a man who once landed airplanes on the deck of a bobbing aircraft carrier, a man who flew a Lear jet for four governors of Tennessee, a man trained to protect his country in time of war. He was the hero in the family, the top officer, the one with the career, long before he saved my life and my career.

Sometimes I worry that people will judge Ken harshly because they see us arguing. What's the saying—they fight like an old married couple? Well, that's exactly what we are, an old married couple. And you can tell.

Somebody meeting us for the first time will hear us bickering, and will discreetly ask somebody close to me, "Is that a result of the accident?" and anybody in my family will say, "No, they've always bickered." And that's a fact.

I read once that arguing is a sign of a healthy marriage. If that's the case, then I would say we have an abundance of good health in our marriage. We got started bickering when we were dating and didn't want anybody to know. We tried arguing to fool people, and it got to be such a habit that we couldn't stop.

We have all seen one too many show-business movies where the man gets a complex because his wife is the star. That is emphatically not the case here. Ken is very intelligent. He knows a lot about science and business and history. He's so sure of himself. It does not bother him to be called Mr. Mandrell.

Ken remembers flying one of our governors around and being asked what his wife did for a living.

"She's a country-music singer," Ken said. "Her name is Barbara Mandrell."

"Hmm, I don't recognize the name," the man said.

"You will," Ken said. "You will."

He was happy when it did happen for me. I've seen it when one partner does resent the other one because of success. I've also seen it when one partner consciously stays out of the limelight so the other partner can have center stage. We see it, but we don't know the history.

It is not easy for either of us to try to live a normal life. Tons of pressure get piled on Ken, and tons on me. We cannot let it out on others because we will be judged by the public, so we take it out on each other.

When my hectic life gets the best of me, I break down. But once I cry and get it out, Ken comforts me. I have the luxury of crying, yelling, screaming, because of the strong man I married. I can do that behind closed doors, which is not very kind to him, but that's the way it is.

They tell me that while I was out of my head in the hospital, I let Ken have it, both barrels, all eight cylinders, three shifts a day. He was it. He's been it for me for a long time.

It figures that we were introduced by my father. Daddy hired Ken—although not as a prospective husband, I hasten to add.

After I had played the Vegas shows and made the tour with Johnny Cash, it was pretty clear that I had a certain attraction as a child novelty act, but Daddy and Momma were not about to let me traipse around the country for long. It was also clear that I could not make much money or gain much experience even closer to home in California, because there were a lot of clubs where a minor could not be booked.

However, there was one type of club where a minor could perform, if she was in the company of adults—the military camps. With that in mind, Daddy gave up his job with Standel to open a music supply store in Oceanside, not far from Camp Pendleton, Miramar, San Diego, and inland service bases. Camp Pendleton had different clubs for enlisted men, officers and noncommissioned officers, female officers—marvelous opportunities to work in a wholesome environment.

To back me up, Daddy formed a small group, the Mandrell Family Band, with me doing my things on saxophone, steel guitar, and singing, Daddy singing and playing rhythm guitar and serving as master of ceremonies, and Momma playing bass. You're not going to believe it, but this sedate little lady wiggled so much while playing bass that the band gave her the nickname of Swivel Hips.

We also had Bill Hendricks, Daddy's partner in Oceanside Music Supply, who played saxophone and clarinet, and later we hired Brian Lonbeck, a high-school boy who drove down from Los Angeles on weekends and played a double-necked Joe Maphis–model guitar.

After a while, we needed a drummer. There was a college boy who worked across the street at Safeway, who played in a country band on weekends. His name was Ken Dudney, and I thought he was cute. He was also seven and a half years older than me.

Ken used to wander into the store, to buy drums or a ukulele, and Daddy would brag about his three daughters, including his oldest daughter who played in the band. Daddy offered him a job, and I met him when Ken came down wearing a suit to take some publicity pictures at the store.

Later, he told me that when he first saw me he thought to himself, "Wow, this is a cute little girl." The way he puts it, he was young for his age and I was old for mine. He didn't know I was only fourteen.

Ken had lived in the Northwest, and when his parents divorced, he lived in Richland, Washington, with his aunt and uncle, Martha and Jim Stifter. Then he lived with his father in Topeka,

Kansas, during his first year in college. Now he was in California, going to college and working two or three jobs. He could read music, had played some light opera, and he had danced ballet.

One of the things that attracted me to Ken—even before I knew it—was my feeling that he was intelligent, informed, learned. He was a college boy, and we did not have many of those in the family at the time. I mean, he was not a showoff or a braggart, but he just carried himself in a way that told you he knew some things, he had taken some courses, he had studied, he had read some books. We all have our areas of expertise. I have mine, and obviously Daddy and Momma have theirs, but Ken knew a lot I didn't. I don't think I could have fallen in love with a man I didn't respect that way.

Ken seemed pretty grown up to me, although I was not a little baby anymore. I wasn't particularly precocious because of performing in Las Vegas. That was a pretty wholesome environment, with good people keeping an eye on me and probably shielding me from growing up too soon. But nature has a way of arriving right on time.

When I was in the fourth grade, I brought home a note that said we were going to see a movie about a woman's monthly cycle. Momma said, "You're going to learn about the birds and the bees," and I, with my usual confident attitude, announced, "Oh, I already know about the birds and the bees," so she signed the note that said it was all right to see the movie.

The truth was, I didn't know anything about the birds and the bees. As a matter of fact, I didn't know anything about sex, either. I thought the movie was very interesting, but it didn't tell us very much. One of my girlfriends in the fourth grade knew a whole lot more than the movie covered, and when she told me what it was all about, I said, "I don't believe it. You must be crazy. How disgusting. How horrible."

My parents hadn't told me a whole lot, but they got along so well that I grew up with a healthy, positive feeling about marriage. And they certainly monitored us closely. When I was around twelve, Daddy told me I should start wearing a brassiere. At first I was so proud of being able to wear one that I would deliberately let the strap hang out of my sleeveless blouse.

Not long after that, I was staying with Al and Ena Long, a

wonderful couple who were friends of the family, while my parents went back to Illinois because Grandpa McGill had passed away. While I was staying at their house, I called Ena in and said, "Aunt Ena, I just started my period." She said, "Well, fine, good." And I said, "No, ma'am, you don't understand, this is my first time." So she had to give me a little advice, and I thought, How terrible to make somebody else get involved in something that personal; but I'll always remember how helpful and sweet she was.

Years later, I looked forward to my one and only daughter growing up, and I wanted to make sure she was prepared, so I used to talk to her about becoming a young woman. And yet she was staying with Newt and Janice Lovvorn on the night Matthew graduated from high school. Janice and I used to say, "What are we going to do with our daughters when the time comes?" That night she called me at home and said, "You know how we always say, 'What are we going to do'? Well, our Jaime . . ." So I wasn't there for Jaime, either. Janice turned out to be Ena for my daughter.

Anyway, I was a big girl by the time Ken arrived in our lives. I had a "boyfriend," Danny Sneed, who played the steel guitar, but we communicated mostly through little notes in the mail. I think we saw each other alone three times, and I had never dated anybody seriously—certainly not anybody twenty-one.

Ken was really nice to all of us. When we would travel on weekends, he would fuss with Louise and Irlene more than he paid attention to me. He would take us to the movies or out for ice cream, never showing me any special attention. Both Louise and Irlene swear they had already picked Ken out for their future husband.

There was one little complication for little Louise and little Irlene. This poor, shy, backward boy already had a girlfriend—a beautiful young woman his own age, who danced in the same ballet group. Ken had taken up ballet as therapy for arthritic feet he had gotten working as a gardener and watering the plants. For a while, he had to walk with canes; that's how bad it was. Ballet was supposed to keep the feet supple. Maybe it did or maybe it didn't. Anyway, he was engaged. And she was beautiful.

One day Ken was driving me somewhere and he picked her up in his car. I can still remember getting jealous at the way she sat next to him and put her hand on his knee. I could have scratched her pretty brown eyes out. She was this beautiful girl with these pretty legs with shorts on, and I just didn't like her at all.

Not long after that, my cousin Danny Pollard took me, Louise, and Irlene to the drive-in movie to see *Days of Wine and Roses.* At intermission, when the lights came on, I saw Ken's car.

You couldn't miss it—an orange 1955 Oldsmobile that had been in a few wrecks in its time, and whose back wheels were a foot or two to the left of the front wheels. Ken was regularly being stopped by the Highway Patrol and being told, "Do you know that car is going down the road sideways?" And Ken would say, "No, officer, really?"

This was definitely his car. There weren't two like it. And when the lights went on for intermission, these two heads were really enjoying a big, long kiss. I knew it was her by her shadow. Ever since then, I've hated that movie. Ken says I was spying on him, but, really, we just happened to be there.

I probably was pretty ornery when the two of them were together. I'd like to think I had something to do with them breaking up, but Ken says I can't take the credit for that. They would fight about things other than me, and she would throw his engagement ring in his general direction, and he would scoop it up and loyally bring it back to her the next day.

The trick was to catch him between retrieving the ring and giving it back to her.

When Ken turned twenty-two, I thought I would impress this man, and I baked him a birthday cake and decorated it myself. I took the whipped-cream dispenser and wrote, "Happy 22TH Birthday." Now, that was not on purpose. I was too stupid to spell it right.

Shortly afterward, Ken asked me to give him a lesson on the steel guitar. He had never shown any interest in me before, and I didn't think he was about to start now, so I gave him a lesson in an empty rehearsal room.

Afterward, Ken said, "When are you going to give me my birthday kiss? You never did give me my birthday kiss." He was sitting in an easy chair. There is some difference of opinion as to who reached out to whom, but the end result was, I sprawled down on his lap and kissed him right on the mouth.

I am not trying to embellish things, but I just melted. I didn't know there was a kiss like this. And to this day, he is a great kisser. Boom. I saw fireworks.

Meantime, Ken told me later, he was thinking, "Gollllly, I could be thrown in jail for what I'm thinking, let alone kissing this fourteen-year-old girl."

There were a few reasons why it didn't go any further: The Law. Religion. Irby Mandrell's Well-Known Sense of Right and Wrong. And Mary Mandrell's Frying Pan. We didn't discuss the feeling between the two of us. We just knew it was there.

We gave it a few chances to go away. Ken's fiancée had done her occasional ring-throwing number and he had given it back. She tossed it one more time—and he held on to it for a while.

However, being fourteen and fickle, now that Ken was not engaged, I was more than willing to bequeath him to Louise and Irlene. So I gave the poor guy a hard time.

When my eighth-grade graduation came around, I wanted my parents to buy me a wrist corsage, but they didn't. And I was so snippy about it that when Ken came over that night and gave me a regular corsage, I decided I didn't like him anymore. Being a mature, twenty-two-year-old man, Ken was polite to me. He wasn't rude, but he also wasn't interested in me.

Naturally, after being ignored for a few days, I fell, and when I fell, I fell head over heels. He knew how to catch me. Since I knew he didn't care for me, I went after him. And after that, we were boyfriend and girlfriend, 1963 style.

It certainly did not strike me as unusual to be going out with an older man. I felt grown up because I was a performer. Besides, women do grow up young. My mother had been sixteen when she was married and Loretta Lynn was not quite fourteen when she married Mooney.

And Juliet was only fourteen when she met Romeo. Of course, you could say, "Look what happened to them." And you might be right.

We didn't make a big show of our feelings, and because we started out so innocently in the same band, nobody had a clue about how we felt, for a while. We must have seemed like big brother and little sister to people. Ken sold that lopsided Olds and bought an old seven-passenger Cadillac limousine, dark blue, which he used to pick me up at high school. One day he jumped out of the driver's seat wearing a chauffeur's hat and came around and opened the back door. My high-school sensibilities acted up and I was embarrassed.

"Get in this car," I hissed. "Just get in this car."

That's how we related. Not quite Romeo and Juliet.

Ken didn't have any money but he had a lot of charm. He'd say, "I'm taking you out to eat. I just got paid, so you can have a nice dinner tonight—anything you want." I'd know it was true, so I would order steak. Then he would tell the waiter, "Oh, she had a steak, I guess I'll just have a hamburger. That's all I can afford now." He liked to embarrass me with his jokes. Still does.

When our band played the military base, we'd work forty-five minutes and take fifteen-minute breaks, and Ken would ask me to dance to the music of the jukebox. He could never dance the funky stuff I liked, but he is the most beautiful slow dancer. He'd make me feel like the queen of the world.

I soon discovered he had an odd sense of humor. He is such a tease. He would ask me, "Barbara, would you like to dance?" and I would say yes, and he would say, "Well, keep sitting there and maybe somebody will ask you."

(He's done that to me a million times and I'm sick of it, but I still fall for it. On our twenty-second anniversary recently, all three of our children were home. I asked Matthew to run out and buy something from Bonanza for dinner, and I set the table on our screened-in porch. I put out my presents to Ken, and we ate this nice dinner which I didn't have to cook. Afterward, I gave him a music box that was a cable car. You wind it up and it plays, "I Left My Heart in San Francisco," which is our song. We have a deal between us that whenever that song is played, whether we can dance or not, even if we're in a car or at a show, he has to ask me to dance, and I have to say yes, and if we're in a place where we can dance, we must dance.

(On the night of our anniversary, he looked at me with that music box playing and he said, "Barbara, would you like to dance?" and he took me by the hand, and we started dancing on the porch, and it was pretty with the candles lit, and I'm just paying attention to dancing with him, and when the music box wound down, all three of our children had quietly left the porch, so we could be together. That was so sweet of the kids, because there have only been four or five anniversaries when we could be together.)

It took me a while to get used to his odd sense of humor.

Sometimes we'd be dancing to something slow and romantic, and suddenly he would say in a rather loud voice, "What'd you say, Barbara? No, I will *not* buy you a beer." And heads would turn, because most people there knew I was not old enough to drink. He just did it to tease me.

After a while, we decided we really did not want people to know we were boyfriend and girlfriend, and that it would be good to argue a little bit. So we began to bicker, criticizing each other, playing can-you-top-this? Wouldn't you know it, we got into the habit and we're still doing it. Two officers trying to lead the same company.

We were still together when I got to high school, looking forward to spending the rest of our lives together. I would sit in class and practice writing my name: Mrs. Kenneth Lee Dudney, or Mrs. Kenneth L. Dudney, or Mrs. Barbara Dudney. Pages of it. As much as I loved music, I just wanted to be his wife. That's all I cared about. When people would comment that youth goes by so fast, all I could think was, "You're crazy, this time goes on forever."

Our romance wasn't always perfect. One time I threatened to break up with him, and I finally did, and I went out with somebody else. Ken came over to my house and asked me whether I kissed the other boy good night. I remember I was combing my hair standing at the sink in my parents' bathroom. When I said I did, Ken slapped me and sent me sprawling clear into the bathtub. Then he started crying. He was very upset at what he had done.

Another time, I got mad at him and hauled off and slapped him. He slapped me back.

"I can't believe you'd slap a lady," I said.

"The moment you slapped me, you ceased to be a lady," he said.

We got that stuff out of our system early. We know better now.

When I was around sixteen, we started making plans to get married. He took the ring his fiancée had given back to him, and a jeweler gave him credit toward a ring Ken had designed for me. His lucky number is thirteen, so he had arranged for twelve tiny diamonds and a single one-third carat in the middle.

In October of 1965, when I was not yet seventeen, Ken was accepted into a program that trained you to fly, and if you passed the test you became a naval officer. He went away to training, and was able to pay off the ring. At my request, and against his better judgment, I kept it at home in my drawer. At night, I would put it on and sleep with it on, and then put it back in my drawer when I went to school.

My parents knew we had been going out, but they did not know how serious we were. They loved Ken, and rented him a guest house we owned, charging him pennies. But we didn't want to tempt fate until I was graduated from high school and old enough to get married. My immature teenage thinking was, "It's not fair that I can't be engaged. Of course, I'm going to finish high school." I resented that I couldn't be engaged.

One morning, while Ken was in Florida in Navy training—I'm sure it was God's plan—I forgot and left the ring out. While I was at school, my mother found it. I got a call at school to call home. I still remember, it was a rainy day. I went home and my parents said they had always believed me, always trusted me, but now they were upset at finding the engagement ring.

I pleaded with them and said I was not going to get married until I finished high school, but they said it was still another year and a half before I would be graduated and they said I could not be engaged.

My parents said I had to call Ken's mother and take the ring down to Escondido and give it to her to hold for Ken. My father contacted Ken down in Pensacola, and told him he was not to see me or call me or write me in any form. Daddy reminded Ken that you had to be twenty-one to be legal in this state, and Daddy said he would contact Ken's commanding officer and get him in trouble. Daddy did not have to add that the news would not do any good for Ken's career as a potential Navy pilot.

I have never told this story in public before. Up until now, our marriage has always sounded like peaches-and-cream, like Ken-and-Barbie. But there was nothing plastic about the pain all of us felt at the time. I know I was upset, and Ken was sad, and my parents were hurt and angry to find out about the ring.

Some members of the family are not comfortable with my bringing up this conflict from so many years ago. They are afraid somebody is going to look bad—me, or Ken, or my parents, or all of us.

But you know what? Looking back, I think we all acted extremely well. Ken and I were treating our courtship with strong Christian respect. Momma and Daddy had their rules about my finishing school and waiting until I was eighteen. And I respect that.

If I were to find an engagement ring in Jaime's room when she turns sixteen, I guess I would probably get her a private tutor to come to our house to teach her, and I would probably never let her get through the two armed police guards I would hire to make sure she could never leave our house to go anywhere, ever. So I think my parents were pretty understanding at the time.

I have no problem finally telling this story. The important thing is, I obeyed my parents. Of course, at the time I thought my life was over.

15

"I THOUGHT SHE DIED"

KEN SAYS HE BUCKLED when he got the call from R.C. The first words he heard were "There's been an accident, the driver of the other car was killed." But then he heard R.C. saying, "But everybody's going to be all right." That made him feel a little better, until he realized I was going to the hospital with head injuries and broken bones.

Somehow, Ken managed to wrap up all his business in the next hour or two and still was able to catch the red-eye from Seattle to Atlanta, arriving in Nashville just after dawn. He rushed to the hospital, but I don't remember him arriving.

I do know that long before my memory began again, while I was still in deep trauma, I was aware of a strong presence by my side. That presence was so strong that I was able to focus my pain and my anger and my fear on it.

From what I am told, I was sweet with Louise and Irlene

and our parents. I was moody with the doctors and the nurses—cooperative at times, mean at other times. But with Ken I was consistent. Consistently miserable. All the pain I felt, all the anger, all the loss of control, I took out on this big, strong, intelligent man who was coordinating everything.

You explain it. The doctors tell me it is absolutely normal for somebody to lash out after an accident, from any kind of pain. But why would I be worse with the person I love most in the whole world? You could say, "That's human nature." But why?

By the time Ken saw me in the hospital, I was in a tiny glassed-in cubicle in the cardiac unit, in traction, with that pin inserted through the broken femur. I was under medication with intravenous tubes connected to my body.

He says he tried talking to me, but I did not know who he was. I would open my eyes and look around but I was groggy, just out of it. And all the time, people were coming and going because this was the middle of the heart unit, with people requiring constant life-saving care.

In the morning, the neurosurgeon came in, a very nice, intense man. He said, "Hello, Ms. Mandrell, I'm Dr. Bond, do you know where you are?"

Ken says my eyes fluttered, as if I were trying to think, but I only shook my head left and right and wouldn't say anything.

"You've been in an automobile accident," Dr. Bond said. "You're fine. You're in Baptist Hospital."

He left the room and came back ten minutes later.

"Hello, Ms. Mandrell, do you know where you are?" And I said, "Phoenix," which wasn't even accurate, because we were supposed to be in Hutchinson, Kansas. A while later he would ask the same questions and I would answer, "New Orleans," which was a moral victory since I was actually supposed to be in New Orleans.

"No, you're in Baptist Hospital. You've been in a car accident and you're going to be fine. You're in a cardiac-care unit in Baptist Hospital with a broken leg. You're going to be fine. Do you understand?"

Maybe I would nod, and maybe I wouldn't. And sometimes I would cuss. Bad stuff, the kind you hear out in the street—or on some of the cable television channels, for that matter. Really heavyweight cussing.

When I started talking again, the doctor would come in and I would say, "Oh, how are you, nice to see you." But when I would see Ken standing next to the bed, I would yell, "What the hell do you want? Get the hell out of here." And worse. I don't remember any of it. I'm embarrassed because I do not use that language, even when I lose my temper, which has been known to happen. But it just goes to show what is lurking below the surface. I have never been a big fan of psychiatry. Maybe I should be, but it seems like too much double-thinking going on. However, it surely was a revelation to me what kind of garbage and bad behavior floats around in your mind.

Our preacher, Mike Nelson, told Ken about a preacher friend of his who had a head injury, and he cussed like a sailor. I guess nobody's immune.

Ken says the doctors kept waiting for me to snap out of my stupor but as that first full day went by, I showed no signs of recognition or taking information. Up to that point, I guess, they had been concentrating on the obvious open fracture of the femur and the cuts to my legs, arm, and face.

Even though I was out of my mind, I would insist that my ankle hurt, even though there was no swelling, no black and blue marks. So finally they did a scan of my ankle and found out it was broken in five places. It's not surprising they had missed it the first night, given all the other things wrong with me. Anyway, they set it and eventually put it in a cast when I left the hospital.

Not because they discovered it belatedly, but because the blood does not flow easily in the ankle, the healing takes a long, long time. Aside from my head, the broken ankle is the injury I still feel the most. Sometimes I can be bouncing around the house and the ankle just gives out. I try to fake it, but it's all I can do to keep from stumbling to the floor.

What I do not understand is why the ankle has never gone out on me on stage. Not once. I have had it so painful that I couldn't walk off the bus without limping, and I have to wrap it in heating pads. But never has the ankle betrayed me on stage. Don't tell me that's adrenaline. That's God watching over me, just as He was in those days after the wreck.

They were so busy putting me back together again that they assumed I would come out of the fog. But after twenty-four hours had gone by, Ken says, they began voicing concern that my head injury was worse than they expected. He was still in my room at two-thirty in the morning when the doctors decided to wheel me down for a CAT scan of my head. That sounds like a weird time to do anything, but as I was to learn, a hospital is a busy place around the clock, and they have to wait for machines to become available.

After they analyzed the CAT scan, they decided my head injury was worse than expected. There was some fluid in the frontal lobe, but it wasn't anything alarming, and they did not see any blood in the brain. I was lucky, if you stop to think about it. That accident, two cars going fifty-five miles an hour, was the equivalent of hitting a brick wall at a hundred and ten miles an hour. Only that seat belt kept me from being killed. But they now realized I had taken a worse shot than they had thought.

People started coming in, my family, dear friends Tim and Cathy Bucek, other friends, just to try to bring me around, mentally. But I was out of it. Daddy and Louise held a press conference almost right away to express sympathy for Mark White and to say that we would all be okay. Dr. Jones, who was not used to public appearances, was asked to describe my injuries. Although his specialty is bones, he was asked mostly about my head injuries, and he had to keep assuring people that I was not in a coma.

My family and the doctors did what they could to minimize the talk about the damage to my head. We just didn't want to alarm our fans, the people who love us. We wanted to get through it. They said I'd be back in six to eight weeks, but anybody who saw me in the hospital knew it would be longer than that.

President Reagan called from Air Force One, and former President Jimmy Carter also called. Ken had to thank them and say I couldn't quite come to the phone. Good thing. I'd have hated two fine men to have heard my post-wreck vocabulary.

They did not tell me anything about the accident, and I did not ask. I certainly did not read any of the cards and letters coming in. Ken did show me a sampling of the flowers, but I had no way to understand that, within a few days, five hundred floral arrangements had arrived. They could not put many of the flowers in my room because they would deplete the oxygen supply, so they stored them in a room in the basement before finally dividing them among other patients at the hospital. I had no sense of any of it.

I was in outer space. They had all this apparatus hooked into me, including a catheter because I could obviously not get up to go to the bathroom. Still, I had this feeling of urgency that I had to go, and I would try to unhook all the apparatus. They tell me I would swing and push hard on the leg, trying to get out, but I was working against a twenty-two-pound weight and a set of pulleys. I am something of a determined person, in my right mind or out of it, and Ken had to come over and hold me down. Meanwhile, the pin through my leg would hurt like crazy, and from deep in the cave, wherever I was, I knew only one thing—it was all Ken's fault.

"I've got to go to the bathroom," I would shout.

"No, you're going to the bathroom in a bag," Ken would say.

"No, I'm not."

And he would pick up the bag and show it to me and that pacified me, for a few minutes.

Then the doctor would come in and I would ask, "Can you get me out of this?"

"No, you've got to keep that on."

"But I've got to go to the bathroom."

"Well, you are going, you're catheterized," the doctor would say.

"No, my husband took me to the bathroom a while ago."

And Ken would have to explain. This was how we passed the time, for days on end. It was a lot of laughs—particularly for Ken.

Exactly a week after the crash, on September 18, which Dr. Jones just happens to remember because it is his birthday, they had to repair the damage to my broken leg. The Steinman pin was just a device for putting the leg in traction. Now they had to make sure the bone healed.

"It was like planning the invasion of Normandy," Dr. Jones has said. "We had to plan surgery but I didn't tell any of our schedule people because I didn't want to put Barbara's name down on a list. Normally, we do surgery at eight in the morning, but I was low profile about it. I just said we had something special planned that night, and we went and did it.

"We used Room Ten at Baptist, and we gave her a spinal, and I took a drill and backed out the old pin. We perform the repairs by remote control, by propping the patient on her side. It's a most unusual scene, with her contorted. My brother, Frank, who is also an orthopedic surgeon, was working with me. We make a small incision over the hip, into the top end of the thigh bone, and we insert a high-tech drill. Then we watch on TV while the drill does the work. We widen the hole from eight millimeters to eight-and-a-half to nine, and you overdrill slightly.

"Then we insert something called a Sampson nail, a curved nail with sharp flutes. You tap the thing and when it goes into place, everybody gives a hooray. I remember thinking again that this is somebody in the public eye, which just makes the sweat pop out a little more. We worked from eight-thirty until eleven P.M. and the leg looked great."

After the operation, I was still ranting and raving, getting worse. Ken says the night nurse came and tried to control me, but I started pummeling her, cussing her up and down. I was so abusive that they had to call a doctor after midnight, and he prescribed Valium as a sedative. They came in and had to hold me down to give me a shot, and I was still rambling even though they were giving me more Valium intravenously. They tell me I kept ranting and raving until two-thirty in the morning.

"Finally, it was like a light switch had been turned off," Ken has said. "She had been horrible, horrible, and all of a sudden, click, she went out. She was gone, that fast. I thought she died, it was that fast, but I saw her heartbeat on the monitor. And from that moment on, she was fine. She was never like that again.

"When she woke up the next morning, she'd slept, the first time she slept more than two hours. She slept seven or eight hours that night and allowed me to get some sleep. I would only sleep an hour at a time on the chair right next to the bed. They took her into surgery and got her leg pinned, and she didn't go back to the cardiac-care unit again and she began recovering better."

Dr. Jones has said that I was answering some questions rationally even in those first two weeks, particularly about cutting down on the Demerol I was receiving. He said he could tell right away that I am not a person who uses much alcohol or any medication, and he felt I was challenging him to take me off the medication.

"I knew she was a strong person," the doctor said, "but I became aware of her ability to take pain."

The scandal magazines have suggested that I was "addicted" to one drug or another, but that is ridiculous. The doctors were doing their best to find the appropriate level of medication for somebody who has come close to dying in a car crash. Dr. Jones talks about "the Catch-22 of medication," either being in pain or being zonked. For whatever it means, I seemed to gravitate toward pain.

For some head patients, the mixture of pain and medication puts them into a passive state. My body was tied down, but my spirit was raging.

"You were uncontrollable," Ken has told me. "I know you don't like me to use the word 'grotesque,' but that's what it was. We couldn't reason with you. You just wanted to get out of bed. Then you started throwing things at me—trays, drinking cups, anything within reach. You were just sweeping pitchers off the bed stand, out of control. But after they changed the medicine, you calmed down and were never that physically violent again."

That incident finally got to Ken. He went in and had a long talk with the neurosurgeon, who said my behavior was quite logical. The way the doctor explained it, because I know how much Ken loves me, I could vent my anger on Ken. Even in that traumatized state, I did not want to make the other people mad at me, but I knew Ken was always going to be there.

My contention is, why would you do it in front of people you love when you wouldn't do it in front of people you don't love? But I understand what the man meant. Like the song says, you always hurt the one you love. And who did I love more than Ken?

People have asked Ken if there was ever a time when he

thought I might not make it. Ken says, "No, not after the first day. But because they didn't know what was happening with her brain, we didn't know what her situation was going to be. We didn't know if she was ever going to work again."

To me, there were two levels of recovery: whether I was going to survive the accident, and whether I was going to be the same person again.

"She's still not the same person," Ken will say. "There are things about her that are not the same. She doesn't want to hear most of them, but it's true."

He's right on both counts, by the way. I do not want to hear it from anybody else, even from Ken. It makes me furious when he or Daddy say I'm not the same. It's almost like trying to control me, or limit me. But then if you ask me my opinion, I would tell you I am not the same. Gone is the precocious little girl, so optimistic, so energetic, like a teenager out on her first date.

16
HIGH-SCHOOL GIRL

AFTER MOMMA AND DADDY ordered Ken and me to stop seeing each other, Ken tried to call me one time, but I hung up. I didn't want to make things worse. We honored Momma and Daddy by not seeing each other, and I walked around totally lost, convinced that my life had been taken away from me.

I thought I would pine away without Ken, but I had my music, and I was sixteen, and it was California, and it was the Sixties.

I managed to keep busy. Oceanside High School in the middle Sixties could have been the basis for every California teenage movie you ever saw. We had it all.

Half the kids in town were surfers who liked beach clothes, although I was not one of them. The girls wore their hair in the long blond straight fashion of the Sixties, but I liked the other style, where my hair was all done up with kind of a Connie Stevens ponytail, big and tall on top. I also liked wearing lots of makeup, which took some trouble to put on, and you certainly did not want to lie on the beach with that hairdo and that makeup, so I was never one to sunbathe. But there was a lot of talk about getting your rays, and hanging ten, right out of a Beach Boys song, and those kids were my friends.

Living in a Beach Boys song also meant I had some friends with great cars. Brian Lonbeck, one of the guys in our band, had a fantastic Plymouth with a 383 in it, torque flight speed transmission. Another friend had a '66 Dodge with a 426 Hemi in it, dual quads, ram induction, with a Hurst four-speed from the factory. That was my love, drag racing, quarter mile. I loved watching the guys take care of their cars, squirting in the fuel with that plup-plup sound. Not at the track, but on the open road. Stupid, if you look back, but we all survived.

Some of the guys would let me drive their cars. One time, I popped a six-inch wheel stand. We shouldn't have been going that fast, but I learned to handle a car, learned respect for what it could do. A year or two later you wouldn't catch me going those speeds, and when I became a mother I slowed down some more, so you cannot equate my drag-racing days with the accident twenty years later. Apples and bananas. But I've always had a love of speed, which is why I loved flying with the Blue Angels and the Thunderbirds years later, and flying Mach 1.1 speed in the F-18.

I am very pro-military. Always have been. The kids at Oceanside who were surfers, beach kids, didn't like the military. The Vietnam War was cooking up, and the country was becoming divided between the hawks and the doves, and you can guess where I stood on that one. I'd keep my mouth shut when I'd hear people criticize our country and the military, but I do remember one time there were rumors that a motorcycle gang was coming to take over the beach. I have nothing against motorcyclists, not responsible ones, but this was supposed to be a gang, a bunch of tough guys. They were going to take over the beach. And the Marines met them. One of the bases sent out a contingent of Marines, more or less unofficially, just to take their training down at the beach that day. By coincidence. Bunch of guys with bald heads and thick muscles standing around the beach. Hey, welcome to Oceanside. Just passing through? That's nice. After that, the surfers decided they loved those guys in uniform.

My school was so overcrowded with the baby boomers, all the kids who had been born in the first wave after World War II. We were on double shifts, sharing classrooms, so I didn't really know everybody. Nowadays, people come up to me and say they knew me back at Oceanside, and I always say yes, but in truth I was not in the thick of things there.

I was so busy with things outside school. When I was a sophomore in high school, I entered the local beauty pageant, The Fairest of the Fair, which people usually call Miss Oceanside. It wasn't a talent show, just bathing suit and evening gown and personality. I could talk a little, and I figured I had a chance at being one of the runners-up, but I thought the contest was geared toward a couple of the older girls. I remember the night of the contest, when they announced the runners-up, and I was annoyed because they never mentioned me. Ken was working at one of his three jobs that night, and he had just walked through the back door of the auditorium when he heard them announce the winner was . . . Barbara Mandrell.

Because I got along with people, the Chamber of Commerce sent me out to cut ribbons at the openings of every supermarket and boutique for a year. There was not a week that went by that my picture wasn't in the papers at least once. So everybody at the high school knew me and would say, "Hi, Barbara." I really appreciated the friendliness, but now I couldn't tell you the names of a hundred people from those days.

I had a handful of close friends, and some of them were the teachers and ladies who worked in the office. I was old before my time, and I guess I related more to the older women who worked in the cafeteria than I did to the kids hanging out at the beach. Now it's the other way around. I still think of myself as being in my twenties—until I look in the mirror.

Because I was busy playing the military bases on weekends, I went to only one football game when I was in high school—homecoming day, when I had been chosen the freshman princess. But I loved the football players at Oceanside High. We had the top team in the Avocado League, as I recall. Our team was about a third Samoans—smart, fast, tough, great athletes, and nice-looking bodies, too. Put a football uniform on them and they were not afraid of anything. About a third of our team was black, and they were great guys, too, and about a third of the team was white. We must have had some Mexicans, too. I don't remember any racial friction when I was going through high school. It was an upbeat time in that part of California, and I think the winning football teams helped make everybody closer.

I hate to say this, but I was so busy with music that I did not have time to be much of a student. And I'm also ashamed to admit that, from the time I began performing in public at the age of eleven, Momma never asked me to set the table or wash dishes or do any of those household chores. And once my sisters started performing, it was the same for them.

I was supposed to keep my room clean, but I was just like my children: my room was a mess—not just the bed unmade, but things strewn all over. Momma was so shrewd. I came home from school a couple of times and everything I owned was dumped in a pile in the middle of the room. So I had to straighten everything. After that, for about a week, I'd have a nice clean room.

While holding down a full-time job, Momma did all the dirty work around the house. She also encouraged us to have skills and take responsibilities, and she trusted my judgment. I'm not kidding when I say that from the time I was ten, Momma let me pick out her clothes. She loved my taste. If I said, "Take this back," Momma would take it back.

When I was around twelve, I told Momma, "You know, Mom, you'd look cute with that bubble haircut," which was the big fashion at the time. I had never cut hair in my life except to cut my bangs, but my parents had raised us to believe there was nothing we couldn't do. So she said, "Why don't you do it for me?" I put her in a chair with a magazine and a cup of coffee and I cut her hair in a bubble, and everybody who's cut hair knows it's not easy because it's layered. And I'll be danged if I didn't do a good job with it. After that, I was her personal hairdresser, cutting and combing her hair regularly. I also manicured her nails, and she loved it. I loved touching her and doing things for my mom.

When I was around fifteen or sixteen, Momma let me pick out the furnishings for our house in Oceanside. I cannot imagine Jaime decorating a room for me, but Momma trusted my taste. From this, I developed a sense of confidence in myself, that I could do anything.

Confidence is so important. If the people closest to you don't say you look pretty, you never feel pretty. If those closest to you don't brag when you bring home an A or a nice project in school, then you can't have pride in yourself. My mother let us do things, and she also set an example by doing things with her own hands.

For example, for many years, she made all my costumes and

my band's costumes, too. And this while holding down a full-time job, without any housekeeper coming in. We girls were not expected to do many household chores, and to this day I do not know how Momma managed it all.

Our band kept going after Ken went into the service. Daddy had hired another musician, a kid named Mark Peppard, who was younger than I was and had a voice that could tear people up. Ken had even taught him the drums so he could take Ken's place with the band. Daddy says Ken made sure we hired somebody younger, who would not take Ken's place with me. But Ken says not so.

I was making twenty dollars a job, with two jobs every weekend. That wasn't bad money in those days. I was a kid, living at home, my parents providing a roof over my head, so I was able to buy some clothes. At one time I had forty pairs of high heels. Of course, they only cost $6.98 a pair, but that was a lot of money then. We believed in dressing up, not in the blue jeans and yoked shirts and the real hayseed country look, but I could not escape the stigma of being a country singer.

As the Rhonda Kye Fleming and Dennis Morgan song says, "I Was Country (When Country Wasn't Cool)." And let me tell you, in Oceanside, California, in the middle Sixties, country was most emphatically not cool.

Ever since I was eleven and doing the *Town Hall Party* television show every Saturday night up in Los Angeles, I would go back to school on Monday and hear some of the kids go, "*Town Hall Party,* yee-haw" or "Country music, yee-haw." I'd walk down the hall and hear the word "hillbilly." That may not have been a fighting word, but it surely was a cold-stare word. You put country people together, a couple of southerners, maybe, and if one of us calls the other a hillbilly, that's a term of endearment. But it is a derogatory comment from little kids, making fun of somebody else.

Not that I ever lived up in the hills until we built our log house in 1988. But hillbilly isn't just about hills. It's not even regional. It's a state of mind. We were living near the beach in California, but we were hillbillies.

Talk about a split personality. On weekends, I'd be singing and playing backup behind country musicians like Gordon Terry, Joe Maphis, Jimmy Dickens, Eddie Dean and others, while during the school week I was studying classical music with Mr. A. R. Lambson, the most caring teacher I had. I still keep in touch with him.

In the mornings, I would come in early to sing in the a cappella English madrigal group. I loved madrigal singing because the different parts were not all harmony of one melody, but counterparts against each other, and it worked so well. Although I sang in my normal alto on the job, I sang soprano in choir.

Mr. Lambson taught us to study operas in Italian or French or German. Even if you did not understand those languages, you could still enjoy the performance. He also taught us to enjoy classical guitar, which I adore to this day. Last year my band bought me a collection of Andrés Segovia compact disks, and if you should happen to have my phone number, if we have to put you on hold, you'll hear classical guitar, not country.

At the same time, I enjoyed being in the marching bands. That's what I mean when I say I'm a melting pot of all the music I like. I loved the madrigals, but you'd have to say I spent a little more time listening to Elvis. I was too young to remember all the fuss when he broke in, how the television cameras wouldn't show him below the waist because of the "shameful" way he wiggled. Elvis the Pelvis. So what? When I started to follow Elvis, he could do no wrong as far as I was concerned.

Because my career is music, I just marvel at what that man could do. He was consciously marketed as a white man who sang black, but where's the boundary? I never did get to see him perform live, but I used to see him on television and I would marvel at his control of the audience. Even when he would do something I would personally find totally unacceptable in style, he would make it work just fine. The songs, the mannerisms, the patter between songs, the way he'd move a microphone, the way he'd demand something to be done onstage, he could do anything and I would accept it because he was . . . Elvis.

I was a teenager in California when the Beatles came along. I'd hear the little girls shrieking about the Beatles, and I'd ask, "What's a Beatle?" But as soon as I heard the music, I loved them immediately. The first song of theirs I ever heard was "I Saw Her Standing There." I think I was in my bedroom, listening to the radio. The music was great, but I thought their hair was ridiculous. Maybe it was because I was used to seeing Marines at the bases on weekends, but to this day, I prefer short hair on a man. My theory is, if you're a man, look like a man.

But the harmonies? The energy? The little riffs with the French horn or the flute? I loved that stuff. We did "I Saw Her Standing There" in our Mandrell Family Band.

I think a lot of music lovers get too caught up in labels. People don't go to the movies, see a great mystery, and say, "That's it, I am never going to see a western or a comedy or a musical." That would be ridiculous. You'd just keep yourself from enjoying other kinds of movies. It's the same with music.

George Benson is a good example. He's a superb jazz musician but he was controversial because he "sold out" and did popular music. If you go hear him in concert, you'll hear "pure jazz," too, but he gets a variety of people in there and makes 'em like it.

I've been stereotyped by my music all my life, but there was one time back in Oceanside that country music got me out of a jam. Because I could not participate in some of the band concerts, I was about to get an F in one of my music classes (not from Mr. Lambson, I should add). Daddy went down to school to find out what the problem was, but the teacher said he would have to fail me if I did not play in the band concert on Friday night.

Daddy told him we had a concert of our own on Friday night, and that I just didn't have the time to appear at extracurricular activities.

"Besides," Daddy said, "if she's so important to the band, she'd better not get an F."

Then Daddy went to the principal and said he needed me at our concert Friday night because I had to back up our special guest.

"I'm bringing in Tommy Duncan," Daddy said.

"The one who used to sing with Bob Wills?" the principal asked.

"The very one," Daddy said, getting the feeling the principal just might be a reasonable man.

The principal asked how he could get invited to the show, and Daddy said he thought that could be arranged. Then the principal said that if I was so important to the Tommy Duncan show, then I ought to perform at it.

I came home that afternoon and said, "Guess what? They changed the school concert to Thursday."

It was not until nearly twenty-five years later, while we were working on this book, that my parents told me what had really happened between Daddy and the principal. They had so much respect for school that they almost never tried to get me out of anything. That was one of the rare times.

All along, I had thought Daddy had avoided going to the school because he didn't want to risk his business selling instruments to the school district. But Daddy said, "You know me, I never back away from anything."

They were great days, growing up back in Oceanside. At times, I did not realize how much I relied on Daddy and Momma, or how much they were watching over me. I only began to understand it when it was my turn to raise children.

17

MATTHEW AND JAIME

ONE THING THAT PUZZLES me is that I never asked about the children in the days after the accident. I pride myself on being a good mother. I had rushed home from New England just to have twenty-four hours with the two kids, but even when I started to come out of the clouds, I did not show much interest in them.

Ken would come in and find me talking out of my head and he would tell me, "The kids are fine," but I never asked him for details. We've decided that I was too afraid they might have been killed or gravely hurt, and I did not want to know, so I did not ask. I just shoved it out of my mind. Or maybe his telling me they were okay reassured me, and I didn't have to ask. But I'd mumble other stuff and never really ask about them.

It's probably good they did not tell me about Matthew for

a while. He was hurt more than anybody realized. While Jaime remembers details about the accident, Matthew was briefly knocked unconscious and does not remember a thing. It's strange, but Jaime said Matthew was lying on the ground, talking to people, asking them why they were doing this or that, and he was telling them stories and just talking up a blue streak.

He also doesn't remember going to the hospital, yet Jaime said he was alert in the ambulance on the way over to Hendersonville. She can remember a man in the ambulance talking in medical terms, and Matthew asking how I was, and the man saying I was fine.

In the ambulance, Matt asked, "Was it a good wreck?" and somebody said, "There's no such thing as a good wreck." Jaime remembers the nurses trying to fix Matt's face, and trying to put her in a neck brace that was too big. And when she and Matt asked how the other driver was, they were told he was perfectly okay. So they didn't think anything was wrong.

Jaime was nervous that night staying with Ron and Gail Cook, but they reassured her everything was going to be all right, and the next day she went home. She was so stiff that she could hardly walk, so Kathy made her sit in the whirlpool, and that took some of the pain away.

"The phone never did stop ringing," Kathy said. "I gave the same information to everybody. Wayne Newton. Brenda Lee. They all wanted to know what they could do."

The next day, Jaime went back to school. Her friends had heard about the wreck on the news but they still wanted to believe it was another family, another Mandrell. They didn't fully understand what was going on until she came to school. She wasn't sure she could do the work, but she found it was an outlet for her, a way to forget about what had happened.

She still didn't know the man in the other car was dead until Ken came home a day or two later. She said, "Dad, I want to meet the other man," and Ken said, "He died, didn't you know that?" They had kept the news from her, or else she avoided comprehending that part of it, which is only human nature.

Matthew was in worse shape than Jaime because he had been sitting in the front seat. He had a bruised bladder from seat-belt trauma, and the whole area was swollen. He had a black eye and his nose was swollen, and his cheek was broken from hitting the dashboard. The bruised bladder was causing the bile in his system to build up, and he had a tube down his nose and into his stomach to remove the bile. He was in terrible pain.

I think people underestimated how badly Matthew was hurt. When Kathy Brown heard about the accident late Tuesday night, she was told Matt would be out of the hospital the next day. But as soon as she saw him Wednesday, she knew it would be a little longer, and it turned out to be three and a half days.

Ken said he will never forget it as long as he lives, going to the hospital to see this fourteen-year-old boy who has played hockey and tae kwon do and football, and hearing his own son say, "Dad, I wish I had died." As Ken says, that is big-time pain when you are fourteen and wish you were dead.

"Matthew went through all this pain, lying in a different hospital, with everyone giving their attention to Barbara because she was so critical," Momma says. "He was out there by himself most of the time, hurting, and no telling what he was thinking, and the newspaper reports saying he was fine, no problem. It was just like the whole world didn't care about him."

The person who is probably closest to Matthew is Louise. She has loved him and understood him since he was a baby, and that continues now that he is in college. If he has a problem, he will call Louise, which is great, because we all need somebody else besides our parents.

Finally, a day or so after the wreck, Louise realized she had not been paying attention to Matthew, so she went out to see him. She called Momma and said, "You know, Barbara has so many people visiting her, but we all must pay attention to Matt. He thinks he's dying, and none of us is out here."

One of the things that bothered Matthew was seeing that he was in the intensive-care unit. He thought that was a sign he was in worse trouble than he was. But Louise had the perfect comeback for him when he thought he was dying. She said, "Haven't we always given you intensive care?" He had no answer for that.

Everybody started to pay more attention to Matt. I re-

ceived so many flowers that they couldn't put any more in my
room. One huge bouquet came from Lynda Carter, my friend
who used to play Wonder Woman, and it had a huge balloon
attached to it. Momma took my name off the flowers and
brought them out to Matthew to let him know Wonder Woman
was thinking about him.

Maybe thinking about Lynda Carter did the trick. At any
rate, Matthew started to bounce back. They released him, and
Ken took him home. It took him a long time to get over the
bruises, physical and emotional, but he's a good boy, and he'll
be fine. I don't want to minimize the kids' problems and say it
was easy for them. Jaime has seen my personality change, and I
know it bothers her, and Matthew and I have had clashes.

Here's a kid who never had problems, never, but the dashboard was cracked in from the impact with his face. He hasn't
forgotten about it, yet his problems were put on the back
burner because of the seriousness of my injuries. I try to understand Matthew because I know what it's like to crack your head.

As the days went by, Ken told me bits and pieces of how
the children were, but nothing registered. I hardly knew who
was in the room with me, much less remembered information.
But my parents and Ken got the idea that if I saw the kids, that
might get through to me. They were supposed to wait until I
was moved from the cardiac-care unit into a private room, but
they brought Matt and Jaime for a visit.

Daddy says that when they came in, I really didn't seem to
recognize them, but I must have had some kind of maternal instincts because I kept looking at their hands. Mine were cut
from the glass, but I apparently thought I had blisters from
being burned, and I was inspecting their hands to see if they
had blisters.

Jaime says I motioned for her to sit on the bed next to
where I was lying in traction. I said, "You sit here," but she was
hesitant because of all the traction devices. I kept motioning, so
a nurse picked her up and put her on the bed, close to me. Just
then, the doctors had to do something with me, so Jaime had to
hop off again.

"It was really gross," Jaime has said. "Momma looked
pretty bad. Her face didn't look anything like her. Her hair was
way out and everything. Her arm was all in stitches. They had

her leg covered up, I think so we couldn't see. All I could see was her foot hanging out and the bars."

Jaime also remembers me constantly adjusting my position by pulling on a rope of some kind. I don't remember.

Jaime also remembers the nurses bringing in a milkshake, and how I pushed the container toward Jaime to taste. She did not have any appetite for a milkshake, but I kept forcing it at her.

Ken had told them I had a concussion, but there was no way the kids could be prepared for my mood swings or my lack of memory. I was talking nonsense for part of the time they were there. Then, about two hours after they left, somebody mentioned my children and I said, "My children haven't been here." I could not remember a thing about their visit.

They were all beginning to realize this was going to be a long haul for me. The kids would need attention, but taking care of me was a full-time job, particularly for Ken. He had married me in sickness and in health. Up to then, I had been a dynamo. Now he was getting the sickness part.

18
LOVE AND MARRIAGE

I THOUGHT MY LIFE WAS over when Ken was gone, but I discovered that life has a way of going on when you're sixteen. I didn't have many dates with the boys in high school because I wasn't around school that much after classes, but after a few months, a college man asked me out. He had a fabulous sense of humor, which he needed going out with a kid like me.

Our first date was to the drive-in movie. In a way, it was my first real date, with a man asking you out, and the two of you not knowing each other very well, so you have to make small talk. Going out with Ken, I never had felt I was on a date. We just went out. Ken and Barbara.

I didn't know how people acted on a real date, so I kept thinking what I should do next. And when you start thinking, you usually get in trouble. At one point, he pushed in his cigarette lighter. I figured I was going to be a very attractive, wonderful person, a good date, and I was going to light his cigarette. So when I heard the lighter pop, I pulled it out. However, I grabbed the dad-gum radio knob by mistake—pulled it right off the dashboard. We laughed, and he fixed it, and I was embarrassed.

Later he went to the concession stand and bought a couple of cups of cola. I didn't drink all mine, so it was still half full of ice. Sitting next to him, I thought it would be attractive to casually throw the ice out the window on his side. Unfortunately, he had raised his window. This tried his sense of humor, but he thought about it for a few seconds and laughed again. We got along great after that. He was a nice man and taught me how to play golf. We'd go to the driving range and hit a few bucketfuls, and later he trusted me enough to take me on the greens and let me play, and I didn't do anything really dumb.

I was getting to like the idea of dating. I also got to like kissing my date good night. One date complimented me on how well I kissed.

"Is that from playing the saxophone?" he asked.

I didn't want to tell the truth, which was that Ken is an excellent kisser, and I had learned from him. I don't know if it was the kisses or what, but of the six guys I dated, five proposed to me. I was flattered, but I knew I was waiting for Ken, and I guess everybody else did, too. To put it in military terms, this was kind of like marching in place.

Just before I turned eighteen in my senior year in high school, my parents said they had heard from Ken. He was coming home for Christmas.

"Because you're turning eighteen, he's asked permission to take you to church and to see you," my father said. "It's okay with us if you want to."

And I said, "Yes, I do want to see him."

I had wondered if he would forget about me. Would he be angry because I was the stupid one who left the ring out where my parents could find it? Could he still love me? Did I still love him after all this time? The second he walked in, our eyes met, and we were both uncomfortable being around other people because we *knew*. We just knew.

A couple of months later, Ken came home on leave and took me for a drive down by the ocean. He pulled the car behind an underpass, switched off the engine, and he turned to me and said, "Barbara, will you marry me?" And I said yes.

But he did not stop there. He said, "You set the date, or we won't be engaged." We looked ahead and figured the exact date of graduation and the date for our band's trip to Asia. We had been there the summer before, and now we were going back to entertain the troops again. Ken and I wanted two weeks of living together as man and wife before I left for overseas, so we were married ten days before I graduated.

Then he reached into the backseat and handed me an engagement card from his mother. The card said: "I hear you two have to get married—because you love each other so much." Gift-wrapped in the backseat were four stemware glasses. We only have three of them left, but Ken and I used them to toast each other on every anniversary, and to think about his mother. From the moment Ken proposed to me to the day she died in 1982, Beth Kurtz was a lady who could single-handedly demolish any mother-in-law joke you ever heard.

Before he took me home, he made a plan for asking my parents' permission to marry me. I was going to stay in my room, but he had a code: If he said, "Barb, come out here," I should bring the ring, but if he said, "Barbara, come out here," forget the ring. I was in my room praying that everything would go well, but their discussion lasted so long, I fell asleep. Finally, Ken walked into my room and woke me with a kiss and said, "It's all right."

My parents had known all along that Ken and I would get married someday, but that didn't make it easy for my parents to give up their first child. It was a sign of everybody getting older, of things changing, and it was hard for them to adjust to the idea of their little girl growing up and moving out. Yes, it was hard for Daddy to let go of me, but he is a Mandrell, and he did it with great style and pride. I guess that's where I get my cockiness. My mother is more nervous, more introverted, and she wasn't all that comfortable with the idea of a big wedding.

"Why don't you go to the courthouse and get married?" she asked. "Why don't you elope?"

"No," I said, "I want this wedding in the church."

We started planning the wedding at Christmastime. We didn't want to get married right away because Ken had to get his wings as a pilot first, and I was in school, and we wanted a big, traditional wedding. But I couldn't be a June bride, either, because we were leaving for Asia in early June. So we settled on May 28.

I had been planning the wedding in my mind for years, anyway, so it wasn't all that hard to put the plans down on paper. We didn't have much money, but we caught a break in that Ken and all his friends could wear their dress whites from the service. Ken looked so handsome in his uniform, and I guess that was part of the dream, too.

We decided to get married at the First Presbyterian Church in Oceanside, which I had been attending. We would be able to use the church hall for the reception instead of one of those fancy catering halls people use.

My budget for the wedding was three hundred dollars, and we just about made it. That was still pretty inexpensive, even in 1967. My flowers cost thirty dollars, done by a lady who worked out of her home. I had two baskets of flowers on the altar, which they then transferred to the room in the church for the reception. I used daisies because they were cheap and could be dyed any color, and looked pretty. I think I had candles, too. The party cost around a hundred dollars, and we bought my wedding gown for ninety-nine dollars at a shop in Oceanside.

It was a full skirt with a long train and a hoop underneath, all white, the kind of traditional look I always envisioned, with a tight bodice, tight waist. I rented the hoop because I couldn't afford to buy it. And of course it had a veil.

The newspaper described my outfit as a "bouffant gown of chantilly lace and silk organza with a jeweled and beaded bodice, featuring long bridal sleeves, with tiers of chantilly lace, and a watteau chapel train. The fingertip veil was attached to a headpiece of rose nosegay surrounded by petals of lace and baby seed pearls." I carried a corsage bouquet of white, centered with an orchid corsage.

The gown is now in my museum on Music Row in Nashville. You know me, I'm definitely a hands-on person, and I've put in a lot of my time decorating and arranging that museum myself. Just recently, Ken and I were in the museum after hours, putting some new touches on it, and we were reminiscing in front of the display case with the gown and his Navy dress whites.

"I can still get in my wedding dress. Can you get in your dress whites?" I asked, smarty-pants that I am.

My weight has been rearranged a little bit, but I think I could squeeze into it. But Ken can definitely not get into his dress whites. On our tenth wedding anniversary, we rededicated our vows in a lovely ceremony in our home, and the sign on our truck said: "Married—Definitely to Each Other," a reference to my hit record at that time, "Married—But Not to Each Other." Then we took the two kids to Disney World for our anniversary. Well, Ken and I have been talking about how to celebrate our twenty-fifth, and just to provoke him, I said, "Wouldn't it be nice if you could get in your dress whites?" and I'd wear my wedding dress. I'd like him to get down, not for the dress whites, but just so he'd be slim again, and healthier.

Nowadays we bicker about what we're going to wear for our twenty-fifth anniversary. Before we got married, we bickered about other things.

Louise insists that Ken and I actually drove in separate cars to our premarriage meeting with the minister because we were having a tremendous quarrel. Could be.

We were having a horrendous fight about something or other. It doesn't matter about what. But when we zoomed up in separate cars from separate directions, the minister started asking us questions like, "Why do you love her? Why do you want to marry her?" and we looked in each other's eyes and remembered how much in love we were. It's the same thing today. When I heard Ken answer the minister's questions, all signs of being angry just vanished.

We used to apologize so easily, particularly Ken, but I think I was kind of hardheaded, and now he's become more like me. I remember my father told Ken at the wedding reception, "If you and Barbara ever have a serious argument, I can tell you right now, it's your fault because Barbara is never wrong." I guess that's why I'm Daddy's daughter. But most of the time, Ken and I forget our little quarrels about thirty seconds after they're over. We certainly did that day in the minister's office. We were young and about to be married. What else mattered?

We did worry about the weather for the five months before, but it turned out to be a gorgeous sunny day. I remember getting up early that day, the house full of my girlfriends and relatives, which got me into a bit of trouble. The wedding was not until late in the afternoon, so I spent the whole day playing beautician.

Remember, I had been doing Momma's hair and Louise's hair and Irlene's hair since I was a kid, and it wasn't going to be any different just because it was my wedding day. I did ten women's hair when suddenly we looked at the clock and everybody started screaming because I was due at the church in forty-five minutes, and I had about two hours' worth of overhaul to do on myself.

And Momma started getting so nervous that I think she took either a sleeping pill or a tranquilizer just to get through it. It was funny to me because, whether she would admit it or not, she didn't want to let go of me, either. So we were rushing around, and everybody was jumpy, wondering if we'd get to the church on time, but we roared into the parking lot with at least ninety seconds to spare.

Momma was not the only nervous one. Irlene, who was eleven at the time, was one of my attendants. Her little bouquet of flowers was shaking like crazy, and Daddy was standing there at the back of the church watching her shake.

"When you get married, you don't want a big ceremony like this, do you?" he asked, trying to extract a promise out of her in a moment of weakness.

Irlene's voice fluttered the way you do when you try to talk while you are shivering.

"Ooooh, yes, I doooo," she managed to get out.

Now it was my turn to panic. I was all set to walk down the aisle of the church on this day of days when, for the first and only time in my life, my heel broke. Just snapped off. So I was standing there in a wedding gown, with a veil over my perplexed face, holding a heel in one hand and a shoe in the other hand.

Somebody took the shoe out of my hand and called in the Navy. That is to say, all of Ken's guys tackled the problem with the ingenuity of naval officers. The church was very pretty, circular with stained-glass windows, some of them opening onto a garden. I was told later that the guests could see these officers out there in the garden, hammering something. What they were hammering was my shoe. They straightened out the nails, lined up my heel with the shoe, and pounded the heel onto the pavement. Very mechanical instincts, those boys. Meanwhile, I hopped around on one foot in the foyer. Finally, somebody brought the shoe back to me and I prayed, "Dear God, please, let it hold until after it's official."

In my life, working in front of people since I was eleven, I had never, never felt stage fright. When I was in that beauty contest for Miss Oceanside, I remember girls saying to me, "Oooh, I'm so scared," and out of compassion for them I would say, "Oooh, me too." But it was a bunch of bull. I wasn't scared. I wasn't nervous. I kind of liked the idea of showing off in front of people. But now, the idea of walking down the aisle terrified me. I was scared and nervous and I said to Daddy, "So this is what it feels like."

Somehow I managed to put one foot in front of the other, and walked to the altar, where Ken and his best man were waiting. I remember my girlfriend Marty Gillespie sang the Lord's Prayer, and I could feel a tear coming down my face as Reverend Wayne Walker pronounced us man and wife.

Before the wedding, I had thought Ken was crazy trying to give me advice about how to conduct our kiss, but now I'm glad he did, and someday I'll recommend the same thing to my children. A week or two earlier, Ken suggested we rehearse our kiss, which was going to be in front of everybody. And so I started to kiss him, and he said, "No, no, no." Then he said, "Kind of sweet, not in any way passionate," and I said, "Hmmm," thinking this was an interesting new game, but he showed me where to put this hand and that hand, and how to put our lips together, just so. I felt that it was a very short kiss but Ken said, "It shouldn't be any longer. This is a wedding ceremony."

Looking back, I'm glad I married a very mature man because I was too young to realize. I've been to weddings where the kiss went on and on, and I thought to myself, "Ooh, save it for later." So we had this sweet, precious kiss, man and wife, and we went down the aisle and out the back to wait for the honor guard to cross the swords, so we could take pictures. We did all that, and then we were running down the hall to the reception, and my heel broke again. Courtesy of Navy ingenuity, it had held for the entire holy part of the ceremony and now it went.

I had worn orange high heels to get to the church, so I wore them to the reception. And when I took off my garter at the reception, the orange heels showed. And they showed up in the pictures, of course. And one lady said, "Didn't Barbara look pretty, but did you notice she had orange heels on?" That's the thing she probably remembered most from the wedding, how my heels did not match my gown.

Now we were married. We flitted around the reception, having a great time, greeting all the friends and family, and I had not eaten all day. Now it was evening, and Ken and I were planning our getaway. Our honeymoon was going to be spent at an apartment we had rented for two weeks before I went overseas.

Unfortunately, a few people did not want to say good-bye to us. My cousin Danny Pollard and Mark Peppard, one of the guys in the band, followed our car, which was not hard to spot since it was decorated with a just-married sign inside Navy wings, and naturally tin cans clanging off the back bumper. We couldn't lose them, so we showed up at our apartment and there they were. And in they came. Our buddies.

Uncle Al Mandrell and his wife Lynda had given us a gift of three bottles of wine, one wrapped in wedding paper, one in silver, one in gold, for the anniversaries. So here was our wine being chilled for us, and the guys all drank it. I had not eaten all day, so I made a bologna sandwich and had a glass of milk and watched *Gunsmoke* while the guys drank the wine with Ken.

Eventually they left, and I went into the bathroom and got into my nightgown, a long cream-colored gown with a high neck and pink trim, certainly the ugliest nightgown ever created, and also the least provocative. I mean, you could wear it to go outside and get the morning paper, and nobody would look twice at you. Or even once. But at the time it seemed attractive.

The last time I wore that gown was on May 23, 1983, our sixteenth anniversary. I put it on before going to bed and I asked Ken, "Notice anything special?" and he didn't have the slightest idea what I was talking about.

So I put that gown in the museum, too. The lady who works the cash register at the museum, Martha McGown, says that every couple of weeks, somebody grumbles about a wedding nightgown being on display in public.

I don't have to tell you that country music fans can be a strange mixture of prudish and natural. I mean, you've got all these drinkin' songs and cheatin' songs. I'd bet you that three-quarters of the country songs written in the last two decades have the word "body" in them, usually accompanied by adjectives like "tender" or "warm" or "trembling." I mean, we don't leave much to the imagination. On the other hand, you've got gospel songs, which I love, and a strong moral sense running through country music. I figured the gown would amuse people, but as the saying goes, it takes all kinds. So Miss Martha has to calm somebody down and say, "It's really all right, Barbara doesn't mean to offend anybody."

The first time I wore the nightgown, I'd been waiting four years, writing Ken's name over and over again in class, daydreaming about being with him. I certainly thought I was prepared for my wedding night.

It was very natural to want to experience making love with Ken. That's the magic of it, the beauty of it, when you truly love somebody. I'm not a good adviser because I'm such an imperfect person, but I think waiting is the right thing. I believe it's important to marry somebody of the same faith and to enter into it with the belief that it is for life. You must literally make it a lifetime commitment.

The waiting was over now. I brushed my hair and touched up my makeup to prepare myself for my wedding night. I was so in love, so sure that something wonderful, something beautiful, was about to happen. Ken is very sensitive, very romantic, very loving, and he was just wonderful. I was a little scared and nervous, but it was very fleeting. Everything was beautiful, bells ringing, the works. I would not change a thing, except for what happened afterward.

After this earth-shaking, magnificent experience, I was so happy, so fulfilled, that I wanted to stay up all night, talking about our life together. I soon realized I was doing all the talking. And all the listening. Ken was asleep.

How could he? How could he possibly ever sleep again after what had just happened? I was devastated. I cried, but he did not wake up. So I cried louder, but he still didn't wake up. I thought, "How on earth can he sleep after experiencing this lovely moment?"

Next, I went and sat on the couch and cried and cried, and the longer I cried, the more I thought, "This is ridiculous. I'm suffering, heartbroken, and he is asleep." So I got back in the bed and I stopped crying and I started wailing. Finally he woke up. And he was so wonderful, so comforting and apologetic, that naturally I milked it for all the sympathy I could get. And then he reminded me we both had been up for nearly twenty-four hours preparing for the wedding, and it was getting close to dawn, and we had to be up at six o'clock to go over to his mother's house and say good-bye to his aunt and uncle and grandmother who were leaving for Washington.

I understand family loyalties, so I dozed off, but when the alarm clock rang, I started thinking, "I have to get up and go out?" I really didn't want to see anyone because I thought, "They're going to look at me and say, 'I know what you've been doing.'" At eighteen, you're not exactly reasonable, so I was in a bad mood when we went over to his mother's place, and I've never let him forget it. We had been married for twelve hours, and as far as this mature young lady was concerned, the honeymoon was over.

Grandma and Grandpa
Mandrell (The Mandrell
Family)

Grandma and Grandpa McGill (The Mandrell Family)

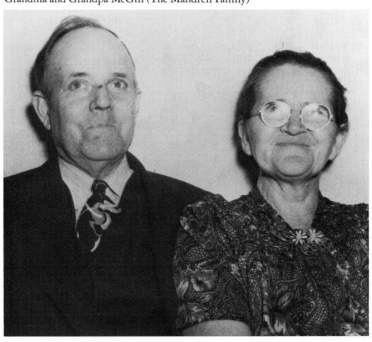

My father, Irby Mandrell, as a Corpus Christi, Texas, police officer (The Mandrell Family)

Irby and Mary Mandrell (Daddy was so proud of those yellow, red, and green boots.) (The Mandrell Family)

May 6, 1949—I was four months old (The Mandrell Family)

Age 3, with Momma in Corpus Christi (The Mandrell Family)

Playing piano at age 2 (Russell McGill)

With Aunt Thelma, holding my sister, her namesake, Thelma Louise Mandrell, and my cousins, Iris and Linda Mandrell (The Mandrell Family)

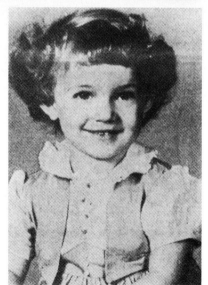

I loved to have my picture taken, even at age 3 (The Mandrell Family)

First grade (The Mandrell Family)

Second grade (The Mandrell Family)

Third grade (The Mandrell Family)

Fifth grade (The Mandrell Family)

Performing in Las Vegas with Bud Isaacs on steel and Johnny Western (who wrote and sang the theme from *Have Gun, Will Travel*, "Paladin") and Bobby Dyson (The Mandrell Family)

With Gordon Terry in January 1962 (Frank Valeri)

Miss Oceanside, California (A Bert Winford Photo from the *Blade-Tribune*)

Daddy helping me during my first recording session, for Mosrite Records, when I was 17 (The Mandrell Family)

My engagement photo 3/30/67 — "All my love and affection, Barbara" (The Mandrell Family)

My favorite picture of Ken, in his flight suit— 1966 (Official Navy Photo)

I was 14, Ken was 21 when we met (The Mandrell Family)

Walking with Daddy down the aisle— he's got The Mandrell Look (Ray Metcalf)

Ken's mother Beth Kurtz (left) and my mother kissing the nervous bride (Ray Metcalf)

May 28, 1967—Married to my Navy pilot in Oceanside, California—the new Mrs. Kenneth Dudney loved those crossed swords! (Ray Metcalf)

Our first year of marriage, at Grandma's house in Washington State
(The Mandrell Family)

I was pregnant with Matthew and we were living in Momma and Daddy's basement apartment (The Mandrell Family)

The first PR photo of the Mandrell Family Band: from left, Momma, Brian Lonbeck, Daddy, Ken, age 21, on drums, and the Sweetheart of Steel herself (Ray Metcalf)

In Vietnam, performing for 9th Infantry Division HQ (Danny Rice)

Irlene, a pregnant Barbara, and Louise before a performance in Germany—Mom made our costumes (The Mandrell Family)

Did my hair weigh more than the banjo? It should have—I paid enough for it! (The Mandrell Family)

With newborn baby Matthew (Ken Dudney)

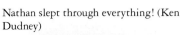

Nathan slept through everything! (Ken Dudney)

My beautiful baby Jaime (Ken Dudney)

our generations of McGill women (Grandma, Momma, me, and Jaime) plus Matthew (The Mandrell Family)

skating party for Matthew's birthday (Wayne Johnson)

Our first new bus—Tennessee Governor Winfield Dunn cuts the ribbon while Daddy and I look on! (The Mandrell Family)

Lynn Anderson, me, and Dolly Parton pose with Daddy the day we ladies were inducted into the Walkway of Stars at the Country Music Hall of Fame (The Mandrell Family)

19
HOSPITAL STORIES

ALL RIGHT, I WASN'T throwing trays around anymore, but that didn't mean I was all there, either. Over the years, we have collected some Barbara Stories. They're funny now, if I'm in the right mood.

Most of the stories come from JoAnn Berry, my friend and my agent, in that order. JoAnn devoted almost every waking moment to me from the moment she heard about the wreck. She's a good old girl from Texas who started off as an assistant to Dick Blake, my booking agent in the early days in Nashville. I remember when she first came around, I gave her such a hard time because I didn't think women were capable enough to handle important jobs (except me, of course). So I treated her like a secretary for a while, until my father said, "You ought to keep an eye on that JoAnn because she's a good one." Now she's the one who takes care of all the details, travels with me, shields me from all harm.

She couldn't do much about the wreck, but as soon as she heard about it, she camped out at Baptist Hospital for the duration. She says it bothered her the way life went on. She'd leave the hospital to run an errand, and the disc jockeys were back to telling jokes and twitting just about anybody in country music. She felt somehow life should stop and get serious until I was better. But how long that would be, nobody knew.

Even while I was still zonked, JoAnn tried to bring me back to reality. She would deal two hands of cards and try to get me to play gin with her. But I couldn't tell the queen of hearts from the two of spades. And that wasn't all I couldn't tell.

One day they had that dreadful elevator music piped into my hospital room, and I cocked my head and said, "I love that music." And JoAnn knows how much I hate canned music.

I listened to that stuff some more, and then I said, "I hope they play 'Amazing Grace' at my funeral."

Yeah, I was a bunch of laughs. Another time, there was a huge clock on the wall and at about ten minutes to seven, I sat up in bed and I said, "I've got to start getting ready."

"Ready for what?" JoAnn asked.

I said, "JoAnn, I'm late."

"No, you don't have a show tonight," JoAnn said.

That held me for a few minutes. But my short-term memory was not my strong point at that time.

A little while later, I looked around and said, "There is no bathroom here. There's no television here. This is the worst clean-up room we've ever had."

For those of you who've never traveled with a bunch of musicians, a clean-up room is the room you hire at a motel when you're touring by bus. It enables you to shower and get dressed before and after the show, before jumping back on the bus again. Sometimes you can't worry about getting a beautiful room, you just stop at a motel close to the theater. In my mind, I was somewhere out on the road.

"Let's just never stay here again," I said, as they tried to hide their smiles.

I didn't always make them smile. There was the time I looked over at JoAnn and I shouted, "Gimme two!"

"Two what?" JoAnn asked.

"Jeez, give me two pictures. What do you think I want?" I

said, referring, I guess, to the photographs I sign and give to people on the bus.

"We don't have any pictures," JoAnn said.

"Yes we do," I snapped. "They're down below."

I thought I was on the bus. Fortunately, Ken was in the room at the time, and he said, "Barbara, I'm sorry, we're out of them."

"You didn't even look!" I screamed.

So he got down on his knees and fumbled around, pretending to be looking in drawers under my hospital bed.

"I looked, we're out," he said.

And I started cussing like a sailor.

Momma tells the story about the time Ken said, "I wish it were me." And I looked up at him and said, "Me, too."

But Irlene tells the best one. This was when the doctor brought in a fresh batch of X rays to show us. I stared at them a long time, and then the doctor announced he had to take them back. I handed them over to him, reluctantly, and then I announced, "Okay, but I get artistic control."

Irlene says, "The thing is, Barbara, you were serious."

20

OUR TWO-WEEK HONEYMOON

By THE TIME WE had been married twenty-four hours, I was already considering divorce, and probably Ken was, too, although he won't admit it. I was disillusioned because Ken had fallen asleep after our first beautiful time together.

By now, of course, I'm used to it. To this day, he still falls asleep. And not just after that. He has never once taken me to a movie that he hasn't fallen asleep. Or even at home. There are some movies he wants to watch, and he'll be wide awake, but eventually he will fall asleep. I cannot do that. If I have started to watch a movie, I must watch until the end, but Ken is snoring away. I don't understand it.

We argue about that, just like we argue about everything else. We are so good at it by now. Unfortunately, we've had a few times when we fought so hard that I thought about divorce. Once in a while, I even said, "That's it. I want a divorce." But Ken doesn't listen to me, he knows it's not true, he knows it's in the heat of the moment. And to give him credit for maturity, or covering up, he's never once said it. It's my line, so to speak.

But I'll bet you any amount of money he was wondering how he could ditch me the first night I prepared dinner for him. I wanted the bells to ring in the kitchen, too. This was our first full evening as Mr. and Mrs. Kenneth Dudney, and I wanted to have steak and baked potato. But I was so stupid, I didn't know there was a difference in the cut of steaks you buy, which is why some cost more than others.

The only steak I could afford was a round steak. And since we both ate our steak well done in those days, I put it under the broiler and seasoned it with garlic salt. Nowadays, I'd know you had to pound it first, or make something else out of it, like a stew, but I just broiled it until there was no way to cut it. So we sort of had beef jerky that night. And I was disappointed because I wanted to impress him.

It's too bad I wasn't taking home economics that semester. It would have come in handy, but I had too many other courses to finish. I had put off taking science until my senior year, and you can't graduate unless you pass science. I was getting a bad grade, and my teacher said, "You'll have to get a B on the final test to pass the course." I could just see myself failing to graduate, and having to come back for another semester.

Fortunately for me, the test was on engines, and because I was really into drag racing, I felt I had a shot at a B. I had wanted to take auto mechanics, but they wouldn't allow me to take the class because, they said, I'd have no place to change. Nowadays, I'd challenge that little bit of excuse. But at the time, my mind was on getting out of high school.

How wonderful it was to be married to a man who was a Navy jet pilot and who understood the science of engines. So we sat together on the couch and studied the textbook until Ken was sure I would get a B. Now tell me, how many other girls spend the second night of their honeymoon studying jet engines?

Ken's knowledge got me a passing grade in science, but soon we were arguing again. This time it was over a stupid little habit I had developed. Cigarettes.

That's what I said. Cigarettes. Little Miss Perfect has a bad habit. The only way I want to talk about this is if everybody understands what a bad habit it is. I would not want one person to think that smoking is good or glamorous or healthy just because Barbara Mandrell has got the habit. Do as I say, not as I do. Besides, maybe I've quit by the time you read this. I hope so.

I started when I was seventeen. Daddy always smoked, and I'm a daddy's girl, and I guess I got used to being around the smell of it. I had a girlfriend who smoked, and she was so pretty that I thought it was cool. We were in the Philippines, the summer before my senior year in high school, and Daddy left some cigarettes in the room. I took a drag off one and, unfortunately for me, I did it right. I did not choke. Even with a rather strong gagging reflex, I could inhale. I liked it. I was a big girl. I'd steal one once in a while. A month later, I was hooked.

When Ken and I got back together the December I turned eighteen, he found out I was smoking. He hated cigarettes and wanted me to quit. In fact, he made me promise to quit smoking or he wouldn't marry me. So I promised. Meant it, too.

But in those first ten days of being married, I'd come back from high school to our little apartment, and I'd sneak a smoke while fixing dinner. I felt so grown up in every other way that smoking seemed to go along with it. It was dumb, but that's what I thought.

One night while Ken was out, I started to get into bed to wait for him. Instead, I found my cigarettes torn into little pieces and stacked on the bed, along with a note saying, "You can choose between sleeping with me or the cigarettes."

That was a tough one. I thought about it for a while and then I got a blanket and stretched out on the couch.

By the next day, I was back to wanting a divorce. I wanted to go home to Momma and Daddy. I don't know why. I guess it was the realization, I'm not with my Momma and Daddy anymore. I had always been so grown up, but the truth is, I was just a baby of eighteen. And I think Ken realized it, too.

Of course, I didn't go home to Daddy and Momma for more than a quick cup of coffee because they would have tossed me out on my backside and told me to grow up. I had a lot of that to do.

I was so proud of myself, not just being Barbara Mandrell, but also Mrs. Kenneth L. Dudney, which was my new legal name.

I'm still extremely proud of being Ken's wife, but I think it would have been easier if I had kept my maiden name for all the legal papers. I can never remember whether I am Barbara Mandrell, or Barbara Mandrell Dudney, or Barbara Ann Dudney, or Mrs. Kenneth Dudney, on my driver's license, or voter registration, or whatever.

Recently I signed a Visa receipt, "Love, Barbara Mandrell," as if it was an autograph for a fan. I'm so used to signing different things—cocktail napkins, postcards, handkerchiefs—that I just took it and signed it. The saleswoman looked at me as if I were nuts, but they accepted it. The charge showed up on my next bill all the same.

Back when I was eighteen, I was just getting used to my married identity when I embarrassed myself, right after graduation. The graduation was so pretty, with several hundred boys and girls, the girls in white caps and gowns and the guys in emerald green, the ocean in the background, my husband and my parents in the audience. We did end up with one Polaroid picture of me receiving my diploma, just to prove I finally made it. Then we took more pictures by a big band shell down by the beach, and when we went back to the car, there was an envelope with a graduation card from my parents, and it contained money, which we needed quite badly.

The big tradition in that part of California is to go to Disneyland after graduation, but what with Ken being nearly twenty-six, and our being with another Navy couple in their mid-twenties, we really didn't want to go to Disneyland. We wanted to go dancing, but we couldn't get in because one of us—the new graduate—was far under twenty-one.

In my newfound wisdom, I said, "You know, Tijuana is only a few hours away. You can go to clubs there." I was an old married lady, and I was cool. So we drove down to Tijuana, less than two hours away, and we went to a likely-looking club. They all ordered a drink, something like a Tom Collins. And I said, "Well, that sounds good, I'll try that."

I should mention that I do not tolerate much alcohol, then or now. The Tom Collins seemed fine, and we started dancing, and I said to Ken, "Hey, nobody cares how you look, let's boogie down." Naturally, the dancing made me thirsty, and somebody else ordered a different drink, perhaps a rum and Coke, and I tried that, and I kept dancing, and all of a sudden, boom, I felt real tipsy.

So I went outside, where they have a donkey and a sombrero, and somebody will take your picture to prove you were in Tijuana. I said, "That'll be fun, let's do that," but I was in high heels, and I slipped off the curb and twisted my ankle, though not as severely as I might have, considering I was out of control on a few drinks.

"Ken, we'd better go home," I said. "I'm not feeling too good."

He picked me up and carried me to the car, but meanwhile, a lady of the evening hollered at him in a Mexican accent, "She get sickee? She pass out?" I was lying in his arms with my head on his chest, and I snapped to and said, "No, I'm not sickee and I'm not passing out—and leave him alone."

I must have been a sight. I have never been so sick in my life, hugging the toilet all night long, but that wasn't the end of it. The next morning, one of my best girlfriends, Karen Molloy, was getting married. She is a Roman Catholic, and it was going to be a nuptial mass. I never got any sleep, and I had to do my makeup, my hair and go to the wedding, which was being held at one of our California missions, San Luis Rey.

This was one of the missions where the Indians dance every few hours on a platform. And only a few yards away, they were holding a Catholic wedding, which produced the unusual sound effects of: "Do you take this woman to be your lawfully wedded wife?" and "Hey-yah, hey-yah, yah-yah-yah." And with my headache, it sounded as if the Indians were dancing on my forehead. Finally, the priest sent an altar boy out to ask them to stop for a while, which they did.

"How horrible," I had always felt, whenever I saw someone drunk. This time I didn't plan it, but I got myself so sick. I discovered it really isn't smart to party down and drink everything in sight. I found out the hard way. I tell this story for two reasons: one, to remind people that Snow White is not exactly perfect, and, two, to perhaps save somebody else from the same feeling of Indians dancing on their heads.

Bad cooking. Smoking. Hangover. And *I* was the one having the temper tantrum about wanting a divorce. The wonder is that this grown man, this Navy officer, put up with me. If he had shuffled me back to Momma after a couple of weeks, nobody would have blamed him.

But I guess I instinctively knew when I married him that this was a man so secure that he would give me room to grow. I have great respect for men who are kind to people, protective of their families. My father's such a strong man, physically, and mentally he's very much his own man, very strong-willed. That's where I get it, I know that. And I can see why I fell in love with Ken, because Ken's that same way. He's so much better educated than me, and patient, and he has a great sense of humor. He's needed it.

When people hear that I got married at eighteen, and that in fact Ken and I started dating when I was fourteen, they ask me, "What would you do if Jaime, at age fourteen, wanted to date a twenty-two-year-old man?"

I usually say, "Well, if it was another Ken Dudney, I'd be all for it." What I usually add silently is, "From what I see and hear, there aren't any more like him."

21
WAKING UP

THE FIRST THING I can remember is the twenty-fifth of September, 1984. There was a man standing by my bed, identifying himself as Dr. David Jones, my orthopedist, but he could have been the David Jones who used to be the head of the Joint Chiefs of Staff, or he could have been the David Jones who was the national editor of *The New York Times,* or he could have been one of the thousand David Joneses in the country of Wales. I wouldn't have known him from Adam. I had just landed from the moon. Of course, I had been seeing him, and talking to him, for the past two weeks, but I did not remember him.

"Miss Mandrell," he said, "we've had you on Demerol and then Valium. Now I would like just to put you on Tylenol. Is that all right with you?"

"Of course," I said.

That is the first memory I have since driving along Gallatin Road two weeks earlier. Everything in between is hearsay. You could tell me I did Vegas in between, and I'd have to believe you.

People had started to wonder if I'd ever snap back. My father admits now that he was starting to make trade-offs in his mind. Very early, when my leg was broken and I was still in the cardiac-care unit, my father found himself praying over me.

"I looked at her and I knew the leg was real bad, and she was still out of it," Daddy has said. "She'd say things, but she didn't know what she was saying. So I just told the Lord, 'If she has to lose her memory or her brain versus the leg, please make it the leg.' I was so afraid when she came out of it that she would never be the same person again. With a head injury, you worry about those things."

Momma has said, "She was in so much pain that I was sitting there one night thinking, 'She's going to lose it. How much more can she take of this before losing it?' "

They would have to do simple things for me. One day when I was really nervous, before I snapped out of it, Daddy suddenly got the idea of putting a cigarette in my mouth, but Ken had the same idea and he did it. Maybe it helped hold my sanity, just doing something familiar like that.

I soon discovered I was still numb in a few spots around the lips. Later, I learned I had been all cut up inside my mouth, but thank God it was not worse. I still have three dots near my mouth, but I just use a little more makeup than I used to do, the kind women use to hide the bags under our eyes, but it could have been so much worse. To this day, I have numbness on my lower lip and part of my chin.

They started telling me a little about the accident, although they glossed over the part about the young man being killed. And as the cobwebs started to clear, I started to take stock of my injuries.

They had put me in traction with a pin running straight through the broken bone. During my lucid moments, Ken described how they had drilled a hole in my hip bone and inserted that Sampson nail.

"What did I look like those first couple of weeks?" I asked my parents.

"Like you had been in a boxing match and somebody had laid a couple of good ones on your chin," my father said.

My mother told me about the time I was screaming because I "couldn't get comfortable," and one of the nurses said, "Just pray about it, Barbara," and my mother thought, "For goodness' sake, don't you have any sense? She's lying there out of her head, in all kinds of pain, and you're telling her to pray? Everybody else should be praying for her."

But nurses are great people, and most of them do understand pain. I was just starting to find that out. I began to realize what had been going on during the two weeks I was in a fog. They had been starting therapy on my leg but I was too messed up to help them.

My whole leg was black and blue from the blood vessels being broken, and everything was stiff, so they started getting me up on crutches and moving me into the other room to sit down, just to get me into different positions. My knee had been gouged by the dashboard, and they had pulled all kinds of black plastic out of it. So I had to start exercising the knee.

Linda Fowler, the head therapist, used to come in a couple of times a day and try to manipulate my leg, but I did not cooperate much. Ken was the only person who could touch me without hurting me at times, but he was not a therapist. There were also times when he tried to move me, and I would just swing on him, but I guess I knew I could get away with hitting him, and I couldn't get away with hitting the doctors or the nurses.

Ken would hold my knee with his left hand, and he would feel any small motion in there, and he would hold the leg out as far as I would allow. Sometimes he would make me stand up, and support myself with my arms and upper body, and he would feel my leg and lock my knee as tight as he could and force me to push against him. It was as if someone took a knife and jammed me in my knee, and Ken was the only one who could do it.

Sometimes, however, I would belt him and scream, using my new-found vocabulary. I'm sure there are people at Baptist Hospital who still say, "Oh, sure, that Barbara Mandrell. Huggy-kissy on television, but scratchy-yelly in her hospital room." And they'd be right.

In between therapy sessions, I began finding out all kinds of things. For example: I discovered that my aunt Thelma had been there. Apparently, they all took shifts at the hospital, and they had rooms at the Hermitage Hotel, and they sometimes stayed at the office, too. Well, Aunt Thelma did, too. She would sit by my bed and talk to me, and I would nod to her, and the last thing she said before she left was, "Well at least Barbara knew I was here."

A few weeks later, somebody said Thelma had been at the hospital, and I couldn't believe it.

I had a lot of catching up to do. But I went real slow, and I wasn't overly gracious about it. It wasn't that I didn't love other people, but I just didn't want to think about other people. My parents and Ken wanted to tell me about the abundance of flowers, and more mail than anybody had received in the history of Nashville, but all I wanted to say was, "Who cares?"

Now that my head is on straight, I feel gratitude, but at the time, not only didn't I care, I didn't want to hear about it. It's a beautiful memory now, but I didn't care at the time about the expense and the trouble taken by radio station KFDI in Wichita, Kansas, where I was supposed to have played the Kansas State Fair. They rented a billboard right outside my window at Baptist Hospital that said, "Get well, Barbara." But my attitude at the time was, "So what? I don't care! Don't pay attention to me! God, just let me stop hurting!"

22

ENTERTAINING THE TROOPS

AFTER TWO WEEKS OF marriage, I was an old married lady of eighteen. In fact, I was so married that I said good-bye to Ken and took a business trip for the next three months.

This wasn't just any trip. This was to Southeast Asia while the Vietnam War was going on. I must admit, I felt pretty smug that I was going back to Asia, and Ken, the jet pilot, was still based in the States. It sort of fit my hawk image.

I have felt close to the military ever since hearing Daddy's war stories and seeing him in his police uniform. In high school, not only did I get teased by some of my classmates for being country, but I was also teased for entertaining "jar-heads"—you know, Marines. Well, I love country music and I love the Armed Forces, and I was proud to bring one to the other.

The war was very divisive while I was still in high school. People I knew protested the war, and people I knew participated in the war. I won't claim I had all the answers, but I supported whatever my country did. Plus, I got to know these guys who were going over. They were my age. They were my friends.

I have such vivid memories of watching them assemble for war. My family's band would arrive at one of the bases like Camp Pendleton while it was still daylight, and we would see a training field, wall to wall with Marines in formation, in full combat uniform, getting ready to ship out. They were eighteen years old, maybe, and getting ready to go where they might have to die. Our men.

I would get a lump in my throat, standing there with my little guitar, watching these guys carrying their bags onto buses. Even if we didn't know their names, we entertained them every week, knew their faces. We loved them very much. Sometimes we had only seen them in civilian clothes, but now we saw them in combat uniform, and it definitely got our attention, to think about what they were about to do. We were honored to play for them in the bases in California, and we were honored to be asked to go to Southeast Asia.

My father's private contacts for the military bases also booked acts into Vietnam. We weren't part of any USO tour. We were independent entertainers, getting paid a certain fee for performing. San Diego. Los Angeles. Vietnam. I mean, they checked us out, told us the rules, made us sign some papers, gave us visas and a million shots and bottles of salt tablets, but we weren't always escorted by the military.

We made our first trip the summer after junior year in high school. Then we were invited back again after my graduation. I'm going to be perfectly honest and say that the two years have blended together in my memory, so I'm not even going to try to separate them.

I had watched television and I had read the papers and magazines, but the first time I flew into Vietnam, it was like jumping smack-dab into the middle of a movie with both feet. We were flying commercial into Saigon, and the plane just suddenly dove down from the sky and landed, without the graceful approaches they use in the States. Daddy didn't have to explain to us why the pilot dove down like that. The pilot did not want to be a target until the last possible minute.

When we landed, we felt it just couldn't possibly be real. In any direction, I could see machine guns and tanks, men in uniform, definitely on guard. Then we went to downtown Saigon, that bustling city the Vietnamese and French had built. We could see it must have been fun at one time, but it was a war zone now—sandbags and metal bunkers in front of the best hotels. The Vietcong would just lob a grenade or fire a machine gun into the lobby of the hotels.

Right away, Daddy said, "Whenever you leave the hotel, you keep a black scarf on your head, and don't dally. Don't call any attention to yourself." My thoughts at that time were, "Oh, Dad, don't be ridiculous," but because he was my dad, I did it. I was thinking I had done such a nice job with my hair, why would I want to cover it up? But the point was not to be conspicuous, not to look too western. I got the feeling things were not too wonderful in Vietnam.

The hotel we stayed in, the Majestic, was right across the street from a park. Anytime they captured Vietcong arms and ammunition, they would put them on display out in the open to raise the morale of the American and the Vietnamese people. It sounds like a good idea, except that some of it was live stuff. One night, somebody told us, they had found a fuse with fifteen minutes to go before it would have blown up five or six blocks. And this was one of the best hotels in the capital.

We stayed in Saigon for a while but our job was to go from base to base, entertaining the troops. A little different from California, since there was a war going on, but the guys were the same. I felt comfortable being around the military. Of course, we knew they were from all over the States, white and black and Hispanic, some of them just in their late teens and some of them into their thirties, so we tried to do pop and rock 'n' roll and rhythm and blues, which was not hard, considering that is some of my favorite music.

Sometimes when people comment that my shows jump around from one style to another, I say, Right, because I know how broad the taste of the American public is. I have been out there, all over the States and in Asia, too. I know what the guys like.

And there are a lot of misconceptions. A lot of people have said that blacks don't care for country music, but the truth is, we have black fans now, and we did then. When we played at Pendleton, there were two black sergeants who used to be in the front row at nearly every show. They would follow us from club to club because they really liked country music, and they liked us.

We hit Okinawa on one of our trips, and we stayed in the hotel there. One of those sergeants was sitting at the bar, and he was absolutely thrilled to see us. We were happy to see him, too—until he told us his buddy had been killed in Vietnam.

We never could get used to that, week in and week out, people sitting right there at the front table and everything, and then we'd run into one of them and find out somebody'd been killed. It comes home hard.

We were not in Asia long before we realized the men knew the score, too. Some of them would talk openly about this possibly being their last contact with Americans. They wanted to have our support, knowing they might never leave there alive. Very often, they'd pull off their unit crests and other medals from their uniforms and pin them on us. I've got so many of them in my museum in Nashville, and many more at home. Each of those medals has a story, a face, behind it.

I don't mean to make it all sound tearful, either. These were strong, healthy, normal guys, a long way from home. When they wanted to meet us, it wasn't always homesickness that was doing the talking. I was eighteen and blonde. Momma was around thirty-five and wearing her hair blonde. We did not lack for attention.

There was one base where the manager didn't want me and Momma talking to the guys or dancing with them or anything. Daddy said, "Well, we're leaving then. If we can't mingle with the men then we're leaving," so of course the manager had to relent. Daddy wasn't worried about the men dancing or talking with us, and the men almost always behaved.

Almost. There was one time on the second tour when we hadn't taken a bath or a shower for days at a time. We would literally take a sponge bath with a little water scooped out of a helmet. Finally, we got to one base that had a shower built into a Quonset hut. Momma and I made sure it was not a mirage, and then we asked if we could use the shower, and they said they would put a guard on the door to make sure we'd have privacy. We did not have to be invited twice.

Momma and I were standing in the shower naked, and we started to hear giggles. I looked at her and she looked at me. Then we heard scratching sounds, like somebody brushing up against a wall. Finally, we figured out there were showers on the other side of the wall, and that a couple of guys were peeking through the showers.

Anybody who knows my mother will appreciate the punch line to this story because she is one of the most shy, modest people you could imagine. We started yelling and grabbing towels at the same time, and the chief came running over trying to save us, but of course the guys in the other shower had somehow disappeared. With all this commotion going on, I looked at Momma, figuring she would be terrified, but she just shrugged and said, "Well, we came over here to entertain the guys."

Good thing they didn't see us dressing. Sometimes we got paid in cash, and Momma and I used to carry the gate receipts in our bras.

Showering for the troops was going a bit far, maybe, but we did try to give the guys what they wanted, whether it was music or a touch of femininity or humor. Daddy had one joke he told everywhere: A Red Cross lady asked a gate guard for directions, and in return the guard asked her for a date.

"Oh, I don't go out with anything lower than a second lieutenant," the Red Cross lady said.

"Oh, that's no problem," the enlisted man said. "There isn't anything lower than a second lieutenant."

The men always loved that one. (On a Navy base, of course, Daddy would change the second lieutenant to an ensign.) Of the hundreds of times that Daddy told that story, he met only one lieutenant who complained about it. Daddy said, "Lieutenant, don't come talking to me. You were in the enlisted club, and I believe you're a lieutenant."

No two shows were ever the same because we were booked all over Asia by civilian bookers rather than the USO. Sometimes we had good facilities and sometimes not. We were transported by helicopter a lot—sometimes armed and other times personnel carriers or surveillance helicopters. And there were times, too, when we would get someplace and they couldn't move us because they needed the helicopter to pick up injured men. I mean, we were in the middle of the war. Sometimes the Aero-Evac would come back for us and there would be blood on the floor.

At the Bien Hoa Air Force Base, just outside Saigon, we

played an afternoon show when the temperature was around a hundred and twenty. Oh, they had air conditioning, all right— open windows halfway up the wall—but unfortunately, the men outside were standing on wooden boxes, looking in, so the air was not circulating. Daddy's philosophy has always been that a band should look like a band, so he and the boys kept their coats on. I was placed slightly behind Daddy, and I could see his dark serge western jacket with gold trim getting darker and darker from sweat until you could see the drops falling from the tails of his coat.

Finally, Daddy said, "Hey, fellas, we're not going to look like a nice Stateside band today. We're going to take our coats off." That was a pretty rash act for Daddy. However, there wasn't much I could do about my solid gold lamé dress. After about two hours in that heat, I just flat keeled over. They plopped me onto one of those hospital gurneys, and hustled me into one of the few places with real air conditioning—a library, Daddy recalls.

As soon as I was back on my feet, the club manager said the base had changed shifts, and a lot of new guys had come over to see us perform. He asked, "What would we have to pay you all to get you to play another show?" Remember, this was not a USO tour, we were booked independently. Daddy answered, "Nothing. We've already made our money for today." Of course, the guy who was booking us went crazy because Daddy wouldn't charge them anything, but we played at that club for six hours, and then they couldn't get us back to Saigon that night because it had gotten dark and you couldn't travel the roads at night because of Charlie— the Vietcong. So they bunked us for the night in the pilots' house trailers. Momma still talks about hearing mortar shells, being tired but afraid to sleep because you could hear these whistles, followed by an explosion. We were afraid because they were going out over our trailer. That sound really drives you nuts. The guys tried to calm us by saying that as long as you can hear them, it's all right. I don't know if I believed that.

We began to realize what a difficult war this was. From a few thousand feet, our helicopter people had trouble telling who we were. How were they possibly supposed to know who was Vietcong and who was friendly to us? Daddy, who fought in World War II, said it was easier to fight in Japan than in Europe, because in Europe you might not be able to distinguish between a German and an Englishman from a hundred yards away, but in Japan you could tell. In Vietnam, how could you tell? The same people who help build something today might sneak out at night and help blow it up. The same people. You just didn't know. On one trip I asked, "How do I recognize a Vietcong?"

"Well, if you see somebody in silk pajamas and he's got a gun, he's a Vietcong."

Wonderful. We'd be driving along the road or through a town and you'd see people in silk pajamas. Everywhere. You wouldn't see the gun, but how did you know what was hidden in the basket, or in the little fishing boat, or under his clothing? That was the point. You didn't know.

On one of our trips down the Mekong Delta, an Army sergeant was carrying an automatic rifle with a .45 strapped on his hip. We were riding a big van with side doors that slid open.

"You know how to use this?" the sergeant asked.

"I believe so," Daddy said.

"Well, if anything happens, just reach for it," the driver said.

About a month after that, a rock 'n' roll group was ambushed on the same road. The only one who survived was the girl singer, who lay still and pretended she was dead. I always thought it was the same sergeant and the same bus we rode in.

One thing I noticed right away was that I wasn't afraid. I was curious. I think I could have been a soldier. They still don't want women in combat positions, but I think that's silly. Who is to say a man is not going to become emotional? What makes them think a woman is going to have a problem? That's just a stereotype. You never know what you're going to do until you do it. I love to target shoot, and I don't want to kill a human being, but if I was placed in a situation where my life, or my family, or my country was in danger, God forbid anybody should get in my way.

It was fun most of the time, but I guess we showed a certain amount of guts just being there. John Wayne went over and entertained the troops, and when he came back, he was on the Carson show and Johnny asked him, "Weren't you scared to be in Vietnam?"

"No," he said, "there was a group over there with a thirteen-year-old drummer, so I figured if a thirteen-year-old could take it, I could." That made Mark Peppard proud, although he was actually fourteen, and it made the rest of us proud, too, since we loved John Wayne.

We wound up in some pretty wild places. One time we landed in a helicopter at a tiny camp, where we were supposed to transfer to another place. The few soldiers told Daddy that they never got to see a show because their camp was too small.

"You got electricity?" Daddy said.

They wired us up, and gave us a tent for changing, and they removed a tent from a platform to make a stage. Right in the noonday sun, while the guys were coming in from the field, we did a show for a handful of people, who were so elated at being noticed. It still gives me goose bumps thinking about it.

We'd meet thousands of guys, and most of them were terrific. The Vietnam veteran has gotten a bad rap from the way the war turned out, and from some of the movies, but most of the guys I met did not seem like psychos and killers and lunatics. Most of them seemed like guys from home. And if I hadn't been in love with Ken, I might have paid even more attention to them.

The first summer we went to Vietnam, I was single. If we stayed in a nice hotel in Saigon, we'd run into officers. Of course, most of them were more interested in Momma.

We still talk about the time Momma got on this hotel elevator with those beautiful French wrought-iron gates. There were two officers on the elevator and the major asked if she was going to the tearoom. She said yes, and he said he'd see her up there. And just when she got off on her floor, the other officer, a captain, yelled, "And bring the other girl with you." Momma said the major was a very good-looking guy, with dark Italian features. Anyway, she came back up to our room and she told Daddy, "I think I just made a date."

Daddy was a good sport about it, but Momma didn't keep the date. I did check out the Air Force captain, however, and got invited to meet him for a drink in the hotel tearoom. Earlier that same day, I had met an Army pilot whom I liked, but now I liked the Air Force captain even better. The Army pilot asked me to have a soda with him in the lounge. Like any seventeen-year-old, I couldn't make up my mind, so I split my time between them. Finally, I rushed up to my parents' room and I said, "Daddy, you've got to tell me what to do. There's an Army pilot downstairs in the lounge and we kind of have a date. But then I met this Air Force pilot upstairs, and I really like him, so I keep going back and forth."

Daddy replied: "You got yourself into this. Now you can get yourself out."

So I had to pretend I had the worst case of dysentery there ever was. And finally I managed to get rid of the pilot downstairs by saying, "My dad said I had to go to bed."

The second trip I was married, so it was easy to tell guys, "Hey, I'm a married woman," and they almost always respected that. So I didn't have to worry about getting involved with one of them. I could fall in love with all of them—guys from the farms and the ghettos, guys from the north and the south, tough guys, innocent guys, and all of them there mainly because their country had asked them to do it.

The debate still goes on about what we were doing there. I have always tried to avoid making controversial or political statements. I mean, who am I? An entertainer. Do I have any more right to make a statement than anybody else? I don't like it when celebrities, whether they be athletes or entertainers or writers, endorse somebody for office. I mean, who cares? That's the wonderful thing about America. I get to go in that little booth and pull that lever. Boom. That's between me and the voting machine, and that's my right. My forefathers earned it for me.

I'll admit I did get upset when people spoke out against the war. No tact, no regard for their own men who were fighting the war. I mean they were fighting for us. I didn't like knowing it would go out over the radio, and these men would hear it. It was the most unsupportive, unappreciative thing they could have done. I feel that even if you had these feelings, you could have prefaced the negative position with something positive about the men who were over there. I did not appreciate that. That made me angry. Why didn't they say how great our men were?

Here I am with a nineteen-year-old son, and someday I may have to put my money where my mouth is. I didn't like it when men skipped to Canada or burned their draft cards because I believe that if you live here, you obey the law. That's my upbringing, and that's also Scripture. You obey the law of your country.

The men I saw over there were amazing. Their morale was better than it has been portrayed, but they didn't like what they heard from home. They would ask us, "Gee, don't they love us? Don't they know we're only doing what we're told?"

I tried to tell them that the press liked to report what was negative, but that the vast majority was for them, and grateful that it was just a few who were saying this negative stuff.

I wanted to believe it was just a few back home, and so did the military men. You send anybody that far from home, he wants to think people are behind him. They would see a seventeen-year-old American girl and her daddy and her momma who looked better than she did, and they said wonderful things to us.

One young man came up to my father and said, "I look at you and your wife and daughter and these two young men and that shows me what I'm fighting for. Now I remember. It's the family. It's freedom."

Their attitude was just wonderful, most of the time, but they couldn't help but feel things were stacked against them. I remember talking to some pilots about how they felt flying over Hanoi, knowing they couldn't bomb it, and yet thinking, "There it is." They could see it: the arms, the ammunition, the fuel, just sitting in the streets—the stuff they were going to use on their buddies.

Excuse me for feeling strongly on this subject, but if you ask me to lay my life on the line, and you start taking away my weapons, my way of protecting myself, that makes me very angry. It was like saying the other guy can keep his weapons but you can't.

I'm not saying our boys were angels. One time we did a show and guys were drinking beer, having a party, and I'm sorry I saw it but two guys started a fight and one guy broke a big beer bottle and slashed the other guy across the face. I never saw hand-to-hand combat with the enemy, but I saw it between two of our own.

They had their moments of exploding, taking it out on each other. And you could understand when you heard about the poisoned sticks the Vietcong stuck in the ground. Men would fall in a trap onto these sharpened bamboo poles, the punji sticks, which would cut right through them.

One thing I learned from Vietnam is that I am not totally a soft, loving person. There was a jail for prisoners of war at Long Binh—they called it LBJ, in honor of the President who had sent them to Vietnam. It was a chain-link fence with walls and a roof and picnic tables and army cots and blankets and pillows, the same stuff our men had. The Vietcong prisoners in there were getting the same food we were, not the rotten fish heads and a spoon of rice they gave our men.

I got angry when I saw how we were treating those prisoners while our men were being put in dark, dingy holes with rotten food, where people beat them up. Maybe our guys did some of that when there were no visitors.

I've had people tell me that some of our troops would take a prisoner up in a helicopter and if he wouldn't talk, they would drop him out. Maybe that was true and maybe it wasn't, but I've heard stories about what the Vietcong did, and when I saw this nice jail with Vietcong prisoners on a picnic, I didn't like it.

And yet I never felt any hate for the Vietnamese. To this day, when I think of them, I think of gentleness and discipline and kindness. I met one woman who was my age, and I've prayed for her and her family because we don't know what happened when the Communists took over. And all the people in Saigon and out in the countryside. What became of them?

The second time we went to Vietnam, we stayed in a villa for a while. A Vietnamese family did the housework and the cooking, preparing American food so we would feel at home. There was a daughter who was my age, who went to school and worked in the villa. She was trying to earn enough money to buy an umbrella for the heavy rains in the monsoon season. Before I left, I bought her an umbrella, and it was as if I had given her a car.

That family was so wonderful, so kind, and when Vietnam went over to the Communists, I prayed so much for them. Because they were close to the Americans, there is no telling what happened to them.

I think of them whenever I hear about Vietnamese people moving to the United States and Canada. I hope they made it. It's too bad we couldn't move the whole country to Texas, Montana, Wyoming, Canada, wherever there is space. They were good people who got caught in the middle. I admire the Oriental belief in respecting one's elders, but I still feel America is by far the greatest place. If Americans could travel to other parts of the world, they would want to kiss the ground when they got home.

But I came to realize it was pretty complicated. I understood that we were protecting a nation from going Communist, but other people said it wasn't so simple.

I hope we never forget those men, who answered the call when they were asked to put their lives on the line. I often think of those men, but I have not yet been able to visit the Vietnam Memorial, the wall in Washington, D.C., engraved with the names of all the soldiers who died there. I don't know if I could. We used to see the caskets being put on planes back to the States. We have our own memories of Vietnam.

One thing that stands out in my mind more than anything else was the time we were at a hospital and I saw this one black soldier with IVs stuck in him. We stopped by his bedside and I bent down to see what he wanted. He asked me to sing "Danny Boy," the Irish song about a father whose son went off to war. It's the one they sing in bars, and everybody cries.

I knew the song. I did not know if I could sing it to a dying soldier. But somehow I did. The man fixed his eyes on me the whole time I was singing. I have no idea how I managed not to break into tears, but I finished the song and said good-bye. They told me he died just a few hours later. I've never heard that song since that I didn't think of him, dying in a strange place. God gave me the courage to sing to him. I know God was with that soldier too.

23
FINDING OUT

I WAS LYING IN THE hospital bed, the television blaring. I was not really watching the news—until I heard my name. The announcer said I was still recovering in the hospital, and then he added:

"The other driver was killed."

I started to weep. Ken and the nurse came over and tried to calm me down, but I was out of control. This was more than two weeks after the accident, and I had just come out of my fog. Ken says I heard people on television talking about the accident during the first week, but it just didn't register with me. I had no memory of the accident—and I hadn't been asking any questions, either. Now I felt grief, and after that, my second reaction was to ask if the wreck was my fault. Ken assured me it wasn't.

I had to deal with the fact that somebody had died. Who was he? What caused it? Did he suffer? Did he leave a family? How were they taking it? Did people blame me? Was there anything we could do? What about my children?

All these questions, all these emotions, came flooding into

my mind, but I was in no shape to express them. I was still
groggy from the accident, parts of my mind still not working to
capacity. But now I knew the extra sadness that other people
had been carrying around, the news they had tried to keep from
me. Other people had been hurt by this wreck. Another family
had been crushed.

While my family was worrying about me and the children,
the family of Mark White was just beginning to mourn its loss.
I think there is nothing worse than the pain of losing a child,
and my sympathies still go out to the White family.

At the same time, the police began investigating the cause
of the crash. I remember none of it. But the police and my lawyers and other witnesses have put together many details. Eventually, a report would be filed.

The report would say that Mark White, a mathematics
major at the University of Tennessee in Knoxville, had worked
from seven until three-thirty that day. Later, he was driving on
the Gallatin Pike.

The police diagram of the accident area shows five lanes—
two in each direction and a middle one, for turning. I know the
road because I drove it almost every day I was home. The turn
lane was always clearly marked.

The police report says I was traveling eastbound in the left
or "inside" lane. According to two witnesses, my car was following theirs. The police report says the White car, a red 1981 Subaru, was heading westbound in the left or "inside" lane.

After consulting witnesses, the police determined that exactly 142 feet from the point of impact, the White car moved to
the left into the turn lane and "began heading directly towards"
the vehicle in front of me. The report adds that the driver
ahead of me "swerved to the right & avoided collision" with the
White car, which then "continued its path" and struck mine.

From all I can gather, I never saw him coming, at least
until the other car swerved, and the White car was right on me.
Matthew and Jaime seem to think I gasped just before impact. I
have no recollection.

The report said there were no skid marks to indicate the
young man had tried to brake his car.

The police laboratory returned reports that neither Mark
White nor I had any trace of alcohol or drugs in our systems.

In a report written by one officer, it said two witnesses recalled "the driver was sitting straight up in the driver's seat, the driver had both hands on the steering wheel & was looking straight ahead as if 'statue like.' "

The report said the witnesses told an officer that the White vehicle "did not appear to be traveling at a high or excessive rate of speed, there was no sign that #2 was applying his brakes prior to impact & it appeared #2 was traveling in a straight line."

One officer returned the next day at exactly the same time and drove westbound along 31E, to see if the late-afternoon sun had been a problem. The report said, "The sun was not presenting a visibility problem for west-bound vehicles upon 31E at this particular time period."

The examination of the White car determined its wheels were turned very slightly "towards the left of the vehicle" and that there was no evidence of any braking activity, nor any indication of brake problems. The speedometer was positioned between fifty-five and sixty miles per hour.

The officer then looked in the backseat and found the following:

(item) "a dark-colored bow (as in bow & arrow)."

(item) "an ashtray containing numerous brown-colored cigarette butts."

The officer also found:

(item) ". . . in the front passenger seat, a blue-colored pamphlet, 'About facing death as a Christian.' "

What does any of this mean? We turned the reports over to our lawyers, who felt the main issue was that I was exactly where I had the right to be, driving legally, and that the White car was where it should not have been.

If he had been drunk or on drugs, that would have been another story. That was not the case. What was his state of mind that day? Could he have had a fight with a girlfriend? Was there any pattern of erratic behavior? Did he fall asleep? We may never know the answers.

It seems certain to me that he never knew whom he hit. There is not the slightest suggestion that anything happened to us because I am Barbara Mandrell, the country singer. He probably never saw my car until the vehicle ahead of me swerved. I could not take it personally. I could only take it as terrible luck for all of us.

Why was his car in that lane? In some ways, I would like to know. In other ways, it almost doesn't matter. To this day, it grieves me to think of the loss of that other family. I hope they know we pray for them.

Every year that September 11 anniversary comes right after Nathan's birthday, and on the same day as the birthday of Randy Wright, my close friend who was our drummer and band manager for many years. It's also the birthday of Will Lunsford, a boy from Texas I call my third son.

But my main theme for that day, between me and the Lord, is to pray for that young man on the Gallatin Pike, and for his parents, and their love for him.

24

MY FIRST
RETIREMENT

BY THE TIME I was eighteen, I had reached three milestones in life:

I was married.

I had a hit record.

And I retired from show business.

That's an unusual combination any way you look at it. The record was a modest little thing I had done for Semi Mosley, who made Mosrite guitars and was a dear friend of ours through Daddy's work with the Standel amplifiers. As a sideline, Semi had started a record label called Mosrite, and when I was seventeen, he let me make a record under Daddy's supervision.

I went to RCA Victor in Hollywood, where they had the backup group that sang with Dean Martin and many other artists. Bob Morris played bass and a fellow named Glen Campbell played guitar. The song was called "Queen for a Day," it was written by

Freddy Hart, and we put it together and I didn't think much more of it.

But the summer we went to Asia, we stopped in Okinawa and Daddy called me into his room. He said, "Look at this." Then he showed me a copy of *Billboard*, the show-business weekly paper.

"Your record made the charts," Daddy said.

"The what?" I asked.

Then he explained the record had slipped into the top one hundred singles on the weekly charts, but it did not seem real to me while we were in Vietnam.

After we got back, we got more excited about it. I can remember Daddy stopping the car while we were driving in California, just to make sure the station playing it didn't fade off the car radio.

Then the record actually hit number one on radio station WJJD in Chicago, which was country at that time. I flew into Chicago to do a TV show called *Country Swing Around*. I was still a naive little girl from California who worked for her daddy, but there I was with a number-one record and Merle Haggard was a guest on that same show. Still I was the top dog because I had the number-one record in the area.

After being on that show, I got into the swing of it. In fact, I began suggesting that Daddy pay me more money every week, but we were still a family group, so he didn't go along with that. We pushed that family record as a unit. Louise and Irlene would get on the phone and call the stations all day long.

You had to know the managers were saying to themselves, "It's those Mandrell girls from Oceanside again. You'd think they'd disguise their voices or have their friends call." But we were so young, we just plowed right ahead. I mean, it was something right out of a television skit that we might invent twelve or thirteen years later, but it was an example of how Louise and Irlene have always been in my corner.

The record stayed on the charts only a few weeks, and then it disappeared. Then I decided to disappear along with it. When we went over to Asia the second time, I knew it was going to be the end of my career, such as it was.

We had never tried to do anything nationally—mostly military bases and clubs on the West Coast. Most people don't know this, but when I was around fifteen, I had an offer to play steel guitar for Loretta Lynn, who was thinking of putting together an all-girl band. Daddy turned it down because we really didn't plan for me to have a career in music. It was just for fun.

Our band was a small family business, but the way Daddy looked at it, you build a business until it gets to a certain point, but then you must have the business increase or decrease. There is no holding even. Even if you're the only good music store in town, you're still going to have to have more people come in. He got tired of wondering where his new customers were coming from, and he could see the band was a shaky proposition because I wanted to be with Ken. Everything had reached a plateau and Daddy thought it was time to get out of it, go do something else, like when Daddy sold his music store. So—no more Mandrell Family Band.

Music had been a nice way to help the family while I was in high school, but now I was Mrs. Kenneth Dudney, the wife of a Navy pilot. I was going to follow him wherever his career took him. We were going to have babies and my singing would be confined to lullabies or maybe a solo in the church choir.

That was fine with my parents. My mother had done her bit, learning to play bass, dyeing her hair blond, flying all over the world, having soldiers play Peeping Tom in the shower.

My father, far from being a stage father, was opting for a solid life. When Ken asked Daddy about us getting married, Ken said, "I'll never butt in on her career because I know you've planned it that way." But Daddy wasn't pushing a show-business career on me. He had heard of some prime land in western Tennessee, and he was going to build a home for the family and then go into the home-construction business.

Our minds were made up as we finished our last show in Korea. Daddy went around to each of us and said, "This is our last night. Each of you choose what song you want to do." So we each sang our farewell song. I can remember being up there singing my last song, but darned if I can remember what it was.

Then we headed back to the rest of our lives. For my mother, that seemed like one flight too long. To this day, Momma is petrified of flying. After more than a hundred hours of flying on these two tours in the Orient—the monsoons and the abrupt landings and flying over oceans and mountains, always with the possibility somebody might try to shoot you down—well, if you were the least bit afraid of flying, all this could put you over the edge.

On that last trip, Daddy promised if Momma would just make the flight from Guam to Honolulu, he would take a boat back to the mainland. She agreed, but she was still frightened, so she went to see a doctor, who gave her these wonderful pills. She took one pill before she got on the plane. She took another pill when we were in the air. And by the time we were approaching Honolulu, my mother, who does not drink, was, shall we say, very relaxed.

Momma is so straitlaced, such an absolute lady, that what followed seems even more ridiculous. As we began to descend, my dad said, "Barbara, you have got to help me with your mother."

"What are you talking about?"

"She is just out of it on these pills."

I took her into the rest room on the plane and I sat her down and washed her face with cold water and fussed with her hair and tried to talk to her, but she was still half asleep. When we landed in Honolulu, we had to go through customs. Daddy said, "Your mother's worse," so I took her into the rest room and washed her face and combed her hair again, and I raised my voice, saying, "Mother, would you please wake up? We've got to go through customs. Would you please just come out of it?" And people looked at me and thought Mother was drunk or something.

I walked her to the area where Daddy was pushing the shopping cart through customs. It was slightly downhill, and I hooked her arms on the cart, but then I had to turn around to do something, and I looked up, and, oh my word, there went my mother with the cart—rolling toward the customs desk. It looked like a scene right out of *I Love Lucy*.

We caught her at the conveyor belt, where the customs officer was. Daddy was handling everything—until he noticed that the conveyor belt had started up, and that Momma was sitting on it. She rolled directly in front of the customs officer. The belt stopped.

"Hi," Momma said.

"Where'd you get that watch?" he asked.

"I don't know," she said. And she stuck it right in his face and said, "You see."

I couldn't believe it. It was so out of character. The man smiled and waved us through. At least the pills got her through what she believed was her last flight.

Surprise. Daddy had tickets for the flight from Hawaii to Los Angeles. He said there weren't any passenger boats at that time. We had to take his word for it.

I got back to Seattle to meet Ken, and I hung up my picks. Just nailed them to the wall, as the baseball players say. Ken and I had survived our stormy two-week honeymoon in our temporary apartment in California. Now it was time to get serious about this marriage stuff.

Ken was taking a big ribbing from his Navy buddies, who knew I was in Vietnam.

"Where's your wife, Ken? Over fighting the war for you?"

Not that he was exactly going on a picnic. He had gotten his orders to go to Whidbey Island, Washington, where he was the first ensign assigned to pilot the A-3, a tanker nicknamed the Whale, originally a bomber, doing midair refueling. It was the largest jet aboard a carrier, and his job was to plop that thing down on a carrier out in the middle of the ocean.

While practicing his landings and takeoffs, Ken had found time to go house hunting. Base housing was all gone, so we were allowed something like a hundred and forty-five dollars a month. Ken had found a summer beach house on a bay near Coupeville, with the most beautiful view of a mountain. It was already furnished, so I spent my days rattling around, rearranging furniture, or walking the beach picking up firewood, which burned pretty colors even if it wasn't the healthiest or safest thing to burn. And it was free.

I was used to being busy, going to high school, playing the bases on weekends, being on television, traveling to Asia, but I didn't miss it. I was happy. We got a wonderful black dog, Scheherazade, half Labrador, who was my baby. I'd sit for hours and hold this big Labrador on my lap. I'd open the sliding glass door and let in the fresh salt air. I took a patch cord and hooked up one of my old Standel amplifiers with a beige plastic thirty-nine-dollar record player and listened to my one Aretha Franklin album and my one Andy Williams album and my one Wes Montgomery album, "A Day in the Life," over and over again, while I was cooking and cleaning and waiting for Ken to come home for lunch. I liked lunch.

One day Ken made the mistake of coming home for lunch in his flight suit. There was a mark at the bridge of his nose, where the oxygen mask had rubbed up against him—a sign of danger, like a dueling scar or something. For reasons I cannot explain, I was, shall we say, *stimulated* by the mark on his nose.

His flight suit had all the zippers in the world, and I started unzipping all of them. Ken said, "Barbara, I am a pilot and I have got to go back to work," but he was late getting back to work that day. And a few other days, too.

I was a newlywed. I thought, "You're married, you make love every night, and at lunchtime, too." Sometimes at night, Ken would say to me (we laugh about it today), "Barbara, I have got to get up at five in the morning and my life depends on how alert I am, so would you please leave me alone? This is dangerous stuff I have to do."

Not me. I didn't have anything to do except clean house and wait for Ken. He was my life. And I was so in love—like a little bee around Ken. Even today, we're very affectionate people. I think I drove him crazy.

After I'd let him go back to work, I started exploring the area. It was a big island, with mountains in the distance, always something different around each curve in the road. One of the first times out, I made a few turns and was admiring the scenery so much that I, well, to tell you the truth, I got lost, which is really hard to do in Coupeville.

No problem. I stopped at a service station and I suddenly realized that not only did I not know where I was, I could not remember my address . . . or my phone number . . . or Ken's number at work. Truth is, I didn't know anything. I was starting to cry when the attendant came out and said, "Can I help you?"

"Can you tell me where I live?" I blurted.

"What?" he asked, looking behind him.

"Are we on *Candid Camera?*" he added.

When he figured out I was serious, he let me look at the map, and while I described how the land was shaped, with the beach houses, he was able to pinpoint it for me, and give me directions.

Dumb? Yeah. Another time, Ken was away on maneuvers for a month but, mathematical wizard that he is, he had figured out to the penny that we could just afford new tires for our Chevy

II, which was going around with baldies on it. All I needed to do was have the tires changed.

The new tires were in the trunk, doing me a lot of good, the day Arlene Dickey and I decided to go shopping. Arlene was my friend next door, a little older than me, and we had fun together. We'd get our housework done and go next door for coffee, something I looked forward to every day. This day we stashed my laundry in the back of my car and went shopping with her four-month-old baby.

In Washington, there is something called black ice—when the oil seeps up into the highway in the rain and becomes slicker than ice. I was heading down a two-lane highway, and a truck was coming in my direction, and my car started to get away from me, fishtailing from side to side, right toward the truck. I had always been told that if you take the wheels and set 'em, real quickly, the tires would grab, so I tried it, but nothing happened. On the side of the road was a pine forest, and just before I hit the truck, I jerked the car the opposite way and we crashed into the trees. Wham.

The whole backseat of the car was full of four big Navy duffel bags full of dirty clothes. The car was still running. I screamed Arlene's name and asked, "Are you all right?" and I started screaming, "Where's the baby?"

My car was upside down, and I tried to turn off the ignition, but you know the sound when you turn the key the wrong way. I finally got it turned off, and the baby was in the backseat with the dirty clothes, and there was nothing wrong with him. Arlene's ankle was sprained and I had a bad bruise behind my left ear from my head hitting the window, and I couldn't stop crying from worrying about the baby.

After I was checked out at the naval hospital, I was taken to the home of Mary Bottenburg, whose husband was the commanding officer of Ken's squadron. And she took care of me for a while, until Captain Jack Quinn, the commanding officer, came around and asked about my car insurance. I didn't know where anything was, so Captain Quinn and his wife, Betty, two super people, came to my house and searched for the papers. I was just a stupid eighteen-year-old kid.

I was beginning to appreciate how the military pulls together, and I needed all the help, because right after this, my dog Scheherazade got loose and was killed by a car. It was Mary Bottenburg who had to break the news to me. I didn't have any children of my own, and to me, it was the same thing. When they told me Sher was dead, with not a mark on her, I really lost it. They had me stay the night because I was in no shape to go home.

I was still in rough shape the next day, and I went to see the naval chaplain to talk about my accident and Sher being killed. When I saw the chaplain, I asked, "Why did God let me lose control of that car and crash?" The chaplain was a naval officer, and he gave it to me straight. He said, "It wasn't God's fault. He didn't do it. You were the one who didn't change your tires. You were the one who had bald tires on the car. You were the one who made it happen."

And I asked, "Why did God let Sher get killed?" And he said, "You let Sher out, and a human being was driving too fast. You can't blame God for that. We all have the ability to make choices. We're all going down the road. We all choose left or right. God is omnipotent. He knows what road we're going to choose, but He lets us choose. He doesn't do bad things."

When the chaplain told me that, it gave me such peace. It brought me back to reality, brought me to my senses. I was heartbroken, blaming my Heavenly Father, but then I found out that I had messed up. Instead of blaming God, I should ask Him to help me be better in my actions.

I also don't believe God looks down and says, "Zap! I'm going to give that person cancer," or, "Zap! I'm going to give that person a heart attack." That's the way it is. There are these things, germs, diseases, accidents, in this life. I know that God and only God can give us the strength to cope with these phenomenally difficult things. As a Christian, I was raised to believe that if you have faith the size of a mustard seed, you can move a mountain.

I am proud that when bad times came to me, as much as I retreated into myself, as depressed as I got, I never asked why God had done this to me. I didn't look at it as a test of me or my faith. In fact, I could have done without it.

25
GOING HOME

As soon as my head cleared, I began asking to go home. The doctors decided I could recuperate just as well in my bedroom as I could in the hospital. They told me it would be a few days yet, but they also ordered me to have my bags packed, both literally and mentally.

They had been so great about security, keeping out the television crews and the reporters and the well-meaning fans who wanted to encourage me, and now they managed to keep my departure a secret—even from me. Dr. Jones has said that with the "normal" patient, you only have to worry whether there is enough help at home, but that with the so-called "celebrity" patient, the doctors also have to worry about security and publicity, all the extra distractions in a very public life. But after checking with Ken, he knew my family could protect me, keep me safe.

One night Dr. Jones was at a reception at the hospital, and he told his office nurse, Sheila Dennis, "Tonight's the night." They alerted Ken and they visited my room. Dr. Jones said,

"It's time to go." I was glad to think about my room at home, about crawling back deep into my cave.

Rousing every extra bit of security, they put me on a stretcher and carried me to the ambulance, laid me flat. This scared me because I had never been in an ambulance before, not that I could remember. The trip from the wreck did not exist in my mind. All I could think was that this was my first ride since the accident, so out of the blue, I blurted out to the driver, "Do you have a seat belt on?" I don't even remember the answer.

With Ken and Dr. Jones in Ken's van, Sheila Dennis accompanied me for the forty-five minutes out to Gallatin. I had never realized what a rough ride you get in those ambulances—bump-bump, I could feel it all through my body. I was still hurting so badly that all I could think was, "I wish I hadn't said I wanted to go home."

But this was the best way to do it, for somebody as wounded as me. It was stealing away in the night, and that was fine by me. I was rapidly becoming a person who did not want anyone around, no squad of hospital staff, no fans, no reporters, no television crews, no nothing. It was just great. I could suffer, I could cringe, I could yell out from pain, and there was nobody there to see it and hear it.

They had no time to prepare anything at home. No banners. No balloons. No cake. Kathy was there with the children, and I got to see my dogs and my cats, but it was no big deal. I didn't care. For the first time in my life, I did not care.

I would like to say there was a sense of being glad to be alive. I would like to say I felt, "This is my home, my family, my life starting all over again." I was the peppy one, the positive one. Not anymore. I was just anxious to get into my little hole in the ground. I wanted to go home and pull the curtains and shut out the world.

2̲6

AN OFFICER'S WIFE

S HORTLY AFTER WE SETTLED on Whidbey Island, Ken bought
me a book with a title something like *Etiquette and Protocol for an
Officer's Wife.* I said, "You've got to be crazy. If they don't like
me the way I am, that's tough." That was the eighteen-year-old in
me—as well as the Mandrell. And Ken said, "No, you really must
read this."

So I read it. Learning to be a Navy wife got pretty intricate.
The Navy does not exactly run those aircraft carriers on spur-of-
the-moment decisions, and life on a naval base was about as complicated. Nothing happens without a set of rules—not even a
friendly visit.

Shortly after I arrived at the base, Ken was supposed to introduce me to his new commanding officer, Captain Quinn. Ken
told me all the rules. When you visit his home, you will notice a
little silver tray where you are supposed to slip your calling card:
Ensign Kenneth Dudney and Mrs. B. Dudney. But the rule is,
you cannot do it while they are looking. You are supposed to be
subtle and just drop it.

We managed the calling card all right, but we had more trouble with the fifteen-minute rule. Ken explained to me that Navy protocol says you are expected to stay fifteen or perhaps twenty minutes, not more, not less. That was fine. We sat down, sipped our drinks and started to make small talk.

Actually, the day I knew we had an appointment to visit the Quinns, I had seen Mrs. Quinn in the supermarket and had introduced myself to her. I said, "I'm the one who's going to be at your house tonight." She was very warm, and I was comfortable talking to her. And when we arrived at their house, Captain Quinn and I soon discovered we had a lot in common, too—all of Asia in common.

Captain Quinn and I had been to the same places—Subic Bay in the Philippines, Vietnam, Thailand, Korea. We had all kinds of "war stories" to swap. There I was, eighteen years old, having a great old time trading tales of the grand old hotels and the landing strips and the people. And I could see Ken was panicked.

At exactly seventeen minutes and thirty seconds, Ken looked at his watch, cleared his throat and said, "Well, ahem, we really must be going." But Captain Quinn and his wife, Betty, just waved him off. No problem. Let's talk. In his cool way, every five minutes or so, Ken said, "Well, we must leave now," and they would wave him down.

After two hours, the captain and his wife shook our hands and said they had a great time. But all the way home, Ken was trying to figure how far they could bust him for overstaying his visit. He saw his career going down the drain.

In fact, he was doing fine. Ken was training to fly the KA3B, the largest craft able to land on aircraft carriers. If he was more than three feet off center, he was in big trouble. As it was, the planes had to catch a giant cable just right, or they'd be out over the ocean again, with a limited amount of fuel to come around. Or they'd crash.

Ken would make two hundred and seventeen of those landings on aircraft carriers—and live to tell me about it. But we had no guarantee about it then. The planes were for refueling, designed for action in a place like Vietnam. They would try to stay outside the shooting range and wait for the fighters to go in, and then Ken would hook up with them and refuel them. It was hazardous work.

Also, because Ken was the first ensign to fly the A-3 right

out of flight school, he often got the hardest details. All the other pilots were either commanders or lieutenant commanders, many of them out of Annapolis. The most difficult details would often go to the low man on the totem pole. Let Dudney do it. More than half his flights were at night, which is a high ratio, but he never complained because he loved what he was doing.

He had his career, I had mine. Mine was being an officer's wife. As an eighteen-year-old, just out of high school, I was thrown in with women who were five and ten years older than me. In fact, because my mother is only seventeen years older than me, some of my girlfriends were my mother's age. And I was expected to have the same manners, observe the same rituals, as these grown women.

In the Navy, there is a tradition known as the wetting-down party, where you celebrate somebody's making a new rank. The wives tended to like that ritual, and sometimes we would celebrate even when our husbands were out to sea. So I decided it was my turn to throw a wetting-down party in my little beach house.

I remember being nervous about making a good party because the women were all so senior to me, and they all had beautiful homes, and they all knew how to throw a party. I wanted everything to be just right. I wanted to appear worldly and smart and mature. And generous. I wanted to appear generous.

Since it was my party, and since I was the bartender, and since I didn't know anything about alcohol, I figured I would just use my common sense and everything would be fine. If somebody ordered rum and Coke, I'd fill half the glass with rum and half the glass with Coke. Made sense to me. Vodka tonic? Half and half. Sounded right.

Within an hour, those women were having a great time. It ended up with us playing Twister, a game where you spin a red marker on the floor and then you have to put your feet and hands down wherever the marker points. It brings out the contortionist in you, that's for sure. After one of my drinks, we all discovered joints we never knew we had. We had the best time, and all because I was too stupid to know how to mix drinks. Of course, how they felt the next day is another story.

Fortunately, I don't think I had one drink. I was too busy running the party, and besides, I remembered my episode right after my wedding. I am what I laughingly call a cheap drunk, and most of the time I remember it. My friends thought it was wonderful—at least until later. Bartender was one of the jobs they didn't quite spell out in *Etiquette and Protocol for an Officer's Wife.*

I didn't mess up often. Service wives could be a tremendous asset to their husbands' careers, the way I saw Betty Quinn doing for her husband. She was so smart and so tactful and so loyal—officer material herself. Very few wives had jobs, much less "careers." I didn't get much of it, but I think I could have dealt with the officer who said, "Hey, you're a wife, and wives are supposed to be seen but not heard. Talk to my wife about drapes while I talk to your husband about pitch and roll." I would have been enough of an actress to be manipulative, to get that officer to want to speak to me. It would have been a challenge. And I would have let him know that Ken Dudney was the best pilot in the Navy. Because he was.

Nowadays, from what I hear, Navy wives have their own careers, don't have to pitch in around the base. But the way the Navy was in those days, a Navy wife could help or hurt her husband's career. I'm generalizing like crazy here, but I found there were wives who wore their husband's bars. They were the officers. As a rule, the friendliest, warmest, most easygoing, down-to-earth wives were the lowest-ranking officers' wives and the higher-ranking, like Mrs. Quinn. But there would be a point where a man was concerned about promotion, and all of a sudden his wife would start acting like "Mrs. Lieutenant Such-and-Such." It's that way in business, too. The wife of the chief executive officer usually knows who she is. In show business, it often works the same way. The greatest performers are the most secure. I mean, everybody has an ego, but some people handle it better. Bob Hope. Minnie Pearl. Roy Acuff. Lucille Ball. On that level. So easy to talk to. So human.

I think I could have handled being the wife of an admiral, because that's exactly what I would have been. And I would have liked it. Those stupid little things I did would have done nothing but help Ken, because even at eighteen, I think I had a sense of how the Navy worked.

Of course, I didn't much love it when the Navy assigned Ken to the Mediterranean for a nine-month cruise. I had gotten used to having him home every night for dinner (to say nothing of lunch!). What would I do for nine months while he was away? Well, I would visit my parents. They were living in a state I had never visited before. Tennessee.

27
LIVING IN DARKNESS

ONE MORNING IN EARLY October, Ken came into the room and opened the blinds, letting in the bright fall sunshine.

"Close those blinds!" I shouted.

Snarled. Yelled. Screamed. You name it. I was in a foul mood, and Ken got the brunt of it.

"But Barbara, it's a gorgeous day outside," Ken said, pointing to the sun shining on Old Hickory Lake just outside my window.

"Ken," I said in cutting tones. "I do not want to see. I hurt all over and I don't care!"

"If you say so," he said, closing the blinds.

The pain was making me withdraw from everybody. I was just discovering that when you are in pain, even sunlight adds to it. I had always thought I could force my way through anything, but I was becoming a recluse.

Everything was difficult. I was on crutches, and Ken had to

help me get to the bathroom. He even rigged a way for me to take a bath by installing handrails and putting me in the bathtub and then putting a little white plastic stool for my leg, so the cast would not get wet, but it had to be done ever so carefully or I would scream in pain.

It was hard to sort out the pain. But when I learned to deal with the pain in my bruised knees, the pain in my broken femur, the pain in my broken ankle, the constant headaches, there was another pain that was excruciating—the pain in my tailbone, like a twenty-four-hour alarm clock, never stopping. Ken would rub the tailbone area for me, and I would try lying in different ways, but I couldn't lie on my stomach, couldn't lie on my side, couldn't turn the knee too much. And could not sleep.

The television had to be on twenty-four hours a day. Every single day, I'd watch *Little House on the Prairie* and *M*A*S*H* and the Nashville Network. Television was my life, twenty-four hours a day. I used to like to read in bed, Louis L'Amour westerns, but now I had no desire to read.

I would try heating pads, pillows, but there was no position I could lie in that was comfortable. Then to my horror I discovered that if I dozed off in a certain position, my mouth was so numb on the left side from the accident that I would drool slightly. I was so disgusted and embarrassed that I did not want anybody to see me.

I'm a woman, and we all care how we look. I couldn't talk without stuttering, and I certainly did not want anybody to see me that way.

My world was that bed. I didn't want anybody around, just my immediate family and my closest friends. I could not think of anything. It was horrible. Horrible. Being home made no difference.

I had never been so depressed. I would not allow anybody to talk to me but my precious family. Poor Martha Smothers, our housekeeper at the time, brought me my food and I would hardly acknowledge her. But Martha was wise enough just to carry in the tray and tiptoe out again, and act like everything was normal.

Ken had to work to pry me out of my room. He would lift me out of the bed, prop me on my walker, and say: "We're going to take just a short walk into the library and then we're going to go right back."

Later, he would have Martha put lunch on the back terrace, to make me get out in the fresh air.

"I don't want to do this," I griped. "I hate doing this. Why don't you leave me alone?"

But he would not leave me alone. Very seldom do I remember him not being with me in that darkened room. Anything I needed, he did. He talked to me: "Are you comfortable?" He bought one of these foam-rubber cushions to help keep my body from getting sore from lying down day after day. He would rub the tailbone for me, rub my shoulder.

He put up with the TV in our bedroom being on twenty-four hours a day. That way, when I woke up every hour or less all through the night, there was the TV.

Nobody else could move me. Kathy Brown would try, but I would say, "If you hurt my leg, I'm going to hit you." And naturally, that would make her nervous. How could it not?

Ken was still trying to understand what I was going through. We had never experienced anything like this. I had gone through childbirth but I had never known an injury.

Oh, sure, when we were getting ready to go on my first tour of the Orient, my dad had said to me, "If you don't stop playing softball at this very moment, you're going to break a finger." Sure enough, I broke my finger.

That night, we had a job at a military club near our home. The finger was so swollen and hurt so much, I had a splint on it, but I took it off so Daddy wouldn't see. So I put the pick on and I hung in there. Once I had proven I could do my job, then I told him. And he said, "I told you so." I toughed my way through that one. This was different.

Ken did not realize how serious it was until he happened to talk to Bill Anderson, an old friend and one of the most gifted songwriters and singers in Nashville. Bill's wife, Becky, had also been in a car wreck and had suffered a head injury. Bill talked to Ken and they discovered a lot of similarities— problems with memory, speech, temper. Becky is better now, too, but it made both husbands a little more comfortable at the time to know what could happen after a head injury, even if the doctors said we were going to be fine. At the time, it didn't look that way.

28
A LITTLE VISIT TO TENNESSEE

"HEY, IT'S SATURDAY," DADDY said. "Let's go to the Opry."

If you were a tourist visiting India, you wouldn't miss the Taj Mahal. If you were visiting Paris, you wouldn't miss the Cathedral of Notre Dame. And if you were visiting Nashville for the first time in your life, you'd want to see the Grand Ole Opry.

The Opry is the living heart of country music. The mother church. It is a live show coming from Nashville on radio station WSM, sixty-five on your dial. Now it comes from the new auditorium on Opryland, and that's fine, but there are some of us who still close our eyes and pretend we're in the old red-brick church downtown. The Ryman.

We were raised on the belief that the Ryman was the center of the world for country music. You had the Louisiana Hayride and the Wheeling Jamboree on WWVA and the Renfro Valley Barn Dance out of Kentucky and the Eighth Street Theater in

Chicago and the National Barn Dance and of course the Town Hall in California, where I had performed.

When I was working in Las Vegas and California, I had met a lot of the stars from the Opry, but I had never been there. We could not pick it up on the radio in California, but we would catch it when we were visiting our families in the Midwest. Anybody who had ever heard Minnie Pearl cackle "How-dee" or Roy Acuff sing "The Wabash Cannonball" has a deep belief that someday she will visit the Opry. And this was my chance.

As soon as Ken had gone off on active duty, I joined my family in western Tennessee. I had never been in the state before, although Daddy's father came from Sumner County, just outside Nashville. It had always seemed like a distant, romantic, but also very familiar state. I always knew I'd visit there someday.

My folks were living in the western part of the state, in a town named Newbern, where Daddy had been planning to live peacefully, building homes with his brother, going to church, and raising the two girls.

However, Semi Mosley, the man who had released my first record—and as far as I could see, my only record—asked Daddy to go to work for him. Mr. Mosley still sold his Mosrite musical instruments, and was having trouble with some accounts out in the field, so he asked Daddy to go out and do a little "trouble-shooting."

Fortunately, that was the only thing Daddy had to shoot. He would go into a store where there were close to fifty guitars, and the salesman had told the owner, "You keep them and I'll just draw off this stock and you don't have to pay for them." The business was really messed up. Daddy would either collect for the instruments or he would ship them back to Mr. Mosley.

When I got there, the family was preparing to accompany Daddy on a business trip through the South, in the trailer. It was like old times, back with Louise and Irlene, who were getting to be teenagers. I have such beautiful memories of that trip, pulling over and finding a nice rest area, and Daddy cranking up the generator for the stove, and Momma frying potatoes. I can't say I missed the performing. It was just fun being together again.

On the way back, Daddy stopped off in Nashville on business. We also had time to visit with our country friends—Uncle Joe and Aunt Rosie Maphis, Betty and Merle Travis, and Gordon and Virginia Terry, those great people who had fussed over me when I was little. We stayed in a trailer park, right next to Buck Trent, who played banjo with Porter Waggoner, and I got to meet him.

After being in town for a few days, Daddy noticed it was Friday and he invited me along to the Opry. I thought of myself as a kind of hillbilly from California, but I honestly admit I expected to see people barefoot and wearing burlap sacks in the streets of Nashville. Instead, the men wore jackets and called other people "sir" and "ma'am" and worked at things like the state government and publishing companies. There was a kind of conservative politeness to everything. I liked Nashville right away. But where were the hillbillies?

Maybe we'd see some hillbillies at the Ryman. Daddy and I had no problem buying tickets for the upper deck. The rows were still the old church pews, but now each place was marked off with a painted number.

From our vantage point in the balcony, we could see the stage, with the famous backdrops they would lower for each quarter-hour segment. One segment was sponsored by Pet Milk, one by Goo-Goo Candy Bars ("Go get a Goo-Goo! They're goo-o-od!"), and one segment by the insurance company that owned the Opry. You could even see the radio microphones with the world-famous call letters WSM, which subtly advertise the insurance company's slogan: "We Shield Millions."

Before the Opry would begin that night, they were taping the Porter Waggoner Show, with his singing partner, a little old country girl from East Tennessee. Her name was Dolly Parton. My, she was great. Beautiful and great. Bright and chipper and with that voice like a fiddle. And she'd written songs like "Coat of Many Colors" and "Butterfly" and "Jolene" that make you laugh and cry and think.

I have never told people that it was Dolly on the stage that night. As I sat there in the balcony and peered down, I had the overwhelming sensation that I wanted to be on that stage. I hope it doesn't sound conceited, comparing myself to Dolly or anybody else, because I'm not. I just suddenly wanted to perform again.

"Daddy, I can do that," I whispered. "I want to get back in music if you'll manage me."

I'll never forget his words. It was almost as if he had prepared them, although he swears to this day he had never considered the possibility.

"I'd bet my last penny on you," he said.

And he danged near did. His last penny, and his health, and the future of the whole family. Lots of times it would have been easier to give up. But Daddy committed himself as abruptly as I had decided to try music again.

"I'll just sell the house and we'll go for it," he said.

We stayed for the regular Opry show. I have a vague recollection of Roy Acuff and Minnie Pearl, Grandpa Jones and Stringbean, some clog dancers, bluegrass groups, some of the regulars, and I think Porter and Dolly came on, although don't hold me to it. I just gaped at these famous names. You could see them milling around on the far side, near the dressing rooms, just hanging out, very informal. The studio audience was part of the show. The illusion on the radio was one of a grandiose hall, with everything running like clockwork, but you'd see performers and friends mingling at the edges of the stage, chatting while the next act went on. This was it. We were at the Ryman. The center of the world.

We went home that night and broke the news to Momma and the girls. I kept waiting for somebody to say, "Wait a minute. What about our plans? What about *my* life?" But nobody did. It was just sort of understood that I was the firstborn, the Sweetheart of the Steel Guitar. I was Big Sister. Everybody in the family was excited about my going back into show business again.

Except Ken. He was in Europe, trying to work his way up to Navy captain. I'd have to break the news to him one of these days.

29
THERAPY

ONE OUTSIDER WAS ALLOWED to pierce my cave, my hideaway. That was my physical therapist. It was not my idea. I was so badly stunned that I just wanted to retreat, with no thought of bouncing around again.

You are talking about one of the most active people you ever met. I never met a celebrity ballgame that I didn't like. I've run sprints and ridden in bike races for charity. I took spring training with the Los Angeles Dodgers, doing all the exercises along with my pal Steve Yeager. If you visited my house, I'd jump up and clean the table. Can't stand being still.

Now my legs did not move easily. It wasn't that I wanted to do anything about it, but my family and my doctors knew I had to get my legs working again—not so I could perform again, but so I could move normally.

In the hospital, I used to scream and holler when Linda Fowler would give me therapy, but I didn't know nothin' about pain until I got home.

By now, my knee could still move only fifteen degrees. All

of the quad muscles were torn up, all the knee muscles had atrophied. It wasn't so much that they hurt. They just wouldn't move, as if they were rusty.

As good as he was, Ken was not trained to administer the intricate therapy. Dr. Jones said we needed an expert, a private therapist who would come to the house every day.

Her name was Martha Goodpasture. I cannot even remember what she looked like, except how she smiled at me in such a pleasant way while causing me unprecedented pain.

I would be lying in bed, and she would take hold of my leg and try to bend it as far as it would go. I would be moaning from pain, expecting that at any moment the leg was going to snap in two. She would push the leg to the point where it doesn't go any more—and then she would push it some more.

There were adhesions in the muscles, and she would have to break them loose. She would push on the leg and you would hear this sound—snap, crackle, pop, like a doggone bowl of Rice Krispies in the commercial.

"Aaaagh!" I would scream.

And she would smile at me and say, "Let's try it again."

This lady was not afraid of me. She just kept coming at me. I remember vividly telling myself I was not going to cry out loud, but no matter how hard I tried, I'd grab the headboard of the bed and the tears would just roll down my face while she pushed.

The next time she would take out her measuring device and find I had gained a millimeter of flexibility. "It's working," she would tell me. Then she would put her hands on my leg again and start pushing.

She was very much like a drill sergeant with me. She would never take no for an answer and she would never give in. No matter what excuse I would attempt, she had my number. Headache? Tired? Sick to my stomach? She would just start pushing.

"I love you," I told her, "but I'd love to put you through the wall. If it were up to me, I'd never let you in my house again."

And she would smile. And keep pushing.

This just wasn't me. I had always been game for anything. Childbirth. Do it. Pneumonia. I'll get over it, or I'll die. Exhaustion. Just let me sleep. But I was discovering we all have different sides to us, that you never know how you will react to a new situation.

Ken would leave the room because he couldn't bear to watch. When Martha was gone, Ken would make bad jokes that she must have learned her trade from the Gestapo. But she knew what she had to do to make me well.

In between, we got to talking, and I learned that she was Christian, my sister in Christ. As much pain as she gave me, she was very loving to me at the same time.

I told her one day, "I love you. I think you're a wonderful person."

Of course, at the same time I was thinking, "Maybe you could get a flat tire tomorrow. Or the flu. Nothing serious. Just stay home."

But she'd be back, with that pleasant smile and those strong hands and a will like iron.

30

WORKING AGAIN

I BROKE THE NEWS TO Ken by telephone that I was thinking
of singing again. He did not sound surprised. He was on maneuvers
in Europe, having interesting little meetings with Soviet ships out
in the Mediterranean, and he seemed glad to know I was going
to be busy.

"I promised your father I would never get in the way of your
career," Ken said. "And I meant it. You do whatever you want.
I'll see you soon."

He would never back down from that promise, either, even
though it would cost him his own career as a Navy officer. I will
never be able to make that up to him. I could not have done the
same thing if the roles were reversed.

Daddy and I began making plans for my return to music.
Gordon Terry was playing the fiddle at the Black Poodle, a
country-music place in Printer's Alley, the entertainment block in
the center of old Nashville.

Gordon volunteered to let me sing a couple of songs on his
part of the show, and I did. The crowd seemed to like me because

the owner wanted to know if there was any chance of my coming in and entertaining for a couple of weeks. Yeah, I would say there was.

I was going to stay in Nashville so I could start performing, and Daddy had to arrange to leave his job with Mosrite. Uncle Joe and Aunt Rosie Maphis were going on the road so I couldn't stay with them, but Betty and Merle Travis offered me a place, so I lived with them for many weeks. After that I moved in with Gordon and Virginia Terry.

Virginia is only the best cook in the entire world. She would fix a meal at three in the afternoon and then she would put away the leftovers for after you finished working. Just the best. And Gordon and I would play Yahtzee or poker—great fun. I remember Gordon got furious with me one time we were playing some kind of game and I did not know who Tojo was. He said, "There's no excuse for not knowing he was the Japanese leader during World War Two," and I said, "Well, I wasn't born during World War Two," and we'd go on like that . . . the best times. Betty and Uncle Merle lived in a fancy house by the lake, and he knew so much about animals. They had a poodle and I had a cat, and he said, "If you leave them alone, they will work it out," which was true.

It took over a month for Daddy to finish up and move the family to Nashville, where we lived in a travel trailer until he rented Mother Maybelle Carter's house.

I began working that club in Printer's Alley, which was exactly that, a narrow little alley smack in the middle of the city, only a few blocks from the Ryman, only a few blocks from Tootsie's Orchid Lounge, where Tootsie Bess herself would jab a patron with her ever-ready hatpin, whether he was a bum off the sidewalk or the biggest name in country music. Tootsie Bess wielded an equal-opportunity hatpin.

The clubs in Printer's Alley were not that much different from most of the military clubs we had played out west, with beer being sloshed around and maybe a fight breaking out here and there, but the civilians expressed themselves a bit more fully, without worrying about the intervention of the Military Police or shore patrol. People wandered from club to club, and so did the top entertainers in the business. On a nice evening, you had the feeling you were in the center of the universe.

One night while I was working the Black Poodle, Daddy came backstage and said, "Brenda Lee is out there."

I said, "Wow!"

I had been a fan of hers since I was ten or eleven, watching her on television. I would stand in front of the mirror, singing along to her songs like "A Good Man Is Hard to Find," imitating the way she would always keep the microphone in one hand, never moving it from one hand to the other, which is so distracting. I learned that from her. Once I sang at an album store and they gave me my choice of two albums. I remember taking "Grandma, What Great Songs You Sing" and "Emotions," two great Brenda Lee albums.

Now she was sitting in the Black Poodle—and I was excited. That's the ham in me, the competitive side, but I always loved to perform for other artists. In the old days, when I was a kid, I wanted to go out there and show 'em what I could do.

I went out there, and I could spot Brenda sitting at a table. She's tiny, but you could see heads turning to see how she liked this little blonde kid at the microphone. And let me tell you, Brenda was the first one to applaud and the last to stop. You could hear her yell "All right!" and "Woowee!" the way we hillbillies do. Along with servicemen, she was the best audience I ever had.

After the show, I got to meet her. She was so gracious, so encouraging. A few months later, I received an invitation to her baby shower. I remember how awestruck I was at her mansion, with antiques everywhere. She was so natural, with no shoes on, and she set her plate right on her pregnant tummy, which formed a natural shelf.

Since that first meeting, we have always been in touch. Whenever she puts up hot peppers, she sends a jar to me because she knows I like spicy foods. And she's such a pro. When Louise and Irlene and I had the television show, you bet she was on my A List. Scott Salmon, our choreographer, would tell her to do something once and she could do it, boom, just like that.

Other professionals visited my show. One of the great steel players in Nashville, Lloyd Green, was touring the alley one night. With my reverence for great steel players, if I had known he was in the audience, I might have been nervous—or, as hammy as I was, I might have picked better.

That very same night, Lloyd Green went on Ralph Emery's

talk show on WSM. That show was an institution wherever those 50,000 clear-channel watts would take it. And in a dozen states or more, people heard Lloyd Green say, "I just came from hearing this girl play steel down in Printer's Alley." And that was the start of a great friendship with Ralph, too.

Green also mentioned my name to Billy Sherrill, the record producer at CBS–Epic. The next night, three different record guys came to see me in the alley, and we must have received seven or eight business cards in those first few weeks. Daddy and Gordon Terry knew which ones were fly-by-nighters and which ones were serious. One man from Capitol offered to bring us out to Los Angeles, but we wanted to work with Billy Sherrill, who had such a great reputation right in town. I was going to be on records.

Later, I got to meet Lloyd Green when he worked on one of my records as a studio musician, and I thanked him for helping me. And Green told me this story: He had been a shoe salesman who came to Nashville to try to be a session musician. He had no place to stay, but a friend of his put him up. When he told his friend, "I can never thank you enough," the friend replied, "Yes, there is. Help other people." That story made such an impression on me. I hope I've passed on Lloyd Green's favor to somebody else.

With a record contract being worked out, Daddy and I had to plan the rest of my revived career. Daddy had been around the business long enough to know that you had to go out on the road to meet your fans and plug your records. You couldn't just play the clubs in Nashville and wait for it to happen.

Sometimes I worked at fashionable golf and tennis clubs, singing pop music with Boyce Hawkins, who has since passed away. Boyce played organ and piano and had great musicians behind him, and I would sing songs like "The Shadow of Your Smile" and "The More I See You," old pop tunes, for fifty dollars a job, and grateful for it. It helped me buy a used car, which Daddy and I drove on some of our first road dates.

We'd put the instruments in the trunk of the car and Daddy and I went wherever they would have us. With all due respect, sometimes the club musicians didn't know my material, so we'd go in and Daddy would have to play rhythm guitar just so the house musicians would stay in tempo with me.

I don't think I could have survived in the business if I had to play with house bands every night. It was just too hard getting to know each other so you could play a few songs together. Fortunately, I did not have to improvise for long. As soon as Daddy moved the family to Nashville, he began doing the booking and playing rhythm guitar behind me. Then he hired a lead guitar-singer named Kent Morrison, who had a nice voice and came from a good family.

In the spring of 1969, we brought in a dark-haired girl bass player who was all of fifteen years old—Louise. Sissy had been practicing in the basement of our rented house in Madison, developing her own skills and just waiting for us to start up another band. She says she always knew I would go back to singing again. How come I didn't know it?

We also began to work in a drummer, a prodigy hardly into her teens—Irlene. She had been pounding away at the drums in the basement, not about to let the rest of the family take off without her. Those two girls gave up a normal life, with dates and sports and parties, in order to be part of the band. And they did it for free. We had to pay Kent a salary because he wasn't family, and we couldn't expect him to work for free. But we needed at least three bookings a month just to break even. And it took a lot more than that for them to get paid. Yet they worked hard, just to build something, and the closeness of the three of us would shine through on television many years later.

But for now, there were no promises. We began a tour of Texas, traveling in a Ford station wagon and later hooking a trailer on it to carry more equipment. In Nashville, I was mostly a nobody, so it was miraculous that Daddy was even able to get dates for me. When he called people to talk about a date, he had to talk pretty quickly about my appearances in Las Vegas and on the old *Town Hall Parties* and *Five Star Jubilees.* He wasn't lying, but that had been a few years back. I wasn't eleven anymore, no longer a novelty act. I was a grown woman. Would people pay to watch a short blonde steel player sing with her family playing behind her? Daddy talked and talked, and got us booked wherever he could. I've always been grateful to Bill Anderson, that talented songwriter and singer and former journalism major from the University of Georgia, for putting me on his television show in the early years.

In the summer of 1969, Columbia released my first single, "I've Been Lovin' You Too Long" and "Baby, Come Home." It attracted enough attention for us to keep going, but we just barely made enough money to cover gasoline and food. Any profits we made, we plowed back into the show. Maybe because of his military background, Daddy was a firm believer in our looking like a unit. He'd say, "What uniform are you wearing? Are you going to change into civilian clothes right after the show?" Not costumes, but uniforms. Daddy figured when you say "band," you think of a marching band, and they're always in uniform.

We did not have money for store-bought outfits, so Momma would go to Starr Fabrics in Hendersonville and make the uniforms for us. Sometimes I would draw a design and she'd put together a few patterns. The guitar player and Daddy would buy their uniforms from the manufacturers—creamy white and black uniforms.

Uncle Merle Travis used to say: "When the curtain opens, the first thing people deserve is a costume, a group that looks like they know each other. You don't want to look like you just got through overhauling the bus." From the beginning, we didn't even wear blue jeans while traveling.

When we were on a package show, with many different names and stars, we might be the cheapest paid and the least famous, but I'll guarantee you we presented ourselves the best. We would sink our money into better instruments or a better sound system, because a lot of the little places did not have their own systems. We wanted to come off as a class operation, and Daddy's lesson still goes today: every year I insist on putting more money into the lights and the props and the costumes. Oops, the uniforms.

I got used to uniforms because I was back to playing for military audiences. A friend of ours named Pop Phillips said he could book me on bases in Europe, which I did not mind a bit, since I happened to know a Navy pilot over there.

31

"I AM NOT BARBARA MANDRELL"

"**B**ARBARA, WOULD YOU SIGN these pictures?"

JoAnn Berry held out a stack of glossy photographs of a blonde woman. Underneath was printed the name Barbara Mandrell.

I pushed the photographs away.

"I am not going to sign them," I said.

JoAnn looked at me to see if I was joking, but obviously I was not. I was not speaking in riddles, or trying to make some complicated point. That smiling woman with the makeup and the well-coiffed hair had nothing to do with this broken hulk slouching around in the darkness.

"I am *not* Barbara Mandrell."

I was not the woman in the photograph. She was somebody I did not know, but was constantly being compared to. People wanted me to be her, but I couldn't be—and I resented everybody who tried.

It got so bad that I even resented the fans who drove up outside the house. This house on Old Hickory Lake had been our dream. We had spotted it while living in the neighborhood, and eventually we traded houses with the people who lived in it. We had a pool and a helicopter pad and play houses for the kids, and a big enough lawn to convince ourselves we were living way out in the country.

The house was included on the celebrity map that tourists could buy in Nashville. Tour buses would park up on the road and everybody would scramble to one side of the bus and look out. Or cars would pull up along the fence and people would peer through the iron grille fence. We had never minded it, even when sometimes at night people would break off the sharp little decorative points on the wrought-iron fence to take home as a souvenir of Barbara Mandrell's house. In the old days, it had been reassuring to see them waiting outside when I came back from an awards ceremony, and once in a while I would enjoy walking up to the fence to sign an autograph.

We had electronic security at the house, a closed-circuit camera that showed everything that moved on the road and near the gate. Sometimes they would push the buzzer to try to visit us, and it would be annoying when we were eating dinner, but we were glad to know somebody cared. They were the reason I had this lovely house on Old Hickory Lake, so once in a while I would wander out to say hello. Not anymore.

After the car crash, Ken fixed the system so I would not hear the telephone or the buzzer from the front gate. I just wanted the world to go away and leave me alone.

My bedroom faced the lake, but other rooms were open toward the street. Or if you'd go outside, the fans would be there. The old Barbara would have smiled and waved. This Barbara wanted to hide.

It seemed as if the tour buses just multiplied after the accident. They would pull up and you could hear the guide talking about me and the wreck. They were fans, God bless them, but when I craved privacy more than at any time in my life, they were always there.

I think my fans will understand that the flow of visitors became something of an obsession with me. Sometimes I would sit in front of the monitor and watch the cars and buses parked up front.

"What do they want from me?" I would groan. "Why don't they just leave me alone?"

This was not the hambone Barbara Mandrell we all knew and loved. Or at least knew and tolerated. This was a reclusive, cranky Barbara Mandrell. I would tell myself, "If it were not for those fans, I wouldn't have the security camera, wouldn't have the gate, wouldn't have the house. So what's your problem?" But I couldn't help myself. That's how I felt.

Now, I would go into a rage when somebody would stop at the gate. The security monitor was below my television set, which I lived with. Even if the fans didn't buzz the gate, even if they just parked to look down at the house, I would think to myself, "They're watching me. They're thinking about me. Leave me alone."

Sometimes I would say it out loud to Ken or JoAnn or Kathy—and catch them looking strangely at me. I had always been so loyal about my fans. I had signed autographs for these fans until the last one left the hall, and I loved them for their attention. But now they made me so nervous, so frustrated. I absolutely could not deal with people. I could not make small talk.

When I had to visit the doctors' offices, it was arranged that Ken would walk me through the back door because I just didn't want to be around people. I didn't want to be around the outside world.

One day while I was home, the post office delivered fifty thousand pieces of mail, more mail than any person in Nashville had ever received. Ken brought it to our house in the helicopter, right onto the landing pad alongside the lake. Bags and bags of it, incredible. But I could not cope with reading mail, and finally it was given to the fan club to answer. If people did not get an answer, I just hope they understand.

Everything was out of focus. I had never been very heavy, but now I was just skin and bones from lying around not eating.

On the other hand, Kathy Brown gained fifty pounds sitting around with me in the darkened room. Somebody had to eat all the good cooking, and Kathy seemed to be elected. Later, Ken and she would both go on a Nutri-System diet to lose the weight they had gained. Kathy kept hers off; Ken didn't.

Others who were gaining weight were my animals, because they virtually slept in the bed with me. I'd feed them part of my meals, plus they had their own bowls and trays right around the bed. It got so that the room smelled like a menagerie, but I never noticed.

I was oblivious to a lot of things. Other things I shut out on purpose. And the things I noticed made me nervous, like the people driving on the road outside my house. The fans were lucky they didn't see me when my moods swung back and forth. My kids saw me up close. They were not so lucky.

32

EUROPE

WHEN KEN WAS SENT to the Mediterranean for a nine-month cruise, I was devastated. But after he had been gone a few weeks, he called to say he had arranged for me to visit him while his ship was stationed in the Gulf of Juan, near Nice, France.

We found a cheap round-trip fare to Luxembourg, and then I was supposed to fly to Nice, but things got complicated and I did not arrive on the right plane. Ken went out to the airport and waited for three planes, but I was not on any of them. He went back to the hotel where he had reserved a room for seven dollars a night and he wondered if he should cancel the reservation, since his ship was anchored just offshore.

He watched the shore patrol check the bars, where guys were going to find prostitutes, and he was just about to cancel our room when a taxi pulled up and out I jumped. Ken said, "Hey, lady, can I help you?" He was so cute.

He gave me a present, a black negligee from Frederick's of Hollywood, that he had ordered from a catalogue. We stayed together that night and others that followed. He would have to take the "liberty launch" back to the ship every morning to make sure his leave had not been changed. Then he'd come right back to the hotel. He would play his ukulele and we would walk along the beach and we'd buy bread and cheese and have picnics in the park.

One day I was walking by myself when an American sailor spotted me. Thinking I was French, he said with a deep southern accent, "Oui, oui, Mam'zelle." In my best southern accent, I replied, "Oui, oui, yourself, sailor." We both laughed.

Ken and I had a great time for a few days in Nice, and then it was time for me to go to work. I flew up to Germany and auditioned with Pat Patterson's band, playing in an empty hall. When we finished the set, Pop Phillips said, "Yes, I think I can book this." Not only could he, but he paid me a hundred dollars a show. And he had seventeen of them for me. I thought I could handle that.

I played those seventeen shows for good old boys at military bases and clubs, just as if I had been playing along the coast of California. They paid me in cash, and I flew down to Genoa, where Ken's ship was now based. You could tell our priorities had changed just slightly. When we got to the hotel room, we both sat down on the bed—and counted out seventeen hundred dollars. Neither of us had ever seen that much money. Right away, Ken put most of it in the hotel safe, but he kept a little so we could live it up, by our humble standards.

So we did. We'd walk around the harbor to a nice restaurant and sit down and order a meal. Rubes that we were, we didn't know about a traditional Italian meal. We would order pasta, maybe a little salad, and we noticed the waiter was still tapping his pad. What else? Maybe a glass of wine? Some chocolate ice cream for dessert. And coffee. But still the waiter didn't seem pleased. It took us two or three meals at these restaurants before we looked around and noticed everybody had a main course of wonderful veal chops or chicken or fish. We just hadn't realized the pasta was only a starter in Italy. But we got into it after that, long meals down by the waterfront, just a young American couple loving Italy and being together.

Also in Genoa, Ken took me to dinner in the officers' mess on the ship. I had been around the military most of my life but I had never seen such a sight—the linen tablecloths and napkins, the silver and the china. It was magnificent. Talk about officers and gentlemen. The men would all stand behind their chairs and the captain would come in. It was really exciting. I whispered to Ken, "You get to eat in a place like this, on a ship?" The men wore dress whites, holiday whites, and I'm a sucker for uniforms. But Ken told me they did not exactly eat like this all the time. This was for company, when their wives or other guests were visiting.

I got to visit the carrier one other time, but only because Ken goofed and nearly got us both in a lot of trouble. This was in Italy, when he took the liberty launch at seven in the morning for people who had stayed onshore the night before. He took me on the launch, and said, "I'm only going to have to check in. Liberty starts at eight o'clock. We'll get right on and come back."

What he did not know was that the night before, they had passed a rule that visitors could not come aboard until ten. And for very good reason. I was idly watching the planes, not knowing what I was seeing, when Ken suddenly grabbed me and hustled me down the corridor.

"Cover your eyes," he said.

We ducked down some more stairs until we reached his room. His urgency scared me half to death.

"What's going on?" I asked.

"Don't say a word," Ken said.

Later he told me that he noticed they were moving the A-4s around on the flight deck in case of attack, so they were ready to go out at any time. Not even Ken was supposed to see them, although he had a high security clearance. He could tell from the Marine guards around them all the time that he had no need to know about this stuff. He was just a refueling pilot and he knew those planes had something more volatile than fuel on them.

He slipped me straight into his room, which he shared with another man, who wasn't there. We stayed in the room until the maneuvering was over on deck, and the ten o'clock whistle sounded. Then we went back to shore, just like on normal liberty.

It wasn't until later that Ken even dared tell me I had come close to seeing nuclear bombs. I didn't want to jeopardize his security, but being on the same ship with A-bombs did not bother me in the least. I just figured, "Good, glad we got 'em." I told you, I'm a hawk. I want the big gun, and then I'll be sweet and nice to you. That's me. Walk soft and carry a big stick.

During that stay in Genoa, I embarrassed poor Ken again by chatting with strangers. I was in the lobby of the hotel while Ken was taking care of some business. A really nice man in a Navy officer's uniform struck up a conversation, and I said, "Are you on a carrier? Are you on the U.S.S. *Independence?*" And he said, "Yes, yes."

"Well, so is my husband, Ken Dudney," I said. "Do you happen to know him? He's an ensign."

"I'm not sure I do," the man said. "It's a pretty big carrier."

Well, we were chatting about the carrier and how lovely the F-4's nose looks, all curved down, and then we got to chatting about country music, which was his favorite. All of a sudden, I spotted Ken walking up to us, looking like he'd just seen a ghost.

I introduced the two of them, and we talked for a while. When we had left, Ken said, "Barbara, that was Captain Matthews, the captain of my ship." I said, "Well, he seems like a real nice fellow." Rank made Ken nervous, and rightfully so, and I guess he was worried about what his stupid little nineteen-year-old wife had said, but truthfully, I was an asset to Ken's career. I could talk to these men because I had been there, had traveled to Asia and Europe, had performed under trying conditions, and was pretty confident about myself. And I believe officers like Quinn and Matthews were secure enough to pick up on it.

As confident as I was talking with these wonderful top officers, I was also a young wife who couldn't stand being away from her husband. On our last night together in Genoa, we took a walk around the town and Ken carved our initials on a tree near the harbor. We went back to the hotel and watched the minutes tick away until the eleven-thirty launch. I started crying, and he could only reassure me that he'd see me again in a few months, which seemed like forever. As the moment approached, I was wailing.

With five minutes left before the launch departed, Ken kissed me good-bye and closed the door to our room. I was crying so loudly that I had to put a pillow over my head, but that didn't stop the screams. As he descended in the hotel elevator, Ken could still hear me crying.

33

KEN STARTS TO WORRY

AFTER I HAD BEEN home for a few weeks, it became clear that the old peppy Barbara was not suddenly reappearing.

I had always felt that if you were depressed, sad, lonely, unhappy, you just got yourself a project, you got busy, you got off your butt, so to speak. But I was in serious pain, and it was not only physical.

It's natural that somebody in pain is going to have depressed feelings like that, but I had never felt anything like this. I was so used to just bouncing along that I had no way to cope with my feelings.

I had almost always looked forward to tomorrow, couldn't wait to get started. This time I had so much pain that I just wanted it to stop, and some of the pain was mental, from the brain. I couldn't say to myself, "The future will be great." Nothing seemed good.

I ached so badly that I wanted to be out of my misery.

Now, what do I mean by that? I think I can honestly say that I never contemplated suicide. I did not want to die. I did not lie there and say, "If I do such-and-such, I won't hurt anymore."

If it had been as simple as turning off a light or pulling a plug, I still wouldn't have done it. To me, if a person commits suicide that is the same as killing somebody. And that is a sin.

In a sense, I was doing a slow version of "turning out the lights" by not wanting my drapes open. Maybe I just wanted to be left alone as a form of trying to "pull the plug." I wanted the world to go away, I know that.

Maybe I was in mourning for Barbara Mandrell the performer, who the world saw as beautiful, talented, energetic, caring, having all the answers, all of the hype—and I could not live up to that anymore. I wouldn't even autograph a picture of that other Barbara Mandrell, which I guess was a form of self-denial.

I did not want to die, but that didn't necessarily mean I wanted to live. I just couldn't see myself living through this business of broken bones, a constant shooting pain in my tailbone, and feeling sad and angry. I couldn't see what was ahead. People would talk about the future and I just didn't care. I did not, could not, want a tomorrow because, as far as I could see, tomorrow would be just like today.

To this day, it distresses me to realize that I did not ask God's help at that terrible time in my life. I still wonder why I did not pray. Could not pray. I talked with Mike Nelson, our minister, and I never blamed God for the accident, but it was strange to me now that I didn't pray.

Until the moment of the accident, I had been someone who knew that Jesus was my friend. Even if I was alone, taking a bath, combing my hair, driving a car, out of the blue, when something would go through my mind, I would say, "Thank you, Jesus," and I would talk to Him in passing. We had a relationship, a real relationship.

To this day, I believe my family was spared from death in the wreck because Jaime was reciting her Bible homework in the backseat of the car. And I believe God gave me a warning to put on the seat belts. I have never seen kids playing in a station wagon like that, so God must have given us a way to live through what was about to happen. And I knew that only came from God.

But now as I struggled to recover, though I might pray with Mike, or members of my family, God was not with me in private moments. Did I feel God had abandoned me? Was I angry with God? I can't answer that.

I considered myself a saved Christian from a Pentecostal-style background, but we had attended many different churches. When I was ten, we attended a revival at a Lutheran church in California. On this day they had a guest minister, a missionary who was giving a sermon about the crucifixion of Jesus. My parents were there in another part of the church, and I surely did not want to do this, but when the preacher asked who wanted to repent, I stood up by myself and walked down the aisle and joined other people at the altar.

I hear a lot of people talking these days about being born again. It's a matter of semantics. Speaking strictly for myself, I believe I was born into a Christian life, but I was also born in sin, and I must ask to be saved because we are all sinners. There's a bumper sticker you see all the time that says: "Christians Aren't Perfect—Only Forgiven." I also believe you have to work at being forgiven.

That sermon about the crucifixion was so real, so vivid, that even before my accident I could not watch the film *Jesus of Nazareth* or any other film with the crucifixion in it without crying. Such agony and pain for a living human being to endure, even though He was also the son of God. I am not a Bible scholar, but from what I have, the crucifixion took nine hours, while I cannot even watch a film for six minutes of His suffering without crying.

Sometimes I hear people argue about what is the exact truth in the Bible. We go to a unidenominational church, which is open to all kinds of Christians, who interpret the Bible in different ways. We believe the Bible is God's holy word, but my Uncle Ira, who was a marvelous minister, used to say, "Rather than taking somebody else's word for it, read it. Read it for what it says. Consider what was going on, and where they were, and who said it, and who they were talking to. Read it like it was any other book."

I believe in the power of prayer. When my father had

open-heart surgery, I got down on my knees and I prayed for one solid hour for his recovery. But now in my time of trouble, I did not pray.

I knew people were concerned about my physical health, but I was so out of it that I didn't realize how concerned people were about my mental and emotional health as well.

We are not very much into psychology in my family. We're mostly from the old school. This is what's right. This is what's wrong. You do your job. You don't hurt other people. You don't complain. You get through. So there was no immediate call for me to talk out my troubles, no friendly family counselor. We had friends, we had ministers, we had family. What else was there?

It entered other people's minds that I might try to harm myself. We always have pistols in the house to protect ourselves as a last resort. Ken told me recently, "Barbara, I don't know if you noticed, but after you came home from the hospital, I emptied the pistols and I locked them away in a closet. I just didn't want them lying around the bedroom."

I had never missed the pistols. Never thought of using them. But I can see Ken's point in hiding them. I was a girl who did not have a great will to live.

34

A FEW DATES IN THE NORTHWEST

W<small>HEN KEN'S HITCH IN</small> Europe was over, he was assigned back to Washington, so Daddy promptly booked some dates out in the Pacific Northwest. Nobody knew me as a performer out there, but my second single, "Playing Around With Love" and "I Almost Lost My Mind," began to get some plays, and I was able to combine business with pleasure.

Ken was facing combat in Southeast Asia, and he insisted that I work hard on my career so I wouldn't worry about him. Like any wife, I was scared about what might happen to him in combat, and I was happy that he was able to spend the entire Northwest tour with me.

Eventually, I had to go back to Nashville. When I got there, I did not feel very well. I figured maybe it was a bug I picked up out on the West Coast. After a few days, while I was describing my symptoms to Momma, she said, "You'd better see a doctor."

I said, "Uh-oh."

Up to now, I hadn't contacted a gynecologist in Nashville. I had always been backward about seeing a doctor, which I do not recommend to other women. The first time I had seen a gynecologist was when I was getting married and I needed a blood test and a prescription for birth-control pills. I was eighteen and scared to death, which any woman can appreciate. I had never been examined before, and it was horrible. You know it's necessary, you want to get married, so you get up the guts to do it.

After I started on the pills, my parents found me hugging the toilet. I couldn't stand the pills, but I felt I had to hang in there because we were only going to be together for two weeks after we were married, so then I could stop for a couple of months while we went overseas. When we got close to home, in Hawaii, I started taking them again, and I could not even keep down juice and crackers. Nothing worked, so my father forbade me to take those pills anymore.

When I got back with Ken in Washington State, he made me go to a doctor for a milder pill, but I did not like taking his advice. Because Ken is seven and a half years older, I hated any insinuations that I wasn't mature. But now I was a Navy wife, and Ken took me down to the medical center. I was complaining the whole way, until Ken said to me, "Oh, grow up."

Well, that was the wrong thing to say to me. It crushed me. Until a doctor walked from one end of the room to the other and the nurse told me he was the gynecologist. Talk about a hunk, I mean, he was handsome, as good-looking as a movie star. I turned to Ken and said, "Well, I think I just grew up. I think I'll be just fine." I got the last word, gave him a zinger, like a normal wife.

I was still nervous about seeing the doctor, but he gave me some pills that worked better, and life went on. I was supposed to take them every day. Of course, I might have forgotten for a day on that tour of the Northwest.

Now I was back in Nashville, seeing Newton Lovvorn. He was very businesslike as he asked me the pertinent questions: "When was the last time you this? When was the last time you that?"

And I said, "I don't know." I never knew. Who can keep track?

"All I know is, it either happened in Oregon, Washington, or Canada."

"Oh," he said.

He did a few tests and later he broke the news to me. It was an overcast day, just like in the movies, the day I found out. I have never had such a battle with my emotions. Happy? Ken and I wanted to have a family, two or three children at least. Gloomy? I had just started a singing career and Ken was facing overseas duty.

I called Ken to tell him about the baby, and he boosted my spirits because he was so excited. Even though this was not a planned bundle of joy, he was thrilled to think we were going to start a family.

A few days later he called me with some news. Because of a budget cutback, the Navy was laying off three thousand reserve officers, including a number of pilots. Even though the war in Vietnam was still raging, any pilot who had put in five years could leave without serving the last year of his hitch.

To me, it was news from heaven. It had nothing to do with patriotism. I loved being a Navy wife and Ken loved the Navy, too, but we could not stand these long separations—nine months or a year while he was out on a cruise. Ken had been gearing up for possible combat duty in Southeast Asia. We would have accepted it if he had gotten orders to report to Vietnam because we never questioned what our country was doing. But as a pregnant woman who missed her husband, I said to myself, "Thank you, Lord." The Navy was not asking Ken to leave. He could have pursued a career, but at this crucial moment he was being given a choice. It was a tough decision for him because he loved the military almost as much as he loved me. If he had stayed, he would be a retired admiral by now. I never forget that. But I was resuming a career, and he was as supportive of me as I had been of him. And now we had a third party to consider. He signed the paper to leave the Navy. Does he still think about it? I know he does.

I had my own struggle with my emotions, but my parents did not let me see their mixed feelings. One day I asked Momma, "Is Daddy as happy as he seems about the baby?" and she said, "Yes, Barbara, he's worried about your career and the business, but yes, he's genuinely excited."

Bless my father's heart. He had changed businesses several times to keep us going. He had traveled with me, shabby motels and flat tires and me crying because we didn't have enough money.

It was real scary for him, but my father said, "It might be hard, but it will be wonderful when it happens." And my mother said the same. Maybe when they were away from me they expressed their concern, but to my face they were positive. I went through moments of being happy, more moments of being scared, scared, scared.

You know the term mixed emotions? When you love a man, and you love children, and you have always dreamed of having a baby, you know this is what you want. But absolutely not at that time. There was no way we could afford this baby. But God knows the answers, and we don't.

Speaking strictly for myself, I would not have been tempted to go for an abortion if it had been easy at the time. From my standpoint, life is life. From the moment of conception, I believe, there is a soul inside your body. Matt was Matt, Jaime was Jaime, Nathaniel was Nathaniel. There was not a lot of controversy about abortion back in 1969. You got pregnant, you had a baby. I still believe that, unless there's a situation that seriously endangers the mother. And I don't mean inconvenience.

Dr. Lovvorn set a tentative due date of May 8 and Ken and I rented two bedrooms downstairs in my parents' house. For the first three months, I had morning sickness, so I didn't have to worry about gaining weight. I didn't show my pregnancy until my fourth or fifth month. I was still performing, and I was glad that I still fit into my costumes.

When I started to show, Momma sewed some extra room into the front of my outfits. At one club, somebody stole my slacks and I remember thinking, "Won't he be surprised when he finds it's a maternity outfit."

Halfway through, I began feeling little fingers and feet, moving around, touching me from the inside. I felt so blessed, so fortunate, it was like a sign from within. I'd be sitting there, quiet as can be, and all of a sudden, this little life within me gave a kick, and I'd automatically jump and say, "Oh!"

I didn't know what I would do in the middle of a love song if I jumped and said, "Oh!" But for some strange reason, none of my three children ever kicked when I was onstage. I guess they knew I was working.

When I was home, there were six of us waiting on the baby. It was going to be the first grandchild, so Daddy and Momma were excited, and so were Louise and Irlene, and of course Ken.

It was as if I had five doting mothers, all waiting on me.

But I didn't get my way in everything. Momma was always on me for eating sweets. She is a health nut, anyway, and now she was nagging me not to gain weight because it would cause stretch marks and the weight would be hard to lose after the baby was born.

"Eat something good for you," she would say. And she would leave notes in the cookie jar that said, "Get out of the cookie jar, Barbara."

One day she and the girls caught me in the cabinet, looking for something. My back was turned to them, and Momma said, "Barbara, turn around." Before I did, I crammed the whole doughnut in my mouth and tried to gobble it down, but when I turned around, you could still see the doughnut stuck in my teeth.

I woke up on May 8, Mother's Day, and found our toy terrier, Dinky-Doo, licking my hand. The bed was wet, which made me furious until I realized my water had broken in my sleep. We called the doctor's office and they said to rush to the hospital, but the contractions were so slow that I took time to have a bath and color my hair. I wanted to look nice for the big event. I had read the book about childbirth, and I was convinced it was going to be a cinch.

I dried my hair and set it and put on my makeup, ironed a maternity blouse, keeping a towel between my legs the entire time. This was my first baby and I felt a little discomfort but no hard labor. It started at seven in the morning and I didn't get to Nashville Memorial Hospital until eleven. A nurse, Mrs. Gannon, said, "Where have you been?" I think she got the picture when she saw how dolled up I was.

They took an X ray and offered me a shot for the pain, but I declined because I didn't want to miss the great moment. But the great moment was not happening. We went on for a while, and they tried to induce labor, but nothing was happening. After nine and a half hours of labor, I remember opening my eyes and seeing Ken and Momma standing over me. The hospital only allowed the husband into the labor room, so I figured that there must be a reason they allowed Momma in.

"This is it, I'm dying," I reasoned. "Momma nearly died having me, and now the same thing is going to happen to me."

I was more than a little panicked, and not doped up enough to relax. Dr. Lovvorn was with me, and he asked me some questions, and then he told me my bone structure just wasn't big enough to allow the baby to pass. There was just not enough room. The way I remember it, you are supposed to dilate to ten, and the most I dilated was to two or three.

I was convinced I was going to die.

"Everything's going to be fine," Dr. Lovvorn said. "I'm going to give you a C-section."

"A what?" I asked.

"A cesarean section," Dr. Lovvorn said.

I guess I hadn't read the whole book, after all. I had skipped over the chapter on cesarean sections because I didn't think it applied to me. It took Dr. Lovvorn a few moments to explain to me he was going to operate through my abdominal walls to deliver the baby the way Julius Caesar was supposed to have been delivered two thousand years earlier. Of course, they did not have anesthesia in those days, which was too bad for the mother. If this had happened even a century earlier, I would have been a dead woman.

I was game for this C-section, whatever it was, because I thought I was going to die. Just being in the hospital gave me the willies because I had never stayed overnight for anything except to have my tonsils out. (My mother, Louise, Irlene and I all had our tonsils out at once, and Daddy had said it was the quietest the house had ever been.) I was still resisting the big shot because I like to have control over things, but Dr. Lovvorn said he was going to have to knock me out.

Just before the anesthetist gave me a shot, Dr. Lovvorn said, "Don't worry about the C-section. I'll give you the incision, and you'll be able to wear a bikini." I know this sounds like an old joke, but I actually said, "That's great, Doctor, because I've never worn a bikini before." And on that note, I retired for the duration.

When I awoke it was still Mother's Day, and I was now the mother of a healthy little boy. I was so proud and happy to be a mother, to have given Ken a baby boy, to have started a new generation in the family, but I would also have to say I was relieved it was over, that I hadn't died. Matthew's birthday is always celebrated on May 8, but I think about it every Mother's Day, too. I was born on Christmas Day and Matthew on Mother's Day, but I wouldn't rate either day as a day off. And after having a C-section on Mother's Day, I wasn't looking to fill up all the other holidays with operations or births, either.

When I got out of the recovery room, they could not let me hold the baby and feed him because I was hooked up to the IV machine and was still taking a drug for the pain from the C-section. My roommate had her baby, this precious little thing, and I was feeling terribly deprived until one of the nurses walked in with my baby and said, "Oh, I'm sorry, I didn't know you couldn't have your baby just yet." But since she goofed and brought him in, she stood there and let me hold him.

We had already decided on the names for him. We both loved the name Matthew because it is Biblical, and it's my father's middle name. I also wanted to name our first son after Ken and his father, but I didn't think Matthew Kenneth sounded exactly right, so we named him Kenneth Matthew but agreed ahead of time to call him Matthew, which we always have.

I felt so proud to be married and holding this beautiful little boy. Ken brought me one rose and he said, "One baby, one rose, happy Mother's Day." He also brought a bottle of nail polish I wanted and he painted my fingernails and toenails for me.

It was the neatest Mother's Day you could imagine—until somebody broke the news to me that a C-section was more expensive than a regular birth. We had just barely scraped together eight hundred dollars to pay for the delivery, and now we owed five hundred dollars more. Dr. Lovvorn, who was just starting out and needed the money as much as we did, was very agreeable to letting us pay for it on time.

I wanted to save every dollar I could by getting out of the hospital early, but anytime you have abdominal surgery, you have problems getting your system to work again, so they wouldn't let me out. Every night I would pray to get rid of the gas, and I would try not to cry so my roommate could get some sleep, but it was very painful. Finally, things got better, and when I got out of the bathroom, my roommate and I started laughing, which I do not recommend after a C-section. You do not want to cough, either.

I wanted my stomach muscles to heal as soon as possible. We had not made any bookings on either side of the birth date, but now we had the cesarean bill to pay. I had to get back on the road again as soon as possible. I was going to have a career in show business and I was going to take care of my growing family. I would make some money and I would protect my children. I was twenty-one. How easy it all seemed.

35
MATT

As SOON AS I got home from the hospital, I was pretty ob-
sessive about having the kids around me, as if I was afraid to be
apart from them, or perhaps it was some kind of guilt over what
had happened. I would lie in bed, watching *Nashville Now*, and
I would insist that Matt or Jaime sit and watch with me. They
obviously had their own things to do, games or homework or
listening to their own music, but I would not let them get away.

If Jaime said, "I'm going to leave now," I would say, "No,
you sit there." If she made an excuse like, "I have to go to the
bathroom," I would say, "Well, you hurry back."

When Ken and the therapist started prodding me to get
around on the crutches, everybody else in the family got en-
thused that I was getting back to my old self. But even as my
body began to heal a little bit, my emotional state was rocky,
particularly with Ken and the kids.

If I was in the kitchen, I would give orders like, "Clear the
table." The kids would clear the table and then I would say,
"Go clean your room." Obviously, things were getting done

without me. But if Matt or Jaime said, "I already did that," or "Which room do you want me to do?" I would start yelling and have a tantrum.

I tried to monitor everything the kids did. Maybe it was because I had been driving when they had been hurt. I don't know. But I wanted to be in control.

I would ask to see their homework. If Jaime wrote a note in longhand, I would say, "Oh, Jaime, you wrote this so nice." But if there was the slightest smudge, I'd raise my voice and say, "You're wasting paper. You should erase it."

Irlene remembers how I had to get involved in every little thing. One day I was trying to help Jaime with her homework when Matthew came in to take care of some poison ivy. I told him to go upstairs and put some lotion on, and he said, "I already have lotion for that." I got mad and said, "Go up there now and put what I said on it."

It had to be doubly hard on Matthew because he had been injured worse than people realized. I kept trying to tell Ken or anybody who would listen to me, "I know Matt's head hit the dashboard, too. If I feel the way I feel from getting hit on the head like that, if I'm having difficulty emotionally, he must be, too."

So I would alternate between yelling at Matt and feeling sorry for him. It's hard enough for kids to grow up. Part of them wants to stay young and be a child and the other part wants to grow up, to separate. This accident just complicated all the normal changes that take place between parents and children.

Up until then, Matthew had always been a good student, obedient at home, thoughtful and polite, do whatever you asked of him, and always answer "Yes, sir" and "No, ma'am," because that's what we expected of him. He was so disciplined in what he did, maybe from studying the martial arts. And he still seemed so young to me. He was fourteen, but his face had been so youthful, so unblemished by anything. Now he looked like he had been through a war.

On the wall in my room, I have school pictures taken two weeks after the wreck, and you can see the scars on Matt's face. Jaime still says that every time she sees that picture, she can see

Matt's face immediately after the wreck with the scratches and the blood pouring out.

Matthew had never been a reader, but he had always been a diligent student. Now he was going through some traumatic times. The teachers were sending reports home about failing grades and difficult relationships with students and teachers. It was like night and day.

We went along with it for a while, assuming it was a natural reaction to being hurt in the car, then seeing me hurt so badly, and reacting badly afterward. We also figured it was normal teenage moodiness, but when it persisted, we began to worry.

I was always raised to do your best, work hard, be polite, tough your way through problems. Less talk, more action. I'm not crazy about counseling, but we did take Matt to a psychiatrist who specialized in adolescents. Matt said it didn't do him any good, that all they did was have him talk, but how can you know what the lasting benefits were?

Did he feel guilty in some way because I was hurt? Was he mad at me because he got hurt while I was driving? Was he upset because he felt people had not paid enough attention to him immediately after the crash? Was he angry at me because of my bad moods? I don't know. Maybe he started withdrawing a little, finding his own space in the world. That's normal with children. Eventually, Matt joined a church youth group and spent more time with other kids, and he began to relax a little. He started playing football at the high school and socializing and doing his schoolwork again. But I'm sure he could never totally forget those terrible months.

36

THE EDUCATION OF
A COUNTRY SINGER

WE PLAYED WHEREVER WE could get a booking back around 1970. We had to. Sometimes I would go off and play a date by myself because that's what they were paying for. And sometimes Louise would go with me because I couldn't stand playing in front of a different bass player every date. I was my own steel player on these engagements, still thinking of myself as a musician. Singing was an interesting new sideline at the time. If times got rough, I figured I could always make it as a steel player.

It wasn't easy being accepted as a female steel player. Back on that earlier tour of the Northwest, we played a date in British Columbia. I got along great with the house steel player when we arrived. He was real friendly and we traded advice about the instrument. But after my first show, he kind of grunted at me. Had I done something wrong?

When it was time for the second show, the house band members asked me where the steel player was. I said, "Oh, he said he was going to your bus."

"We don't have a bus," they said.

Guess he didn't like nineteen-year-old girl steel players.

In my latest road show, I do a number with all my Do-Rites chanting, "We don't allow no girl pickers 'round here." Well, they do if she's the boss lady. The routine gives me a great chance to play all my instruments in duets with my talented band members. Back then, however, we were inventing the wheel.

There were times when I worked at bars, which were a challenge. It wasn't always pleasant when some good old boy had too much beer, but I was trying to build my career and I wanted people to remember me as being friendly, so I'd kind of smile and back off.

More than any other form of music, country music is based upon a long, personal relationship with the fans. We all say that we are nothing without the fans—and it is true. The fans will drive hundreds of miles to watch you perform. Then they will call up and pester the radio stations to play your records.

And believe me, there is nothing more thrilling than hearing your record on the radio. I had been delighted when my little Mosrite record got some plays back in California. Now, my first record for Columbia was starting to get around. I recorded "I've Been Loving You Too Long," the old Otis Redding song, in 1969, and it went to seventy-something in *Billboard*. I remember driving across the Bootheel of Missouri in our old Ford and hearing it on the local station. Daddy always pulled over on the side of the road until the record was over. We knew that wherever your record was being played, there were fans who might like to hear you sing it in person.

When I broke in, it was an accepted fact that you had to be "out there" to be a recording star. You couldn't just say, "I am an artist," and work out of the studio. You had to work the little clubs and the high-school gymnasiums and the picnic groves because that's where your fans were. And God bless them, you could come back the next year and the same fans would turn out.

I learned early in the country business that the fans really do know us, really do love us, and they want to be noticed in return. They wanted to know we were not any better than they were, that we were human. It meant you didn't have to be perfect, as long as you were yourself. When I was doing a show, I would choose somebody right up front as the surrogate fan. You hug the lady in the front row who is taking your picture, and everybody in the place feels hugged. You give your guitar pick to the man who's been smiling at you all night. You give your monogrammed towel to the little girl in the pretty pink dress—you stop the show and call her Punkin—and people know where you come from.

In country music, you belong to the fans. The fans belong to you. And I was fortunate to have had Daddy repeating that lesson to me as I went along.

Because I had started off as a child prodigy, a novelty act, I was still discovering what my adult role would be as an entertainer. I didn't think a married twenty-one-year-old blonde could get by smiling and being cute.

Daddy's theory was that I could get away with singing cheatin' songs because I was from such a wholesome background, with a good marriage, and looked like I just came from church. It's a paradox, but it's true: Cheatin' songs are a staple of country music, but usually it was the men who were singing them.

You'd hear George Jones or Merle Haggard or Waylon Jennings, all the bad boys, singing about slippin' around, runnin' around, and people would say, "Well, that's human nature." But back then, if a woman would sing a cheatin' song, not everybody would take kindly to it. I know, it's a double standard, but so much of life is—particularly in the part of the world called Middle America, where country music thrives. "Men aren't supposed to run around, it's sinful, but, well, you know men," they say.

If a woman sang about it, she had to suffer and cry and get hurt as a result of her sin. And somehow, the message of the song would get passed on to the singer. But Daddy had the feeling that I could get away with singing cheatin' songs because people knew it wasn't really me.

I guess it couldn't have been me, because I've never thought of myself as a sex symbol. And I guess neither has my audience. I'm so doggone wholesome, so Miss Goody Two-Shoes, that men just don't go following me offstage. Not that I want them to. But couldn't they just pretend?

I have a male friend who says women don't begin to get interesting until they turn thirty-five. I never thought about that until I got close to that age, and men started to look differently

at me and tell me I looked sexy, or asked what perfume was I
using, or was I doing my hair a different way. I kind of liked it,
you know?

Maybe when I was younger I was always working so hard, or
had just finished changing diapers and people could tell, but I
never considered myself a sex symbol, even when I was singing
cheatin' songs. Perhaps I shouldn't admit this—it's not good for
my image as an entertainer—but I have only been propositioned
twice in my whole life. Except for Ken, of course, and I don't
think your husband counts.

The first time was on one of my trips to Vietnam, when I was
seventeen or eighteen. I went out to shop in Saigon and was
standing on a street corner, waiting for the light to change. You
have to remember there were many Frenchwomen in that town
who had stayed to do one kind of business or another. You also
have to remember that in Europe, people used to think I might
be French. So I could understand that this American man, whose
branch of service shall remain nameless, walked up to me on the
street corner and spoke to me in broken English.

"You . . . like . . . go . . . with . . . me?" he asked very slowly.

That was bad enough, but the dad-gum fool only offered me
twenty dollars. Twenty dollars! Can you believe it? I said to him
in a very soft voice, "I am sorry to tell you this, but I am American,
and you really offended me." He was shocked, bless his heart,
and he quickly disappeared among the bicycles and rickshas and
taxicabs.

Later, I had other men get overly friendly, if you know what
I mean, but they always stopped a little bit short of asking the
direct question. I guess they got my message.

One man did not get that message. Not at first. He is a very
wealthy, prominent man in one of America's major cities. I met
him through my work—and that's not much of a clue. He knows
Ken as well as he knows me, but he had no qualms about asking
me out to dinner. A private dinner. Just him and me. At his place.
I'm not stupid. I knew what he had in mind, and I tried to be
polite in refusing, but he could tell I was offended, and I was. I
had respect for this man, and it severed what could have been a
friendship.

And yet it's kind of funny. You wear pretty outfits, you get
comfortable with showing your shoulders and your knees, you put

on makeup, you sing cheatin' songs, you spend a lot of time away from your husband, you miss being with him, and you have standards as thick and solid as a cement wall. But still, in some little corner of your mind, you like to fantasize that men are interested in you. And when it happens, you are hurt.

I have even asked girlfriends why men never approach me. Am I that unattractive? Even a male friend told me, "Most people conduct themselves differently around you. They consider what you go for and what you don't."

I'm not stupid. I know there's drugs around, but guess who never hears of it. We have rules about no drinking the day of a show, not even a sip, and I will never tolerate anybody in my band being involved with drugs, ever. So people who know don't do anything around me.

Still, I like it when men joke with me, tell me, "Wow, you look great," or "Hey, how come you're only friendly to me when Ken's around?" I like that kind of thing. All girls like that. That's an innocent stroking of one's ego. But I guess I discourage that. It goes with the franchise.

I'm not a total Miss Priss. I mean it. I like masculine, military kind of guys, with relatively short hair. Kind of like my husband.

For years, until he grew a mustache, I had a huge crush on Chad Everett, the actor who starred on *Medical Center*. I love doctors anyway, but that's another story. Chad Everett was so handsome that when Ken and I did the game show *Tattletales* and he was asked, "Who does your wife have a crush on?" Ken did not hesitate. He said, "If I was taking one thing out of the house during a fire, it would be the television set with Chad Everett on it." He got that right.

Ogling an actor on TV is about it for me, however. Except when I'm up onstage doing a cheatin' song. I learned early in my career that you have to feel it for the three minutes you're singing it. It's absolutely necessary. You hear of actors and actresses becoming the characters they portray. It's the same with music. Any singer worth her salt better be living it. How can I make you believe me if I don't feel it?

I'm a real lyric freak. The words are so important to me. When I sing a gospel tune, I am not just singing a pretty song, I am singing about the Lord, in whom I believe. That's real. That's permanent. But when I am up on the stage, singin' about slippin' out the back door, I have to believe it for those three minutes.

Another thing I learned early in my career was that it was not enough to make good records. Daddy firmly believed that when you appear in front of people, you had to give them a show.

"People don't just buy a ticket to come hear you sing," Daddy said many times. "They buy a ticket to come be entertained by you. Don't try for perfect music on the stage. Just get it close to the record, get it good, and get it where people will enjoy it, but people will almost forget about listening to you if you've got enough entertainment going on on the stage."

Daddy meant that our uniforms had to look good, our sound system had to be the best, and we had to be rehearsed. He did not like it when we improvised onstage. I learned to hate watching other people dance and sing to their own prerecorded music. Even on my television or Las Vegas shows later in my career, I never used prerecorded music. I think the imperfections are part of a live show. For sound, you cannot beat a record or a tape or nowadays a compact disk. But for watching, there is nothing like a live, expanded version of your best material.

And what was my best material? Rose Maphis used to tell me and Daddy that if I was going to do standards, only do men's songs, not other women's songs. This worked for me tremendously right away. When I started out, obviously I did not have a huge backlog of "Barbara Mandrell's Greatest Hits" to perform. The idea was to perform old country hits, but only hits by men.

I still believe in this. If I went out onstage and sang "Butterfly," you know they'd be comparing my version to Dolly's. Should I sing "Coal Miner's Daughter"? It doesn't make any difference how well I might do the song, another lady has recorded it. Nailed it to the wall. There is no woman in the world who can sing "Stand By Your Man" as well as Tammy Wynette. Why should I even try somebody else's song and make you think of her? And the fans are accustomed to the arrangement that came with the hit, and yours will not be as good.

Instead, I picked up men's songs. Merle Haggard's "I'm an Okie from Muskogee." Don Gibson's "Oh, Lonesome Me." Or songs that weren't associated with men or women, just old standards like "Columbus Stockade Blues."

I truly believe that once I've sung a song, and it's a hit, then nobody, not even the greatest, could do it better. One time we were working in New Orleans and wandering around Bourbon Street, just dropping into places. We walked into one club where the door was up near the stage, and as soon as I put my foot through the door, I could hear a girl singer doing one of my songs—I can't remember which one, but it was mine.

I guess I froze, and the singer turned sideways and saw me standing there, and I swear she totally forgot the words. Just blanked out and kept moving her lips, the way you do when you can't come up with the lyrics. I just backed right out the door. I wanted to move on and not be recognized at the time.

The funny thing was, her band members had their backs to me, so they never saw me. I can just imagine her trying to explain to that band later why she blanked out: "Barbara Mandrell walked right through that door, honest, while I was singing that Barbara Mandrell song." They probably thought she was hallucinating.

While she was trying to catch up with her own show, we went to Preservation Hall to hear the old black jazz musicians. My Uncle Al was a dixieland jazz drummer and he always told me about Preservation Hall, and when he died my aunt Lynda gave me his great jazz record collection. I remember standing there with tears streaming down my face, listening to those wonderful old musicians and thinking, "Well, Uncle Al, I finally got here."

We did whatever we could those first few years. Ken got out of the service. We had a baby. A lot of long drives on the road. The bus always breaking down. Bills stacking up. The usual legend of the overnight success.

I didn't know how long it would take and I often wished it would happen faster, but now I realize I was learning. I don't buy the old theory of paying your dues. This is about show business—creativity, talent, personality, not just sticking a card into a time clock—but I do feel you've got to go to school. You've got to get an education in your craft.

This way, I became an entertainer before I became a hot recording artist. It's an important difference to me. I loved being in charge out in front of a crowd. I expect my doctors to be in charge, to make me feel they know what they're doing. They are professionals. Same thing with my attorney. That's the same way I want people to feel about me.

I want to earn my money. That's the only way I can be happy and feel good. I may be tired but, boy, do I feel good inside when I know I have kicked it. And there are times when I say, "Why didn't I push it harder?"

The audiences were basically the same all over the country— good people, nice people. Sometimes a really tough audience would make me ask, "Why can't I give 'em more?" I'd think to myself, "Are they a painting out there?" But I took it as a dare. By golly, I'd give just as much. I would entertain them. And sooner or later, it would pay off.

37
JAIME

WHEN I WAS TALKING with Jaime recently, she said something I had never heard before. She said, "Momma, I feel like I lost a whole year of my life because of that accident."

That is a hard thing for a child to face, the gap of a year when nothing seemed normal, when her entire concept of family life was disrupted. Other people go through it, some lots worse, but you never think it will happen to you.

She was eight and a half years old, and life had always been fairly easy for her. We had certainly been prepared for her coming on the scene. We had planned her February birth around the slowest month of the year for bookings, and I kept working as long as I dared.

Up to the wreck, the only dangerous moments Jaime ever had were before she was born. Louise, Irlene, and I played a tour in Germany very late in 1975, and I was seven months pregnant. First we had a scare when one club manager said some political activists had vowed to stop the country-music show from going on that night. Don't ask me why. We were told that if we saw waiters in civilian white shirts and black slacks, they were really military police. I was really nervous, but we went on with the show, and nothing happened.

Now it was time to come home. We'd been there a month and I was nearly eight months pregnant. I was very emotional. I wanted to see my husband and I wanted to have my baby. All of a sudden, the lady at the airline desk asked, "Where's the note from your doctor?" I tried to suck in my stomach, but I had this horrible vision of having to have my baby in Germany. I tried to bluff by saying huffily, "Well, excuse me, but just how far along do you think I am?" and that bought me a few seconds.

Fortunately, at that moment, Leon Bollinger showed up, carrying a leather boot bag, shaped exactly like a pair of boots. He sized up the situation and plopped his boot bag down on the counter, as if it contained forceps and other obstetrical tools, and he said to the agent, "Excuse me, I'm her doctor, may I be of some assistance to you?" And she said, "Well, if you're the doctor, no problem."

Doctor? Leon was my guitar player. But he's the main reason Jaime was born in Nashville, not West Germany.

There is also a show-biz story to how Jaime was named. While I was pregnant, Ken and Matt and I were visiting the Lovvorns, and Janice was also pregnant. Everybody else went inside for dinner, and I stayed behind to watch another minute of the old television show, *The Six-Million-Dollar Man.* He had a bionic partner, played by beautiful Lindsay Wagner, and in this episode they were both strapped to hospital gurneys. While I was watching, Lee Majors turned to his partner and whispered her name.

"Jaime," he said, ever so gently, pronouncing it "Jay-mee." But it was spelled Jaime.

I walked into the kitchen and announced, "I know exactly what I want her name to be—Jaime." I liked the spelling, after the French way for saying "I love," which is "J'aime." I also announced that her middle name would be Nicole, because Ken's family name had originally been French, and was pronounced something like "Doo-dawn." So we made a clean sweep, three

French names, although Jaime Nicole Dudney doesn't sound very French when pronounced in the local Middle Tennessee twang.

The kids knew me at home as Mom, as a real mother, but they also saw me as a celebrity, which we tried to downplay as much as possible.

We always explained to our children that nobody is more important than anybody else, but they've been around celebrations and award shows, and have seen people doing favors for us, so they couldn't help but think it extended to all parts of our life. One time when Matt was quite young, we were standing in line at a restaurant and they said it would be fifteen minutes before we were seated. As soon as the manager walked away, Matt whispered, "Do you think we should tell 'em who we are?" Ken said, "Who are we, Matt?" And Matt said, "Oh, you know." Ken said, "No, we'll wait like everybody else."

Now there was another obstacle to keep us from living a normal life. The two children had to deal with television pictures of a wrecked car and what people were saying about me. We were news, bad news.

Jaime had trouble with the reality of the accident. She remembers looking at the pictures on television and thinking, "That's some other wreck," until she heard the name "Barbara Mandrell." She hadn't realized how bad it was until she heard somebody on television say, "Barbara Mandrell is in critical condition and her son, Matt, is in intensive care."

Jaime also had to deal with my unpredictable behavior. It started with me babbling, "I'm Santa Claus" at the wreck, and it continued when they came to the hospital. Sometimes I reacted as if they were fans, and other times I acted like an obsessed supermother. I don't think a child can ever forget seeing a parent like that. Up to then, I had always presented this image of trying to be perfect. But when you lose your temper, scream, throw things, you have no claim on perfection, no matter what the reason.

Jaime hates her school pictures from that year, with her face looking kind of frozen and scared. She had done some acting on the television show and some modeling, and she was used to looking critically at her own photographs. Now she saw herself looking pained and vulnerable, her mother unable to offer any consolation. I only found out much later how she was walking ever so stiffly for weeks afterward, with red marks across her neck from the shoulder straps of her seat belt.

In a way, the accident brought Matt and Jaime a little closer together. They used to fight, the way some brothers and sisters do, but she said she felt sorry for Matt when he was recovering from his injuries.

She was never the kind of kid to lash out, the way some young children do. She had been raised to know that if she smarted off, she would get spanked. She's said that when I was yelling at her she would go to her room and scream.

The only person she talked to was the lawyer, and that was about the details of the accident. There was nobody at home or school who drew her out about her feelings, to help her express what she was going through.

"I knew inside that it wasn't Momma talking, that it was the head condition," Jaime said recently. "At the time, I just wished it would go away, that Momma would come back. I knew she couldn't help it, but I wished that it would stop."

Jaime stayed in her room a lot, focusing on reading and homework, so nobody could tell if she was upset or not.

Momma and Daddy were great with the kids. They would try every excuse to get the kids out and away from the house. Or they would stay and fuss over the kids. I found out later that my Momma would tuck Jaime into bed at night because Jaime had been having nightmares about fires. Momma told her, "That's because you go to bed thinking about something like that." So they began saying their prayers together. Momma would say one, and Jaime would say one, like "I thank God for my health," and Momma would thank God for her family, until Jaime fell asleep.

"I've tried to block it out of my memory," Jaime has said to me. She also says I've gotten "a lot better in the past year or so," but she admits she still gets "frustrated" because she knows that it's "not really Mom" who's getting upset. But it *is* me. That's the way I am.

I was not much good for prayers or guidance at the time. I am so thankful that Momma and Daddy and Ken were around to watch over the children and to ask for God's help. My kids needed all the help they could get.

38

RALPH, MR. ACUFF, AND MINNIE

WHEN I FIRST SETTLED in Nashville, I could not sleep at night. It was not anxiety over my career. That would take care of itself. I was missing my sleep because of Ralph Emery's talk show on radio station WSM.

Ralph had an open-door policy, so he never knew who was going to pop in, and neither did the audience. You just had to keep tuned in to see what happened. These new talk hosts on television and radio like to shock, but twenty years ago, Ralph Emery was so good at getting musicians to talk about themselves. He could zing you, but he was also sensitive. He loves country music, and he could give your career a tremendous boost if he liked your work.

While I was just starting in Printer's Alley, Merle Travis arranged for me to be on Ralph's afternoon TV show. We started talking about the old *Town Hall Party* and, God bless him, he put one and one together and remembered that Tex Ritter had brought him my dinky little Mosrite record a few years earlier, and he used to play it on the air. So he treated me like an old Nashville hand, rather than some tourist with a cardboard suitcase who just wandered into Music Row.

To most people, I was still Barbara Who? But Ralph invited me on his radio show the same night as Tammy Wynette, who was in the midst of three consecutive years as top female vocalist, in her "Stand By Your Man" years of glory. I was so proud to be on the same show as Tammy, and pleased to get a call from a record producer afterward.

After that, I became a regular visitor to Ralph's shows. We became friends, and he's been accused of mentioning me too often, but there are dozens of other people he likes too. He has a great reputation wherever that 50,000-watt clear-channel station goes. I would be an ingrate and a fool if I did not acknowledge that Ralph Emery helped me tremendously.

Being on Ralph's show did not hurt my standing with the people at the Grand Ole Opry, either. We were invited to be on the show for the first time in May of 1971.

Louise and Irlene and Daddy and I were just in awe as we drove to the old brick church in downtown Nashville.

I thought I'd be nervous when I got backstage, but it was just the opposite. We were directed to a few square feet behind the curtain where everybody just hung out. It was hard to feel nervous standing cheek to jowl with the biggest names in show business. It's been so long that I cannot swear who was backstage on our very first night, but it's a safe bet to say that on any given night, you'd mill around alongside Roy Acuff, Minnie Pearl, Bill Monroe, Marty Robbins, Johnny Cash, Kitty Wells, Loretta Lynn, Tammy Wynette, Stringbean, Grandpa Jones and Del Wood, The Queen of the Ivories, plus an assortment of pickers, singers, and clog dancers in gaudy costumes. You talked with whomever you were squished next to. Great way to make friends.

In case you needed to put a little powder on your face, there was one—count it, one—bathroom per gender. I minded my own business the first few times I was there, but let me tell you something, familiarity does not breed contempt, at least not backstage at the Opry. You cannot imagine how leveling it was to see Dolly perched on a toilet seat, Connie Smith leaning against a sink, and

Tammy scrooched up in a corner, because that's all the room there was.

That first night, we went out and sang a song or two. I looked up and saw the familiar backdrops for Goo Goo Candy Bars, peeked out of the corner of my eye and saw Mr. Acuff counting the house, and I thought, "Oh, my, it's the Grand Ole Opry." But then I realized these folks had driven in from Nebraska and Alabama and Rhode Island and Oklahoma. They were the same fans I had been playing for in tiny high-school gymnasiums. This was their mother church, their temple, their Mecca. This was home. It didn't make sense to be nervous at home.

I got to feel comfortable backstage at the Ryman on Friday and Saturday nights. You would not pass up a big payday or a big tour to play the Ryman, but you didn't mind being in Nashville on a weekend, either, just to be around all these great people.

After a year or two, Mister Acuff and Bud Wendell, the manager, asked me to be a member of the Opry. They prepared me for it offstage, but then Mister Acuff popped the question again onstage, heard by millions of people in WSM's huge reception area. It was the ultimate acceptance in the country business, and you'd better believe I said yes. Now I felt I had made it.

But there is another part to the story about me and the Opry. When I was asked, my father and I accepted immediately. But being the assertive, ambitious person that I am, I asked, "Oh, yes, I'd love to be a member. What do I have to do?" And they said I had to make a certain number of appearances per year to be called a member.

But I wasn't finished.

"What do you have to do to be a host of a segment?" I asked.

Somebody said you had to gain enough national stature, which sounded fair to me.

Oh, yes, and you also had to be a man.

I bit my tongue, but in the back of my mind, I knew I would change that someday. I do not consider myself a feminist—I hate labels—but I wanted to do it for myself, and for all women.

Soon afterward, a woman did play host to a segment because the man who was scheduled did not show. But that wasn't quite the same as being booked and announced in advance as a host.

A few years later, I got enough national recognition that I said, "Okay, I want to be the host," and they scheduled me to do so. While I was onstage, I remembered when somebody had said only a man could be the host. But once I had been a scheduled host, I didn't have any desire to do it again. As a performer, I'd prefer to be on Mister Acuff's segment of the show. That's as good as it gets.

I'm sorry if I sound like a little girl but I still cannot bring myself to call him anything but Mister Acuff. He is the backbone of the Grand Ole Opry, as well as the first living member ever voted into the Country Music Hall of Fame. Sometimes he was the master of ceremonies at the Opry and sometimes he sang "The Great Speckled Bird." Sometimes he just twirled his yo-yo and sometimes just counted the house with his businessman's eyes. Some hillbilly. Mister Acuff was so courtly, so gracious, that you felt like you were being welcomed into the board meeting of a bank by the chairman of the board, which was not far from the truth.

Mister Acuff stands for the tradition of the Opry, but he also knows when to bend the rules a little. Ever since I joined the Opry, I had never agitated to play my saxophone because I had joined knowing the rules against horns. However, in 1982 I had a hit record called "Till You're Gone," which had a saxophone break on it. I played the sax break whenever we did the song live, although not on the record itself. The Opry is always great about letting you play your current hit record, to plug it, but when I told them what I was going to play that night, I didn't list "Till You're Gone." It was no big deal.

By that time, of course, we had moved out from the Ryman to the fancy new Opry at Opryland, where we have a lot of space, but in keeping with tradition, the girls still share one makeup room. Mister Acuff knocked on the door to the new ladies' room and he said he wanted me to get my saxophone out of the bus and perform my song on the show. This was Roy Acuff asking me. Nobody felt more special and important than I did that night. That's better than the Good Housekeeping Seal of Approval. So I hauled in my sax and played my little solo, and another little rule was broken, or bent.

One thing people do not know about Mister Acuff, because he is venerable and dignified and not a very big man, is that he once was a promising baseball player. He always likes to perform in celebrity softball games. When I was doing my charity game for organ transplants, I asked him to pinch-hit for me. Well over seventy, he made a base hit. He is a special man to me. I am in awe of Mister Acuff.

There is one other person I put into this category, and that is my girlfriend Minnie Pearl. Like everybody else, I grew up with this image of a hillbilly woman with a goofus smile on her face, the $1.98 price tag hanging off her straw hat, and her piercing greeting of "How-*dee!*"

Some hillbilly. The first time I spotted her backstage, she was wearing the hat with the price tag, but carrying herself like a queen. If not a queen, then the best teacher everybody remembers from high school, the dean of students. I checked it out and found she is a graduate of Belmont College in Nashville, and she was indeed a drama teacher before she found her calling as a comedienne.

Her real name is Sarah Ophelia Colley Cannon, and she plays tennis at the country club. JoAnn Berry plays doubles with her and says, "I'm usually on the other team, and once in a while I cannot control where I hit the ball, and I may hit it down anybody's throat. When I do it to Minnie, she will say in that gravelly stage voice of hers, 'My former friend, JoAnn.' She is quite good and quite competitive at tennis. Minnie is also the kind of friend you are lucky to count on one hand, in a lifetime."

I second the motion. To me, it is hard to remember that she is a number of years older than me. I always admired her, but then we became true girlfriends through lunches with JoAnn. She's really like a teeny-bopper with all that energy and a sense of humor, so curious about things. And great with kids. She never had children of her own, but she has mothered a couple of generations of Nashville women.

One time we were on the same bill in St. Louis on Easter weekend. It could have been sad being away from home on Easter, but Minnie helped us dye the eggs in our tour bus and we had them backstage at the Fox Theater. She turned the dressing room of the theater into a little bit of home. And she was so great with Jaime, who was traveling with me.

Jaime adores Minnie so much that she would tell Minnie her best kids' jokes. On that trip to St. Louis, Jaime told Minnie a joke backstage. Wouldn't you know it, a few weeks later at the Opry matinee, Minnie called Jaime out onstage and introduced her and asked her to tell the story. It was like the two of them were having their own private little conversation, only in front of a thousand people.

The joke was about the little potato who told the mother potato she wanted to get married.

"Who do you want to marry?" the big potato asked.

"I want to marry Dan Rather."

"You can't marry Dan Rather."

"Why not?"

"Because you are an Irish tater and he's a common tater."

Well, you had to be there. Minnie came offstage and said, "She's just like Barbara." She thinks Jaime has enough poise to be a performer.

One time I said I didn't think I'd want any of my children going into show business because I knew how hard it is. Minnie pulled me over in the kitchen and just let it rip. She said I shouldn't discourage my children's dreams because I would not have liked to be limited when I was a child. She doesn't spare the wisdom, or the punches. That's why she's my girlfriend. She's a role model for me. We talk on the telephone and I can share my deepest feelings about show business.

I would like to think that if I'm really lucky when I grow up, I might be something like Minnie. She has taught me so many things. She's finally Minnie to me, but sometimes when I'm sitting around gabbing with her, I suddenly get this moment of panic and I realize, "Oh, my goodness, I am talking to Minnie Pearl!"

39

A PICNIC WITH MINNIE

ONE LOVELY OCTOBER DAY in 1984, Ken directed me outside to the deck for lunch. Waiting there were JoAnn and Minnie.

No matter what shape your head is in, you do not run Minnie Pearl off your property. Through the haze, I was glad to see her. I think I was polite.

Minnie sort of tested me out while we ate lunch. Then while we were having coffee, she asked me what I thought about going back to work.

For the first month since coming home from the hospital, I had heard subtle suggestions about working. Nobody was rushing me out the door for a payday, and I'm sure it was in my own best interests, but Daddy and Ken and JoAnn would keep saying things like, "When you go back to work . . ."

They were appealing to the trouper in me, the workaholic,

the compulsive lady who sang until her voice gave out, who signed autographs until her hand cramped up. They just assumed this was the best rehabilitation of all for the old firehouse dalmatian. Ring the fire bell and watch Barbara leap on the fire truck.

Normally, that might have worked. This was not normal. Whenever they mentioned working, I'd think, "I'm just trying to live, to make it through the day, and you want me to work?"

Same thing with Minnie. She is my role model in Nashville, the woman I hope I grow up to be. She meant it as a compliment when she talked to me about work. She wanted me to think about going back to entertaining when my body got healed.

"This has been your life," she said. "You've been great at it. You're going to find out that you can't give it up."

"Wanna bet?" I thought. Out loud, I said something like, "I can't."

I was pretty blunt with Minnie because I knew she could take it. She could also give it back.

She told me that she had been ill at one point in her life, and she said it took people close to her to draw her out, to get her back to work. She said she had the same reaction I did. She told me I would snap out of it.

I told her I did not want to perform again.

"She did that," I said, meaning that other Barbara Mandrell. "I can't do that."

Minnie just smiled and shook her head. I was in no mood to think positively, but just having Minnie Pearl sitting there on my deck, giving me advice, meant so much to me.

"You'll see," she said. "This is your business. You can't give it up."

In fact, I thought I had given it up. That Barbara Mandrell was history.

40
BUS STORIES

EVEN BEFORE WE MADE it to the Opry, there was a tangible sign that we might be getting somewhere. That sign was a clunky old 1948 Silversides bus we had bought in the spring of 1970.

We couldn't afford one of those luxury models the stars were using, with the custom bedroom in the back and the high-tech electronic gear up front, but it was a bus, and it was a big step in our lives.

On one level, it is a status symbol that you can afford a bus. Plus, it is a great advertisement for your show, having your name written on the front and the sides, whizzing around the country, watching people's heads turn as you drive past. On a more practical level, you are now able to travel and sleep and talk and eat exactly as you want.

It was only two years since I'd started traveling in our family car, barely able to meet expenses. Even when we graduated to a car and trailer, Momma remembers us picking up a check for seven hundred and fifty dollars, and the man saying, "You are the most underpaid act." It was a compliment, if you stop to think about it.

We saved up enough of those "underpaid" checks to pay for the old Silversides, designed during World War II by Greyhound and built by General Motors. It weighed more than a new bus because it had honeycomb metal sides where the passengers sit. They don't protect people like that today. When they ran right, those old Silversides would outrun almost any bus on the ground.

This one was supposed to have been overhauled, which was a lie. Daddy and his nephew, Charles Ott, took it down to the boatyards outside Little Rock and stripped it down, but the weather was so bad that they finally had to run it up to Nashville and finish the interior—pieces of plywood all over our backyard.

We three girls had a room that was literally only big enough for three stacked bunks, with the hallway running down the side. We had a little closet and a mirror and just enough room to stand there and get in and out of the bunk.

I can still feel the prickly sensation of getting down from the bunk and having my feet rub against the wall, picking up splinters. But we had a full kitchen, and that was important because we didn't like to eat out, and it was cheaper to cook.

Daddy put a generator on the bus so we had electricity. In the back, he and Momma had a double bed with a red bedspread on it.

Daddy was not about to let anybody else drive our bus because he was afraid they would tear something up. So he was it. Besides, we couldn't afford a driver.

We spent the next few years bombing up and down the country. Daddy had started out as my hero when I was a little girl and he was still my hero as he sat behind the wheel of the old Silversides.

He'd been driving around the country so long that he knew all the towns along the way. Daddy would park in a shopping center and we'd go to the movies while he would catch two or three hours of sleep. Then Momma would wake him up and he would eat and start driving again.

One of the first trips we made was to the fair buyers' convention in Texas at the time I was pregnant. This convention was very important to us because the people attending were in a position to hire us if they liked our work. We wanted to look like a big-time act, so Momma made white and purple outfits for the girls, and we went out and bought a set of white pants for Daddy and Cliff Parker, who was playing guitar with us. Cliff was a big fun-loving guy with a great sense of humor. It was a ridiculous trip from the start, with me having morning sickness and Momma having to make clothes that fit me.

I wasn't the only one with morning sickness. The bus started having sympathy pains in Arkansas, and Daddy thought we had taken on bad fuel, so he would swerve back and forth on the road to try to mix the fuel. We got as far as Texarkana, and the bus just wasn't going any farther.

We had been booked to perform early in the day, so Daddy hired a man with a truck and a car to take us, and he said, "All right, in an hour we've got to be ready to go. Don't forget your uniforms." We had no generator, and just a tiny bit of battery light in the bus, but the sun was coming up so my sisters and I used God's own light to put on our makeup. My hair was wet, and I was down on my hands and knees, pregnant, by the sofa, trying to dry my hair from the heat from the butane heater, which I do not recommend. And all the time, Daddy was telling us to look presentable because the fair buyers' conventions were always held in nice hotels, and we had to make a good impression.

We finally got there, with maybe an hour before we had to perform, and just after we got into our dressing room, a nice woman, an official with the convention, asked, "Would you-all like to eat?" We had now gone close to forty-eight hours with no sleep and no food.

"Oh, no, that's quite all right, we don't need anything."

Guess who said that?

Louise and Irlene and Momma and Daddy looked at me like they were going to kill me, and Cliff looked at me like I was crazy.

"Are you sure?" she asked.

"No, thank you, ma'am, we've got to go over our show list," I said, wanting to impress everybody with how hard we prepared. We needed to go over the list because Cliff was new with us.

We dressed in our new outfits. The women's clothes were fine, but I had gone shopping for new slacks for Daddy and Cliff, and found these snazzy white pants in J. C. Penney. The slacks were a bit dazzling, and we all laughed as Cliff and Daddy walked into the room and Daddy said, "Here's the two quarts of milk you ordered," because they did look like milkmen. It wasn't so funny when we realized you could see their underwear through the white pants. Cliff was wearing boxer shorts and you could see the pattern on them. Stripes, as I recall. But it was all we had. The show had to go on.

Somehow, we managed to do a good show, and we were booked for lots of dates because of it.

When the show was over, we found a café. By now, it was over fifty hours without food.

"What do you want?" the waitress asked.

"The left side of the menu," said Cliff, who was a big man and a big eater. Then he got serious: "If you can, bring me some tacos and stuff right now while I'm waiting on my dinner."

That was life in the big time with our tour bus. At times it seemed remarkably like the old days in the car.

One of our epic trips was playing Amarillo with Sonny James and Margo Smith, then starting out about seven o'clock for our next show, which was in Seattle. Sound far away? It was even farther than you think because there was a heavy snowstorm in the Rockies, and Daddy had to cut out west to avoid it.

Daddy started driving. Amarillo. Tucson. Phoenix. He stopped for two hours of sleep, then drove north to Las Vegas.

By now, the weather was getting cold, and the generator was not working right, so we did not have any electricity in the bus. We ran out of butane for the heater, and there was no place to get it filled up. So the bus was getting cold.

We were all wrapped up in blankets while Daddy had put on a couple of pairs of socks, two pair of pants. The driver's compartment was the coldest part of the bus because the air just blew in there. The bus was already twenty years old at the time, and all the original rubber seals had dried and cracked, letting the air come in.

How cold was it? A pot with three inches of water sitting in the kitchen sink, approximately twelve feet from the windshield, was frozen solid.

Somewhere along the road, Daddy got out and tried to mess with the generator, but it just sputtered. He got mad and kicked the side of the bus as hard as he could. He thought he had broken his toes. Otherwise, he felt better.

Daddy was having trouble seeing out the front of the bus because the heating system was out. He told us to get some after-shave lotion and put it on the windshield, which was frosting up from the inside. The wipers outside were taking snow, so Daddy had to stop periodically and clean them off. Then he would get back on the bus, determined he was going to make it to Seattle. All of a sudden, the windshield wiper came right around and started wiping the side window where he was sitting. He managed to fix it, but we all said that if we lived through that, we could live through anything.

We reached Twin Falls, Idaho, and pushed on to Pendleton, Oregon. We got to Seattle about four o'clock the day of the show—just enough time to check in to the Holiday Inn, go straight to the auditorium, set up our gear, and do the show. We didn't leave the auditorium until sometime between eleven and twelve. Daddy had driven three days on two hours of sleep.

Another epic trip came in the summer of 1970, six weeks after Matthew was born. We could not afford for me to stay home anymore, so we just lugged him on the road with us—and I've been traveling with one or more of my children most of the time since then.

That first trip, we packed Matthew in a cute cardboard baby-holder the hospital had given us, all blue with a mattress inside, the perfect size for an infant. We just nestled him in the space behind the driver's seat, no big deal.

About ten years later, I would make the mistake of telling this story to a writer from one of the tabloid magazines. A week or two later, the front-page headline said:

BARBARA MANDRELL: I WAS FORCED TO KEEP
MY BABY IN A CARDBOARD BOX

Well, it was true, but the headline made it seem worse than it was. Jaime was about four at the time, and she asked us, quite seriously, if we had kept her in a cardboard box, too. We said no, that was just for Matthew's first few weeks on the road.

The cardboard era ended as we headed west on Interstate 80 from Chicago toward Las Vegas. Daddy sensed a problem, so he hopped out and discovered the rear end had a grease fire. He grabbed the fire extinguisher and put that out.

He had just had the bus serviced, but the mechanic had not bothered to lubricate the rear end because the springs in the old bus were a little weak, and you needed a floor jack to raise it, and he had been too lazy to do it.

The rear end burned out on a long straight incline, somewhere between Laramie and Cheyenne. We absolutely had to get to Las Vegas, so we started unpacking the bus.

One thing about Nashville buses is that you don't carry suitcases because your clothes are all in your closet. Daddy, who has memorized every stage and loading platform and motel parking lot in North America, happened to know there was a set of drums on the stage in Las Vegas.

We unloaded Irlene's drums from the cases and put the drums in bins under the bus. Then we took the drum cases and loaded all of our clothes in them. Daddy tried to get a rental car but the rodeo was going on in Cheyenne, and it was impossible. He could not get an airplane, either, so we waited for a Greyhound bus.

I will never forget us sitting around the coffee shop in Cheyenne when Daddy got the news that it would cost eighteen hundred dollars to fix that rear end. I remember thinking, "There's no way. That's the end of everything." We had about a hundred dollars that was supposed to carry us to Las Vegas. This was just too much.

Momma always had the final say on money matters because Momma is the practical one, the family bookkeeper. Daddy had taken some money out of the music store and turned it over to her. She knew how much we had in reserve back home, and she would never let us get over our heads. We looked across at Momma and waited for her signal that our careers were over. But Momma allowed as how she had put a little aside, enough for a new rear end, so it was not the end of the world. We got on the Greyhound, our careers still intact.

It was impossible to keep Matthew's formula fresh on these long hauls, and when it spoiled, we had to have more. Every time the Greyhound bus pulled into a station, Daddy would run for the closest drugstore and get Matthew some more.

Another problem arose when we had to change buses at a transfer point. Kent, our guitar player, left the costume bag on the bus, which was headed toward San Francisco. So he had to go on to the next stop, where the bag was left for him, and he got to Las Vegas just in time. Kent was a great guy, raised in a gospel-music family, and you could not be upset with him. Daddy just waited at the bus station for him, and they went straight to the job with the uniforms.

Talk about hillbillies. My second record, "Playing Around with Love," had just reached number thirteen across the nation, and Daddy had been able to book us in Vegas on the basis of a hit record. According to the giant billboard outside the Golden Nugget, we were big-timers, but here we were rolling into Las Vegas on a Greyhound bus with drum cases for our luggage and me, the glamorous blonde star herself, carrying a newborn baby with formula on his face and the distinct scent of diapers coming from every one of us.

Everything was so messed up, you had to laugh—unless you happened to be a high-roller spending a few hundred dollars a night at the Golden Nugget and saw these hillbillies straggle off the bus.

Well, nobody canceled their reservations at the sight of us, so we played the show. The next day, Daddy rode the Greyhound back to Cheyenne to get our own bus fixed.

The old bus lived to break down again. We played with Conway Twitty and Hank Williams, Jr., in Davenport, Iowa, and were heading for Buck Lake Ranch in central Ohio. We got to Gary, Indiana, and as Daddy drove up an incline into a truck stop, the radiator slipped and got into the fan. It was Sunday morning. The bus was going nowhere. One service station rented cars, but the agent said he couldn't give us his last car because the last customer had switched some old junk tires onto it, and he was afraid to rent it.

After convincing him to let us have it, Daddy hitched a U-Haul trailer to the car and drove on to Buck Lake Ranch. When we arrived, we tried to find some rooms for changing. Meanwhile, Daddy was stretched out in the front seat, trying to sleep. Suddenly he heard a peck on the window. It was Conway Twitty.

"Come over here," Conway said, motioning to his own brand-new MCI bus. He led Daddy to the back of the bus and pointed to his bed, all made up with clean sheets, with the blinds drawn and the air conditioner on.

"You go to sleep here," Conway said. "I'll wake you up thirty minutes before you have to go onstage."

We hadn't known Conway very well up until then. After that, we knew all there was to know about him.

Sometimes even Daddy made a mistake. One time he drove right past a fair out in Illinois, saying, "Tomorrow night we're going to be in Caving Rock, but after that we're going to be right back here at this fair." We drove on to Caving Rock in the morning, but Julian Thorpe, a great musician working with us, woke up and asked, "Where are we?"

"Caving Rock," Daddy said.

"We don't play here tonight," Julian said. We had to turn around and drive all the way back to that fair we had passed the night before.

I'd like to say it only happened once. I can't. One time we drove from Nashville, heading north up Interstate 81 to play a convention in upstate New York. We turned east on the Thruway and arrived in Schenectady.

"Where's the Ramada Inn?" Daddy asked at the toll booth.

"I don't know of one here," the man said.

Daddy went off to a pay phone. The nearest Ramada Inn was in Syracuse. We had driven two blocks past that Ramada Inn two hours earlier. So Daddy turned around in the wee hours of the morning and drove back to Syracuse, the snow blowing like the dickens.

We drove that old bus into the fall of 1972 because Daddy knew how to baby it. On the long trips, I would bring a pillow and sit on the floor right alongside Daddy. Every so often I'd wet a washcloth and wash Daddy's face and neck, and I'd sit there for hours and we would plan a new bus.

We'd fantasize about a new Custom Coach with custom-made bunks along both sides, and a custom bedroom in the back. We'd argue about colors, from tasteful silver to gaudy maroon. We'd plan what we'd stock in the galley—fresh fruits and vegetables for the health freaks, sausage and eggs for Daddy. We'd discuss what kind of sound system we'd put in, where the speakers would be. A color television set. Couldn't do without that. Sophisticated recording units so we could work on the show while motoring across country. Intercoms. Telephones. The electronic age was just starting, but we knew people who had these gadgets in their buses. And it wasn't totally frivolous for us to be dreaming about our ultimate bus. The bus was part office, part home. We spent so much of our lives in it.

Sometimes I'd even say to Daddy, "And a relief driver for you," and he'd kind of grunt and say, "Ummmm." Daddy said he couldn't afford to hire a driver, and he wouldn't trust anybody else anyway. So we'd argue about it for a while. Anything to keep him awake, this tough guy who held our future in his very capable hands.

41

SHOWING MY FACE

THERE WERE RUMORS FLYING all over Nashville that my face was so badly smashed that I could never appear in public again. There were also rumors that I was a total vegetable, unable to walk or talk.

Daddy and Louise had made public appearances after the accident, saying that I just needed some recuperation time, but they never let on that I had serious brain trauma. With the rumors flying, Daddy and Ken suggested that I make a short appearance on television, just to show that I was getting around.

Actually, I wasn't getting around, and I didn't care, because all I wanted was to be in my darkened room. And I had a terror of appearing on television because I had developed a terrible stuttering problem.

Whenever I was under stress, I would start to stutter on the simplest words. I would get words backwards. If I meant my elbow, I would say my knee. Sometimes I was aware of it, and other times I was not, and Ken would point it out to me.

There was no way I was going to do live television, but

then I was asked to make a brief appearance on the annual Country Music Association awards show in mid-October.

Somebody in the family pointed out that this was one of the rare times that I happened to have a lot of projects "in the can," as we say. I had done a television movie that appeared right after the wreck, and I had two albums ready to go, which was very rare for me, because I'm usually pushing deadline. So this was a chance to remind everybody that I was still "out there" in the marketplace. Even in my doldrums, I could appreciate that.

So I agreed to appear via a satellite feed on the live network show. It was all carefully worked out, where I would be sitting on my couch, with my ankle in a cast and the kids and Ken sitting around me.

But I was so nervous that I made a few demands. The only way I could do it was to have Dr. David Jones sitting just out of camera range, keeping a medical eye on me. God bless him, Dr. Jones agreed to be with me, and gave me a cortisone shot that starts with a numbing injection, so my tailbone would not hurt for about thirty minutes.

Also, I insisted on having cue cards because of my speech problems. Lee Greenwood, my partner on the hit duet "To Me," was going to interview me and then sing the song to me. I did not trust myself to memorize the answers, nor did I trust myself to speak off the cuff, which normally I can do.

The television people were a little surprised when we asked for the cue cards, but Daddy said, "She's got to have them." A lot of people in my business have to use cue cards and nobody questions it, so it wasn't as if we were asking for something unprofessional. It's just that I had never needed them before, and everyone knew it. I think some of the television people began to raise their eyebrows, realizing I was hurt worse than we had let on.

We got the questions in advance and had my answers inked up in large letters. I just prayed that I wouldn't stutter when I read the cards.

The day of the show, they brought in my hair and makeup people. It was nice to see these familiar faces, even if I was too nervous to show it at the time.

A few minutes before my segment began, they propped me

up on the couch. Ken was the only one who could prop my leg
on the ottoman, with the cast sort of tucked underneath, so nobody would pay much attention to it. Then my family sat
around me, and we all put on our best show-biz smiles. Maybe
I looked serene and comfortable, sitting on the couch, but the
truth is, I couldn't have moved if I wanted to. And the smile
was just fixed on my face. I was scared, even knowing my family was with me and Dr. Jones was a few feet away. This was
more than I could handle. I was too boggled to say a prayer,
but God was with me.

When the lights went on, I could hear Lee Greenwood
talking to me, and I could read my cards—simple little sen-
tences like, "I feel fine," and "I want to thank everybody." Just
four or five remarks like that, and I did it fine, no stuttering.
Then Lee sang our song by himself on the show, and then it
was over.

I guess we proved I was not totally out of it. But as soon as
the cameras were off, Bobbe Joy washed my face and I asked
Ken to help me back into the bedroom. He helped me remove
my pretty outfit and eased me back into my old pajamas, and I
thought, "Huh, if they only knew."

42

THE GIRLS GROW UP

ONE OF THE NICEST things about those early years on the bus was being together with Louise and Irlene, just as we had been as children. I was married and had a child, but I was still able to play Big Sister to the hilt, coaching my sisters about their roles in the band but also relying on them for help with Matthew.

We would arrive at an auditorium or a state fair, and I would bustle around making appearances with the disc jockeys and the reporters while Louise and Irlene would take Matt out to the midway for a sampling of the local cuisine. Louise became like a second mother to Matthew, providing discipline as well as love, and that continues to this day.

Maybe I felt we would all go touring together for the rest of our careers, but it didn't quite work out that way. My two sisters were not put on this earth to be loving sidekicks to me. Hardly. They had to grow up in their own ways, as painful as the separation might be.

Early in 1971, Louise fell in love with Ronny Shaw, a talented musician who opened the show for us and then sang harmony and played rhythm in the band. He also stayed at the house with us in Madison. I thought Ronny was one of the best singers ever, with a very romantic voice, and he was a great guy.

I also thought Louise was way too young to marry, and I told her so. She was still only sixteen, but she looked older than that, and how do you argue with somebody who believes she is ready to be a wife and a mother? Louise and I were close, and I reminded her that Momma and Daddy had forced me to wait until I was eighteen before I could marry Ken. But times were different now, things were moving fast. We weren't rooted in a home, living so-called normal lives anymore. Besides, Ronny was so in love with Louise, and she was so in love with him, and he came from a strong religious background, and we were sure they would work it out.

They were married on June 16, 1971, with Irlene and I acting as maid and matron of honor. For a while, they continued with the band, but by the end of 1971, you could see that Ronny was homesick for Texas. He persuaded Louise to give up music and opt for a more stable life. Because she loved her husband so much, Louise agreed to leave the band and give up her music career. In Texas, she worked in a store and decorated a new home and tried to start a new way of life for herself.

I felt so empty and sad without my sister near me. She's my sister—and a darned good bass player. I felt a tremendous sense of loss, because we'd always talked to each other, always known what the other one was feeling. I just didn't like being so far from her. Yes, I know, I had moved away to Washington after I got married, but very quickly it had all worked out that we would be reunited in Nashville.

The Mandrells were meant to be together. I missed Louise terribly, and we didn't have enough money to afford regular telephone calls. Neither of us are what you call diligent letter writers, either, so for almost an entire year we were hardly in touch. As time went on, I developed an ominous feeling that things weren't right with Louise.

She tried working at a couple of jobs, but she was used to the excitement and the challenge of being a musician. After being away for a year, Louise more or less told Ronny that she was coming to visit us right after Christmas of 1972. She stayed in Nashville for a while, and although she didn't say it, you could tell things weren't working out. She had been too young, and they just didn't have that much in common. As talented as he was, Ronny wanted to settle down. And Louise wasn't ready for that kind of quiet life.

Ronny joined her in Las Vegas and played with us for a while, but the marriage was over. Ronny found somebody else who matched his religious and social beliefs, and Louise was devastated. As she has made public, it was only her faith, living day by day in prayer, that pulled her through a terrible time.

I was absolutely stunned. To me, the greatest women in the world are Louise and Irlene. This may sound arrogant in print, but I told her, "Louise, you're so wonderful, you're so good, I can't believe Ronny is letting this happen." I feel about my sisters the way a mother feels about her children. You don't mess with the momma lion. I try to forgive and forget, and I totally love Ronny, but I also thought he was stupid for letting Louise get away.

A few years later, however, I thought Louise was stupid for marrying somebody else, more or less on the rebound. While performing with Stu Phillips, a great friend, she met a musician and decided to get married. Oh, please, Louise, I thought. This marriage was worse than the first one, without the good intentions that one had. This husband really treated Louise badly, but fortunately she was smart enough to get away from it, which some women don't.

Louise's problems hit me harder than anything that had happened in my personal life. How could these two men not appreciate this beautiful, intelligent, giving woman? Louise started to turn bitter after the second marriage broke up. She will tell you that I took her aside and told her she was too doggone talented to be moping around. I also told her she needed her own identity, that she should get out and sing and perform on her own. In 1977, she formed a group called Louise Mandrell and the Country Classics, and began touring. I could see the old spunky Louise starting to bounce back.

Now it was time for Irlene to start growing up—and out. Just like Louise, she had grown up somewhat in my shadow, because I was older and pushier than the two of them. Irlene was not blessed with a soloist singing voice, but she had made herself into a professional drummer, and she had beauty and a comic touch that made her unique—part Ringo Starr and part Goldie Hawn, if that makes any sense.

Irlene never gave me the feeling she resented my getting so much attention. In a lot of ways, she is the most relaxed of the three of us. I'm always fussing about something and Louise is usually rehearsing dance or music for her show, or decorating a house. Irlene was more laid back, more satisfied with herself day by day. She never let anybody put pressure on her to match her two older sisters. She was Ene. That was good enough for her—and me, too.

But I wasn't prepared for Irlene to fall in love with my bass player. Ric Boyer had joined the Do-Rites after a very strange audition. He came to the house to play for me and Daddy at a time when some men were working on the roof. Uncle Joe Maphis was also visiting the house, and he was dressed in old clothes, kinda like the roofers. While Ric was tuning up, Uncle Joe wandered in and said, "Mind if I pick a little?" Daddy said, "Sure," so Joe started to play, and Ric thought to himself, "Well, I'd better hang it up and go home to St. Louis if the roofers in Nashville can pick like this." We told him it was all right, that it was really Joe Maphis and not a roofer.

Ric Boyer became one of the greatest musicians I ever had in my band. He could pick and he could sing and he was a real asset to the group. But he is also ten years older than Irlene, and he had been married before, and he had four kids.

Maybe it was because of Louise's two marriages going bad, but I resented Ric. As far as I was concerned, he was too old for my sister, and besides that, nobody was good enough for her. Daddy also did not approve.

The message was pretty clear. Ric Boyer was no longer welcome in my group. Irlene left the band and so did Ric, which was the biggest disruption we had ever had in the family, even more abrupt than when Louise had moved to Texas. But when you find somebody you want to be your lifemate, that's the way it is. Irlene did what she had to do.

It was so horrible for me because normally we saw each other every day, and if not, we'd call each other on the phone. We had grown up together, we had been on the road together for years, and I hated to be separated from her. So I did the worst possible thing. I transferred my hatred from the situation to the individual.

I have hated very few people in my life. I consider it a wasteful and improper emotion. But I now hated Ric Boyer. I knew it was wrong to hate him, and I prayed to God for me to stop. I had always believed that if I passed away in the middle of the night, I would go directly to be with the Lord in Heaven. I had been assured of my salvation, assured of my being right with the Lord. But now I did not have it.

This went on night after night for about a week. I could not sleep at night. I would pray, but I still couldn't sleep because I had no earthly idea why I didn't have God's assurance anymore.

"What have I done, Lord?" I prayed. "What is wrong with me?"

One night, when Ken was asleep, I was watching one of the preachers on television, very quiet so as not to disturb Ken. I was lying in bed, praying for answers, weeping and crying and asking, "God, please show me why I don't have this peace and assurance. What have I done wrong? What is wrong with me?"

I'm not saying this television preacher had all the answers, but I believe God can change anything and everything. The preacher started reading Scripture, so it was God's word I was hearing, not the word of another person like me and you. The Scripture was about how we cannot ask God to forgive us and to love us unless we can forgive and love others. The preacher went on to say that you cannot hate somebody, that you have to genuinely, sincerely, realistically, with all your heart, love everybody, and love them so much that you pray for them and care about them.

I instantly began to pray. And I not only forgave this other person for separating me from my sister, but I also loved him and prayed for him and for his well-being. I thanked God for showing me this. Finally I had peace of mind again.

The very next day I was downtown. I had not seen Ric or Irlene for quite some time, but as I was parking my car to go to my parents' office, Ric pulled right across from me and parked his car.

A day earlier, I might have turned my back. This time, I did not hesitate for one second. The most natural thing I could do was to immediately walk over to Ric and put my arms around his neck and kiss him and start asking him how he was and how my sister was and tell him how I loved him and how I loved Irlene.

I think he was a little surprised, seeing as how I hadn't talked to him in months. He told me they were going to be married, and I shocked him again by offering our home for the wedding.

Ric is not performing these days because he has a new profession: photographer. He took the cover photo for this book, many of the portraits in our home, and three recent album covers. I predict he will be a major photographer in Nashville in years to come.

Irlene showed us a lot of strength in her loyalty to her husband. She showed us even more strength when their first child died before birth. Her hopes had been so high, and now she had to endure the pain of eleven hours of labor and delivery, yet she was stronger than I ever could have been. There were tears, but she remained faithful. Our minister, Mike Nelson, came to pray with us. I watched my little sister prepare to give birth, and I started sobbing, but she was so brave. Soon we discovered that the child had been a boy, and Momma and I began crying again. As soon as she could speak, Irlene began comforting us, if you can imagine that.

A few years later, Irlene got pregnant again. She wasn't due until January, but Dr. Lovvorn said he might have to induce the baby the day after Christmas. I said, "Let's do it on my birthday," as if it were my child, and Newt said, "Barbara, you know I wouldn't mind having Christmas with Janice and our two girls," which I could understand, but I said, "Of course, but you still could go down there and deliver the baby later in the day, or something." You know how friends are. I was serious and he was serious.

I said, "Newt, I'm telling you right now, she is going to go into labor on Christmas Day." So I was not surprised when we were out in Aspen on Christmas, and the phone rang, and she was going into labor, and Deric Mandrell Boyer was born. In January of 1988, they had a daughter, Vanessa Mandrell Boyer.

Having given Irlene some free advice, I promptly went out and dispensed some advice to Louise, too. In June of 1978, just after she came out with her first record, Louise was performing at Fan Fair when she met a songwriter and performer named

R. C. Bannon, a handsome guy with long, dark hair. She was a little suspicious of him at first, as she recalled in her own book, *The Mandrell Family Album:*

"We actually just got on the interstate and drove toward Kentucky," she wrote of the first time they went out. "I decided I would have to scare this guy into believing I was a good girl so he would turn around and take me home. I talked about my faith, the Bible, and the Lord. I was sure he wouldn't try to kiss me if I told him about my religion. My tactic would get rid of this guy for good.

" 'I tell you, Louise, I sure am glad that I asked you out. We have a lot in common,' R.C. said. 'My daddy is a preacher, and I *really* grew up in the church. . . .' "

Louise was still upset about her two marriages going bad, and she was not looking to get involved with another musician. I seconded the motion on that one, but R.C. pursued her so ardently that she began to realize what she might have been missing the first two times. They were married on February 26, 1979, and soon moved in right near Ken and me.

It didn't take me long to appreciate this talented guy out of Texas who had written Ronnie Milsap's hit, "Only One Love in My Life," and also had a record of his own song, "It Doesn't Matter Anymore." R.C. fit in with our family right away, and there would come a time when he would also be a huge asset in our television show.

Now they are parents, too. They adopted a baby girl, Nicole, to bring the grandchildren total up to six, at latest count. And R.C. has helped Louise rebuild her career. She and her group put on one of the best shows you will ever see, with great musical skill and energy.

Just as important, R.C. had brought the smile back to Louise's pretty face. She has been able to smile and play, as well as take over some responsibilities in the family.

Louise had no way of knowing this when she met R.C., but five years later she would play a major role in holding me together.

43
LOUISE SOCKS IT TO ME

I WENT BACK TO MY room after that staged television appearance, determined to keep almost everybody out of my life. But I could not duck my sisters.

Louise had assumed a leadership role as soon as I got hurt, staying with me in the ambulance, trying to keep the photographers away from me, and giving press conferences that tried to reassure people I would be all right.

She would fly home from her concerts even if she only had twelve hours to spare, bringing me expensive gifts like beautiful silk nightgowns—a bit more glamorous than my personal style, flannel—or fashionable Lladró statues, that I only appreciated later.

When I insisted on staying moled up in the darkness, Louise became upset.

"Louise, she doesn't realize what she's doing," Momma told

her. "She's not Barbara. You can talk to her where nobody else could. If I were in her shoes, I would want you to tell me."

That wasn't true. I did not appreciate Ken or Daddy trying to talk me into getting around. I thought I must be crazy, and I did not miss any of the things that used to mean so much to me. I couldn't have cared less. All I knew was that I was lying there hurting, and thinking, "I'll get through today and then maybe I can get through tonight."

I couldn't realize at the time how much pain everybody else was feeling. Irlene was still sad about having to cover up the extent of my head injuries.

When people said, "It's a good thing it was just a minor injury," she wanted to tell them, "Oh, it's not what you think. It's really bad and we're really worried." It was hard on her to be so concerned and not able to show it to other people.

But my father explained it to me this way: "A lot of your fans love you like you're family. It hurt us to go through it, and we saw no reason to hurt the fans, too."

Louise and Irlene had to shoulder the pain without being able to share it with many of our friends. The accident had destroyed the balance, the symmetry, the kind of blind trust that we were as strong as the unbroken lines of a triangle.

"It was something we could not share with Barbara," Louise said recently. "It was her pain. We wanted to help her through it, but only she knows how she feels. It's easy for us to say, 'Come on, let us share it with you,' but you can't share physical pain. For the first time, I feel a little bit separated from Barbara."

Like a lot of other people in the family, Irlene would become upset at seeing me snap at Ken and jump all over the kids for silly little things. Irlene understood that I was in pain, but she also knew something had changed.

"Because of what I thought of you, it just broke a bubble to see you hurting like that," Irlene said. "I thought of how much you meant to so many people, and I felt, 'My God, if it can happen to her, it can happen to us.'

"One thing changed in my life when you had the wreck," Irlene added. "I got scared for myself. I still am. It's like when you're a kid and you think things are not going to happen to you. As I got older, I thought they could but probably wouldn't. I thought everything had always happened good for you. Now, I started to think, if this could happen to Barbara, it could happen to other people. I try not to feel that way but I'm real nervous about things."

Irlene went on: "One day, in grade school, you came to help my class. You played games with us in a circle. And everybody thought you were really neat. Even back then, it was like, you were a star and I was proud that people knew you were my sister. Not because you were teaching us but because you were special.

"But from the moment you had the wreck, something was gone. A special spirit. A bubble burst. You were a superstar for me in a different respect—almost a spiritual thing."

I had no way of knowing how much my sisters were suffering—until Louise confronted me.

After I got better, Louise had a conversation with somebody from one of those tabloid newspapers. I can't blame her for talking to the reporter. We've always tried to be cooperative, and we know how nice the press has been to us. Sure, they'd love to find dirt on us, but because there isn't much to find, they've gone with what they had.

This time Louise gave them a little extra. She is perhaps the most verbal, most introspective of the sisters, a seeker, a thinker. Maybe she was subconsciously trying to send me a message. If she couldn't get through to me in conversation, maybe she could reach me through the printed word. She saw the advance copy of the paper and she called me right away to explain that it was going to be in there. She knew I wouldn't be too thrilled with it.

The headline said: "I LOST MY SISTER," and the quote right underneath it said, "My Sister Died—Louise Mandrell." She had said similar things to me, but seeing it in print was a shocker.

Louise was quoted saying that I used to be one way, but now that person had been killed in the wreck and had been replaced by this other sister. I had come to know what she meant, but still . . . I told her I knew how those kinds of papers were, and not to worry.

When Louise came back from the road, she visited me. She sat on the edge of the bed and started crying.

"I don't know how to tell you this, but you are a differnt sister than I used to have," she said. "You are not fun anymore."

I did not take it well.

"Louise, I do not want to have fun," I said. "My back and my ankle and my tailbone hurt me so much there is not one minute in a twenty-four-hour day that I do not hurt. Nothing, nothing, is fun to me right now. Just living is an ordeal, just existing."

"I just want to get my sister back," she said, sobbing.

"I'm still your sister," I said. "I'm still Barbara."

She was desperately trying to get me to respond, but I didn't even have enough spunk to fight back. I just felt sad and disappointed that she did not think I was the same person.

Of course, looking at it now, I was not the same person. I did not like hearing it, but I *was* different. Maybe she was right, but I was right, too.

There have been times since when I was acting silly, or coming on like Bossy Big Sister again, and I would look at Louise and ask, "Is that fun enough for you?" But at the time, I didn't think anything would ever be fun again.

44

THE DO-RITES

WITH LOUISE AND IRLENE leading their own lives, I had to rebuild my band. I had come up with the name Do-Rites, after an early single of mine called the Do-Right-Woman and the Do-Right-Man. The name also suggested the image I wanted for my band—no drinking around the show, no drugs at all, bright costumes, no jeans, no excessively long hair. A clean-cut look. I wanted my musicians to be an extension of the family.

And believe me, a band quickly becomes your extended family. You know all about them, their families, their ambitions, their quirks. You know which ones snore and which ones like to stay up late. It gets pretty intimate on the road, even with a new bus, which we had finally managed in December of 1972.

Daddy had met a friendly banker named Clarence Reynolds, who thought we were a good risk for a bus loan. We bought a Custom Coach made in Columbus, Ohio, and we put a ribbon on it and the governor of Tennessee, Winfield Dunn, cut the ribbon in a big party out in front of the Commerce Union Bank. We knew Governor Dunn because Ken had been his pilot. I got my

Uncle Al to design my name on the side of the bus—it was artistic, and good publicity, too.

Now that the girls were not traveling with me, I had to go out and find the best musicians we could attract to Nashville. With almost no exceptions, these men became part of my family, the brothers I had never had. I loved their energy, their independence, their love of sports, and the challenge of working with new musicians who thought they were hot stuff.

One of our first new members was Dennis McCall, a bass player with a creative mind who used to tell Matthew stories to keep him happy backstage. Dennis would begin making up some wild adventure story, and other members of the band would sort of edge over, trying to listen in. He's a backup singer over at the Grand Ole Opry now. We also had Lonnie Webb, who later went to work for The Nashville Network.

Deep down in my heart, I still consider myself a steel guitar player who branched out a bit. I wasn't having just any steel man on that bus with me. In 1975, we found Mike (Cookie Monster) Jones, a burly guy out of Quincy, Illinois, who used to be with Charlie Louvin's group before he joined me. And I haven't let him get away.

After being so well received in Asia, I had no qualms about taking my music across the Atlantic. I had enjoyed playing at the bases when Ken was in the service, and our family band had been given a great reception in 1970.

Just so I wouldn't get a swelled head, I did find a few places where Barbara Mandrell was not universally loved. It happened twice, actually, at Montreux, Switzerland, and at the Wembley indoor arena in London, England.

I was honored when I was invited to a country-music segment of the famous jazz festival at Montreux. I knew they were discerning fans who were used to the great jazz musicians from the United States. I never claimed to be Ella Fitzgerald or Count Basie, but I grew up listening to jazz, and I thought the Do-Rites could play some country sounds that would impress these people.

Besides, I hate the whole idea of labels. Where does country leave off and pop music begin? What was Elvis? Where does pop leave off and folk begin? Don't attach labels to things. Just listen and enjoy it.

We got to Montreux, a beautiful town alongside a lake in the

French-speaking part of the country. Gorgeous mountains. Lovely homes. We were on the same bill as Roy Clark, Doc Watson, the Oak Ridge Boys, Clarence Gatemouth Brown, some of the great names in the diverse field known as country music. I thought people would have an open mind about us, but the purists were out in force.

I played a song or two and I couldn't believe it. People started rattling around and walking out and some of them even booed. It had never happened to me before. I've heard that some people take classical music and opera so seriously that they will boo or hiss if they don't like a performer. I've heard that Bob Dylan's fans booed when he started using an electric guitar during the height of the folk-music craze. It was a big controversy—Dylan goes electric! Horrors. But I'd never seen anything like that in country music.

I don't even like rudeness at sports events. Root for your own team, but don't boo the other guys. I have too much respect for the professionalism of anybody to boo them. When I watch tennis in America, I'm appalled at the rudeness. Granted, some of the new tennis players are pretty obnoxious, but my theory is, if there's somebody you don't like, keep your mouth shut. Don't be like them.

I would have said that even before I saw people walking out at Montreux. They just thought banjos and steel guitars were too pop. I didn't know what to do.

If an audience is slow to respond, I'll try to coax them and love them and work them into a better mood. I've heard about singers just walking off the stage because they didn't like the audience. I can't do that. I was raised to entertain an audience, not confront it. If they don't like me, that breaks my heart, but I'm not going to take them on.

I cut my show short a little, and obviously did not perform an encore. After me came the Oak Ridge Boys, who were booed from their first song. Then Roy Clark went on. You can say what you want about Barbara Mandrell and the Oak Ridge Boys, but to me, Roy Clark is the most versatile performer in country music. He can play most instruments and he has that wonderful voice. You know what? They didn't like him much, either.

Roy did not feel the same constraints I did. He let them have it. He told them they were not only rude to him, but they had been rude to his friends, too. I never figured out what nationalities were doing the booing, but they could understand English. They quieted down after that.

How bad was it? Cookie, my steel player, had been around the block a few times by then, but he was so shaken by the poor reception that he broke out in hives.

At Montreux, we were "too country." At Wembley, we were "not country enough." I had always heard what great country fans there are in the United Kingdom. But the fans at the annual indoor country festival at Wembley had their own image of country.

I guess we should have known before the concert began from the way they were dressed—shirts with leather fringes and yokes, boots, cowboy hats, and little plastic pistols in holsters. I loved it. I thought it was great. They were making a statement that they were more country than the Americans. But in their own way, they were intolerant.

They just hadn't kept up with the evolution of country music into the middle Seventies. My band was dressed in costumes made by Harvey Krantz, designer to the stars. They were wearing purple with rhinestones all over them, real hippy-dippy looking, bell-bottoms, loud, not one country yoke to be seen.

The way we started the show back then was to have the band play an overture, with a lot of different themes mixed together. One of our big sounds was the "Theme from SWAT." So here was a band in purple suits playing show-business themes, and the old-fashioned country fans did not know what to think. They did not boo us but they were decidedly distant.

I remember thinking, "What makes them the judge of country music? Whose music is it, anyway?"

Historically, I guess it's true that American country music has its roots in the people who came over from England, Ireland, Scotland, and Wales and settled in the Appalachian Mountains and then moved out west.

But I say that country music is pure American, and it continues to evolve. Bill Monroe incorporated the banjo into country music and gave a name to bluegrass music through his group, the Bluegrass Boys, from Kentucky. When I first followed country music with my Daddy, we were listening to Webb Pierce and Hank Williams, Ernest Tubb and Kitty Wells. Now that's as country as it gets. Those are my roots. But country music continued to change and grow, and my music evolved in its own way.

If I had done "Big Big Love," the things I used to do many years before, or "Please Release Me," kick it on steel, I could have wrapped them around my finger. "Little Red Wagon." But to me that would have been selling out because it was not the music I was playing by the mid-Seventies. I said, "Let's show 'em what Barbara Mandrell is all about. Let's give 'em what we give people back home."

To me, country music is an art form, always changing. Even classical music doesn't sound the same from one decade to another. The instruments and the arrangements have evolved from one century to the next. Musicians are artists in some small way, and we do not want to do the same thing from week to week. This is supposed to be a "creative" business.

Well, I learned my lesson. We were invited back the next year, and I gave in. I bent, I broke, I did what they wanted. Older tunes. Less complicated arrangements. Their yoked shirts and little toy pistols told me what they wanted. The customer is always right. Boys, I said, it is 1953. The big record on the jukebox is "It Don't Hurt Any More." I may sound cynical, but they loved us.

One of the reasons I like to give a diverse show is because of the talent of my musicians. The faces may change as guys get better offers, or decide to stick closer to home, but I am always carrying a talented group of musicians. Sometimes I get sad when I think about all the great guys who have worked with me, but then we find somebody else with terrific potential, and in a few weeks I'm comfortable with him, too. Still, I never quite get over all the great guys who moved on.

Once in a while I still get together with Gene Miller, who went to California to pursue his career. If you would say to me that I could hear only five more singers before I died, one of them would be Gene. I think Gene will be a giant rock 'n' roll star. I once had him do a duet with me on the television series, as a guest star, not a member of my band. He brought down the house. I used to tell him, "You're going to be a great star. One day I'll go backstage to say hello and you'll say, 'Barbara who?'"

Another talented guy was Gary Smith, who later went with Dolly's show. Gary was like a baby when he joined the Do-Rites, but he became very mature, showing a great talent for piano after coming up through gospel music.

We had a major loss in the summer of 1989 when Randy

Wright decided to work in Nashville. Randy was more than just my drummer. He was my liaison man with the band, the one who would visit with me before and after each show, sitting around with me and JoAnn. After every show, Randy would study the tape, just to see if there was anything we needed to work on. He was a beautiful singer who had done some singles for MCA and hit the charts with a few of them. But he decided he wanted more security, so he joined the Do-Rites. Randy went back with me to the high-school gyms and the county fairs, playing in front of two hundred people, and we used to laugh about it sitting around a luxurious dressing room in Las Vegas. But I would notice him growing wistful because he missed his family, and I was not totally surprised when he decided to work on corporate promotions, so he could get off the road.

You never truly replace a Randy Wright, but Randy helped set up auditions for a new drummer, and the boys voted on the six finalists. Their vote was unanimous for Doug Dimmell out of Kansas, who has a peculiar specialty of taping electronic drums to his legs, playing a solo while moving around the stage.

It was the same way earlier when Dennis McCall left us. Louise had a fantastic bass player named Charlie Bundy, who happened to be born in the same hospital as Louise in Corpus Cristi. I would never think of taking a musician away from my sister, but Louise is generous almost to a fault.

In fact, the only arguments I ever have with my sisters are about who is giving what to whom. We all want to outdo each other. Well, she outdid me this time. She said Charlie was so good that he deserved to make more money than she could afford. That, to me, is the ultimate generosity. I am not sure I would willingly give up a musician to anybody.

Charlie has been a great asset to me, because his baby face made him a perfect partner for an occasional joke onstage. As the bass player, he stands closest to me, and he can put down his instrument and help get me a towel or a glass of water or take presents when the fans hand them to me.

More important, he is a superb musician. When he joined us, I was trying to develop more of a rhythm-and-blues sound, with those wonderful bass licks with the thumb, like the black blues musicians do. I explained that I wanted some of those bass licks that go dum-dum-dum. Charlie said, "I don't do it," and I said, "I want it, Charlie," and he worked at it and he got it, and now it's used all the time. They will give me what they don't think they can give.

In addition to being the backup driver for the band's bus, Charlie is also a serious reader who keeps himself busy on the road reading John Irving novels or the national edition of *The New York Times.*

Mike "Cookie Monster" Jones has been with me the longest now, fifteen years. He's just a rock of stability back there on the steel. When we went to Hollywood a few years after he joined me, I would have to play a steel solo on the show. Cookie would work it all out for me, and teach me a few new things. I'm partial to steel players anyway, so Cookie is special to me. I see a lot of Cookie because one of his side jobs is to drive my bus from the hotel to the show, while Danny Wright is resting.

My other current musicians are: Lonnie Hayes out of Illinois, who is often singled out for praise by reviewers for playing the fiddle, banjo, and guitar; Nick Uhrig, with his great smile, who does all that beautiful high-pitched backup singing; David Salyer from Dayton, Ohio, who plays banjo and guitar like a dream and often manages to find a five- or ten-mile race wherever we are performing on weekends; Dino Pastin, the big handsome keyboard man who stops the show when he stands out in the spotlight playing his saxophone; and Christopher Walters, a piano player from New Orleans who also does the arrangements for the house orchestras when I play hotels in Las Vegas or Atlantic City.

When I started working on this book, I kept talking about all those great musicians who had moved on to other opportunities and I began to have the fantasy of staging a reunion: Daddy and Momma, of course, and Louise and Irlene, and all those guys from the early years, all my Do-Rites, Randy and Gene and the current ones. I was thinking about all those people onstage, like one of those anniversary productions of *A Chorus Line,* with everybody performing together.

But I did better. Instead of asking them to perform, we arranged a twentieth anniversary party in December of 1989, inviting everybody who had ever performed with me. To our knowledge, there had never been a band reunion in Nashville. It added up to over forty, when you figured even people who had filled in for a short time, but they were Do-Rites, too. Louise even called her first husband, Ronny Shaw, and assured him he was welcome, and he honored us by coming and having a good time.

The whole gang poured into the great hall of our new home, and for four short hours we were a family again. I ran around in a black-and-white T-shirt that had the familiar backstage refrain, "It's Okay . . . I'm with the Band." I took a lot of photographs, watching Do-Rites from different decades introduce each other and play a song together.

It was gratifying to me how easily everybody got along— telling me we all must have been doing something right over the years. Guys who had been fired, guys who had quit, the current gang, they all seemed to have a common point of view. They even got me and Louise up there to sing a duet of "Night Life," and we all told the old bus stories all over again, and caught up on what everybody was doing. There were a lot of laughs. We tried to overlook the bad times, particularly the time I had to disband my Do-Rites.

45

BREAKING UP THE BAND

ON THE FIRST DAY of November in 1984, I did the hardest thing I had ever done in my life. I broke up my band.

I called them to the house and closed the doors, just me and them. No Daddy, no JoAnn, no Ken, no nobody, and I told them the truth. It hurt me worse than the car accident because I didn't remember that. This one I went into with my eyes open. Full of tears, but open.

These were my brothers. These were my friends. These were my colleagues. And I was telling them the show was over.

"Boys, I have no idea if I'm ever going to perform again," I said. "I hate to do this, but we cannot keep the group together."

I told them I would keep them on salary until the first of the year, and we would do everything possible to get them placed in Nashville. But I understood if they got better jobs and never came back.

I looked around the room, not knowing if I was saying good-bye to them for the last time. Maybe the next time I saw them, they would be working somewhere else, and I would be paying to get in. Maybe they would become big stars. I hoped so. But I was afraid I was letting some of them in for hard times.

Cookie had just taken his kid to a Halloween party the night before. While he was sitting in my room, he thought, "This is some trick-or-treat."

I made no promises about ever getting together again. It had to be that way. We had no idea how my health would be, whether I could ever get up onstage again. Ken and I had saved some money, but we were facing monstrous medical bills with a lot of questions about insurance. I was basically without a living. How could I keep my boys around for the show that might never happen again?

When they left, I went back to my room and sobbed some more. I was beginning to realize that the accident did not just change my life. It had disrupted the lives of dozens of good people around me. People had been so good to me in my career and now I felt I was letting them down.

46

IT STARTS TO HAPPEN

SOMEBODY WHO KNOWS ME pretty well says his lasting image of me in the early Seventies was standing backstage at the Ryman, watching the other performers. I've always been so active that I don't think of myself as ever standing around, but I know what my friend means.

I was kind of on the edge of the inner circle of country music. I was on the Opry, I was a regular in Nashville, I was playing good places. But it was Loretta Lynn and Dolly Parton, Conway Twitty and Johnny Cash who were having the hit records and being discovered by people outside country music.

I never felt like an outsider because I had been part of the scene for so many years. Who else in her early twenties had worked with Patsy Cline, Johnny Cash, Tex Ritter, Red Foley, Jimmy Dickens?

But that didn't guarantee you anything on your own. Olivia

Newton-John from Australia came in and swept the awards one year. People got uptight because she not only wasn't from Nashville, she wasn't even from the United States, and it wasn't quite clear if she actually sang country or not. But I've always asked, What is country music, anyway? Is it Kitty Wells or Crystal Gayle? Hank Williams or Ronnie Milsap? And who cares?

To some degree, country music is whoever happens to be hot in Nashville and on country stations at the time. It may sound cocky, but I always felt I was going to make it. If I was observing backstage at the Opry, maybe it was to see how other people handled success.

If I could have written my future, I would have had my first record become number one, but now I'm glad God had a slower plan for me. When it finally happened, people knew the name Barbara Mandrell from my being out there for five years, my name written in script across the side of the bus, crossing the country on the interstates.

My first #1 hit record was in 1973: "The Midnight Oil," a pretty sultry number about two people seeing each other late at night. I wouldn't be foolish enough to say it was just my singing, or the words and music written by Joe Allen, or even the great production by Billy Sherrill.

Part of that record's success had to do with the amount of promotion we did. We did not believe that my record company, which was Columbia at the time, was doing enough for the record. We had all these ideas and all this energy, and their people would shrug and say, "We know how to do these things." Well, that wasn't good enough for Daddy. He bought up two thousand little kerosene lamps, and we sent them to radio stations all over the country with a nice card that I signed, saying, "Here's something to burn your midnight oil in." We also bought advertising in the major magazines, to call their attention to the song.

If the record was selling, it was because people were buying it, real people who discovered they liked my voice and maybe even me. Before long I had a fan club, loyal men and women all over the world, ten thousand of them now. For a long time, my mother-in-law, Beth Kurtz, ran the club, but after she died, the job was taken over by Mary Lynn West, who sends out newsletters and autographed pictures to all members.

So many times a fan will walk up to me and show me the

photograph from my club and ask me to autograph it, and I say, "I already did," and they say, "No, I mean really sign it." I've heard about machines that will sign your name exactly the way you do, but I won't do it because I think your signature should be authentic. Still, people don't believe me.

We have a fan club breakfast every year, at the Opryland Hotel during Fan Fair, the big blast for fans every June. I put it together, using songs and jokes they never see us do when they come to my concerts, and Ken serves as master of ceremonies. My ten thousand club members are the backbone of the people who buy my records. They are my career, and I love them for it.

After those fans put my record at number one in *Billboard,* Daddy walked into the office of Billy Sherrill, my producer and friend, and said we wanted out. This was nothing against Billy, who has had a great career in country music and who made me an offer when I was just singing down in Printer's Alley. Columbia has been one of the great labels, but at that stage in my career, I was just a little fish. Daddy gave Billy a letter asking for a release from the label. Billy understood the situation, and he would have released us, but his New York office would not let me out of my contract.

The New York office. The phrase itself sent terror deep into my heart. People are nice wherever you go, but the idea of taking on the New York office of anything frightened me. There was only one thing to do: Get a New York lawyer. We had been using Pryor, Cashman, Sherman & Flynn, a big-time law firm in New York, and when I wanted to get my release from CBS, Gideon Cashman introduced me to Alan Siegel, his partner, who specialized in entertainment law.

We flew up to New York, and from the moment I met Alan, I felt better about the whole deal. He insisted we be exactly on time at the record company office, and he gave me confidence as we struggled through the crowds on the sidewalk.

When we got there, the man I had to see was not there yet. He was due any minute, as the saying goes. Alan told the secretary that he was very upset because his client had come all the way from Nashville for this appointment. Alan did not think we could sit around and wait.

"We're out of here," Alan told the secretary. "We're going to lunch."

After lunch, we went back to Alan's office. On the way, Alan said, "So-and-so is going to call you. You'll say you are devastated. This is a perfect example of why you don't feel comfortable with their record company, of why you want out."

And that's exactly what happened. We said we would not cut any more records for them, and for eighteen months, I did not issue a single record. I got on the syndicated country shows, which helped keep me alive in front of the people. The deejays would go back and play my old records, and somehow I got more jobs at higher prices. But I was defying common wisdom—and I don't recommend it.

After eighteen months, Alan Siegel finally got my release. We've been together ever since. He has taught me to be strong, to have the courage of my convictions. He says the thing he likes about me is that I won't back down. He can go in and state our fair demand, and know that I will not vacillate behind him.

We signed with ABC/DOT in 1975, and my first song with them, "Standing Room Only," also went to number one.

It was at this time that I met Tom Collins, who would be my producer until the end of 1989. He was having some major successes with Johnny Rodriguez and Ronnie Milsap and other artists, and he had the reputation as somebody who could get a great deal out of an artist. I looked him up. He is from Lenoir City in the eastern part of Tennessee and graduated from the university in Knoxville in 1970, with plans to be a dentist. To make some money, he got a job in Nashville, and has been in country music ever since.

Tom and I talked for a while and he tried to tell me that I was a better singer than I gave myself credit for. He told me early on: "Barbara, I just counted up the number of blonde singers in country music, and there are thirteen of them up near the top. What makes you different? In my opinion, you have an appeal to a lot of people because you can sing songs that are close to rhythm and blues and because you can handle questionable songs."

When I asked what he meant, Tom said that even though my image was the all-American girl, there was something in my voice that would enable me to get even more out of cheating songs like "The Midnight Oil." Also, I was still playing high-school gyms for two thousand dollars a show, and Tom felt I could do better than that.

After my first song for ABC/DOT, "Standing Room Only," I then did a song called "That's What Friends Are For"—not the pop song that came ten years later, but a song about a woman whose man is stolen by her best friend. It had more of a pop sound, and Tom and I both loved it, yet it was not one of my biggest records. Still, I loved the mood of the song, the turnaround about friendship, all these things she did for us and I did for her, and he did, " 'cause that's what friends are for." At the end, when she's taking him from me, I sing, "If that's what friends are for, I don't need them anymore." I just thought it was a great song.

Tom has close contacts with songwriters like Rhonda Kye Fleming and Dennis Morgan, who later would write hit songs for me. One of them was "Sleeping Single in a Double Bed," a brassy up-tempo lament about the breakup of a love affair. Another hit from them was "I Was Country (When Country Wasn't Cool)," which was perfect for me because it was really the story of my growing up in California during the Sixties. While the rest of the world was into the Beatles, I was into (sigh) George Jones.

After that, I heard a song called "Woman to Woman," which had a strong rhythm-and-blues sound to it. I brought it to Tom's attention, and we listened to a version of it, but it had a portion where the performer recites the lyrics. Tom loved that part, and he wanted me to do our own version of the recitation on the beginning.

"There's no way," I told him. "I love the song, but I'm not somebody who can recite. That would be great for other performers, but it would sound corny if I did it."

Tom said, "You can do it. Go into the recording session and do it because I asked you to do it. When it's over and you don't like it, we won't use it."

So I went in there and I did the recitation. It was not easy keeping a straight face, but when I heard the first playback of it, I loved it, and we released it that way.

One day Tom got a call from Detroit. My record had become popular on the local rhythm-and-blues station. I do not need to tell you that R&B is a business term for black. This is Motown. The Supremes. Berry Gordy. Where Aretha Franklin sang in the choir in her daddy's church. Now I was on the R&B charts.

This sounded like an amazing chance to sell a lot of records, but the punchline was, my album was ordered by one of the record stores, and the manager took one look at Miss Oceanside, California, and he called up and said, "Man, we can't rack this," meaning they could not sell it in the store. People on the radio had thought I was black. Talk about compliments. Even though people in Detroit were not accustomed to buying records by blonde country singers, my album did slip onto the R&B charts, so it was on all four charts at once.

Then in 1979, Tom found the old Luther Ingram song called "If Loving You Is Wrong, I Don't Want to Be Right." I flipped over it and said, "Yeah, let's do it," because it felt right up my alley. But when we went to record it, I was having such difficulty making it happen. We did several takes, and finally Tom said, "Just pay attention to the song and what you're singing. Forget everything else." He dimmed the lights in the studio and he had the engineer dim the lights where he was sitting. Tom said, "Forget everybody and everything and just think about this song and put it in the groove." With his help, I did, and that song became a crossover hit too.

Tom's impact on my career began during the old *Urban Cowboy* days, when country became popular in the big cities. You had lawyers and stockbrokers wearing boots and yoked shirts and lining up at country bars all over the place. We had been averaging three hundred thousand sales per album, but my sales jumped up to half a million partially because of the Urban Cowboy trend. Tom and I sure didn't create the trend, but he knew how to take advantage of it.

Tom and I disagreed many times on which song should be the single, or how we should handle the instrumental break in the middle, or what kind of instrument should be used. But it was a marvelous working relationship because I was not afraid to argue with him and he was not afraid to argue with me. Very often, we didn't even know what we were doing until were in the midst of it, but that is my way of being creative—being under the gun and making it happen.

We worked together for a long time but at the end of 1989, Tom and I decided I should work with Jimmy Bowen, one of the top producers in Nashville. I'll always be grateful to Tom Collins for all those years.

I was also fortunate to work with two other fine people in the business. Jim Foglesong, a very cultured gentleman with a background in classical music, became my record president, and he was instrumental in the success of these records. ABC/DOT was eventually bought by MCA, and Jim went over to Capital Records, where I followed him a while later, and we worked together until he took another position in 1990.

I'd like to say that in all my years of working with Jim Foglesong he has never lied to me. Not true. He did lie to me once. We were at a party and somebody was playing oldies, so Jim and I engaged in a contest of "Name That Tune." I would have to modestly report that I was naming more tunes than Mr. Foglesong, but then he switched the rules and started naming publishers and years. Tree Publishing. 1962. How could I match that? I couldn't. I only found out later that he had been making it up as he went along. Otherwise, he is a most honorable man.

Also in the mid-Seventies, Daddy was contacted by Dick Blake, who had a booking agency in town. He said I could be on the same bookings as the Statler Brothers, the most popular group in country, if I joined Dick's agency.

Dick Blake became a dear friend to us. He and my father got along great because they had both been in World War II. Dick was a survivor of the Bataan Death March, during which he had been bayoneted in the chest, so now he had only one lung. He was very thin, and not very robust, and you could tell he had really been through it. Sitting on his boat out at the lake, he would sometimes have to take a whiff from the oxygen tank.

But it did not take away from his business sense or his humor. Oh, he'd try to snow me once in a while and talk me into things I didn't want to do, but that's part of the business. The main thing is, he would never lie. He traveled with the Statlers to settle up their accounts at the end of the show, and when he lost his strength, he started to send JoAnn Berry out on the road. I guess that's why Dick Blake was so good as a talent agent. He knew talent off the stage as well as on it.

Funny? You'd be sitting around his office near quitting time, and he'd look at his watch and say in this raspy voice of his, "Five-thirty, hah! You'll hear 'em leaving the parking lot so fast you could get killed by flying gravel." He had everything figured out. When he died in October of 1983, we were fortunate that JoAnn was in place. I'm just grateful that guys like Tom Collins, Jim Foglesong, and Dick Blake were there when I needed them.

47

IGNORING SOME ADVICE

O<small>N ONE OF MY</small> trips to see Dr. Bond, my neurosurgeon, I admitted I was concerned about the way I felt and acted. Dr. Bond spent over an hour talking with me, saying, "No, you're not crazy. You've done what I call 'maturing.' The way you think and feel now was inevitable. You were always going to think and feel that way, but it would have taken you probably twenty more years."

I took that to mean that we all grow at different rates. Sometimes we stay the same for a long time. Other times we grow up suddenly, or are forced to grow up. Sometimes we take a step backwards. The senior citizen who measures everything so carefully might have been impulsive at the age of twenty, but slowly over the years that person became steadier.

I also asked Dr. Bond why the thought of performing even

in the future scared me to death. He told me it was because I had lost my self-confidence.

Dr. Bond suggested that the sooner I got back to my familiar pace, the better I might recover, emotionally and mentally. Everybody in my family translated this to mean I should go back to work again.

I wasn't having any of it. I had no desire to get back onstage. I still had too much physical pain to even think about it, and I couldn't remember things I had just heard ten minutes earlier, much less song lyrics or stage directions. So I just gave everybody a flat-out no. But they kept bringing it up.

Ken, Daddy, Louise, Irlene, JoAnn, Tim and Cathy Bucek—all of them tried to suggest going back. I don't think it was because of all the money I brought in, or because I was the star who made everybody else's lives go round. Nothing like that. Their advice was well intentioned. They wanted what was best for me. They felt that trying to perform again would be therapy for me. My response was, "Never." I no longer felt the need to entertain people. That part of my life was over.

One time we were having the same old discussion, and they were trying to prod me into trying one performance.

"No!" I shouted. "I am not going back. I am going to stay in my room until I feel better."

48

MY BIG BROTHERS

GROWING UP WITH TWO younger sisters, I often wondered what it would have been like if I'd had brothers. Daddy said it never mattered to him because he taught us the same things that he would have taught a boy, and I appreciate knowing he felt that way. And I cannot imagine loving anybody more than my two sisters. But brothers? It would have to be different.

I found out just how different it was in the fall of 1978 when Dick Blake booked me to open for the Statler Brothers, four zany guys who had taken over as country music's most popular group in 1965 with "Flowers on the Wall," and followed it up with hit after hit.

Not content with being the top group in Nashville, the Statlers created another group called Lester (Roadhog) Moran and His Cadillac Cowboys, whose biggest achievement was appearing on the local radio station, WEAK out of Rainbow Valley, until they finally appeared on albums called "Country Music Then and Now" in 1972 and "Alive at the Johnny Mack Brown High School."

I got such a kick out of the Cowboys that Cookie, my steel

man, can still crack me up during my solo by muttering "Nice pickin', Wichita"—Wichita being one of the characters in the Cowboys. One year, we took out an advertisement in the *Music City News,* posing for a photograph as Ruby Lee and the Swinging Strings, your basic tacky group, expressing our deep respect for the Cowboys. Daddy posed in the photograph, sticking out his belly over his belt.

You know what? They never mentioned it to me, like the guys in the dugout who won't shake a teammate's hand when he hits a home run. You cannot one-up the Statlers. And hardly anybody else ever wondered just who Ruby Lee and the Swinging Strings were. Maybe the moral was that it is not easy to satirize country music.

It isn't easy for the Statlers to have two personalities. You can't just turn it on. I mean, it probably takes Paul Rubens all day to become Peewee Herman. The Statlers were so besieged with requests to be Lester and the Cowboys that they seriously considered killing them off in a bus wreck.

The Statlers were plenty funny on their own. I loved traveling around with them for more than two years, opening their shows and hanging around with them afterward.

Yes, they are a little crazy. It was disconcerting to be warming up my voice backstage and suddenly think I was hearing an echo. However, it would turn out to be Lou DeWitt, with his wonderful tenor-falsetto voice.

It was hard to take yourself too seriously playing with these boys. I would spend two hours getting dressed and putting on my makeup and fixing my hair. A few minutes before my showtime, Phil or Harold or Don would walk by and glance at his watch and say something like, "Hey, Barbara, shouldn't you be getting ready? It's almost showtime." And I could not help but jerk my head around and check out the nearest mirror, thinking, "Do I look that bad?" They liked to give me a hard time, which I needed when we were doing thirty dates in thirty days.

The Statlers have an incredible library of old cowboy movies, so after the show, Daddy and I would go over to their bus and sit up for hours watching Roy Rogers or Tom Mix or Hopalong Cassidy.

Being with them exposed me to a lot of fans I hadn't met yet. And we were a great combination, a blonde girl with her own band, and four crazy guys closing. We were sold out almost all the time, with an enormous number of people coming to see them but maybe liking Barbara Mandrell, too, when they left.

The Statlers were very complimentary to me. They knew I had high goals for myself, and, out of love, they deflated me every chance they got—in jest. One of them told me, "You know, you don't deserve to be the Queen of Country Music, but we'll call you Queenie."

That got to be my nickname. Harold, Lou, Don, and Phil started it, and now other people call me Queenie too. There is another Queenie in the world, however: JoAnn Berry's oldest Yorkshire terrier is named after me. I think it's a compliment.

The boys gave me more than a nickname. Bless their hearts, they gave me pneumonia, too. At least, I blame them for it.

The first winter I worked with them, we were playing a lot of arenas that were also used for ice hockey. Naturally, they didn't take down the ice if they just had a show coming through for one night, so they would put the stage right over the ice. My feet would be so cold that my head would feel hot.

I started out with a cold and then I graduated to the flu, with a roaring temperature. We left Jaime home and Momma went on the trip just to take care of me. Nobody can break a fever like my mother. She'd keep me warm and feed me fluids and soup and fuss over me for a few hours just to get me back out onstage again. I'd sit up and try to get dressed, but then I would have to lie down again for fifteen minutes. People suggested that I take a few days off, but that isn't the way I operate.

We came home from the road on a Sunday night and I took a bath, but I was so hot that I could not climb out of the tub. Ken took my temperature, and discovered it was 104.5, so we rushed to the hospital. By that time, I was so weak I could not stand up for the X ray. At first, they thought I might have Legionnaire's Disease, but eventually they determined I had viral pneumonia and that I had lost the left lung and half the right one. For the next forty-eight hours, they were pumping me full of penicillin, and I decided viral pneumonia was the way to go, because I was so tired I didn't care.

Tammy Wynette had been traveling with the Statlers and she had gotten sick, so I tried making a joke that if you worked with the Statler Brothers you got sick. But I felt too weak to laugh.

The doctors said I had to lie in bed for six weeks and just sleep and eat, but I was back with the Statlers before long. I was having too much fun to stay away.

Appearing with the Statlers was one of the best things that ever could have happened to me. I was nominated twice for Female Vocalist of the Year and I did not get it, but I was not too disappointed because I knew I had plenty of time. In the fall of 1979, I won it on my third nomination, and established a tradition by crying onstage. Some performers laugh, some get serious, some make speeches, some lose the power to talk. I cry. I couldn't fake it or plan it, that's just the way I am. I sobbed in 1979 and I have sobbed any other time I won an award. I ain't that good an actor.

I even cried when the Statlers gave me an award. Yes, they did, bless their hearts. One year I went to their Fourth of July celebration and in return they gave me a plaque. It said: "To The Only Statler Sister We Have."

49

A Prayer in a Coffee Shop

After a month at home, I was able to walk around a little, and strong enough to go for rides in the car. But as my broken bones healed, the pain seemed to collect at the base of my spine. For reasons nobody could explain, I had a constant sharp pain in my tailbone. The doctors had checked and could come up with no explanation.

"Is it connected to the broken bones?" I asked. "Will it go away when they get better?"

"We wish we could tell you," they said. But they made no guarantees. They told me that with tailbones you just don't know.

I have such great respect for doctors that it worried me that they could make no promises. I knew I was in trouble if the best doctors in Nashville could not come up with any plan for the tailbone. I would wake up with the pain and go to sleep with it. I felt sometimes that if I would doze off, maybe I would wake up and it would be gone. But even in my sleep I could feel this drilling sensation deep in my lower back. There was no position that would make any difference. Ken would rub it, but almost as a diversion. It never stopped.

Up to that point, I had blocked off my active prayer to God. I don't know why. I didn't blame God for what had happened to me. Mike Nelson, my friend and preacher, visited the house and prayed for me. He was patient and understanding. He knew what I was going through. He never told me what I should do, which to me is the best way to handle somebody. It would not have worked for Mike or anybody else to say I was neglecting my faith.

We attended the Hendersonville Chapel, a unidenominational church near our home, because of the great preacher, Mike Nelson. We have dedicated our children in front of the congregation, promising to raise our children in the love of Jesus, in a Christian home. I felt very close to Mike because he once told me what I did was so wonderful because it reached people he could not reach. I do at least one gospel song in each show, not to try to evangelize anybody else but just to give witness about where Barbara Mandrell is coming from.

Almost always, people enjoy gospel as music, but once in a great while, I see people walking out during a gospel song and I wonder if they are tired or ill or have to go to the bathroom, or what. Or is it because they don't like gospel? I believe you can appreciate other religions' music, and I don't mind letting people know that my life is built on Christ.

In those dark days, I neglected Jesus. I could not find the words, either on my lips or in my heart.

One day I was twirling the dials and I spotted one of the television preachers. It doesn't matter which one. Just hearing him talking about prayer reminded me that I had not prayed for a healing of my pain.

I have often watched healing programs on television. People would make prayer requests for healing, and they would report later that they felt better. I believe in faith healing. I believe God can make you better. I also believe in great doctors and medicine.

My awareness of healing goes back to when I was a little

girl and Momma and Daddy took me to a tent meeting of Oral Roberts. For some reason, I have a vivid memory of the tent leaking because it was raining so hard. I remember being mad at myself for falling asleep in this humid tent. I remember Oral Roberts saying, "Through my faith, He has healed me."

After I spotted a healing service on television, JoAnn mentioned that a preacher friend of hers was coming to Nashville. They had been friends when they were kids back in Texas, and now he had a ministry traveling around the country.

JoAnn said she and her friend had been raised in the tradition of tent meetings and healing, which I respect. She thought it might be good if I met him. I was not ready for any kind of public meetings . . . MIRACLE! BARBARA WALKS DOWN AISLE BY HERSELF! the gossip tabloids would have said—but I agreed to meet with him.

No tent meetings. No fire and brimstone. We met at the coffee shop of the Hyatt: JoAnn, Ken, the preacher, and I.

He was a pleasant-looking man, with none of the flashiness of the public preacher. Sitting at the coffee shop, he could have been talking to us about mutual funds or the Tennessee Vols.

"This is not about me," he said. "It has nothing to do with me. It's only the Lord Jesus doing this."

He made biblical references about when Jesus cursed a fig tree as he and his disciples were walking down the road. They were astonished that nothing happened to the tree when He cursed it, but a few days later, they were walking past the same tree and they noticed it was withering and dying—because He cursed its roots. Even though I had not been praying to Christ to heal me in the past days, I was now ready to pray for it.

The preacher said, "Your child asks you for something, maybe a sandwich, and you're going to give it to him, but maybe you're doing something else. If the kid keeps asking, 'Please give me a sandwich, I asked for a sandwich, please give me a sandwich,' you don't like it. You say, 'Please be patient.' You're talking about our Heavenly Father. Maybe He wants you to be patient. Maybe it wouldn't do any good for you to keep asking Him. Who knows, maybe the Lord is going to take away your pain instantly. Maybe He's going to curse the roots of the tree. Just accept it."

His attitude made me feel good because he did not make

me feel guilty that I had not been down on my knees praying.

He did not raise his voice or wave his hands. He was not impassioned, the way you imagine healing preachers to be. The four of us held hands only at the end when we prayed for a few minutes. It was very matter-of-fact. And my tailbone did not feel any better when we left the Hyatt. I was still hurting, but something else felt good. I did not feel the urgency anymore that maybe I was doing something wrong. I realized it was in God's hands. I had always trusted God. I still trusted Him. And that made me feel immensely better.

I accepted the healing, knowing the pain would go away in God's time, and I thanked Him for it.

50

DADDY GIVES US A SCARE

I TOLD YOU THE MANDRELLS are stubborn. This will give you an idea. In March of 1975, I was playing some dates in Florida while worrying about Daddy back home in Nashville. He hadn't been feeling well, and he denied it to all of us, but I am Daddy's oldest daughter, and I know this man.

He was home at night and started having sharp pains. Momma, who keeps up on medical details, was worried it was a heart attack, and she began calling the doctor.

"Mary, I am fifty-one years old," Daddy said. "I know when I need a doctor. Hang up that phone."

Don't you love it? He's having chest pains, but he's in control.

The next morning, while Daddy was resting, Momma called Ken and told him about the pains the night before. She said, "Ken, Louise has all her stuff out here in the van, and I know Irby is going to unload it today."

She added, "I know it's his heart, but I can't get him to go to the doctor."

This is how things work in our family: Momma called Ken. Ken called me. And I called Daddy from Florida. I was due to go to England to play the Wembley Festival, and Daddy was supposed to join me.

I told Daddy, "I am not getting on that plane to England unless you go see a doctor. I'll cancel out."

On the other end of the phone, I could hear a flat, hard tone, like you hear from a police officer telling you to fish out your driver's license.

"You will go," he said. "You are contracted to do it, and you will go."

"No, sir, I will not get on that plane unless you go see a doctor."

This is what they call a standoff in western movies, two people covering each other, both ready to fire.

You put us in the same room and you can feel our wills butting up against each other. We will give each other these sideways stares—the Mandrell Look—and you can feel the electricity.

"No, ma'am, that's not the way it is."

"Excuse me, but that's how I remember it."

"Well, you remember it wrong."

There are times when I think I'm too close to my parents. I was a daddy's girl when I was growing up, and here I am crossing forty and I am still a daddy's girl. Maybe that's not a good thing, but I know I cannot help it. In a perfect world, every child ideally would be attached to her parents. But I'm not so sure I haven't gone overboard on my dependence on Momma as well as Daddy. Momma had gone through surgery back in 1973, and had terrible pain while she healed. I used to sit there and rub her back and brush her hair, trying not to show my sadness and also my fear.

The fact is, I cannot accept the idea of losing either my mother or my father. It gives me a cold shiver, and that was long before my nervous system was changed by the wreck. I mean, your parents are the most important people in your life. Fortunately, Momma never had another scare after that operation. Now we were worried about Daddy.

This wasn't the first time he had been sick. When he was forty-nine, he and Momma were sitting around the house when he experienced a sharp strangling feeling near his throat. He thought it was something minor, something he had eaten, and he stood up to go to the rest room, but he went down in a heap. Ronny Shaw happened to be there, and he started pounding Daddy on the back, assuming Daddy had swallowed something the wrong way. When Daddy woke up, Ronny had loosened Daddy's teeth and given him a black eye by batting him around.

For two years, Daddy thought he had nearly strangled, and that Ronny had dislodged a bit of food. It turned out that Ronny probably did save his life—but by kick-starting Daddy's heart rather than dislodging a food particle.

Now Daddy was having chest pains. And from my motel room in Florida, I threatened to cancel my dates in Europe if he did not go to the doctor. After all these years, Daddy knows when I am not bluffing.

"Okay, I'll go to the doctor," he said.

The doctor put him on a treadmill, checked the results, and ordered him to go directly to the hospital. Instead, Daddy went home to take care of a few business details.

He called me back that afternoon.

"Hi, Dad, how are you?"

"I'm fine," he said. "I have to have open heart surgery."

I rushed home to Nashville, only to find that Daddy had to wait a few days for the surgery. I could not imagine having to wait around a hospital for probably the most major surgery in your life, but Daddy was so incredibly brave.

As the days dragged on, Daddy would leave silly notes by his bed or on the door: PARTY FROM 9:00 UNTIL ??? BRING YOUR OWN BOOZE. The nurses used to come down the hall just to see his latest sign.

Daddy did not always have the good lines. One day he got into a conversation with a janitor who was about his age and had a friendly face.

"How're you feeling?" the man asked.

"I'm feeling pretty good," Daddy said.

"What are you in for?" the janitor asked.

"Heart surgery."

"I'll pray for you," the man said.

"I appreciate that," Daddy said, "but there's really not much to it. It's like pulling a tooth."

"Yessuh," the janitor said. "I know what they tell you. They only tell you about the ones that come out the front door. They don't tell you 'bout the ones they take out the back door."

On that encouraging note, Daddy had the operation on March 27. I vowed I would not leave for England until we knew the results of the operation. My flight out of Nashville was the day of the surgery. If I didn't make that flight, I would not be able to perform in London, but that wasn't important to me. I packed my bags and went to the hospital, where we all paced around the waiting room until the surgeon told us Daddy was coming out of surgery.

Everybody said Daddy would want me to go to London, so I literally went directly from the waiting room to the airport. But I vowed I would not get on the plane until I heard more news from the recovery room. People on the flight from Nashville to New York told me they knew Daddy was all right when they saw me smiling as I boarded the plane.

Now I can tell the legend of Daddy the patient. He had heard people groaning and moaning in the recovery room, and while he did not minimize the pain they were in, he made up his mind he was not going to be like that. So while he was being wheeled from the operating room to the recovery room, he noticed that the nurse pushing his cart was named Molly.

"Oh me, oh my, Miss Molly, I'm in love with you," Daddy started singing.

And while the cart was squeaking down the hallway, he switched to, "I'm Back in the Saddle Again." She hollered back, "My Lord, what have we got here?"

The nurses knew they had a live one. His first couple of days were rough. Don't forget, in this operation they saw your breastbone wide open and pull it back in vise grips while they operate on your heart. It takes a while for your system to recover. But before long, they were able to remove the tubes from Daddy's nose and throat, which meant he could talk again. A mixed blessing.

"Am I gonna be all right?" Daddy asked one nurse.

"Oh, yes, you're going to be fine," she said, getting suckered right in.

"Am I going to be able to play the piano?"

"Sure you are," she said.

"Great," Daddy replied. "I've always wanted to play the piano."

This is one of the world's oldest and worst jokes, but Daddy managed to pull it off one more time.

Of course, he was not exactly a model patient. They told him he could not have his beloved cigarettes in the hospital, but he reasoned they had not said anything specifically about cigars, so maybe they were a healthful substitute. His brother Al was a willing accomplice, bringing a full box of stinkers up to the room. The chief nurse got wind of the problem and confiscated the cigars and chewed Daddy out, which slowed him down for an hour or two.

We laughed about that while Daddy was mending. We were still laughing when Daddy came home from the hospital. He was tough. He went back on the road six days later.

About six weeks after the operation, Daddy went out to try to wash the bus before we went out to play a date outside Nashville. But he had to quit because his arms were hurting and he was sweating all over. Momma tried to talk him out of going out that night, but he insisted on going. She called Dr. Lovvorn after he left, and she was not surprised at what happened later.

We played the show and got back on the bus for the two-hour drive back home. We knew Daddy was hurting when he started popping the nitroglycerine pills. Then a few minutes later, Daddy told our driver: "Roll this thing!"

We wanted to get back to Baptist Hospital rather than some little hospital out in the country.

"Floor it!" I told the driver. "I'll pay for the speeding ticket."

We figured we wouldn't get but two or three miles down the interstate before a police car would stop us, and they would either put Daddy in the car, or call for an ambulance, or give us an escort all the way to Nashville. But wouldn't you know it, we didn't see a police car all the way to Nashville.

For two hours, Daddy put his head down at the table and just waited. We knew he was having a heart attack, in horrendous pain, but he wouldn't say a word until the bus rolled up to Baptist.

They unloaded Daddy, and ran him through the angiogram and the arteriogram again. Dr. Harris looked at the results on a large screen, not knowing that Daddy was watching.

"You know, Doc, I'd hate to be in your shoes," Daddy said.

"Why?"

"Well, I'd hate to have to tell a guy he's going to have to go through those bypasses again."

"Who told you?" the doctor blurted.

"Nobody, but I could see it on the screen," Daddy said. "It's all stopped up, like a little bit of muddy water getting into a bigger body of water and just swirling around a little."

The doctor said the bypass was not working, possibly because Daddy had been so active that he created scar tissue, adhesions, around the surgery.

So Daddy went back into surgery. Once again, they had to make a huge incision on the inside of the thigh, to take out a vein. Only, of course, they used the other leg. A couple of days after the operation, Daddy was in the intensive care unit and a young nurse was looking after him.

The bandage was low enough that you could see the top of the livid scar on his chest.

"Oh, your scar is looking good," the nurse said.

"Yeah, the doctor is trying something new with me," Daddy said, sensing he had found the right audience.

"The doctor believes that if you just set your mind to it, you can heal yourself. Even while I'm talking with you, I'm saying to myself, 'My leg is getting well, my leg is getting well.' Let me show you how it's working."

And he pulled down the covers and showed her the scar on his left leg, which was now six weeks old.

The young nurse was amazed at the healing only two days after the operation.

"Can I show some other nurses?" she asked.

"Why, sure," Daddy agreed.

She rounded up three other student nurses, who also inspected Daddy's "healing." This struck the chief nurse so funny that she had to duck down in her nursing station so nobody could see her laughing. When she was able to talk again, she said: "Let Mr. Mandrell show you his other leg," and the young nurses laughed, knowing they had been suckered.

They kept him in the hospital five weeks, making sure he did not develop adhesions this time around. Finally, he was getting so itchy to go back to work that they sent him home.

"I had that operation to live," he told us. "A lot of people have that operation to be an invalid, but I did it so I could get back to what I wanted to do."

We assumed he meant running the family business, but he added, "I want sausage, I want bacon and eggs, I want cigarettes. That's the reason I had the bypass. If I didn't want to live and enjoy life, I could have died without the bypass."

As soon as they turned him loose, he went right back to his pack a day, and all the food that wasn't good for him. We tried to lecture him, but he wouldn't listen. He's a Mandrell. He's my dad.

51
TO GRANDMOTHER'S HOUSE WE GO

EVERYBODY KEPT TELLING ME I ought to get out and do more, and I kept putting them off, but finally I found something I really wanted to do—complete the log cabin we were building for Ken's grandmother out in Washington State.

This was where Ken had been when I had the wreck—about eight miles from the Canadian border, out in the middle of nowhere. We go camping every summer, using the river for our refrigerator, building a toilet, so to speak, back in the woods, and just really roughing it. And we love that. It is so different from our regular working world. You see me gutting fish or digging a trench, dirt on my face, calluses on my hands, and you know I am country.

A couple of months earlier on our summer camping trip, I had gone for a walk with Ken's grandmother, who confided in me that her daughter was trying to talk her into moving into

Richland, where there would be more conveniences for somebody in her eighties. But Grandma liked it out in the woods. And she said she had always wanted to live in a log cabin, the way they did in the old days.

That night, Ken and I had talked it over and decided to build a log cabin for her—but a modern one in Richland, so her family wouldn't have to worry about whether she had light and heat. We talked it over with Ken's aunt and uncle, Martha and Jim Stifter, who thought it was a good idea, too.

We found a company that built very modern but rustic-looking log houses, fashioning the logs with chain saws, if you can believe that. We arranged for the house to be built, and Ken had closed the deal in the hours after learning of my accident, which had happened while I was out buying things for the house.

Somehow, we managed to keep the house a secret from Grandma. She never knew that Ken had been out there to arrange for a house for her.

By Thanksgiving, the cabin would be finished, and now I found some enthusiasm for finishing the job I had started. I stopped thinking so much about Barbara and started thinking about Grandma Johnson.

While I was still confined to my bed for much of the day, we flew in a woman from North Carolina who showed us what fabric and furniture could be ordered for Grandma's house. I did the selecting and ordering from my bed. A few weeks later, we heard it was arriving at the cabin. The old perfectionist in me was starting to assert herself. I wanted the cabin to be perfect when Grandma walked in. All she would have to do was bring her toiletry items and her clothes, and turn the key and there it would be ready. Even the groceries would all be there.

This was fun. This was a project. This was life. My mind was engaged for the first time. Barbara Mandrell still did not exist. She was somebody who had gone away. But this energetic little busybody, even lying on her back, could fuss over architect drawings and fabric samples and mail-order catalogues. This was great.

What wasn't so great was the moment when we had to get from Nashville to Washington State. What's the old saying, the spirit was willing but the flesh was weak? Not only my flesh was weak, but also my bones and my muscles and my lungs and my heart. I was in pitiful shape. Everything hurt.

Ken and I with my longtime producer Tom Collins (The Mandrell Family)

With Billy Sherrill in the studio (Ken Dudney)

With my lawyer Alan Siegel (The Mandrell Family)

Working on a new album at Sound Stage Studios, May 25, 1990, with James Stroud (left) and Jimmy Bowen, my producers (© 1990 Beth Gwinn)

I had a wonderful time when my girlfriend Minnie
Pearl was a guest on the TV show (Jimmy Wagner)

This is the wallet photo that gave birth to the
Barbara Mandrell and The Mandrell Sisters TV
show (Dennis Carney)

Jaime, who played young Irlene on the TV show, with one of her favorite aunts (Ric Boyer)

Jack Regas, who directed the TV show (The Mandrell Family)

Laughing with the four best brothers a girl could ever have — The Statlers (Courtesy Jim Owens Entertainment)

With Uncle Joe and Aunt Rose
Maphis, godparents to
Matthew (Ken Dudney)

With Newt and Janice Lovvorn, who are Jaime's
godparents (The Mandrell Family)

With Tim and Cathy Bucek, Nathan's godparents, at
the John Denver Celebrity Ski Race (The Mandrell
Family)

In 1983, performing a gospel song with Bobby Jones and New Life (Susan Osterhaut)

Accepting the 1981 Country Music Association Entertainer of the Year Award (the first person ever to win two years in a row!) (Ricky Rogers, Staff Photographer, *The Tennessean*)

With Norman Hamlet (3rd from left), who taught me steel guitar, and (from left to right) Gordon Terry, Merle Travis, and Joe Maphis, who gave me the chance to perform (The Mandrell Family)

Daddy and his daughters (Judy Mock)

Appearing with Lucille Ball on one of her television specials (The Mandrell Family)

Roy Rogers teaching me to trapshoot (Ken Dudney)

An "Officer and a Gentlewoman" on a Bob Hope television special (The Mandrell Family)

The Mandrell sisters congratulating a Special Olympics champion (The Mandrell Family)

When I went to spring training with the Los Angeles Dodgers, I took batting practice with Steve Yeager (Ken Dudney)

My dance partner Vince Paterson could make anyone look like Ginger Rogers!
(Ric Boyer)

With Lt. Col. D.L. (Boss) Smith, USAF
Thunderbirds (Official USAF Photo)

Ready to fly! (Official USAF Photo)

Flying with the Blue Angels—a Navy pilot
at last (Official Navy Photo)

Admiral Richard Macke and I, ready to fly an
F-18 and land on an aircraft carrier—my
dream of a lifetime! (Official Navy Photo)

Shaking hands with President Ronald Reagan
(Official White House Photo)

en and I with First Lady Barbara
ush (Official White House Photo)

With former First Lady Nancy Reagan
(JoAnn Berry)

We celebrated the Fourth of July during our annual Grandma Esther Johnson family reunion
(Martha Stifter)

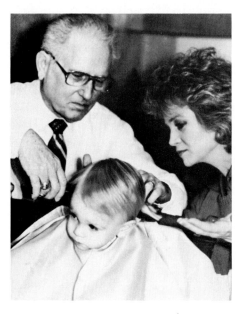

Uncle Ira was the first to cut Nathan's hair, just
as he did Matthew's (Ken Dudney)

Firefighters and police officers at the scene of the wreck (Official Photo, Hendersonville, Tennessee Police Department)

I did this public service poster on behalf of seatbelts — did you buckle up today? (Ric Boyer)

Please buckle up.

You may never get another chance.

"My children, Matt and Jaime, and I were not safety belt users. But minutes before this crash, we put them on. Experts tell us we'd have been killed without safety belts. I share this with you out of love. So please buckle up. You may never get another chance."

Barbara Mandrell

Barbara Mandrell

American Academy of Orthopaedic Surgeons   National Safety Council   United States Department of Transportation
National Highway Traffic Safety Administration

Matthew, Jaime, and Nathan with their other mother, Kathy
Brown Shannon (Ric Boyer)

The Do-Rites plus JoAnn and me in Las Vegas; back row: Doug Dimmel, Dino Pastin, Lonny
Hayes, Chris Walters, Mike Jones, Nick Uhrig; front row: Charlie Bundy, Barbara Mandrell,
JoAnn Berry, and Dave Salyer (Courtesy Bally's Casino, Las Vegas)

Irlene and Ric, with daughter Vanessa and son Deric (Ric Boyer)

R.C. and Louise with daughter Nicole (Ric Boyer)

My family today
(Ric Boyer)

Our home, Fontanel (Ken Dudney)

Mother and Daddy (Ric Boyer)

Somehow we got to the airport, me twitching in fear whenever another car came into view. Then I propped my leg up in the first-class section, but was still in torment all the way to Dallas.

If you've ever had to change planes in the new Dallas–Fort Worth airport, you know how far it can be from one gate to another. When we got there, Ken had arranged for a wheelchair and one of those electric carts to move me from one gate to another. I put up an argument, with the same strong temper I had developed since the wreck.

"I am not getting in a wheelchair," I snapped at Ken. "And I am not riding in one of those carts."

"But Barbara, it's twenty-three gates away," Ken reasoned.

"I don't care how far it is, I'm walking," I said.

"You can't walk that far."

"Yes I can."

"You're being unreasonable."

"Don't tell me that. Ken, we have time between our flights. And I am not going to have people looking at me and saying, 'Huh, she thinks she's better than us, hitching a ride in that cart while the rest of us have to walk.' "

"Barbara, you've been in an accident. Everybody knows that. You don't mind when you see somebody who is disabled getting a ride."

"That's different," I said.

We must have bickered for ten minutes before Ken said, "Look, we don't have all that time. Get in the cart."

So I did, complaining all the way.

When we landed in Washington, we then had to take one of those little commuter planes to Richland. I sat in the front seat, my leg straight out because I still couldn't bend it. By the time we got to Richland, I was just miserable, and the pain and the fatigue stayed with me for days. My tailbone was still hurting me and I couldn't sleep.

Ask Ken how I was on that trip and he'll tell you: "Hell on wheels." If he says so, I guess I was. I would tell the builders, "Put such and such over there," and they would try to explain to me why it couldn't be done, and I'd get mad at Ken, and he would have to take their part and explain it to me.

But at least the old energy was starting to kick in. I remember moving sacks of groceries into the pantry when I could barely balance myself. Would it have been better for Daddy and Ken to have said, "You can't run around doing this stuff"? Not really. The doctors said I couldn't do any harm to my body, and it would be better for my head to be out in the normal flow of life as quickly as possible. So everybody had to put up with one aching, cranky lady.

I was doing all right until the boxes arrived with the antiques I had bought the day of the wreck. I must admit, I got a knot in my stomach thinking about that woman bustling around the Antique Mall, pulling her two children in her wake, enjoying her one day at home. I envied that woman, with her energy and her painlessness, her happiness and her optimism. I did not know if she would ever come back.

But at least I had a project. We finished the house the day Grandma's daughter, Virginia, drove her over from Spokane. We met Grandma at the family house and Ken said, "Grandma, we want you to come with us now. We've got something we want to show you." Ken drove about a mile and a half up the gravel road, and he stopped on the rise, before you could see the house.

"Grandma, what you're about to see will belong to you for the rest of your life," Ken said.

She didn't know what we were up to, but then he drove up to this log house, with its three bedrooms and three baths, landscaping and underground sprinklers, not exactly a rural log cabin. We took her inside, showed her the furniture, the lace table spread, and she kept catching her breath and saying "Oh, my." She thought it was beautiful, but she had a hard time realizing that it belonged to her.

It's hard to change habits. Grandma loved the house, and Virginia and the rest of the family saw to it that she was comfortable in the log house through the cold Washington winters. But as soon as the snow melts, she's back to the family homestead again, ninety-one years old and content with the old ways. We'll always be glad we did it. It gave Grandma a warm place to live in the winter, and gave me something to take my mind off my pain.

52

AN OFFER WE
COULDN'T REFUSE

WITH OUR FAMILIES AND our careers keeping us busy, Louise
and Irlene and I kept promising we would ditch our husbands,
just temporarily, and spend a weekend together, telling stories
and laughing and playing with animals, like kids again.

We finally did start seeing more of each other, but it was not
exactly a vacation. It happened this way:

In October of 1979, I was honored as the Female Vocalist of
the Year by the Country Music Association.

When they called my name, I cried because this had been
one of my major goals as a performer. I also remember thinking,
"It's much more fun than watching somebody else win." I knew,
because I had been nominated three times and hadn't won.

Believe me, all nominees who don't win should be given an
Oscar. You smile and you applaud for your peers and life goes
on, and everybody says, "Isn't that great?" but deep down inside,

it's like falling off a big cliff. You hit the bottom. It's kind of like the Super Bowl. You talk about who won last year, but who did they play?

I have always said that I don't compete with anyone but me. But. There have been times when I have lost—and isn't that a terrible word, lost?—and I've played mental games with myself to soften the blow. I'd say, yeah, she did such-and-such, or yeah, he was so-and-so, but you cannot deny it's a competition. They lay it on the line. Who's the best?

Anyway, when they called my name, it was like a dam breaking.

Good things kept happening. That December, the three of us did a Christmas television special. People must have liked us together, because in the spring of 1980, I was voted the Female Artist by *Music City News,* and Louise and R.C. were both nominated for most promising vocalists, and the presenter was a beautiful young model named Irlene. The Mandrell sisters were together again.

That summer, Mike Douglas asked me to be the cohost of his show for a week. Daddy suggested that the three sisters appear together on one segment, me on steel, Irlene on drums, Louise on fiddle. We loved being together, and that feeling of closeness came across on television.

At the same time, a Hollywood producer named Marty Krofft had seen me on television and was trying to get people interested in me. At first, he didn't have much success, but then he found out I had sisters and thought that three Mandrells might be better than one.

Marty inquired if there was a photograph of the three of us. We had made a photograph for our parents, and Momma sent a wallet-sized copy to Marty, who started showing it to television people. Later, the three of us laughed and said we couldn't believe our gift would lead to a television career.

Marty is a very persuasive salesman. After the Douglas show, he invited two of the Mandrell sisters to lunch. He told Louise and Irlene that the three of us belonged together. And he knew the place. Network television.

Louise and Irlene thought that was a very interesting idea. They also knew that Daddy and I thought television was sudden death for singers.

"Barbara will never go for it," Louise told him, knowing that my next goal was to win Entertainer of the Year from the Country Music Association.

It may sound strange, but television has a way of inflating you and then letting the air out. Poof. Andy Warhol once said something about everybody being a celebrity for fifteen minutes. That's the television age. Traditionally in country music, you can last twenty years or longer, as long as you remember your fans. We did not want to jeopardize that.

We had seen great performers, great singers, be immensely popular on television but soon they weren't selling as many records as they used to do. Daddy and Tom Collins and I decided to kick it harder with records, to take advantage of my Female Vocalist Award.

"It's historical," says Jim Fogelsong, who has held my record contract for so many years. "If you turn on the TV and see this person, you're no longer that curious to hear the records. One thing they said about Elvis was that Colonel Tom Parker did not overexpose him."

Then there was the Bale-of-Hay theory. Whenever somebody from country music went on television, they'd get to the television studio and the prop manager would have you standing next to a bale of hay. I am not talking about *Hee Haw.* I'll make jokes in the cornfield on *Hee Haw* anytime because that's the appeal of that show—cornball, old-fashioned, goofus country.

I'm also not knocking bales of hay, but we were traveling with complicated electronic equipment, doing intricate Las Vegas–style shows, wearing designer outfits, and giving people a touch of everything, from country to gospel to blues to rock. I mean, I would slip a madrigal or a riff from classical guitar into my shows, and my fans would love it. We had control of my show—and we didn't have any bales of hay.

Marty Krofft persisted. He suggested that we, as they say in Hollywood, "take a meeting."

It was summertime and we had just bought our first boat and we were heavily into tooling around Old Hickory Lake. We told Marty, "Oh, sure, we'll be in California sometime in the fall. We'll give you a ring."

He said he happened to be coming through Nashville in a few days. He might even stop by Old Hickory Lake.

Marty and a network man found us at the marina. We talked. Daddy and I gave our reasons for not wanting to do television regularly. But they proposed doing six shows, with an option for the rest of the season.

I did not want to leave Nashville. But I could see two good reasons for trying television. Besides the money. First, it would be a challenge to see if we could entertain a broad television audience with its preconceptions about country music. And second, I tried to look at it from Louise and Irlene's point of view.

Louise was just discovering how much singing talent she had, and she always could fiddle like a dream. This girl was a late bloomer. I thought the television camera just might favor a gorgeous brunette.

Irlene was a talented drummer with a beautiful face and figure and a comic touch, and this would be a chance to broaden her skills. As Big Sister, I felt I might be selfish if I turned down six shows, so I said yes.

In October of 1980, all of our hard work paid off. I was named Entertainer of the Year at the Country Music Association Awards. This is absolutely the highest honor a country performer can win, because it says you are not just a singer, not just a musician, not just a personality, not just a voice on records, but an entertainer. You transcend all the categories.

Just look at the people who had won Entertainer of the Year before me: Eddy Arnold, Glen Campbell, Johnny Cash, Merle Haggard, Charley Pride, Loretta Lynn, Roy Clark, Charlie Rich, John Denver, Mel Tillis, Ronnie Milsap, Dolly Parton, and Willie Nelson—an all-star team of country music.

When they called my name, the floodgates opened. Later that night, I wanted everybody to ride this high with me, to stay up all night, saying, "Did you see so-and-so? Did you like such-and-such dress?" But finally everybody was tired, and I went to bed and Ken was already snoring, because he's on a totally different time schedule from me. I just didn't want the night to end.

I had just won the biggest award in my business. Our little excursion to Hollywood? It would be an interesting lark.

53
DADDY GIVES SOME ADVICE

WHEN WE GOT BACK from Washington, I started to settle back into lethargy again, blinds drawn, not seeing people, picking on Ken. But one person would not let me withdraw this time.

That was the one I love too much, the one I listen to—my dad. Up to now, he had been cautious about giving me too much advice. But now he started to pick up the tempo a bit.

"Look, just do a show," he began saying. "Don't let that car crash dictate to you that you're not going to do it anymore. Go back, face it, do it, and if you don't like it then, okay."

Everybody else had suggested that I try making a comeback, and I just shut them off. But I listened to Daddy. I argued with him. I fought him every step of the way. I exaggerated what he was suggesting.

"I will never go back on the road again," I said dramatically.

He was having none of it.

"Barbara, I agree with you. If you don't want to work dates again, don't work. I don't care if it's but one show, but you cannot retire from this business not knowing whether or not you could have done it."

He was smart. He was not appealing to my pride in being a performer. What he said to me was, "Don't let the wreck dictate that you are different in the head than you were. You decide."

Daddy knows, because I am just like him, that I am a person who must make the decisions.

But I was scared.

"What if I forget the lyrics?" I asked him.

This was a realistic fear, because a lot of things had been wiped out of my mind. I could not remember things I used to know. That woman on the records was another person to me. And then there was the physical part.

"What if I cannot stand up?"

He answered, "You can't retire with that doubt in your mind. You've got to prove to yourself that you are either capable of doing another show or you are not, that you didn't just quit."

We would go around and around about it. But Daddy and I are always disagreeing. I don't want to leave the impression that we get into fist fights or raging arguments, but we are so much alike that it is hard for either one to win.

Besides, he used to be much more pliable before I had the wreck. Of course, he says the same thing about me.

"Now it's harder to get her to change her mind, to see the other side of the picture," Daddy says these days.

My theory is, I have always been like him, and the wreck just matured me faster. I just got more like him.

He got me by talking about control. As I sat around the house during December, I began to think, "Maybe he's right. Somehow, some way, maybe I'll manage to do one more show."

54

FORTY MILLION PEOPLE

THREE DAYS AFTER WINNING Entertainer of the Year, I boarded a plane for California. Having been raised by Daddy to obey my elders, to say "Yes, sir" and "No, sir," I maintained the same well-behaved pose when I arrived in Hollywood. For at least fifteen minutes.

I went to Hollywood at a time in my life when I was ready to assert myself. Sure, I was confident from winning the top awards in my business, but it was more than that. I had been paying attention to my elders in show business for a quarter of a century. I was the least political woman you could imagine. Feminism, women's liberation, equal rights, they were just words to me. I was too busy working. But some part of it must have sunk in, because I got to Hollywood and I said, "Hey, I can do this."

I don't mean sing and play the steel guitar. I'd been doing that all my life. I meant ideas and direction and concept. I'd always been envious of Ken because he'd been an officer in the Navy. I watched the men learn to use their authority and I used to say, "Hey, I could be an officer, too." I got to Hollywood and it was as if somebody had commissioned me. You might call it a battle-field commission. There was a war raging once a week—the desperate struggle to put on a variety show. And since it had our name on it, I wanted it to be perfect.

Marty Krofft had a good vision of the three of us, the way we really were. They did not try to invent characters, turn us into the Beverly Hillbillies or the Gabor sisters. We were modern, Middle American women who happened to be in show business.

With due homage to Lucille Ball, that wonderful entertainer who recently passed away, our show was more like three Lucy Ricardos finally getting to do a show down at the club. Only our club was for country music.

The producers and the audience could see that Irlene is crazy like a fox, a beautiful girl with a squeak in her voice, the dumb blonde who can fool you into thinking she doesn't get the point.

It wasn't hard to figure out that Louise is taller, more volup-tuous, a kind of a thinker and dreamer, a balance between Big Sister and Kid Sister. And of course Louise could sing and play the fiddle.

By building up the two of them, it let me emerge as the bossy older sister who is the foil for all the visuals—the pie in the face, the exploding makeup kit, the electrified hair dryer. I was the starchy oldest child, the modern television image of a banker with the black stovepipe hat in the Sunday comics, the one everybody wanted to throw snowballs at.

But if I was the bossy one during the show, you should have seen me backstage. They may not have counted on that part, but it began right away. This show was really about us, so we figured, why not unpack our bags, physically and emotionally, and move in? Remember, we had been in show business all our lives. We had done Christmas shows in our living room when we were kids, when our parents were the only audience. We knew how to take over.

Out of self-preservation, all three of us began coming up with ideas for the show. It was about us. This is what we wanted. In many cases, because we had wonderful writers, I could come up with a small premise and they could find the right words, or we could tailor their ideas to fit ourselves.

Every week, there were decisions to be made. Nobody was saying, "Don't trouble your pretty little head about it. We'll tell you what's going to happen." They did not patronize me. But their openness brought out the officer in me. I was used to making decisions about our road show. This was no different. What songs would we sing this week? The opener? The closer? We had a segment called the Guitar Pull, where we played different instruments each week. Maybe we did Cajun music or western swing or rock 'n' roll. I would have a gut feeling about what worked best. I'd say, "Oh, we played guitar and saxophone last week. Let's do something different this week."

Some things they suggested were good and fine, but here I was, a newcomer, a beginner with my own network show, and I was Barbara with the big mouth. One thing I wanted every week was a gospel medley. Oh, no, they didn't want that. It was too religious. Too many people out there might not have the same religious point of view that we did.

But I argued, "We're not trying to convert anybody, but this show is about us, and this is part of our heritage. Besides, we're talking about music. There isn't anybody in America—Roman Catholic, Jewish, mainstream Protestant, holy roller, atheist, Moslem, Buddhist, Hindu, American Indian, you name it—who has not heard gospel music, who would not enjoy hearing people sing some old-fashioned hymns. People paid twenty dollars to hear the symphony orchestra and the choir and the soloists do *The Messiah*."

The difference seemed to be that television wants to appeal to the broadest possible audience, and its way is to blur the real differences in people. I maintained that nobody would be offended if we performed our kind of music—to entertain, not to proselytize. I stuck to my conviction, and it turned out that the mail was very favorable, that people enjoyed the gospel portion of our show.

We had to put our foot down in other areas. Or pull our necklines up, as the case may be. Sometimes they wanted our dresses cut lower than we wanted. I discovered that television has its own censors, to protect it from offending "the people" out there, but our tastes were even more conservative than the censors'.

There were double entendre jokes that were just not acceptable. When you see what's on television today, you might think, "Who were these girls worrying about offending?" but we were mostly worrying about offending ourselves. There were jokes that were not acceptable, because Barbara and Louise and Irlene were not playing characters, we were playing ourselves. We are three girls from a conservative, southern, Pentecostal background. We know how to have our fun, but our fun was not in off-color jokes. If television was going to present us as the Mandrell Sisters, it had to take the whole package.

This was a variety show, and I wanted control over the variety. This show was like a visit to our houses, into our lives. I wanted to invite people on the show that I might invite to my home. I did not want to make conversation with people I might not ever see in my real life. With very few exceptions, I selected our guests—for obvious reasons, so it would not become a carbon copy of another show.

The first show that went on the air featured Dolly Parton, one of the most talented women in show business and still a country girl from Sevierville, Tennessee. The second show featured Kenny Rogers, a great performer and songwriter, still country. And the next star was the great Bob Hope.

One of my later shows was built around Roy Rogers and Dale Evans. They were my all-time favorite western heroes. I'd go to the movies and watch Mister Rogers round up the bad guys without firing a shot or saying a mean word. Dale Evans was not just a pretty, decorative wife—she could ride a horse, she was part of the team. Later, I got to know them as model human beings, good friends. Can you believe that Roy Rogers took me trap-shooting? This was my show, my home away from home. I wanted them as my guests.

The writers and I came up with a skit with Mister Rogers wearing one of those all-white western suits and coming into this bar where everybody was standing around drinking—milk and soda pop, of course. Louise and Irlene were dressed in white, so naturally they were the good guys, the Mandrell Sisters. Dale Evans and I were wearing black suits, and we were the Evans Gang, and we were the bad guys.

Well, now, when was the last time you ever saw Dale Evans as the bad guy? Roy Rogers stood there singing a song while Dale and I were breaking chairs and throwing guys around. He never missed a beat even while the bar stools were flying. It was all choreographed by the incredible Scott Salmon in such a manner that we tore up the place and never touched Mister Rogers. We learned to use the guest in a different way, to come up with skits you had never seen anywhere else. And believe me, it wasn't easy coming up with that stuff.

While we were busy creating a show, we were also revamping three characters known as the Mandrell Sisters. They might not wear low-cut dresses or tell dirty jokes, but these three old dogs were going to learn a few new tricks. We were going to learn how to move.

It's funny, but I never thought about the way I moved. You just went onstage, you sang your songs, you played your instruments, and you walked off. I soon discovered there was an art to the way you moved your body.

Dancing? Sure, I liked to jitterbug, but nobody ever taught me any steps. I never had time because I was always busy working. But this was a variety show—and one of the varieties was dancing.

I had not thought about dancing until we started working on our first couple of shows. All of a sudden, he was *there,* a handsome guy with a very confident way of moving and a constant smile. Scott Salmon was a country boy from Oklahoma who had danced in New York and California and was now a choreographer for musical shows and movies, but he never forgot his Oklahoma roots. If you ask him, he'll tell you that the proudest moment in his career was being named to the Oklahoma Hall of Fame, an honor usually reserved for football running backs and oil millionaires, not dancers.

We came up with a skit in which Dolly and I were in a store after hours, looking at two mannequins, who of course were a couple of male dancers. While the Beatles song, "Can't Buy Me Love," was playing and we were singing, one of the mannequins moved just a little bit. Dolly and I did a double take, as if to ask, "What's wrong with this picture?" When we left, the two mannequins moved again, just slightly.

It was pretty subtle, and I kept saying, "I don't know if country music fans will accept this." But Scott told us to trust him that it would come across great on the television set, which it did.

That was how I learned you could do great things with just the right movement of your body. These three country girls now believed in choreography.

We had never danced a lick in our lives, but Scott Salmon,

bless his heart, took six left feet and taught us how to dance. Or at least it looked like dancing on television. The next week, Scott spent teaching us to clog dance. It's kind of a mixture of tap dancing and square dancing, with bright costumes. I've always enjoyed watching the great clog dancers perform at the Grand Ole Opry, and we'd talk backstage, but I never envisioned myself out there clog dancing. Well, that's exactly what Scott had in mind. He came up with a clog dance for the three girls, showing us a few moves. He laughs about it now, but after a few hours of practice, we got the flow of it and I wound up saying, "Okay, let's get us three male dancers and let's put on a real big production." As it turned out, that's exactly what Scott had in mind. I was all for it. Let's dance!

It was hard work. Every week we would work and sweat and throw ourselves around. I had bruises on different parts of my body that I did not even know existed. I got to where I was real proud of each bruise. Right bicep? Yeah, I got that from the lift where I had to swing around. Sore arches? Yeah, I got them from the clog dancing. Everything hurt, but I was enjoying discovering a little bit of grace and agility I'd never known before.

I had always enjoyed competing in sports. When I was a kid, I set a school record in the sprints, and I liked playing team sports, too, but I hadn't developed the physical side of my life because I was too busy making music. Now I was discovering how much I liked using my body again. We'd go in and stretch, do our warm-ups, turn on the music—rhythm and blues, rock 'n' roll, classical—and then Scott would come in and say, "All right, girls, here are our steps for this week."

That was another great part of the dancing—being part of a team. We had some great male partners, guys who had danced in Broadway stage shows and Hollywood television shows and movies, guys who knew every trick. I'd stand there and marvel and say, "Wow, I didn't know a human body could do all that."

And they were great guys. I'd never been around dancers. They were not the highest-paid performers in the world, their careers could be over with a torn muscle or losing the bounce in their step, and they had to perform lugging and twirling three absolute novices. They also had a funny, fierce competitive side—and they loved being in front of the camera. We got along tremendously.

Among the guys I worked with were Vince Paterson, my

personal partner for two years on the show, Joey Sheck, Ken Grant, and Steve LaChance, a former state wrestling champion who was such a hunk that the girls used to stand in line to dance with him. And then there was Charles Ward, who had a big role in the John Travolta movie *Stayin' Alive,* a beautiful, talented guy who has since died. What a loss to all of us.

We also had female dancers on the show, and I was always asking them questions. To me, dancers are the most giving people in show business. Or at least they were with me. The way I saw it, my job was to learn from them, to not mess them up. If we were rehearsing something, I could not expect them to follow me. I would always ask them, "How does that work for you?" And they would tell me.

Working with people like these, I looked forward to the dancing as a highlight of the week. It was new, it was different, and it was fun. I could feel myself growing and changing, too.

When we first started, I was very nervous about some of the costumes. I would not wear a low-cut gown because I didn't believe a woman should be showing too much of her body, so when they put me in leotards and tights and shorts cut all the way up to here, I would say, "Scott, I am not going out to rehearsal in *that*!"

My two sisters didn't seem to mind wearing these form-fitting shorts or tights, but I was very self-conscious. I always took pride in my legs, enjoyed running around in tennis shorts or track shorts, but these shorts were . . . short.

The first couple of weeks, whenever I went out to rehearsal, I would pull the leotards down as long as they would go, so they wouldn't cut high like a swimsuit. I was so modest. I'd walk by my sisters and pull down their leotards, too, trying to cover up some more of them too.

I was also worried what Ken would think about me strutting around in dance clothes and being touched by male partners, but when I brought it up to him, he laughed. I had almost forgotten that he had taken up ballet to exercise his arthritic feet. Of course, I had not forgotten that he used to be engaged to that beautiful ballerina. Funny how some things stick in your mind. Anyway, Ken told me, "Barbara, dancing is not like dating or being married. When I used to lift a woman, you didn't think about where you were touching her except if you were getting the step right. You're so nervous about performing that nothing else matters."

At first I thought, "Ken, you're so full of it," but I soon

discovered he was telling the truth. After a few weeks, I was running around in tight clothes and being guided and held and lifted by these incredible male dancers. Little Miss Prude here was touched all over, and guess what? I found out you really don't think about it.

The dancing lessons influenced the way we did the show, the way we strutted our stuff. Scott could turn an ordinary skit into a laugher.

There was another benefit to having my own show: I could live out my fantasies, particularly the one about being a backup singer for Gladys Knight. That's right. For one brief and shining hour, I was a Pip.

Before Gladys came to rehearsals, Scott made videotapes of the Pips, front and back, and I imitated the way they danced while they were singing. So when it was time for rehearsal, I had it down perfectly. Or so I thought. But after one run-through, Scott said to me, "Barbara, it isn't funny because you *are* one of the Pips." I was doing exactly what they were doing. So Scott came up with other things so I was not quite in sync with them. I'd be a step behind, looking from side to side, trying to keep the rhythm. And Gladys would catch me putting out the wrong foot.

Her line was: "Oh, great, the Pips and one Pipsqueak."

(From that show, I got to be such a friend and admirer of Gladys. Just recently she was closing in Las Vegas on the same night that Louise was opening. I found it out while changing planes in Dallas, and I called Gladys in Vegas and I said, "You know, you're my sister and I'm coming to see you, and Louise is my sister, and she's ticked off." I caught Louise the next night.)

The television show was hectic from the first. I realized that I couldn't get it all done in the hours they had described to me. According to Scott, television stars often come in to work at eleven and go home at four. We were trying to come in at ten and go home at six or seven, but even that wasn't working.

Scott would say, "Well, if you want to put that dance number in, you'll have to come in at nine."

So I would say, "What about eight?"

Scott found out we worked hard on the road, too. During the summer break from television, he thought he'd take a short bus trip with me and the Do-Rites through the South. After a few days of one-night shows and all-night bus rides, Scott was relaxing with a book, when all of a sudden . . . But let him tell it:

"I look up," Scott still recalls, "and I realize we are driving into the yard of the Mississippi State Penitentiary, where she is doing a free show. And this was going to be a tough audience, because the black guys were up in front watching this blonde country singer, and they were saying, 'Show me.' She opened with a soul number and you could see them relax and say, 'Hey, this is all right.' After the show, she walked into the crowd and started hugging guys and shaking hands, and the guards were going crazy. Oh, yes. That night, she took us to a baseball game at Atlanta."

Funny thing. Scott hasn't asked to come along on any bus rides recently. He meets me for a night or two in Las Vegas.

The television show was frantic, too. We would be writing the introductions as I came rolling down the stairs from my dressing room, making it up on the spot the way the three of us used to do shows around the house. And the spontaneity, the fun of it, seemed to be catching. People were watching us. Millions of people.

You'd play the Opry or a music hall and be seen by two thousand people, or maybe you'd play an arena and be seen by fifteen thousand people and think it was the biggest crowd in the world. Television measures its audience in millions.

At one point we were told there were forty million viewers watching us. It is a figure you tend to remember—one-sixth of the country at times. Some of them were country folks, some of them city, white, black, Hispanic, Oriental, you name it. We were three country girls and people were watching us all over the country.

We used to imagine all our fans together on one couch, dipping into one big bowl of popcorn, all of them laughing at the same joke, all forty million running to the bathroom during the same commercial.

After a few weeks, we were informed that our show was a big success. Ratings were high, sponsorship was rolling in, and our contract was being extended for the full season. So we tried making it better.

Somewhere during the first year, they brought in a new director, a former dancer and choreographer named Jack Regas, who had a great feel for making music and dance come to life.

After Jack had been with the show one week, Janice, a girl-friend of mine who doesn't know anything about the business, asked me, "Are they spending more money on your show?" I asked her what she meant and she said things just looked more expensive. I said, "The only change we have is a new director named Jack Regas." He made that big a difference. Later he gave me a book about Hollywood movies, and he was in some of the photographs, dancing in some of those great musicals.

There was something else special about Jack. Louise and Ir-lene and I used to pray before every taping, to ask God to help us to be as good as we could be. The first week he was doing the show, Jack, who is a Mormon, saw us praying, and from then on there were four of us praying every time we went to work.

We also could not have done the show without my record producer from Nashville, Tom Collins, who used to fly out every Wednesday and stay up all night mixing the instrumentation that would go behind our live performance on the show. He knew what worked for me, and he had a good feel for television, too. He'd do a brutal workload in forty-eight hours and be back home in Music City on Saturday.

You never saw the names Rahn McDowell and Bobbe Joy on my television credits, but you're seeing them now. They were the personal hairstylist and makeup person for Irlene, Louise, and me. Without them we were just three little girls standing around looking for tickets to the show.

They could not receive credit for the show because they did not belong to unions. I had to hire them personally, and they could not even walk on the set, so they would sit up in my dressing room and Louise, Irlene, and I would have to rush back there whenever we needed emergency road repairs.

Our dressing room was the hub of our California operation at the old Gower Studio on Sunset Boulevard. It was interesting because other shows were going on there, and you never knew who you'd bump into. One day I was wolfing down a piece of fried chicken on our five-minute lunch break, and I heard this voice behind me saying, "Oh, you really shouldn't eat that." The voice was so recognizable, and I turned around to see Richard Simmons, the fitness and nutrition expert.

When we first arrived in Hollywood, they had the three of

us in separate dressing rooms, but we felt it was important that we be together, so we used the largest room for all three of us, and we used one of the others for all our costumes.

To tell you the truth, the bathroom was our business office, just the way the bathroom at the old Ryman Auditorium used to be the meeting place for all the women at the Opry. While I was being made up, Jack Regas would literally sit down on the cover to the toilet and talk over the next skit with me. Or if we had visiting dignitaries like Jim Fogelsong from my record company, he would just have to "pull up a chair" and talk business. On the Mandrell Sisters show, we practiced togetherness.

Part of our extended family was Rahn McDow, who had been doing my hair for as long as I had been coming out to California. He did everything for me—album covers, publicity photos, magazine covers, concerts, studio shows. When I crossed the Rockies, his radar would go off and he would be ready. He was an incredibly warm and capable human being, and it absolutely tore me up a few years ago when he died of lung cancer.

Bobbe Joy has been my close friend almost from the first moment we met. I say "almost" because it took a few minutes for these two tough women to size each other up. The first time we met back in the late Seventies, my record company wanted me to do an album cover on the beach up in Malibu. I'm something of a control freak, so I used to do my own hair and makeup, figuring that if there was something minor wrong at the site, somebody could touch me up. They told me that the company was sending a hairstylist and makeup person and I figured, "Well, they're paying for it but I still have final approval."

When we got to this borrowed beach house, the hairstylist was a very nice Oriental guy, but the makeup person was real bossy. And you know, if there's one thing I cannot stand, it is a bossy woman.

The first thing she did was hand me cleansing cream and say, "Take it all off." What am I, a stripper? Here I'd spent all this time and she said, "I want it clean." In my head, I was thinking, If I don't like the way this comes out, she's gone. She wouldn't even let me sit in front of a mirror at this beach house. She would not let me look. I had worn false eyelashes forever, but she said, "You don't need them." She was polite, but definitely in charge. Next, she plucked my eyebrows, which I did not do very often.

The whole time I was worrying, "Oh, boy, this is going to be terrible," but then I looked in the mirror and I thought, "Wow, who is this gorgeous person?"

For more than a decade now, there has not been a time that I did not use Bobbe for a television show or commercial when I was in California. Sometimes she would come to Nashville or Chicago or New York just to make sure I looked right. And if she cannot make it, I do my face myself. We have also become the best of friends. I've gotten to know her husband, Mitch Dawson, and watched her kids grow. One thing I learned from the first time we met: I get straight answers from Bobbe Joy.

As we prepared for a full season in California, we developed our routine:

On Monday, Scott would work on the dancing and staging.

On Tuesday, we would spend most of the day with Scott, and during the lunch break we would see Bill Hargate, our costume designer, so our costumes would be ready for Thursday.

On Wednesday night, we would go into a recording studio and lay down the music tracks, sometimes until the wee hours of the morning. After a while, I arranged for my tour bus to be parked right behind the studio in a pretty rough section of downtown Hollywood, but Ken stayed with me most of the time, and let's put it this way: I had plenty of protection.

On Thursday, we would try on the costumes, go over the skits, rehearse the songs, and tape some of the show.

On Friday, we would have our live audience and finish the taping.

Sunday morning, it would start all over again, with me thinking, "Oh, my, what are we going to do next week?" R.C. would visit the house then and we would plan future shows.

I was learning how that business worked, watching people come up with unbelievable solutions. I learned that if you work with great people, you can ask for the moon and they will give it to you.

It got to be a case of can-you-top-this? I truly believed there was nothing we could not do, so it opened up my own creativity.

Scott Salmon will never forget coming to work one Monday morning and receiving a message saying, "Can you see me first thing in the morning?" When he found me, I thrust a ripped brown paper grocery bag at him and asked, "Scott, can we do this?"

Just lying in bed the night before, I had concocted an idea for me and Louise and Irlene and the dancers to go through many different styles of dance in one number called "Dancing Cheek-to-Cheek." I figured we could shift from country-western to Charleston to tango to waltz to disco, with appropriate changes in clothing, hair style, and makeup. Now it was up to Scott and the music director to make it work. I had utmost faith in them. Sure enough, it took a day and a half but they came up with it.

Poor Marty Krofft was about to have a hemorrhage, looking at me and Scott as if to say, "What are you doing with my money?" But he got over it. A year later, Scott gave me a Christmas present: He took that brown paper bag with my scribbling all over it and had it framed, with a nice title underneath, and now it's in my museum in Nashville.

I knew the show was catching on when I started receiving letters from places like New York and Chicago and Los Angeles, often from people who said, "I never loved country music before, but now I do because of your show." We were breaking down the stereotypes, proving that there really were no hard borders between different kinds of music.

This was the single most educational thing I had done. I learned to never say never about what I could do. Just a few months before, I had thought of myself as an entertainer, but now I was learning my sisters and I had a creative side. We could put things together in ways we'd never have thought. There were sides to me I hadn't known.

One thing I loved was imitating some of the women I had admired in show business, like Minnie Pearl, that great talent, and Phyllis Diller with that raucous laugh of hers. We did a skit where I pretended to be Phyllis Diller onstage and the real one walked out behind me. Scott said I did things with my body, with pantomime, that reminded him of little things Mary Tyler Moore used to do on her old shows. You know, the signature way she tossed her beret in the air, or poked through a meat counter at the supermarket. But she had a dancer's way of drawing the camera, and Scott kept telling me I had that quality, too, that I didn't know where all this could take me.

I hope this doesn't sound like bragging, but I think we expanded the parameters of what country women could do. When my friends like Dolly Parton and Dottie West saw me dancing on that show, they would say, "Wow, I wish I could do that." My point was, we could. We were not just duded-up women who sang and played guitar. We had more ability than we knew.

One thing I did not want was to let the television show put a distance between me and Nashville. We had seen it happen a couple of times where somebody went out to Hollywood and word would filter back to the Opry that the person had changed. That would not happen with me. I made sure that I still kept some dates at the Opry. Normally, I would show up an hour early just to give me a cushion of time, but now I went there an extra hour early, just to say hello to my friends, to let them know I missed them. I have been guilty of pre-judging other people, and I did not want anybody pre-judging me. To me, the Opry was the mother church, and I wanted to keep my friends in the church.

By the same token, I was very proud of our show. I kept the tapes of the show, but for a long time I didn't watch them. When Nathan started getting older, I would put them in the VCR to amuse him. It was wild. He knew the three of us as Mommy, Aunt Irlene, and Aunt Louise, but suddenly he realized we were also the Mandrell Sisters, doing things a little kid could relate to—laughing, singing, falling down, playing stunts on each other, wearing goofy costumes.

Just in the past few years, watching those old tapes, I have been able to look at the show with a sense of objectivity and say, "Hey, I'm proud. We did a good job." But of course the show had its price. It was costing more time and energy than I had ever bargained for. We were spending fourteen to sixteen hours a day, seven days a week. And my body was starting to feel it.

55

OUR WINTER VACATION

AT CHRISTMAS OF 1984 IT WAS time to go to Aspen, Colorado, where we've been going every December since 1978. Ken had gotten me started skiing, and we had bought a two-bedroom condominium in Snowmass. I had come to love our annual winter vacation, snuggling into the small apartment, just the four of us, and meeting friends out on the slopes.

Among our skiing friends are Ralph and Joy Emery from Nashville. Wanting to repay Ralph for all the kindnesses he had shown me over the years, I had taken him skiing for the first time a few years earlier. He needed a hernia operation at the time, and skiing didn't come easily.

He had seemed to be almost in tears when I saw him in the lodge. Cold weather and falling down and crowds and frustration will do that to you the first time you ski.

"Don't ever tell anybody you know me, let alone claim that you're a friend of mine," he had said, two-thirds in jest.

I couldn't bear to see Ralph unhappy with skiing, so I said, "I'll take you down the bunny slope." We got up this bunny slope and I skied right behind him, like a coach, saying things like, "Push to the left." "Be aggressive." "You're doing great, Ralph."

He had seemed to be getting the hang of it, so I had taken him up a bigger hill. Suddenly, I needed a bathroom back at the lodge, so I shouted out to him, "That's it, you've got it," and I took off down the hill. Well, he made it down fine, and he and Joy and their boys are now magnificent skiers. In fact, our lives are so busy that the only time we really spend together is at Aspen during the Christmas holidays.

This year, of course, there would be no skiing for me. I stayed in my room and lay down on the couch, just aching. Daddy's pep talk about making a comeback seemed as distant as the moon.

People had said, "Boy, it's going to be hard for you the way you love skiing to watch these people ski when all you can do is lie there." But you know what? I didn't miss it at all, didn't care about the skiing, didn't care about any of it.

When you hurt, you just lose interest in life around you. I never realized just how much you lose when you're in pain. When I used to see somebody in a wheelchair or on crutches, I would feel sorry for that person just as any fellow human being would. But now I really care, because now I know.

Since my regular therapist was back in Nashville, I enlisted Matthew, who was fourteen and strong from his hockey and tae kwon do, to perform my exercises with me.

"No matter what I say or do, you are the therapist," I told him. "Don't listen to me. You've been taught what to do. Don't let me talk you out of it."

He was wonderful. Strong and forceful and just a little bit mean. You have to be, to make somebody sit still for all those painful exercises. Ken attempted it, but he was not as good as Matt.

Isn't that funny? Back when I was hurt in the hospital, Ken had been the one who could push me. But by now he had seen me bear so much pain, and he had been the target of my tirades so often, that I think he just didn't want any more trouble.

Maybe it's wishful thinking on my part, being the wife, romantic and all, but I think Ken just didn't want to hurt me.

My teenage son, however, perhaps thinking of all the things Momma had said when he was hurting, and given the license to be tough, had no problem pushing my leg as far as it would go. And farther.

Another thing that made it tough for me being in Aspen was that I couldn't cook. Normally, I cook like crazy out there—great big meals for hungry people who have been out on the slopes all day. This time I couldn't do anything except lie on the couch and hurt and look out the window at the slopes and watch people ski by.

All I knew was that I was lying there hurting. I just wanted to get through each day and then maybe I could get through the night. I did not miss any of the things that used to mean so much to me. And I do mean any.

But God knows, and we don't. On the night of December twenty-third, the children went out to a party at somebody else's house a mile or two away. Ken drove them and promised to pick them up later. He came back to our little apartment, and he lit a fire, and he rubbed my back and he hugged me and told me he loved me.

This is a man who had comforted me through three months of pain, while I had snapped and screamed at him. Another man might have walked out or gotten himself a girlfriend, and a lot of people might have said, "Well, that's life. . . ."

When he hugged me in front of the fireplace, I got the idea there might be a way of letting him know how much I loved him. We had not been together as man and wife since before the accident, and it wasn't easy, and it certainly hurt, but when you love a man, you want to be with him.

Later that night, kind of offhand, I said to Ken, "When I get back to Nashville, I'd better see Newt and get another IUD put in. I can't take care of myself right now, let alone a baby."

56

THE OTHER
MOTHER

WHEN PEOPLE GET NOSTALGIC about the television show, they talk about the three Mandrell sisters, but there would not have been a show without a fourth woman who never got her name in the credits.

Her name was Kathy Brown—Kathy Brown Shannon now. She was married in 1988 and gave us one more year of her life before devoting more time to being a married woman. Without her help for the past ten years, there would have been no career. I wish every working wife could have somebody like Kathy back home. Even though Ken has been great about taking on more roles at home than most men ever do, we both need somebody to watch the kids.

Taking nothing away from Momma, Louise, and Irlene, Kathy has been our kids' second mother. Nathaniel calls Kathy's parents Nanny and Grand-Daddy, an extra set of grandparents for him. Kathy's mother is an artist who carves beautiful artifacts for us and paints attractive signs for birthday parties and other family gatherings.

Kathy became part of the family. Even though Matthew is a college man now, and she's only ten years older than he is, she doesn't hesitate to set him straight when he needs it.

We found Kathy in 1979 when we needed a full-time assistant for me so I could stay on the road and not worry about our two children. My mother-in-law went to the high school in Hendersonville and got a list of girls taking a child-care program, and we called Beverly Bandy. She was terrific, but she wanted to go to college, so she didn't stay with us too long. We asked her to recommend somebody, and she told us about the second girl on our list, Kathy Brown. Looks like we did it alphabetically, but it turned out great.

Kathy was just out of high school, working as a telephone operator at a department store, a sweet girl who had grown up around Nashville. She came from a nice family and was still living at home, and I'm sure they must have had some misgivings about her going to work with somebody in show business, with the hours and the travel and the demands. I interviewed her and I thought she was young, green, but I said to her: "Try it for three months, and if it doesn't work out for you, or for us, we'll know by then." Three months turned into ten years.

Any working mother can appreciate what Kathy meant to my family and my career. She took care of the kids, she did most of the shopping, she watched the house, she took the children to extracurricular activities—she was like an extension of me.

When she started, Kathy's job was to be on call twenty-four hours a day. I told her, "I may have to go on the road at three in the morning, so keep your bags packed." I wanted to bring Jaime with me since she was not in school yet, so Kathy would watch her in the hotel while I was working. Or sometimes we'd leave her home with Matt and Jaime.

There was never one time that she let us down. Any working mother will tell you that she lives in dread of having to rush home from work to solve a domestic problem. I hear the stories. A baby-sitter quits in the middle of the day and a stockbroker has to leave her office and rush home. A baby-sitter doesn't come back at lunchtime and a child is locked out of her home, and a police officer calls the mother at work. Or worse. Neighbors hear children crying because they are terrorized by a baby-sitter. People are just starting to face up to cases of child abuse.

We got the opposite. We found somebody who would take responsibility, who would raise the children the way we wanted. If I wanted my children to say "Yes, sir" and "Yes, ma'am," Kathy made sure they said it.

We also signed a piece of paper giving Kathy the legal right to make medical decisions about the kids. It's happened a few times that she had to take them to a doctor or a hospital because of a fever or something, and we trusted her to make the right decision.

I always hated it when I came home from the road and heard Ken or Kathy talking about something the kids had done for the first time while I was away. I wanted Jaime to travel with me when she was young, the way Matt had done, so Kathy started to go on the road with us.

She had never traveled much, and hadn't been to many hotels and restaurants, and I can still remember her asking, in that sweet Tennessee accent, "Barbara, what is this soup du jour like?" Her parents worried when she would leave a string of motel phone numbers where she would be for the next few weeks. She would travel on the bus with us, sleeping in a bunk alongside seven or eight male musicians, and Kathy said, "They were my brothers. They made sure I was safe wherever we went."

It was another jolt when we asked her to come to California with us. She had to adjust to another way of life. She would go shopping and people would say, "Would you talk to us? We love to hear your accent." She would blush deep red when they said that, but she never told us until later, and she never backed off from doing the shopping.

The first week we were in Beverly Hills, Ken tossed her a thick atlas with the map of every section of Los Angeles. "The only way you're going to learn to drive around here is to do it by yourself," he told her.

She would keep that book open on the seat beside her and navigate her way all over the area, which can be pretty formidable to country people from Nashville. And we put a lot of demands on her. Tae kwon do lessons for Matt, dance lessons for Jaime, shopping, pick somebody up at the studio. She had to know L.A. better than the rest of us.

"The worst was when I was taking Matt to an ice hockey game in Encino," Kathy recalls. "I kept driving and didn't see it, and finally I asked somebody where I was and they said Oxnard. I was almost fifty miles out of the way. I had made a wrong turn and just kept going. Driving back, I was crying and saying, 'Matt, I'm sorry, I made you miss the game,' and he said, 'That's okay, Kathy, that's okay.' But Ken was right. I did learn to get around L.A."

Her job did have its moments. She'll never forget the time I told her to dress up because we were going to a party at the house of Patrick Duffy, the actor. She looked so pretty as she mingled with everybody, and of course I introduced her as "my friend Kathy." She told me later how proud she was to go with us.

It wasn't easy for her because she had her own ways. As long as she traveled with us, she never smoked, and there is no way she could be comfortable around all the smokers in our group. Also, as long as she's been around show business, she is a morning person, a daylight person. She loves to open the blinds and let the sunlight in. At home I'm up by eight o'clock, but on the road my little children and I have become night people. It takes me hours to wind down after a show, and I am used to sleeping in a darkened motel room until noon.

If Kathy and I were sharing a room with Jaime when she was young, or Nathaniel when he came along, Kathy would sometimes go into the tiny bathroom of a Holiday Inn room and read until the baby woke up. Those hours were totally against her own internal time clock, but she was never sulky about it. I hope I was as considerate of her in other ways as she has been of me.

She hated that old haunted house on Rodeo Drive we rented the first year. We all hated it. But she put up with it, even when Ken and I stayed in the bus at the studio overnight. We knew she was there for us, and she was there for me when I came home from the hospital after the wreck. I promised I would be there for her someday when she needed me.

In 1988, Kathy was planning her wedding to Robert Stanton Shannon, who is a pharmacist and also passed the bar to practice law. He is also the brother of our veterinarian.

"Kathy, you're the only woman I know who has three children

and deserves to wear a white wedding gown," I told her, because to me she is like a saint.

With her large number of girlfriends, Kathy paid me the huge honor of asking me to be the matron of honor at her wedding on November 17, 1988. Some matron of honor. We got up to the altar and I was sweating and shaking so badly that I thought she was going to have to calm me down. I bent down to straighten out her train, and she whispered "The ring" and I gave her a blank look. She and I had forgotten the dad-gum ring back in the vestibule.

Quick as a flash, the minister whipped his wedding ring off his finger and handed it to me. I palmed it and presented it to Kathy, and nobody was the wiser for it. My one job, and I blew it. And after all the times she had bailed me out.

I tried to give her more free time once she was married, but it was hard. I depended on her so much. We talked girl talk, and I told her it's good to have a year or two by yourselves before you have children.

Kathy finally resigned at the end of 1989, and I can only be grateful she lasted so long, so faithfully, so skillfully.

We were fortunate to find Jill Stowe, a young woman from Olney, Texas, who had been a special-education major, working with Down's Syndrome children. Jill is a born teacher who listens to children. She's also as sweet and young and innocent as Kathy was when she came to us. We've been blessed to find two women like them to help care for our growing family.

57
It Must Be Allergies

WHEN WE GOT BACK to Nashville after Christmas of 1984, I still had all the pains from the accident. But now I had another problem. I was dizzy and I was losing my appetite.

"I can't stand the smell of my dogs or cats," I told Kathy.

You have to remember, I'd been living with them in my bed for the previous three months, feeding them off my plate, snuggling up with them. Until I went to Aspen, they were extremely familiar smells. Now I was getting sick just being in the room with them.

"I must be developing allergies," I said. "The animals never bothered me before."

As soon as I told Kathy that, I could see her eyes widen.

"Oh, no. I can't believe it," she thought to herself. But she was too discreet to say anything to me at the time.

I didn't even think of mentioning my queasiness when I

went to see the neurosurgeon. All I could think about was the constant slashing pain in my tailbone. The neurosurgeon said, "I want you to see your gynecologist. Sometimes, a tremendous impact like this can force a woman's system out of shape. Maybe there's something inside that's having some bearing on your tailbone."

I went directly from the neurosurgeon to Dr. Lovvorn, figuring I could get another IUD at the same time. He examined me and said, "Barbara, it's one of two things: you're either pregnant or you have a tumor."

A third child was not exactly on our list of priorities. Not since the wreck. A year earlier, I had been crying to have a third child.

When women reach the age of thirty-five, they begin to talk about the biological clock ticking away. Mine was not just ticking; it was clanging like a two-dollar alarm clock. When I turned thirty-five at Christmas 1983, I had wanted to have another child with as much intensity as I had ever felt about anything.

I would see Matthew and Jaime head out for school in the morning, and the house would seem quiet. I couldn't take them on trips anymore because they were getting into the upper grades, playing sports, having their own set of friends. I loved the days when they were little, when I could feed them and play with them and tuck them into bed. No matter what I had done in show business, raising the two children seemed like the most exciting thing I had ever done.

Ever since Jaime was six years old, I had been raising the subject of a third child with Ken. He believed that we had the perfect family already—a son and a daughter, both healthy, both happy. I kept asking him, and finally in April of 1984 I talked him into it.

"You're not just doing this for me, are you?" I asked, and he assured me, no, he was convinced we should have another child.

At first, I couldn't tell if he really believed it, but I took him at his word and I went to the doctor to have the IUD removed. And every month, when I found out I wasn't pregnant, I would start to cry.

It had been easy getting pregnant with Matthew and Jaime, but now nothing was happening. I didn't want to go far past thirty-five to have another baby because it gets a little more tricky the older the mother is. And I wanted another child as soon as possible. Wanted the feeling of being pregnant, of life stirring inside, wanted the feeling of caring for an infant, the smiles, the cries, the looks, the sounds.

That whole summer of 1984, unable to get pregnant, I had been feeling extremely maternal. I'd fuss over the kids' home-work, do chores at home, not for publicity in a women's maga-zine, but because it felt good for me, for Barbara. I still loved being Mrs. Kenneth Dudney, just as I used to write on my note-pad back in high school.

It was that maternal drive that had propelled me home in September of 1984. There wasn't any way I was going to get pregnant, not with Ken out in Washington State, but I could give the kids twenty-four hours of attention, a day of normalcy, could hug them and listen to them.

Now I was injured, cranky, hurting, retired, and just possi-bly pregnant.

"I can't take care of me. How can I take care of a baby?" I asked Ken.

Given a choice between a baby and a tumor, however, we knew which one we would prefer. Ken and I waited in the doc-tor's office while they were evaluating the pregnancy test.

"It's positive," the nurse said, sticking her head in the of-fice.

I hate to sound ignorant, but I am at times, and I didn't know what she meant by positive. Positive I had a tumor? Posi-tive I was pregnant? Besides, I couldn't be pregnant, not from a few moments by the fireplace. I was hurtin'. I had enormously mixed emotions. Being pregnant was last year's desire. All I wanted now was for the pain to stop.

Ken explained to me what positive meant and then Dr. Lovvorn asked, "How do you feel about it?" I said I was scared. I had just so many reasons to be scared. I was on muscle relax-ant and Darvocet. I had just left having my tailbone x-rayed, which is not a great idea for a pregnant woman. In fact, Dr. Lovvorn shared with me many months later that he had been very scared.

At first, he said he wanted to do an ultrasound, and then he said we would do an amniocentesis.

"Isn't that to tell if the baby is retarded?" I asked, and he said yes. Ken and I agreed that even if we found out the baby was retarded, we would still want the baby.

"Fine, we won't do the test," Dr. Lovvorn said. I know him as a friend as well as a doctor, and I knew that our reaction pleased Newt, my friend, as much as it pleased Dr. Lovvorn, my doctor.

Shortly thereafter, we went over and took an ultrasound, and it turned out that Dr. Lovvorn was right on both counts. Not only was I pregnant, but I also had fibroid tumors in my uterus. Fortunately, none was malignant.

Even with my doubts about being able to take care of a baby, I felt that having a child was going to be one of those miracles in life. A double miracle, really. From that one spontaneous moment in Aspen, I found myself pregnant, but also because of that moment, I had gone to the doctor and discovered the tumors, which could have been more dangerous if we had not noticed them.

I hadn't planned on being pregnant, but now I wanted this baby badly. And I would have an opportunity to test how I really felt.

Not long after the diagnosis—and there is no ladylike way to tell this—I was in my bedroom when I experienced a tremendous flow of blood. I called for Ken to come back and we were both scared to death because this was unlike anything I had ever experienced. I called the doctor, who told me to get to the hospital, and all the way over I kept thinking I was miscarrying. Dr. Roger Burris, Newt's colleague, was very concerned. He said he would arrange for an ultrasound first thing in the morning, and that I had to stay in the hospital overnight.

All night long, I prayed and tried to accept that my baby might be dead. I thought that this was a baby I had wanted so much for so many years, and then when I was pregnant, I had been scared to death. It hurt so bad just to exist, but I wanted the baby really badly, and it was hard to face that I might have lost him.

I cannot tell this without starting to cry, but the next morning when I took the ultrasound, it was the first time you could see the shape of a baby—and to me it looked like he was sucking his thumb. He wasn't dead after all. I just thanked God so much for this child. I would always regard the baby as a gift from God.

In the same X ray, I saw the tumors—one of them bigger than the baby. And I thanked God we had discovered them, too.

Any woman who has carried a baby knows that it is not comfortable. But I had performed while pregnant with my two other babies—including the night before I went to the hospital for Jaime.

This time I could barely walk. I'm a short person, but because I was active with my other two babies, I only gained twenty pounds the second time with Jaime and maybe less with Matthew. This time, I gained forty pounds, and for a one-hundred-pound person, we are talking Goodyear blimp. I did not walk, I waddled.

To this day, my dress designer, Bill Hargate, has to remember that my hips and bust are the same measurement but my waist is two inches bigger than it used to be. I guess that's part of being older, but my weight has shifted around. I have a lot of beautiful clothes I can't get into.

I could hardly recognize my shape and my face in the mirror. And I could hardly live with the pain. The added weight put extra pressure on the ankle and the knee, but it also seemed to put more strain on my tailbone. I was just so miserable that I did not know if I could stand the pain.

58
CALIFORNIA LIVING

We PUSHED OURSELVES so hard for the television show—some people would say I pushed everybody—that we all felt drained. At lunchtime, somebody would send out for delicatessen or Chinese food and we would sit around wolfing down a ham sandwich or an egg roll and trying to write a skit at the same time.

"Okay, Irlene is into practical jokes. What can we have her do next?"

We'd all be sitting around trying to invent something funny while we should have been digesting our food. Sometimes Kathy would bring the kids after school just so I could hug them. That kept me going.

We were desperate for material. It never stopped. You'd finish the show on Friday night and on Saturday and Sunday it was, "Oh, dear, what are we going to do this week?"

Plus, we were beating ourselves up physically. The dance routines were hard enough with me trying to run the whole show. Kathy used to help me count the bruises on my body, but when it got up to twenty, we quit. Counting, that is, not dancing.

Alan Siegel, my attorney, was alarmed at the way the dancers would throw me around. He figured one false move and my career was over. You know what we say in show business when we want to wish somebody luck? "Break a leg." Alan was afraid I was going to take it literally.

In our music numbers, we sometimes used tambourines, slapping them against our hips to keep time. The other performers used to wear a pad on one hip to cushion the blow, the way some baseball runners wear hip pads if they try to steal bases a lot, but I didn't, so I had the worst "strawberry" on my hip, as the ball players put it.

The physical and mental exertion started to take its toll.

There was one morning when Ken got up and found me sitting on the bathroom floor, sobbing.

"Honey, what is it?" he asked.

"I can't find a towel," I blurted, between sobs.

When you're trying to push yourself every minute, you have no margin for minor problems. No towel? Wrong mustard on the ham sandwich? Light turns red on Sunset Boulevard while you're running late? Ba-boom.

We thought we were all right when we reached the Christmas break without anybody coming apart. A bunch of us went out to Aspen to go skiing and try to relax. That was my big mistake, relaxing. As soon as I took a deep breath, the world started to spin. We flew back to Los Angeles right after Christmas and I checked into the hospital suffering from exhaustion.

I was a basket case. They put me on Valium, just to get me to relax, but the slightest thing would touch me off. One night in the hospital, I was working the remote control for the television and accidentally pushed the number past Channel Eleven and had to go all the way around again. That was enough to make me cry.

I was allowed no visitors. None. But one night a nurse came by my room and handed me a tiny tape recorder and said, "You're to listen to this." She started the tape, and it began with the *Mission Impossible* music, and the sound of a match striking, and I heard R.C.'s voice saying, "There was a nun trying to get in to see you, disguised as a girl fiddle player, but they caught her down the hall, so we asked this nurse to give it to you."

The message instructed me to go to the window on my left and look out below the street light on the far side of the street and I would see a gorilla who would give me the rest of my message. Then the tape said it was about to self-destruct, and I heard the noise.

So I went to the window, and there under the street light was a gorilla, only I knew it was R.C., who had paid a bloody fortune for this King Kong outfit. He was holding up a sign that said, "Get Well," and Louise was waving, too. Never thought I'd be cheered up by a gorilla.

When I felt better, I went back to the house Ken had rented on Rodeo Drive in Beverly Hills. I had no idea what it cost, and I'm glad I didn't. This mansion had big columns in front, an enormous atrium with trees in it, the whole house built around it. It had magnificent woodwork, antiques I could not begin to appreciate. In one of the dens, with tall windows and lush drapes, there was an old organ.

Our kids felt a little intimidated by the house. They said it felt like a museum. One night the lights in the dining room began to flicker and the organ started making booming noises all by itself. So instead of a museum, we lived in a haunted house.

The police used to patrol both the main street and the alley behind our house. One night, R.C. dressed up in the gorilla suit, sneaked in from the back alley, and went over the back fence and through the back door, just to frighten Jaime, who was about four. Jaime went into shock, but later she thought it was funny. What amazed me was that the police didn't spot him. I mean, they used to stop walkers, joggers, visitors, anything that stirred. But they missed crazy R.C.

Kathy and Matthew and Jaime were not happy about staying alone in that place, which they had to do a couple of nights a week when Ken and I would stay in the bus at the studio. Matthew was twelve, playing ice hockey and doing karate, but he felt uncomfortable in a dark, gloomy house of nine thousand square feet. When you were up in your room, you were alone.

I found out how isolated I was when my voice started to go that winter. One Sunday morning, I was staying in bed for a few hours, and I had a big bell to ring in case I needed anything. Well, I started getting frustrated about something and I began ringing the bell, and nobody heard me, so I kept shaking the bell and starting to weep in anger. Finally, Kathy just happened to be working in the next room and she heard this tiny tinkling sound, and she rushed into my room.

"Nobody heard my bell!" I rasped in a whisper, tears falling down my cheeks.

Kathy apologized and asked what I wanted. Was it a medical emergency? Did I need to contact somebody about the show? Did I have some instructions for the kids?

"I can't get my Coke can open!" I bawled.

That's how bad I was.

Beverly Hills was a bit different from Gallatin. The kids had never been intimidated by the need for security back home. They just kind of ran loose and used common sense. In Beverly Hills, you had the feeling you were in one big security area. Patrols drove up and down the streets. Anybody walking on the sidewalk was checked out. But then at Halloween, after comments that Beverly Hills was inhospitable to visitors, somebody came up with the idea of busing in kids to go trick-or-treating. All the maids were handing out candy to trick-or-treaters from other neighborhoods.

School was a hard adjustment for Matthew. Our children have always been taught to say, "Yes, sir," and "Yes, ma'am." But when Matthew answered his teachers that way in school, kids would laugh at him. I'd explain to him that this was how we expected him to talk to teachers, and not to let the other kids intimidate him.

One evening he came home and he was crying because the teacher had said, "Don't call me 'ma'am.'" I said, "Just tell the teacher that you appreciate how she feels but that your parents demand it of you. It's not because your teachers are better than you, but that they have been around longer than you, and out of respect, you address them that way."

I explained that one day he would be that age, and would appreciate being shown some respect. I never did meet the teacher, but I think Matt continued to call her "ma'am," and maybe she came to like it.

We went back to Nashville as soon as the show and school were over. Louise and I both went on the road with our bands, and she said that it was like going on vacation, just touring and playing the same show every night. We were all full of energy and high hopes as we went back to California for the second year.

We tried to make things easier for ourselves the second time around. R. C. Bannon was helping out with the music, because he knew what would work for us. He is also one of the greatest specialty songwriters in the business. A good example is the song he wrote when I was the host of a Ringling Bros., Barnum & Bailey Circus special. Later, he also wrote a duet for Gunther Gebel-Williams and me.

Because R.C. was family, there was the temptation to work even harder. He would come over to the house on Sunday, and I would still be in bed at noon, just exhausted, not even enough energy to go to church. R.C. would sit on the bed next to me and we would plan the show for a week ahead. Who are the guests going to be? What songs will they need? What instruments should we play? Here's a list. Choose this. Decide that. That would happen seven days a week, including our theoretical Sundays off. When my voice started to go, which it did early in the season, I would write notes to him. No wonder R.C. wrote the song "Family Affair," because that's exactly what that show was.

That second year, we moved to Brentwood, which felt closer in spirit to Tennessee—more open, more sky, less oppressively wealthy. We rented a one-story French provincial house whose doors all opened onto a pool. I loved it there because you could leave the doors and windows open and let the breeze come in.

We started to know our way around this part of California. Matthew had taken up ice hockey back in Nashville, and we wanted to keep him playing. Alan Thicke, the actor-comedian, knew a place where Matthew could skate. Trust a Canadian to know where there is a hockey rink.

Matthew also took up tae kwon do, the Korean martial art, and was so cute practicing his kicks in his ceremonial robe. And Louise, who has always been so close to Matthew, bought him a good pair of roller skates. On Thursdays and Fridays while we were taping our show, you'd see and hear Matthew in the alley behind the studio, roller-skating down the sidewalk.

Things got interesting for Jaime, too, when the writers came up with the idea of a weekly skit about the three of us as little girls. They found look-alikes for me and Louise but they thought Jaime would be perfect for young Irlene.

At first, Jaime wanted no part of it.

"You'd have one of those dressing robes with your name on it," I said.

She didn't care.

"You'd have a dressing room."

She didn't care.

"You could play your aunt Irlene."

She didn't care.

"Your friends back home would see you on television."

She didn't care.

Finally, I said, "You know, you'll make lots of money."

"Okay," she said, "I'll try it."

First, however, they had to hold an audition because not everybody is cut out to be a performer. The director had to see how she looked on the screen. It was just my luck that the day of her audition, the Statler Brothers were making an appearance on the show. My four adopted brothers gave me one hard time about being a typical stage mother.

At the prerecording session on Wednesday night, Kathy Brown came bursting in to say Jaime had gotten the part.

"All right, now, all of you who didn't think Jaime would get the part, raise your hand," said Harold Reid. My pal.

Jaime was very good at her regular skit, and I'm sure she would have done more acting if we'd stayed in California. Even with country music in Nashville, there just aren't as many opportunities for acting as there are in Los Angeles.

Jaime also worked as a model when a boutique wanted to use a little girl in a kind of parody of a *Vogue* fashion advertisement. Bobbe Joy and Rahn McDowell made her up, and I know she's my daughter, but Jaime looked fabulous.

To my shock, a few weeks after the ad appeared, there were a few letters and even a few articles criticizing me because I let my daughter put on makeup and wear clothes like a grownup model. They even equated it to child pornography, having a five-year-old stand there with her hand on her hip.

Where do they get this stuff? I am among the ten most conservative people in North America on a lot of issues. Love. Marriage. Sex. Manners. I could not believe it. I put on makeup when I was five years old and I loved to dress up in Momma's clothes.

What little girls don't? And I thought to myself, "I'm just sorry I wasn't lucky enough to model and get paid for a magazine ad when I was five."

I was beginning to learn the price you pay for performing for forty million people. It was different from performing concerts, because you always assumed that people were your fans, or else they wouldn't have plunked down ten or twenty dollars. You figured they knew who you were, they shared something. You were still relatively private. But when you played to forty million people, you belonged to the general public, which was a lot more diversified than I could have imagined.

We'd get beautiful letters from people, but for the first time in my life I got not only critical letters but also hate mail. You never knew who was watching. If I had a Jewish friend on the show and I kissed her, I would get hate mail from Nazi types. If I had one of my black friends on the show and kissed him, I'd get hate mail from the Ku Klux Klan. It was an education to find out that it is a big country, and not everybody agrees with everything that Barbara says and does.

But I was a big girl. I could live with that. I did not think I could live without my voice.

59

AN OLD ORIENTAL PRACTICE

I WAS PREGNANT, AND MY tailbone still hurt. I did not know how I was going to handle the constant pain.

I discussed it with David Stringfield, the president of Baptist Hospital and a good friend of ours. He is a devout Christian who prays for people when he has a few spare moments. I found out that Mr. Stringfield had included me on a list of people he prays for in his spare time—including while he is showering, which gives you an idea just how disciplined and busy that man is.

Mr. Stringfield suggested that acupuncture might be a way of cutting the pain. I had vaguely heard of acupuncture, knew it involved sticking needles into your body, and I wanted no part of that. But because my pain persisted, I decided to listen as he explained that acupuncture is an ancient Chinese procedure based on stimulating nerves by sticking very thin, very pointed needles into parts of your body.

The Chinese seemed to know points in the feet and hands and other locations on the body that reach the nerves. Many Western doctors do not accept acupuncture, but in some places in Asia it is used in place of anesthesia for major operations.

Because he is a big football fan, David Stringfield had heard about a doctor who had done some work with the Dallas Cowboys. The Dallas doctor, who is Scottish, has a clinic for the treatment of pain. Mr. Stringfield made a call, and the doctor in Dallas agreed to see me.

Even though I was pregnant, I felt strong enough to go to California to make an appearance on the People's Choice Awards. Since my flight made a stop in Dallas, it was easy to make an appointment to see this man.

I can't say I was scared at the prospect of having needles stuck in me. I had had enough pain. More pain didn't scare me. I didn't like the idea, but it didn't scare me. I remember sitting near Florence Henderson on the plane to Dallas, and telling her I was going to stop in Dallas for acupuncture. Anything to stop that pain in my tailbone.

The doctor did not have office hours on the day I arrived in Dallas, and I was just as glad to go to his home anyway, to avoid being noticed. He and his wife, who is a nurse, made me comfortable on a table. I lay on my stomach on the examining table, and he stuck the needles into my lower back. They did not draw blood or even hurt like an injection would. They were thinner than any syringe I had ever seen. He seemed to know what he was doing. But how could I be sure?

While he was sticking in the needles, he explained to me that pain could be eased by just one treatment, but that it wasn't likely. He said it would probably take a number of treatments.

We could not commute to Dallas for treatment, but we asked the doctor in Dallas if we could pay for a trip to Nashville and arrange for a visit to the Opry and some other places and he could show Dr. Jones how to administer the treatment. Up to now, Dr. Jones had been giving me cortisone shots, and also trying three little electrodes, called a TENS Unit, which gave little shocks into a local area, but I hated it and didn't think it did any good.

When he heard about acupuncture, Dr. Jones, bless his heart, probably thought this was poppycock, but he cannot say no to me, and he didn't think it would hurt me. The Dallas doctor and his wife visited Nashville and gave me a treatment while Dr. Jones observed and Ken took photographs of just where the needles were inserted. Ken took the film to a one-hour photo franchise store we owned, and developed them himself. You couldn't see whose bottom it was, but why take chances?

Using the photographs, Dr. Jones gave me several treatments in his office, but then he asked me and Ken if it would be all right if he came to our house because I think he did not want to attract a lot of attention at his office. As soon as we had the routine down, Ken destroyed the photographs and the negatives.

Who am I to know God's plan? Until I started acupuncture, I had pain in my tailbone twenty-four hours a day. After a few sessions with Dr. Jones, something wonderful happened. One morning, my tailbone stopped hurting. For almost an hour, I felt no pain whatsoever. The next day, the pain went away for two hours, then three, and then it was gone.

With me feeling better, it was easier to hold our annual family reunion, which we usually hold in July in Washington State. Since I was pregnant, we invited thirty-odd relatives to the lake for a ten-day party to honor Ken's grandmother, Esther Johnson. We had contests for tennis, fishing, horseshoes, obstacle course, you name it, and we gave prizes for everything. Pregnant and still recuperating from the accident, I was able to take part in things. The old Barbara was coming back.

How much did acupuncture help? I am not recommending it to anybody else. I am not a doctor and I do not take the responsibility for anybody else's health or treatment. I do know that I asked God for healing through prayer, and that He gave it to me. I recommend prayer to anyone. I also know that a doctor in Dallas and a doctor in Nashville performed an ancient Oriental treatment on me, and my pain went away. It has never come back, and I thank God for my healing.

60
HITTING THE WALL

THE NURSE WOULD ARRIVE every Thursday morning while I was getting made up to tape the show. Right on time.

"Excuse me for a minute," I would say, and they would clear out my dressing room.

Zap. The nurse would give me a shot of cortisone right in the backside. It was the only way my throat was going to make it through another show.

I had always known about "Vegas Throat," the affliction that hits every performer who works in the dry climate of Las Vegas. I was developing "TV Throat," the strain of trying to do a variety show once a week, and talking about it all week.

Maybe if I had been less compulsive—walk on the set at ten, walk off at four, like a lot of the big names in the business—I could have made it. But that wouldn't have been me. I was a big girl now, and I wanted control. I was paying for it in the throat.

The shot was timed so it would help my vocal cords while I was in front of the camera all day Thursday and Friday. Most of the time I was doing my best Kenny Rogers imitation, whispering conversation, whispering lyrics or writing notes, but when the taping would start, I'd belt it out.

I've seen singers cancel out of performances because of a hoarse voice but I always laughed at them. I have always been a firm believer in "singing over." Somehow I do it. It's not easy, but I do it. Like a baseball pitcher trying to "muscle it up there" on a day when he doesn't have his stuff, I would just go out there and force my vocal cords.

I had only myself to blame. I was trying to be all things to all people.

The second year began even better than the first one had. I was honored by being the first performer to win Entertainer of the Year twice. I also won my second Female Vocalist of the Year. I flew into Nashville for the annual Country Music Association show, and right back to Los Angeles again. And I had my little extras on the side.

I would give interviews to almost anybody. I would perform in charity ballgames. In the fall I would spend a weekend running a charity concert and golf tournament for homes for children in Alabama. After the concert in Montgomery, I signed autographs until the last fan went home. The next morning I strained my voice charming good old boys into donating hundred-dollar bills for a good cause. On Sunday night, they scraped me onto the plane and shipped me back to Los Angeles. I was up all night being sick, and at eight o'clock the next morning, I was back on Sunset Boulevard, tooting back at the drivers who recognized me. And I loved every minute of it. I am such a ham that I laughed at the people who warned me to slow down.

A writer came out from New York to do a cover piece for a magazine. He spent nearly a week around me, got to know me pretty well, watched the way we live, and wrote a positive article about us. The editor back in New York told him to find more "spice" about me. He called up his friend David Skepner, who was Loretta Lynn's manager for a long time, and he said, "David, tell me the worst possible thing about Barbara."

David gave a long show-business pause and replied, "I'll tell you the worst thing about Barbara. She works too hard. She's going to ruin her voice." That wasn't spicy enough for the editor in New York. She never ran the piece. We Mandrells were too wholesome for her magazine.

Sometimes life went too fast, and I was beginning to resent it. I remembered the first year, how I had been so busy that Momma didn't even tell me Grandma Ada McGill had died. They knew I had no time to get to the funeral because we performed on Saturday night and began planning for the next week on Sunday morning. So they made the decision for me.

This was the woman who had let me play the piano when I was an infant because she claimed I had musical talent. How could she have known? She was a model for me, a woman with over two hundred descendants. I had shared good times and bad times with Grandma McGill. When my uncle Ralph died, that really devastated her because not only did she lose her son, she lost her minister, too.

I sat near Grandma McGill at Uncle Ralph's funeral. His ten children were not happy he was gone, but they believed if you loved the Lord, you had gone to a better place. Uncle Ira Mandrell, Ralph's old friend and Dad's brother, preached the service, standing over Uncle Ralph's casket. He said, "As Brother Ralph always said, 'When I die, before my toes are cold, I'll be with Jesus.' " They really believe that. So for them, there are no tears shed.

But now I was sobbing when I found out Grandma had died. I was crying a lot by then, within the confines of my home, where nobody could see me. I was furious. Not at my mother, and not at Ken, and not at the TV show. Not at anybody or anything, but just at life—at being so dad-gum busy that I couldn't let down a whole company, just blow off a show. I tried to think, "Couldn't I have chartered a Lear jet?" It really hurt me.

Now it was the second year and I was still pushing myself, making myself sick. Each week I would take the cortisone shots and pills, but each week would leave my voice a little worse than the week before. We went back to Aspen for Christmas, me and Louise scribbling notes to each other to save our voices.

We all went shopping one day, and R.C. and Ken couldn't find us. They stopped to ask some strangers if they had seen a blonde and a brunette, and somebody said, "Oh, you mean the Mandrell sisters, and were they writing notes to each other on Mickey Mouse note pads?"

I started seeing a noted doctor in California named Robert J. Feder. We called him a voice doctor but his real title was "oto-laryngologist." He's handled a lot of public figures over the years.

He had a lot of practical recommendations for saving my voice: drink a lot of liquids, preferably warm, and particularly on airplanes, where the relative humidity is around five to ten percent; do not try to talk in loud places like planes and restaurants; do not try to do new things with your voice; avoid irritating habits like gargling or clearing your throat; avoid medications with mint and menthol, even the old standby, cough drops; avoid milk products before using your voice because they produce mucus; and warm up your voice before performing.

Oh, yes, he also told me to stop smoking.

I hate cigarettes. I cannot justify my smoking them. I do not recommend them to anybody. I hate what they do. You cannot tell me that my father's heart condition was not complicated by his smoking. It's absurd that he still smokes. Heart conditions are often hereditary. Lung cancer is as prevalent with women as with men these days. I think about all the people who smoked and came down with lung cancer. Edward R. Murrow. Humphrey Bogart. Arthur Godfrey. The list goes on and on.

I quit once for nine months. Thought I had it beat. Then Janice and Newt Lovvorn lost their infant son. The funeral was supposed to be for family only, but we were family, too. I took one cigarette to steel my nerves, and I was back on cigarettes again. That's no excuse. It just shows what a dreadful habit it is, what an addiction.

I know I'm going to catch flak for admitting this. People in my family are going to say, "Don't even talk about it." But it's been made public before. Someone wrote a magazine article about me, describing how I "took a sip of soda, took a last drag on her cigarette," and went out to do my show. Oh, my gracious, the flak I got. From all sides. People for religious reasons. People for health reasons. How can I be a lady and smoke?

I hate the looks people give me when I smoke. I hate thinking that some people don't want to be around me because I smoke. I hate knowing what people think when they smell the smoke in their hair and on their clothes after they've been with me. I hate thinking about my smoke getting in my kids' lungs. It is so bad. One man sent me a cigarette case, but it was filled with candies. I got the point. We ate the candies and I still smoke.

Lately, I've been playing a power game with myself. I tell myself I've got to stop smoking not because it will kill me but because it is not popular anymore. It offends people. Instead of pleasing people, you are displeasing people. It is not cool. It is ugly. I've been saying all these things to myself. I am a strong person, but I guess the key is doing it for me, just me, not to please anybody else. I know that all things are possible through prayer and faith. So why don't I stop? I guess we all have bad habits. My worst one happens to be an obvious one.

The smoking didn't help my voice. Every Thursday and Friday, the nurse would give me a shot of cortisone, which had a boom effect on the vocal cords about an hour afterward. Then I'd go down to sing. The next few days, I was given pills to come down off the cortisone, and my face would be all puffy. Whenever I play the old tapes of the show, I wince at my puffy face. Also, I had to hire a throat therapist, which was extremely expensive, just to take vocalizing exercises.

And in the end, nothing worked. My voice was getting worse and worse.

Dr. Feder was concerned. He wanted to take a videotape of my vocal cords, which was not easy because I have a horrible gag reflex whenever something's in my throat. He finally managed to get some pictures of the throat, and he called me into his office and told me, "If you don't quit, you'll suffer permanent vocal damage."

Quit? For how long, a week? Actually, he said, he meant quit the television show. Or I might not have a career. Or a voice.

He scared me when he talked about ruining my voice. He scared me so much that I quit my show.

People say, "It must have been very difficult for you to decide to give up your television show," and I say, no, it wasn't difficult at all. The doctor made the decision for me. He said give it up. So I gave it up.

I announced my decision at the Waldorf-Astoria Hotel in New York to an exclusive audience of one, my friend and my attorney, Alan Siegel. I was in New York for the Grammy Awards early in 1982 and we were having dinner in my suite. Between courses, I casually said, "Alan, I'm not doing my show anymore."

Of course, I had three years left on my contract, and we both knew it. Alan was cool. He just kept eating, and finally he said, "You don't want to do it, you don't do it. Meanwhile, your dinner's getting cold."

That's why Alan is such a good show-business lawyer. He understood that no legal contract in the world can force a performer to get out onstage and perform when she doesn't want to, when she can't. He then went out and did the unthinkable: He terminated a successful television show.

Oh, he warned me it would not be easy.

"They will threaten to take your firstborn," Alan told me, which turned out to be only a slight exaggeration. But I couldn't say Alan hadn't warned me.

Marty Krofft was horrified, and so were the people at NBC, who kept asking Alan how much more money I wanted. I guess they don't understand hillbillies. I wasn't inventing a wretched throat just to squeeze more money out of them. I was telling the truth. They kept coming back to Alan asking what my real price was, and he had to keep reminding them that there was not enough money in the mint. All we wanted was out.

They wanted proof. Alan asked Dr. Feder for a letter describing the condition of my throat, and the implications for my career. Dr. Feder wrote a three-page, single-spaced letter that included the sentence, "In reality she would be committing 'Vocal Suicide.' " When the television people saw that letter, they became more conciliatory.

I'd like to think we parted friends. I owe Marty Krofft and NBC a great deal, not so much for the money but for the chance. People will always remember that Irlene and Louise and I once had a television show, that we were funny and we made music. I can show those tapes to Nathan and he knows his mother had another life. And now The Nashville Network is running the shows on Saturday night, so they'll have a new generation of audience.

People still stop me in airports and hotels and say, "Remember the Phyllis Diller imitation?" or "Remember the pie in the face?" I say, yeah, I remember. I remember being totally exhausted and unable to talk, and I remember trying to create a show on the run, and I remember feeling the love of forty million fans. I remember them most of all.

61

A GIFT OF GOD

As THE BIRTH DATE approached, Dr. Lovvorn told me that the fibroid tumors would have to come out while I was having my third C-section. I was only thirty-six years old, and I did not like the finality of a partial hysterectomy. Not that Ken and I wanted a fourth child, but I didn't like the idea that the child-bearing time of my life was officially over.

The more I pay attention to it, the more I notice how many women have trouble having even one child. Louise and R.C. are happy they were able to adopt Nicole, but I know what they went through when they could not have a child of their own.

Given the other kinds of health problems I could have had, I probably should say, "Who am I to gripe about a partial hys-terectomy?" I used to have horrendously bad cramps, and I don't have them anymore, and I don't have to think about birth control or trying to conceive, but still . . .

Knowing that I can't have a baby, knowing that it's not my choice anymore, makes me feel sad at times. I always liked being in control of things, and now I cannot control that. I must admit there are moments now when I feel less of a woman. Some of my doctors have said to me, "At least you won't have that cancer factory inside you. It's just something else that can't go wrong. You might as well be happy." But it's a time of my life that's over. I can't be happy about that.

But I can rejoice in the blessed event of September 6, 1985—a healthy boy, seven pounds, seven ounces, named Nathaniel Mandrell Dudney.

Matthew gave him that name. He doesn't know exactly where he got it, but it was his contribution. Ken and I had wanted Matt and Jaime to feel involved with the newest member of the family, so we challenged them to come up with some good names. Jaime had Natalie for a girl and Matt had Nathaniel.

"Nathaniel doesn't sound like a name for a football player," Ken told Matthew.

"Nathan does," Matthew said.

We didn't tell anybody what our final choice was until the hospital let us show off the baby to our family. We've got a videotape of Ken holding the baby and saying, "I'd like you all to meet Nathaniel Mandrell Dudney," and Ken is choked up—it is so sweet. Jaime had been wearing a button that said IT'S A GIRL, and she walked over and pinned it on Irlene's maternity blouse, which was bulging out pretty good at the time. Except that it was a boy for Irlene that time, also.

We were all delighted with Matthew's choice of a name. Nathaniel is a Biblical name meaning "Gift of God," which he most surely was. He began in a time of sadness and pain, but right from the start, he was a vital, delightful little human being, a reminder that God replenishes the world with love and energy.

He has kept me young, made me feel important in a different way than I ever could up onstage. Nathaniel was the only one of my children that I breast-fed. When I had the first two, I was working and didn't feel I could do it. I didn't want to have to say, "Excuse me, I have to leave the stage, I have to feed the baby."

I remember asking Dr. Lovvorn if the babies would love me any less because they were not breast-fed, and he said, "I'm a bottle baby—and I love my mother." He couldn't have said anything more perfect. But this time I wasn't working, and Ken said to me, "If you want to breast-feed a child, this is it." It was a really wonderful experience for about four months, to have this tiny child so close, so dependent, but there again, God provides.

I had dreaded the moment when I decided to stop doing it. How could I face saying, "This is it, I'm not going to breast-feed him anymore"? But Christmastime was so busy, and I was having to wrap all the presents, and going over my list to make sure I hadn't missed anybody, that I would say, "Oh, Kathy, give him a bottle, I'm too busy." And by the time we got to Aspen, I had started to dry up, and by the time we got back to Nashville, he was totally on the bottle, and I couldn't even remember the last time he had been breast-fed. So there was no big ceremony attached to it.

And when I started back to work, it was amazing how I managed to integrate him into my life. Thank God Kathy Brown Shannon stayed with us through the end of 1989, traveling with me, taking care of Nathan while I was doing my show. He's getting big—hard to believe he was born back in 1985— but he's still my baby. I love being a mother, and I don't want to give up that part of my life.

Just recently, I did a show in Atlantic City and my good friends Alan and Charlotte Siegel drove down from New York to see me. There we were in a glamorous dressing room at one of the top hotels in Atlantic City—down on our hands and knees, putting together a RoboCop toy for Nathaniel. That somehow keeps it in perspective for me.

When I think how many times Ken and I discussed having a third child, it makes me realize that God has answers for all of us. For a while, Ken wasn't sure it was right for us, but all that has changed.

I know it's probably not a great idea, but Ken and I let Nathan in bed with us. We put him in his own bed at night, but sometimes toward morning he comes padding in to us, and we cannot refuse. There is something about knowing he's the last one. We just want him close to us, even when he brings food in with him. I enjoy playing Army-Navy with him outdoors, or sitting and watching old Mandrell Sisters tapes with him—even if he does think Irlene is the funniest one.

Just being with him is great. And I know Ken feels the same way. There have been a zillion times when Ken looks at Nathaniel and then looks at me and says, "Thank you."

62
TRYING TO BE
A CHAMP

My voice healed the summer after we gave up the television show. I promptly forgot what it was like to sit on the bathroom floor, whimpering because I could not find a towel. I wanted to test myself again.

I was like a heavyweight boxer who got knocked out but is confident of regaining the title. I was Muhammad Ali coming back from his suspension. I was Rocky running up the museum steps. I was going to play Las Vegas and do a show nobody had ever seen before.

We called it "The Lady Is a Champ."

My reasoning was this: doing a new variety show every week is too much work, but performing the same show for a couple of weeks, even if I did it twice a day, would be a piece of cake. I wouldn't have to think. I'd just do it. As Phyllis Diller would say: "Hah!"

We already had the expertise. I had my crew from the television show—Bobbe and Rahn, the dancers, Dennis McCarthy, my arranger and conductor, plus the one-and-only Scott Salmon, my choreographer. We would do more and better than any performer had ever done before. Las Vegas was now the American capital of live entertainment and boxing. We were going to knock the town right on its sequined shorts.

I had a fond feeling for Las Vegas because nearly twenty-five years earlier I had made my big-time debut as the eleven-year-old Sweetheart of the Steel Guitar. I had watched the town grow every time I went back, the lights glittering in the desert night, the hotels and the casinos and the restaurants.

Once upon a time, the Mandrell Family Band had hitched up its bus at Kampground of America sites at the edge of Vegas, while we played the smaller lounges. Later, I had filled in for Wayne Newton for a week at the Frontier, but that was just a friendship thing. I was ready to be booked as a headliner now. I was going to work the Strip.

I went out to Vegas to see five shows in three days—Cher, Wayne Newton, Ann-Margret, Tony Orlando, Tom Jones. I took notes, creating things in my head, things that would work for me. Scott joined me on the road and on the bus and we started going over my ideas, some of which were off the wall, but he was used to that.

One of my brainstorms was going from a serious love ballad with Randy Wright directly into a hobo number, "Just Bummin' Around." I asked Scott, "How do I go from one number to the other without going offstage?" and Scott said, "That's his problem," meaning Bill Hargate, the wardrobe designer. We both laughed. We weren't trying to make it difficult for the people we worked with. Just challenging.

Bill could do anything. I wanted to go from a love song in an elegant gown straight to a skit where I played a hobo—without leaving the stage. I mentioned it to Bill, and he and Romaine Johnston, the set designer, found a way. They had four male dancers come on, and I disappeared behind a little shack with smoke coming out from the chimney. While they danced for thirty seconds or a minute, I was behind the shack, ripping off my clothes, hidden from the orchestra and the audience, and jumping into my shabby pants and shirt for the hobo skit. It worked.

We brought in Jack Moulton, a really neat guy out of the New York theater business, who had worked with Sandy Duncan and other stars, to be our stage manager, and hired Vince Paterson, Ken Grant, Joey Sheck, and Charles Ward, four dancers from the television show. We worked for a month at the Debbie Reynolds Rehearsal Hall in California, long days, long nights. I'm not kidding about the boxing motif. I felt like a fighter training for fifteen rounds. Only instead of running and punching the bag, I was dancing and singing.

Las Vegas has become the boxing capital of North America, and I really wanted my show to be like a boxing match. I wanted it to be real. I wanted the audience so close that when I moved my head, there would be sweat flying, just like at the boxing matches. Not to be disgusting about it, but let's face it, when you're up close to performers, you realize how they sometimes spit while they enunciate their words or sing their songs. That's how real I wanted the show to be.

Some experts told me to prerecord some of my vocals, or at least prerecord the backgrounds for the numbers in which I was singing and dancing, so I wouldn't have to work as hard. But I wanted the effort to show. I hate the sterile feeling of prerecording at live shows. I hate lip-synching. I wanted the real thing. I like to hear other performers gasping and grunting. You don't mind it at the tennis matches, when Jimmy Connors puts his whole body and soul into a backhand. Why should we give less? So we prepared to do the show totally live. We had body packs—microphones with built-in power—tucked into my costumes, including an extra in case one went out. I liked it that way. I'd rather see honest mistakes than something plastic.

We left L.A. and came in to Vegas and went to another rehearsal hall at the MGM Grand, where we joined Bobby Jones and the New Life Singers, a great black gospel group that was working with me. (Early in 1984, we would win a Grammy for the gospel duet "I'm So Glad I'm Standing Here Today.")

If I were the jealous type, I would have worried about Bobby and Emily and Francine stealing the show from me, because they are fantastic: great music, great energy, and most of all, great spiritual life. People would say to me, "They're singing gospel only fifty yards from the gambling machines," but let's face it, Christians gamble. Bobby and New Life are entertainers who choose to do black gospel religious songs, but I always got such a kick out of watching people discover them.

When we first timed the show, it was two hours and twenty minutes, and then we cut it back to two hours. Aside from the Young Blades of Bluegrass doing two numbers to give us a break, and Bobby Jones doing one solo, I was on the stage full-time, and when I wasn't on the stage I was making costume changes.

As we approached opening night, I could feel myself getting more and more tired, but I assumed this was just from the physical training. I took this boxing stuff seriously. I was preparing myself to go the full fifteen. I would be in shape when the bell rang.

I don't guess I would make it as a boxing trainer. I wore myself out before the first round. All my life, even when I was running track as a kid, anything I had done was based on great physical conditioning. Sure, I abused my voice with too much work and cigarettes, but my voice had nothing to do with my body. Or so I thought.

I dragged myself through opening night, four hours of shows. I pushed myself through the second night, four more hours.

Up at noon, mope around the room, makeup at four, dressing room at six, first show at eight, second show at midnight, finish at two-thirty. Eat my first full meal and fall asleep at four in the morning. The hum of the air conditioner, closed windows, curtains drawn, wake up at noon and start all over again.

The third night I did something I hate, something I consider totally unprofessional. I canceled the second show. *Miss Mandrell is ill. Your money will be refunded at the box office.* I detested it, but I had no choice. I had bruises you wouldn't believe from the dancing—knee slides, you name it—and my throat was going. We found a doctor who started giving me cortisone shots and the pills to bring me down from them, and I'd try to do my job.

The dancers tried to show me ways to take care of my body. Somebody gave me some green powder for the bath, to heal the bruises, and maybe it worked. But there would be new bruises. Joey Sheck would stretch me for thirty minutes every night, and I'd be relatively limber while I was performing. But my over-thirty muscles would feel worse at the end of the night.

I was surrounded by family and close friends: Bobbe Joy and Rahn McDowell, JoAnn Berry and Daddy and Ken. But I couldn't talk, which meant nobody would visit with me, which kind of took away from the fun of being a performer.

My feet were swelling up worse each day. Somebody told me that if you soaked your feet in chewing tobacco, the swelling would go down. I told one of our drivers, "We need you to run out and pick up thirty packets of chewing tobacco," and he looked at me as if I was nuts, but he went out and found them.

The next question was how we were going to moisten them. I was not about to put that stuff in my mouth, so Kathy and JoAnn started moistening them with tap water and tamping them down, to make them soft. At night when I went to bed, they would pack the tobacco around my feet like a poultice, using Ace bandages. And it was true, the moist tobacco seemed to take the sting out of my feet.

There was one little detail we forgot. During the night, I had to get up to go to the bathroom. Half asleep, I trudged across the bedroom. Squish. Squish. Squish. And when I got back into bed, the tobacco started to leak into the sheets. I was so out of it, I didn't have the slightest idea.

The next morning, I was still in bed when the maid let herself in. She was Oriental and she was having this conversation with Kathy, who has this soft Nashville accent.

"What on floor?"

"Chewin' t'baccah."

Of course, they couldn't understand one word the other said. I'm sure to this day that maid tells her friends, "Ooooh, that Barbara Mandrell."

I wasn't the only one having physical problems, however. I was going offstage one night and I heard somebody shout, "Charles is hurt." He had broken his ankle during the show, and the next night we rechoreographed the routines for three dancers. Some of the musicians were looking a little glassy-eyed as we slogged toward the final round.

On the very last day, we were making plans to fly home on the red-eye. I had gone down with exhaustion before, and I knew the signs—when you're too tired to eat or to dress, and you can barely get the words out of your mouth. I felt it was time to send a warning signal.

"I'm so tired," I told Ken. "I've got to call Newt Lovvorn and ask him to get me into the hospital."

"You'll be fine," Ken said. "You just need to go home and rest."

"I'm telling you, I need to go to the hospital," I said.

I usually try to avoid doctors and hospitals as much as possible. Ask Newt, who tries to get me down for a physical every year. But for some reason, I knew I needed the hospital. I don't remember the last show, I don't remember leaving Las Vegas, I don't remember the flight, and I don't remember checking into the hospital. I do remember suddenly being very hungry, eating all the time, maybe from all that cortisone racing around my system. I remember Tim Bucek bringing me barbecued ribs one night, and how I ate the whole order, and I remember every time I'd open my eyes, JoAnn was sitting by the bed, and I remember the Statler Brothers bringing me a Christmas tree.

I was so worn down that other things would make me sad. We tried to keep it a secret that I was in the hospital, but my mind started going round and round that people would gossip if they found out. This was right after Marty Robbins and Natalie Wood had died, and I had discovered that even when wonderful, talented people die, if they're famous, if they are that horrible word "celebrities," people make jokes about it. And that bothered me a lot.

It's true, you're fair game if you're a "celebrity." I've heard my share of gossip about me and my family. When Ken and I became friendly with Steve Yeager of the Los Angeles Dodgers, you started hearing gossip that Steve and I were having an affair. We'd be hanging around with him and his wife, laughing about it, but people would repeat the story.

In Nashville, you can hear just about anything, much of it absurd. There was a rumor going around that I had an affair with one of the singers—and to tell you the truth, I was doubly offended because he was uglier than dirt. I mean, puh-leeze, couldn't it have been somebody great-looking?

The national tabloids have actually been pretty good to me—there wasn't much controversial about me until the wreck—but I have heard people say, "She couldn't possibly be as nice as she seems." And they're right. Sometimes I'm not. But it's in the privacy of my house, my room. I don't think I have the privilege of being angry or being short-tempered or not feeling well in public. So, yes, I'm not as nice as you might think I am, but my public face is not acting, either. It's another side of me. But give me a little space to be slightly different in private.

Even when there is tragedy, people want to believe the worst.

Natalie Wood had drowned near her boat, and now people were gossiping about her on talk shows. Maybe it was my run-down state, but it really bothered me to hear people talk about her that way, even though I had never met her and I was just a fan. To me, she was Maria in *West Side Story,* a great actress, a beautiful woman, and I felt I could relate to her. Here I was, in the hospital, completely spent, emotionally and physically, and it just hit me hard. What was I doing this for? People don't care.

When Marty Robbins died, I took that hard too. We used to visit backstage at the old Ryman, back when everybody was really like family. He was a wonderful singer and a handsome gent who raced cars for fun, even when he started to have heart problems. I thought he was the greatest, particularly when he sang that romantic ballad "El Paso," about a cowboy dying for the love of a beautiful Mexican woman. And now Marty was gone, too.

I'd been sick before, but this was the first time I had ever been in such a dark mood. Fortunately, after those days in the hospital, my strength started coming back. I still hadn't learned to pace myself.

As soon as I was back home and feeling like myself, I realized I wanted to get the Champ show down on tape, so everybody could see what I had done. I also wanted to bring the show to Nashville. We arranged to tape it for HBO and perform it at the Tennessee Performing Arts Center. In July of 1983, we flew in all the dancers from the Vegas show, but we used our string and horn sections from Nashville. I did a benefit for the Songwriters fund, and that sold out, and then we taped the show twice, both sellouts. As it turned out, the spotlight operators made some mistakes in the first show, so we ended up taking it from only the second show. It was just as we had done it in Vegas—with no breaks for me to change, just full-out, nonstop go.

We sold that tape to HBO, and I am proud that the show is still kicking around, because it shows what I could do at my peak of energy, with great performers from Nashville and out west. I'll always have that as one highlight of my career. I felt I was at my best. There was no reason it couldn't go on and on.

63
THE SUIT

WHILE I WAS STILL in the hospital after having Nathan, I became suspicious when the newspapers stopped appearing in my room. I started to worry when the television was cut off. And I knew something was wrong when my telephone calls started to be screened.

"What's going on?" I asked Ken.

"Oh, you can't be too careful," he said.

I thought that sounded a bit evasive, but I was having a great time feeding and cuddling Nathaniel, so I really didn't care, at first. Then I noticed Ken was staying with me the whole time and Nathaniel was under twenty-four-hour security guard.

I let it pass until I got home and found there were no letters, no cards, and very few telephone calls. I was being protected from something.

"What's going on?" I asked Ken.

"You don't need to know," he said.

I knew I was in the hospital giving birth to Nathan as the

first anniversary of the accident approached. I also knew that because of the Tennessee insurance law, in order to collect from our own insurance policy, we first had to sue the other party in the accident. But I had no idea of the controversy that was being stirred up outside my private quarters.

Nobody could know the prayers I had said for that family. Nobody could know the sadness that settled in me, a sadness I think you can detect in me today. The horror of anybody losing a child cuts right through me. I knew the White family was not wealthy, and I would never approve any plan that would have taken money from their pockets. But the legal and insurance system put us in an adversarial position. Even after I was re-covered from the accident, I was advised not to make contact with them, but I wanted them to know my prayers were with them, that I meant them no harm.

The accident had badly disrupted many other lives, too. I had huge medical bills, of course, and the children had been injured, and then there was the matter of my missing a year and a half of work. Even if I had not gotten pregnant, I could not have worked.

We had many obligations—to band members, office work-ers, household staff, people who relied on us just as we relied on them. We kept as many of them on salary as long as we could. But the bottom line was that the accident had been tre-mendously expensive, to say nothing of the human pain all around.

In the best of worlds, we would have gone to our insurance policy and been compensated, based on the expensive premi-ums we had faithfully paid. This was not the best of worlds. This was the state of Tennessee—and under state law, if you are in an accident, you must sue the other party before you can collect from your own insurance company.

We hired one of the best lawyers in Nashville, Aubrey Harwell, who explained that we had no choice but to sue. I felt dreadful being reminded that a young man had perished in the car that had strayed across two lanes on the Gallatin Pike. But Aubrey Harwell told us we had no legal option. The suit had to be filed within a year of the accident.

Once I got home from having Nathaniel, I pestered Ken

until he admitted that some people had reacted badly to the suit. Some people resented the idea of a performer suing a family that did not have much money and had lost a son.

"But we had no legal choice," I said.

"I know," Ken said, "but everyone else doesn't, and we can't even mention insurance in court. Don't think too much about it. Let the lawyers handle it."

It was easy to put it out of my mind because I had Nathaniel. Ken gave me strict orders not to look at any mail or take any calls from strangers. That wasn't hard because I was into nursing my baby, the first time I had ever done that.

One day while Ken was out, I noticed a couple of letters sitting around the kitchen. I am so used to knowing everything, to being in control of my life, that I could not resist opening a letter. I had been told there were some negative, hateful things being said about me, but I hadn't seen or heard them yet. This was the first. I was devastated.

The letter was from somebody who had been a fan-club member, had been to a number of my shows. He had saved two tickets I had autographed after one of my shows but now he had ripped them into tiny pieces. He gave me a thrashing with this letter, saying, "You're a star. The young man who hit you is dead and you're alive, and his parents are still grieving. . . ."

Ken walked into the kitchen and found me sobbing. He tore the letter into so many little pieces and he tossed it into the trash compactor, and he turned angrily toward me. I had not seen him so mad in a long time.

"I told you not to read any of the mail," he shouted.

He had been protecting me, and I had slipped beyond his protection. Since I was already upset, he went on to tell me how bad it had been:

As soon as the news was announced, people had started calling the radio stations. Obviously, some people understood the way the law worked, but there were enough callers who said they would never buy one of my records or go to one of my shows. The two Nashville papers got a number of calls and letters criticizing me. A disc jockey in Nashville was quoted as saying, "It seems Barbara has really hurt her career. Our station and others were swamped with protest calls against her." And even educated, professional people showed they had no idea of the state insurance law when they asked, "What's going on?"

Since I wasn't getting out, I had no way of knowing it, but my offices were deluged with calls and letters. People would call my museum on Music Row and bawl out the operator. People called up a chain of photo stores we owned. And people who knew that Kathy Brown worked for me gave her an earful. Daddy and Momma got all kinds of nasty stuff at their office. And they protected me by not telling me.

To be fair about it, many of the stations and papers came back with editorials or news items trying to explain the Tennessee law. Ruth Ann Leach wrote a column in the *Nashville Banner* that said:

"The people who know the stuff of which she is made understand that she is acting on the advice of her attorneys now, and if attorneys advise her later to go after the man's house, she will tell them (nicely, of course) that she will not. That nice girl became a victim one year ago, enduring pain, suffering depression, disfigurement, loss of income, and inestimable damage to her remarkable career. She still has a steel rod in her leg, and her life will never be the same. Now she's being victimized further by the Barbara-bashers."

In a guest column in the Nashville paper, Micki Nelson, a free-lance writer, wrote:

"One can sympathize with the grief of the Whites. However, when sympathy manifests itself in criticism of the victim, it becomes questionable. (One might ask if Mandrell's critics, given the same circumstances, would forgo a year's salary out of sympathy for the bereaved.) In this case, it is reasonable to question if some expressions of sympathy merely serve as masks for the antipathy toward wealth."

After I started asking questions, I found out that Aubrey Harwell had spent the weekend fielding telephone calls from at least twenty different stations and papers. He said he had tried to explain the Tennessee law, but he did not want me to discuss my case in public.

That upset me, because it was my name and reputation that were being hurt, so I asked Mr. Harwell, "Can I say, like in the old hymn, 'We'll understand it better bye and bye'?" and he said that would be all right. Then we issued a statement that tried to tell people how I felt. It read:

"I have been deeply hurt—and my family has been hurt, too—that many of the friends and fans who have made me what I am today have the wrong impressions of this legal procedure.

"I say to my fans, 'Please bear with me. Please trust me that I am doing this solely to obtain a legal judgment, not to hurt anyone.' "

In September of 1985, we thought the insurance case would be settled within a few months. As it turns out, while this book was being written, five years after the wreck, the case had still not been settled because of complications involving the insurance company.

Most people have gotten over their initial reaction. My concert and record business goes on. But because so many people still do not understand the reason for the suit, I asked Aubrey Harwell to expain it one more time:

"The whole theory behind the underinsured motorist policy is that if you are in an accident, and that person whose tortious conduct injures you is not insured, and you sue him, your insurance company steps in and defends him—acts as if they have insurance on him," Mr. Harwell said.

"There is some rational basis for the way the Tennessee law works, but it does create a perception in the public eye that is far from accurate. There is a perception that Barbara sued the family, whereas in truth and fact, that was done in name only."

According to Mr. Harwell, the White family did have a small insurance policy, but not enough to pay for the scope of our damages.

"Our position as her counsel is that she should recover for that loss, and that recovery should come from the insurance company to which a lot of money had been paid out in premiums," Mr. Harwell said, referring to the company that had insured us.

However, one of our insurance companies eventually had financial troubles and is now in liquidation in New Jersey. The company tried to claim that the policy did not include uninsured motorist coverage, but in April 1990, a U.S. District Court judge ruled that our policy included ten million dollars of uninsured motorist coverage. There is still a question of how much in net assets our insurance company has left. But since it tried to deny its legal obligations, we can only assume it has some. In the meantime, in order to recover against our insurance company, we must, under state law, sue the estate of the other driver. This puts us in a terrible position of seeming to go after the estate of a poor, young man who died.

As this book was being written, nobody was looking forward to a trial. We would much prefer that a healthy, responsible insurance company pay our legal claims. We don't want to be involved in having to bring up the details of the accident again. It could only be sad for us and traumatic for the White family. There are so many questions about why his car came across two lanes, and my lawyers feel they can prove I could not have avoided that accident. I don't want that. And I hate the impression that we wanted to take anything away from people who have already suffered so much.

64

MAKING A COMEBACK

HAVING A BABY GAVE me the courage to face life again. Feeling Nathan's energy, knowing I had the responsibility, brought back parts of the old Barbara. I could nurse him. I could lug him around. I also began feeling that I could work again.

During the fall of 1985, I kept putting off making a comeback, partially because I had gained forty-five pounds during my pregnancy. I didn't think anybody would want to see me waddle on-stage.

At about the same time, the doctors decided to take the steel pin out of my leg. They made the incision and located the pin, hooked it and pulled it out part way. At that point, the doctor is supposed to unscrew it and, bang, bang, just pull the pin out. Not so easy. Dr. Jones worked for ten minutes banging this pin but he got it out just so far and he couldn't get it any further.

He was beginning to think I would need a whole new wardrobe to accommodate this interesting-looking pin sticking out from behind my hip.

After ten minutes, Dr. Jones was so tired, so sweaty, that he had to rest. He told us later it is not unusual to have a temporary difficulty, but he always knew it would come out. To get a fresh set of arms, Dr. Jones called on his surgical assistant, Kerry Soule, who banged it out the rest of the way. It is a very interesting piece of hardware. They let me have it as a keepsake. No extra charge.

They said I would be able to bounce around now, that I couldn't do any harm to the broken bone. I was running out of excuses for not working. It would also be a good way to lose weight—work off a little nervous tension, do a little exercise.

Everybody had been telling me to make a comeback, just to prove I could do it, and Daddy had nearly convinced me right before I got pregnant. But now I did not want to make excuses. Finally, I got up the nerve.

I had been in touch with Randy Wright over the past year. I knew he was working around town, so I called him up and asked, "How are the boys doing?" He told me most of the guys were still around Nashville, but that we had lost Gary Smith, who was out in California working in television. It is always a blow when I lose a talented guy I love so much, but I had to get past it. I asked Randy if he could reorganize the Do-Rites, and he said he'd get to work on it.

Now I had to get back in shape again. Just taking care of Nathan helped take some of the pounds off. Sometime in the fall, we agreed to do a two-month tour, called the "Get to the Heart Tour," after one of my hit songs written by my friend Norro Wilson. I would make my comeback on February 28, 1986, at the Universal Amphitheater in Studio City just north of Los Angeles.

We rounded up the remaining Do-Rites, and went back to rehearsal. That's when I discovered I had forgotten the lyrics to most of my songs. They were just blown out of the memory bank. It was so bad that Randy had to write the lyrics on a piece of paper, but even that didn't jog my memory.

I would get on the phone and tell Daddy, "I just can't remember my songs anymore," and he'd give me a pep talk that my memory would come back. But it didn't look that way. Some mornings, Ken would drive me down to the rehearsal studio and I would be crying all the way. I could not remember the words to old songs like "Sleeping Single in a Double Bed." How could I go onstage?

Later, JoAnn brought a couple of my old albums, but even when I heard my own voice, the lyrics did not come back to me. I had to learn them all over again. It was an interesting process, because it made me more objective. Since I had never heard the song before, I could be critical, judging whether it was good or bad. Talk about being removed. I was so removed that I was asking, "Is that me?"

Even with the physical therapy and some sessions at the gym, I discovered I couldn't run around in high heels the way I used to. My legs had been banged so badly that I had to wear low-heeled boots just to get around the stage. I felt rusty, like a pair of garden clippers that has been left out in the rain. Ken had people design special ramps so I wouldn't have to climb any stairs onstage, and they also designed six pairs of boots with special braces in the right boot.

I had been prepared for difficulty, but I did not realize my body and my mind would be this bad. Every day, it was hard for me to go back to rehearsal. I would start crying in the morning, and I'd still be crying when I got to the rehearsal hall.

Nothing was the way it used to be. Cookie and Randy got some of my instruments out of storage and brought them out to the house. At first, my fingers did not work. The first time I faced the steel guitar, I couldn't remember anything I was doing. Somehow, I remembered a song called "Sleepwalk," which was a hit by Santo and Johnny in the late Sixties, but the instrumentals I had been doing at the time of the crash—vanished, history.

And there was real pain in my fingers and arms and chest just from trying to play these instruments. I could feel muscles I never knew existed before, all of them squeaking and groaning and pro-testing. You don't realize how complex your fingers are until you try to make them work again.

Also, my lips didn't work perfectly where I had taken some stitches. I don't like to talk about this, but there were still times when I would fall asleep lying on the wrong side and start drooling slightly, like somebody who'd had a stroke. That got better in time, but it was scary, and it did not do wonders for my self-image. It was never a problem when I was awake, when I was sitting up straight or standing, but I'd think about it, feel I was disfigured.

Then I tried to play the saxophone again. This was an instrument I had learned when I was eleven. Now I put it to my lips and I might just as well have been trying to coax sounds from a banana, like on the old episode of *Sesame Street*. The Sweetheart of the Saxophone was having trouble getting notes out of her instrument. My bottom lip that had taken the blow from the steering wheel just didn't want to blow on that mouthpiece.

With all these mechanical problems, I was afraid my skills would never come back. But there was a deeper fear, a vague, murky unspoken fear. I was afraid of making a comeback. I was afraid of crowds. For the first time in my life, I was scared to death of performing—and people.

In my life, up until that time, I had never, not once, not in any shape, form, or fashion had stage fright. Period. Never. Now it was horrible. I would find myself sweating or shivering with the chills. My stomach would be nervous. I'd have to go to the bathroom. I've heard people say that the old Boston Celtics knew that Bill Russell was ready for a big game when they could hear him retching in the bathroom. Not me. I had always been the life of the party. Motormouth. Half an hour before going onstage, I'd be making sure my guests had enough ice in their soft drinks, or I'd be washing dishes, or looking at people's baby photos. Nothing fazed me.

I've heard performers say, "Oh, stage fright gives me that edge I need to get the adrenaline pumping." Shoot, I had never needed that; I got the adrenaline pumping from hearing the crowd on the other side of the curtain.

I never had much use for people who got nervous. Now I was scared. Knee-knocking, hand-shaking, teeth-chattering, stomach-churning scared. And I hated it.

Gene Miller could tell something was wrong. Gene has always been very close to me, and he told me I wasn't feeling very positive.

"I am positive," I told him. "I'm positive I'm not going to do this show."

"Fear doesn't come from God, Barbara," he told me, and we held hands and prayed for strength. But I was not feeling strong as the day approached. Ken prayed with me, Irlene prayed with me, the whole band prayed with me, but I was still jumpy as the date approached.

We went out to California toward the end of February, and

we went into rehearsal for a few days. But my nerves got even worse. And the day of the show I was a mess.

When we got to the auditorium, I had the fantasy of tiptoeing out the back door and not appearing. I wanted to run away. But I had always been taught, to quote Daddy, a man's word is his bond. You commit, you deliver. So I could not run.

When we got to the dressing room, I received a boost of confidence because Rahn McDowell and Bobbe Joy had come over to do my hair and my makeup as a gift for me. Just having these two dear friends touching me gave me a physical boost. But the fear stayed with me.

Ken was pacing around holding Nathaniel, trying to appear calm, but nobody could fool me. They had no idea what would happen. Ken knew my memory was faulty. I was shaking worse than when I was married. The sweats. The chills. The cramps. The constrictions. You name it, I had it.

What made it worse was knowing so many of my friends were showing up to give me support. I used to love playing for other performers, whether it was Brenda Lee in Printer's Alley or one of the gang catching my concert out on the road, but knowing my friends were wearing gowns and tuxedos made me even more afraid of messing up.

Dolly was there to open the show for me, a huge gesture of friendship from a dear friend. The first time we met her, Daddy and I were introduced to her just briefly. A few weeks later, we spotted her in the parking lot of the Country Music Association offices. I was just a nobody at the time, but she chirped, "Well, hi, Barbara. Hi, Irby. How're you-all doing today?" It was like being welcomed into country music. Now she was warming up the crowd for a very frightened woman.

When she dropped by my dressing room, I told her I had stage fright. She gave it one of her East Tennessee guffaws.

"Ha!" she said.

Then she went out and did her opening number.

"I was just talking to Barbara backstage," Dolly told the crowd. "She's afraid people won't like her anymore.

"She must have been hit on the head!" Dolly added.

Everybody laughed.

(Later, when Dolly was backstage, JoAnn told her that I *had* been hit on the head, that it was much worse than we ever let on.

Looking shocked, Dolly replied: "I didn't know. I never would have said that."

Later, I remembered to thank Dolly for opening the show.

"Shucks, honey, I did it for the money," she said, waving her hand.

Then she added brightly, "I do like you, though.")

Now it was my turn. I felt I wanted to throw up. My hands were shaking. I prayed for help. But then I heard the Do-Rites roar into action, I heard the thump of the bass and the quiver of the guitar and the twang of the steel and the roll of the drums and the jangle of the banjo and the honking of the saxophone and the wail of the fiddle, and I was healed. The prayers and the friends and the music and the crowd made me well. God had given me the peace when I needed it most, at show time.

Ralph Emery, who had helped make my career in Nashville, had flown out to introduce me.

"This is more than just a concert," Ralph told the audience. "Many of you came to experience a singer. But what you're going to experience is a fighter."

Because of my stuttering, I had cue cards in the front row. Because my ankle was so weak, I had a brace built into my boot. I had no idea what was going to happen out there.

When I walked onstage, I could hear people cheering for me, could see the faces in the front row. My wits returned to me. I was home.

I worked for over an hour, singing fifteen songs and playing all my instruments. I wanted to thank people for sticking by me, and the best way I could was to give a good show. God and only God allowed me to do that. I had been afraid I could not sing or talk, but my brain worked as soon as the show began. I was even able to make little ad-libs. I was wearing a silver sweater and a silver-spangled blue jacket with blue stretch pants.

"My earrings don't match," I told the crowd. "My boots don't match. And my hair looks like I stuck a finger in a light socket. But, hey, I'm hip."

When the show was over, I was bubbling, filled with more energy than I had felt in eighteen months. The sponsors gave a great party afterward, with champagne and refreshments for guests like Tammy Wynette, Lee Greenwood, Morgan Fairchild, Steve Allen, Jim Nabors, John Schneider, Cesar Romero, Suzanne Somers, and Pat Boone. There was also a big banner that said, "Welcome Back Barbara! Sorry I Couldn't Be With You Tonight—Kenny Rogers."

Tammy brought me flowers after the show and she told people, "I made the trip to show we care. After my last surgery, I was feeling pretty down. Barbara came by the hospital in Florida and just held my hand."

Unfortunately, the show had lasted so long that we had to run to catch the red-eye to Houston, where I was giving another show the next night. I just barely had time to push through the crowd and greet some of my friends before I jumped in the limousine. If we'd been ten minutes later, we wouldn't have made the red-eye and I would have had to sleep at the airport. Rushing for the farthest departure gate in the middle of the night definitely made me realize I was back to the thrills and glamour of show business.

65
MOVING ON

W E DREW 48,266 FANS the next night in the Astrodome, a record for a live show there, and we played another concert in Louisiana the following night and just kept going through the end of April of 1986.

As far as most people were concerned, I was back, but not in my own mind. I was almost embarrassed by the shows I was giving. I had always vowed I would never resort to "my greatest hits" shows that a lot of performers do—let the crowd cheer them, and take the money. Daddy had taught me long ago that to give the people a good night out you've got to give them lights and costumes and action and hard work, not just music.

I could no longer jump around like Mary Lou Retton. I definitely favored my right leg, and I couldn't bring dancers or Las Vegas choreography into my shows. I was back to just being a singer, not an entertainer, and I knew the difference. Half the time I referred to that other performer in the third person. "She" was Barbara Mandrell.

I just didn't have the energy I used to have. I used to go out onstage after each concert, thousands of people, and I would sign autographs. I would just pull up a chair and sign until everybody else went home. The longest I ever did was for four hours. I chose to do it. I would think, "Those people have stood there all this long time just to get me to sign my name on this picture or book. They're the ones who are really giving." At least I had a chair and they were standing. But after the wreck, JoAnn and Louise and some of the guys just flat out told me I could not do it anymore. I could not do four months on the road, really hitting it, if I had to sign after each show. I hate to have limits placed on me, but I had to stop signing, and I hoped my fans would understand.

Another change was that I could not drive a car. I hated that. I resented that I depended on Ken and Kathy and my parents. I resented that accident because it took away one of my freedoms.

I used to get in a car by myself, just me, and just go. I'd have someplace to go, but it was my time. Turn on the radio, laugh, sing, talk to myself, pray, take stock of my life, just look around. That wreck took it away from me.

Even when somebody else was driving, I'd be fidgeting and twitching the whole way. Danny Wright was now the only driver I trusted handling our bus. He had other things to do with his life, but he more or less stayed on as a favor to me. He was very conscious of my fears, and he was very careful and smooth, but sometimes when somebody else caused him to brake real fast, I would go, "Uh," and flinch. But knowing Danny was at the wheel gave me the luxury of being able to sleep.

To this day, I have no recollection of that car crashing into me, but for a long time, whenever I saw an oncoming car at a certain angle, I instinctively flinched. There must be something in my subconscious that remembers.

Ever since the wreck, whenever I am furnished with a limousine, there must be seat belts on the passenger seats. If there are not, I will refuse to ride in the car. I just can't help it.

There was something else I missed: reading. I used to curl up with a book at night before going to sleep, but now I could not concentrate on the printed word. Just could not focus. I assumed it was from the head injury, but that didn't make me feel any better about not reading.

At least I was back performing and meeting great people. That had started even before my comeback tour, when I was invited to The White House for a State dinner for the Peruvian president. I was nervous about going, but as soon as we arrived we spotted Nancy Lopez, the championship golfer, and her husband, Ray Knight, the baseball player, who are one of the nicest couples we have ever met.

The four of us wanted to sit together during dinner, but we were all given cards for different tables. My table was right up front, and I looked around to see who would be sitting with us, and there was Mr. Reagan himself, standing up to greet me.

"Oh, my," I said.

Ken took one look at where I was headed, and he repeated, with emphasis, "Oh, my!"

I was so nervous being at the table with the President that I tried to catch Ken's eye at his table. Instead, I saw Vice President Bush, who blew a kiss at me. He represents Houston, the city where I was born, and he is a real country music fan.

When we were leaving, one of the military escorts told me the President wanted to see me. I said it must be a mistake, because I had just been sitting with the President. The escort said, "No, ma'am, it's not a mistake." So we walked back to the President, who told me, "I want you to know, when you were hurt, Nancy and I prayed for you." I was so in awe of the President putting his hands on my shoulders and looking me in the eye that I forgot to thank him for calling Ken at the hospital.

I am not a political person, but I try to judge people on how they appear when I meet them. Mr. Reagan knew exactly who I was, and what I had gone through. The man had been shot while President, and he had undergone serious operations, yet he showed his concern about other people.

Because I am a woman, I reserve a special place for female heroes, or heroines, I guess you'd call them. My first heroine was Minnie Pearl, of course, but now that she's my girlfriend, that puts her in a different category. So I would say I have four heroines who are not from country music.

One of my idols has been Corrie Ten Boom, a Dutch writer who often explored spiritual values. I once read a beautiful book of hers called *The Hiding Place,* about how she was imprisoned during the war, and how she had been horrified at being put in a building just teeming with bugs. But when the German soldiers rampaged through the camp, they did not come near Corrie Ten

Boom and her people because they were staying in this disgusting
building. So she learned to give thanks for everything God gave
her—even bugs.

Not too long ago, I gained another idol. Right after the dinner
at The White House, I wanted to give a special present to Louise,
who loves history and collects autographed photographs. I was at
a benefit for Ronald McDonald House, which helps families with
very ill children, and Mrs. Reagan was there. I took a chance and
I asked her if she could arrange for the President to autograph a
photo for Louise. She smiled and said she would take care of it.

Three days later, it was announced that Mrs. Reagan had to
go in for breast surgery. She had to have known that day we met
that she was facing surgery. Had to. But she was so pleasant you
could not tell anything more was on her mind than raising money
for charity and getting me an autographed photograph of her husband. I had never seen her look so beautiful. Shortly after that,
her mother died, and I just figured, "She has so many things to
worry about, I won't even think of that photograph again." Guess
what. A few weeks later, the autographed photo arrived. In the
middle of everything else, Mrs. Reagan had taken time for my
little request.

I also admire Barbara Bush, who, after her husband became
President, was gracious enough to invite us into the actual living
quarters of The White House, to see her needlepoint rug and
meet Millie, her springer spaniel. Did you know that three Secret
Service men take Millie for her walk on the White House lawn?
Mrs. Bush asked me to call her by her first name but I can't. I tell
her, "You're my First Lady."

Another heroine I met in recent years is Eunice Shriver, who
does such a marvelous job for the Special Olympics she helped
to start, along with her husband, Sargent Shriver. She is a Kennedy,
of course, and has such amazing spirit, considering all the troubles
that family has had. I met them at several benefits for the Special
Olympics and eventually they invited me and JoAnn Berry for
lunch in the Senate Dining Room.

They were so gracious, so fascinating, and yet down to earth.
They could tell we were just a couple of country bumpkins, gawk-
ing around at the senators and their guests, and finally Mrs. Shriver
said, "Sargent, tell them about the history of this room." He said,
"I can't even get the waiter to bring me another cup of coffee."

We just roared. They did give us a great tour, and recently I was able to reciprocate by having them as houseguests.

When I realized I was not stuttering anymore, I started to do interviews again. It was difficult if I suddenly had to remember a name or a song title. It was scary how much was gone, but I had to try it.

I had been interviewed by the best in the business—Jane Pauley, Ted Koppel, Ralph Emery—but when I agreed to an interview with Barbara Walters, I was frightened. I knew she had ways of getting you to open up, and I did not know if I could handle it.

The crew came to my house, and I was shaking, but before the cameras ever got set up, she just chatted with me and wrapped me around her finger. We talked about our children, just girl talk, and she was so warm and compassionate that she really got to me.

Plus, I was a fan. I had been watching her for years, seeing how sensitive she was with other people, and now she was fixing her warm, hypnotic eyes on me. Maybe I was vulnerable, just coming out of that terrible time, and for the first time I let somebody get to me. I was not the little stinker I ordinarily am.

When the cameras got rolling, Barbara got me talking about things I wouldn't ordinarily talk about on the air. She asked me about my fears that I would never be well again, about my loss of memory. She even got me to talk about my fights with Ken, how I had yelled at him during my pain after the accident. I had always wanted the public to assume that everything was always a hundred percent ducky with Snow White and her husband. But there was Barbara Walters getting me to admit that sometimes I fight with my husband. At no time did I feel cheapened or used. My defenses were down, true, but I didn't say anything I didn't mean. The fear left me when she interviewed me. With no disrespect to anybody else: Barbara is the best.

Being able to give interviews was one sign I was back in the world again. But in many ways, I had changed irrevocably. I used to be able to scoot around the tennis court. I didn't know dink about hitting the ball, but as for getting from one place to another, I could. Now, because of my ankle pain, I just couldn't move as well as I used to, and I had to conserve my energy, but considering there had been a time when I didn't know if I'd walk again, I was grateful.

I was particularly grateful when I saw the car. That took some doing. I did not want to be reminded of the wreck in any shape or fashion, but I had volunteered to do a public-safety commercial for seat belts, and I felt it would make a stronger impact if I was filmed alongside the car.

The wrecked car has been placed in Irlene's museum in Pigeon Forge, Tennessee. One day, I went out with Ken and the kids and had my photo taken standing next to the thing. As hokey as this sounds, when I saw that car, I wanted to get down on my knees and pray, and I probably would have if my knees had not been shaking so much.

I could not believe that car. Not so much the broken glass and the twisted metal. That was only the exterior. When you look into the driver's seat, there is no room for the driver. No space for legs. I saw where I had been, and what it looked like in there, and I knew that for the rest of my life, when something hurts in my knee and my ankle, I will say to myself, "But I am alive," and I still have my feet and legs. And I will thank God for that.

We did the commercial, and I did a few interviews about how we happened to be wearing seat belts that afternoon. And in the months to come, I began to get awards from organizations like the American Seat Belt Council, the states of New Mexico and North Carolina, Vanderbilt University, and the Benjamin Franklin Literary and Medical Society, all for my work promoting seat belts.

From lobbying for stronger seat-belt laws, I got involved in organ donorship. You know, in case you die suddenly, the little card in your wallet that gives doctors the right to use your organs for transplant to the living. I used to be squeamish about organ donorship, thinking, "Oh, no, I'm not going to be lying on some operating table in bad shape and have somebody decide I'd make a good organ donor." That's what I thought. But I learned they cannot do anything without your signed permission, and obviously not until they know you have died. Besides, your doctor is not the same doctor who does the transplants.

For me, the crucial factor was when our preacher, Mike Nelson, needed a liver transplant. But I've heard of other people needing kidneys or other organs. When I had questions, I went to Vanderbilt, the great university in Nashville, and told them I wanted to do something to raise money and to make the public more aware. First I talked with Dr. Ike Robinson, and he introduced me to Dr. Bill Frist, a heart-lung transplant surgeon, who happens to be a pilot, along with his wife, Karyn.

I told Dr. Frist that I would be the "celebrity" who could get on the tube, and he would be the expert. Together, we could get a lot done. We went on the *Today* show and the *Larry King Show* and all the other talk shows, promoting a celebrity softball game, using people like Ralph Emery, Dick Clark, Bob Costas, and Paul Shaffer as announcers, and we helped raise half a million dollars for the cause, and Bob Hope was my opposing guest captain.

I became a good spokesperson because I had the zeal of a convert. Nowadays people tell me how their lives were saved by seat belts, and I hear stories about people who could not have lived without their organ transplant. Maybe I've helped somebody the way Louise saved me.

66

OUR NEW HOME

NOW THAT I WAS performing again, I tried getting back into the old rituals with friends and family, playing with my animals and being Mrs. Kenneth Dudney, suburban housekeeper.

Although we loved living around Gallatin, things were not quite the same since the wreck. During my recuperation, I had gotten nervous because people could drive right up to the fence and look down into our house, just fifty yards across the lawn. Privacy had never been a big concern of ours before, and now it was. I felt I was living in a fishbowl.

I began to wish I could go outside my house without hearing some tour-bus announcer say, "THERE'S BARBARA NOW! SHE LOOKS PRETTY GOOD CONSIDERING WHAT SHE'S BEEN THROUGH!"

We loved sitting around on our boat at the marina Daddy and Momma owned. The local people knew us and treated us like ourselves, but country music was such a tourist attraction that they would run buses out to Old Hickory Lake.

Daddy told me that one tour guide had said, "Barbara's father owns the marina, and he bought it just because Barbara has this boat, so she would have a place to keep it."

I told Daddy, "Swell. You're sure charging us enough money to keep it there." Which was the dad-gum truth.

When you are in the public eye, you hear so many stories about yourself. Daddy was at a music convention not too long ago, and he was standing near this big old state trooper who didn't know who Daddy was.

"You know, that Barbara Mandrell must be an awfully good person," the trooper said. "She bought a marina up at Old Hickory Lake and gave it to her father."

And Daddy told the man, "I wish she would make the payments."

You learn to laugh at the stories people tell, but after a while you just wish you could walk into a convenience store and buy a quart of milk without having to think about not offending people. Also, you wish you could talk to your husband in public without people listening to your every word.

I always worry about what people will think of me. I don't like going into a parents' meeting at school and having heads turn. In that setting, I'm just a parent, no different from anybody else. I don't like being judged because they see my name in a commercial.

But people make judgments as if you are some different species of life. I used to be convinced that our veterinarian was standoffish because he thought I was acting like a celebrity. But one time my St. Bernard was giving birth to puppies, and Ken was away on business as a state pilot, so I asked Dr. Shannon if he would be there when she went into labor. "No," he said, "she'll know exactly what to do." Ken had even built a whelping crib and left diagrams about what birth would look like, and I started to read frantically.

Brandy kept crying, and I asked my mother-in-law to call Dr. Shannon, but he said everything would be fine. Finally, I shouted, "It's not like the pictures. There's a foot sticking out!" She yelled out that I had to pull that puppy out right away. I pulled it out, but it seemed dead until I tried artificial respiration. There, in my hands, it came to life. It took a breath. When Dr. Shannon arrived, he found me on my knees, giving mouth-to-mouth resuscitation to the sixth puppy, and only the seventh died. Ever since, Dr.

Shannon has been my pal because I think I showed him I wasn't any big deal, just a lady who loves dogs.

We had a lot of adventures in that house, a lot of good times, before the accident. The house itself was great, with all our toys and rooms, and even a separate trophy room for everything the fans had given me. When I opened my museum on Music Row, I felt it was important to put most of the trophies where my fans could see them. We literally took the carpet off the floor and bought the same wallpaper and used the original light fixtures and furniture and piano and just moved all my awards straight from the house.

Moving the trophy room gave me the feeling we could move our entire household. The two older children were going to a good Christian school, a long drive from our house. There were always extracurricular activities over there, so we started to look for a place closer to the school, to cut down on our driving time.

When Ken was flying his helicopter north and west of Nashville, on business with our friend Ron Cook, he spotted a quiet hillside, back behind a farm, where it looked like you could build a house. My girlfriend Janice Lovvorn, who works as a realtor, consulted the topography maps and real-estate surveys and drove Ken into the Whites Creek area.

They stopped near a road marker on the main highway that said: *March 25, 1881. W. L. Earthman, magistrate, Davidson County, arrested Bill Ryan, alias Tom Hill, member of the James Gang. Living in the Edgefield Neighborhood. Frank and Jesse James and Families left Nashville area the next day.*

Hey, if it was good enough for the James Gang, it might be good enough for the Dudney and Mandrell Family. Janice discovered that we would have to buy everything including the woods and the farmhouse and farmland. I've thanked God so many times for that because while the farmhouse had only two bedrooms and one bathroom, it's on the historic register and it's so old and wonderful. We made the deal, and built two more bedrooms in the attic, with closets all the way down the hall and another bathroom upstairs, and we moved into the farmhouse during Matt's senior year of high school, while our new home was being built.

It was wonderful. I have such great memories of being together as a family, being healed from the divisions brought about by the wreck.

One of the customs of Matt's school was that every week a parent of one of the football players would take them to a restaurant for dinner or have the team to their home. I chose to have a sit-down dinner for thirty-odd people in that little farmhouse. I rented tables that were only eighteen inches wide but six feet long, and I moved around my furniture in my little living room and dining room and I cooked spaghetti.

For dessert, I made snowballs, a family specialty, made by literally scooping vanilla ice cream with your hand and making a snowball and rolling it in coconut that you've just roasted. You set it in a bowl of hot fudge and then go to it. The boys loved eating the snowballs almost as much as I loved making them.

Another weekend, Jaime brought the cheerleaders over and I fed them, too. And little Nathan was in the middle of all this activity, getting the feeling of being part of a big family. That little farmhouse reminded us that we enjoy smaller quarters, like the tents we use when we go camping out every summer, and that we surely could live with less if the big bubble ever burst. We had started very modestly, and we hadn't changed that much.

At the same time, we were one of the extremely rare families that ever get to plan a dream house. How can I talk about our new house without sounding like I'm bragging? I cannot. I just hope my friends will understand the hard work and even a bit of the suffering that went into this luxury.

Matthew had always loved the idea of a log house. I used to say, "A log house? Get real," because my taste runs to lovely, formal, fancy, pretty things. Over the years, Irlene and Ric had also talked of building a log house, and I used to humor them by saying, "Oh?" or "Really?"

But my mind had changed after we'd had that log home built for Ken's grandmother out in Washington State. We had realized just how much you could do with logs.

One thing people often ask about log houses is, "What about fire?" Well, I watched a demonstration before I believed it. They made a square pile of about six feet by six feet and set fire to the logs. After six hours at 1800 degrees, the fire had just scarred the edges. The logs don't burn anywhere near as easily as a regular house. But to make sure, we decided to put in an automatic sprinkler system, just like hotels have.

I wanted a few luxuries like an indoor pool, because I think

Nashville is often too hot or too cold to enjoy an outdoor pool. I also wanted a large dining room and a separate area we could call "the great hall," where we could entertain up to a hundred people or so once or twice a year. I also wanted the house to have the feeling of a ski lodge that we enjoy so much in Aspen during the winter.

We gave these ideas to an architect named Seab Tuck, of the firm Tuck Hinton Everton of Nashville. Ken told him we wanted the house to be at least 15,000 square feet, and he told us that a home that size did not exactly come in a kit. He wound up traveling to Montana to see other log homes.

After we made all our specifications, Seab wound up designing a six-bedroom house that was 27,000 square feet. Well, we were close.

The house would be set on the side of the hill, with nothing but woods above it and on both sides, and facing the private road coming in from the main highway. The architect designed a brick base, with glass and logs aboveground. There would be an entry-way from the back, higher up on the hill, with wings on both sides, one for our eating and sleeping areas, one for our entertaining and recreation.

The logs would be hand-crafted, not machine-made, and I requested that some of the cambium be left on the outside, so you can see the darker colors with the light. Some of the logs in the swimming area would be thirty-six feet high, and because of the height of the house, they were at least ten inches wide instead of the normal six to eight inches. They built the rooms up in Montana and then disassembled the logs and put them on semi trucks and hauled them clear across to Nashville. When they got here, they had to cut out all the windows and doors.

There would be plenty of security on all sides, and we even have state-of-the-art closed-circuit cameras around the house, so I know what Nathaniel is doing at every moment, and we have an intercom to buzz the kids down for supper. In back we built a helicopter pad for Ken, and off to the side we built an elaborate playground and jungle gym out of logs for Nathan. We put a shooting range in the basement because marksmanship is a great sport.

We've let our kids try everything from pistols to rifles, and we even have a .357. Daddy held it in Nathan's hands and let him fire it in our range, figuring it would scare him with the heavy concussion and the blue light flashing out the front. We keep most of our guns locked up in the range, of course, but we do keep a pistol in the house for protection.

Recently, I moved it higher to keep it away from Nathan, after a good friend of ours was killed when his pistol accidentally hit the floor and fired, and he bled to death before he could get help. But I still defend my right to have guns around the house.

I hope people don't feel we are preoccupied with guns. I think the focus of our lives is indicated in the unique name we came up with for our house. When Nathan was born, Ken and I heard the word for the soft spot on a baby's head. Knowing how soft and sweet a baby's head can be, I fell in love with the name, and that's how our new home came to be named Fontanel, in honor of our three children.

One of my favorite treasures in the hall is the skin of a tiger named Sibra that was preserved when he died—a gift from my good friend Gunther Gebel-Williams. I had gotten friendly with Gunther and his wife, Sigrid, the first time I was the host of the Ringling Bros. Barnum & Bailey Circus special. We found we had a great deal in common, although I tell all my friends in country music, "You think we work hard? Circus people work around the clock."

He must constantly examine his equipment and the animals, because lives depend on it. If Gunther does not get the proper pecking order for the tigers, there's no telling what will happen. When that circus travels to cold places, Gunther will get up at three in the morning just to make sure the heat is on. He'll sleep with the animals if there's any doubt.

Gunther knows how much I love animals. He always has his animals preserved when they die, but this was the first time he had ever given a skin to anybody else. I had a plaque made with Sibra's date of birth and date of death and other information about him. We hung this memorial of a great animal in our great hall.

Another of my favorite decorations is a series of ten acrylic boxes of butterflies. It's particularly dear to my heart because now that we live back in the woods, and I'm driving along my driveway, there are many times when you cannot even ride on the golf cart or the car ever so slowly without stirring up many butterflies.

I love the statues of bears built out of the logs. The artist, a man named Jim Rogers who lives in Montana, does them entirely with a chainsaw. And then he sort of burns the bears a little with a blowtorch to make them darker. I can't believe it's done with a chainsaw.

One thing you'll notice is that there are very few indications that this is the home of a country-music performer. No pool in the shape of a guitar, no musical notes engraved on the front door, no trophy case in the living room. This is the home of Mr. and Mrs. Kenneth Dudney of Nashville. There is a painting of me holding Nathan the night that we had him dedicated (promising to raise him in a Christian home), but you could not tell I am a performer. I try to separate my work from my home life.

We also built cabinets for the service for twelve of Wedgwood china, black and gold, that we started buying in England just a few years ago. It's never been imported to America, so whenever we want to expand the set, we contact the store in England and have it shipped. Two years ago, I didn't have any silver, and some friends bought us place settings to celebrate our twentieth anniversary.

It took us a long time to care about things like china and silver. We were so used to traveling that we usually ate out of cardboard boxes and plastic dishes on the bus. I just wish I used the stuff more, but we still live mostly in the kitchen, eating great meals. I recently bought fifty pewter dishes for the pool area rather than use breakable dishes.

I kept saying we would do some fancy entertaining as soon as life settles down, and I finally got Eunice and Sargent Shriver to visit us in September of 1989. They flew down on a Saturday and we had a dinner party for eighteen people. Right, you guessed it. My Wedgwood service for twelve just wouldn't do for eighteen, so I had to borrow china from a friend of mine, Argie Oman. Momma and I set the table for dinner, although I did have help from a caterer and a florist. And I cooked three other meals in those two days, and made banana boats, my own version of banana splits.

The Shrivers were great houseguests. They made themselves at home, particularly after the dinner party when Minnie Pearl and a few others stood around the piano and started an old-fashioned songfest. After some of the guests had to go home, Eunice was tired and went to sleep—but Sargent came back down in his stockinged feet for a few more songs. On Sunday morning, we went to mass with them.

It was an ecumenical weekend, because on Friday we nailed up the mezuzah, a small box containing a copy of a prayer in Hebrew, which Jews hang up to bless a home and family. Alan and Charlotte Siegel, who had given it to me, were touched as we prayed before putting it alongside our front door, where it will always remain.

I enjoy having company because it reminds me that our house, with all its bathrooms and its toys, was designed for family living— usually right in the kitchen.

It feels like home, but I admit I sometimes get scared when I look at our heat bills and our electrical bills. They are higher than what I used to earn when I was starting out. Maybe I shouldn't even be talking about this, because it sounds like I'm bragging about how much money I make, but there's part of me that says it can't last.

Maybe someday we'll turn the house into a lodge, rent it out to rich people, and we'll live in a log cabin on the property. We live like that every summer. I could live like that again.

67
CHANGES

WE TRIED DESPERATELY TO get the house built before Matthew went off to Abilene Christian University in the fall of 1988. I thought it was important that he got to live in it, to feel, "This is my house, this is my room," instead of going away and coming back and feeling, "Gee, nice house you have here, Mom and Dad." We just made it, and I was grateful for that. He seems to enjoy it every time he comes home, seeing what else was done.

One thing I had to learn was that nothing remains the same. My accident threw things off, but also, people grow and change, whether they are teenagers or the older generation. You look around and somebody is different from a year earlier.

I had always maintained that I kept a fine balance between being a family person and a career person. I always insisted I gave fifty-fifty to each, but after this horrible knock on the head, I saw plainly that I hadn't been fifty-fifty. I had been closer to sixty-forty, in favor of my career. Now I promised myself that I would turn it totally around.

So I tried to stay home more, only to discover that my two

older kids did not need me in quite the same way. Sometimes there were days when I despaired of things ever being the same between me and the kids. Everybody who has teenagers says that's normal, that one day they just start growing up and having their own ideas, wanting their own space. But when I saw it happening, I couldn't help but blame the wreck.

Matthew will tell you he stayed clear of me for a long time, and I cannot say I blame him. I was not fun, I was not nice, I was not the mom he had known. Before the wreck, I always had energy for playing games, for having fun. Sure, I was a strong disciplinarian, I demanded a lot, but I also felt like I was still a girl, their oldest sister as well as their mom. Now I was mostly definitely Mom.

Is a teenage boy going to choose to be around somebody who's going to yell at him—or gush over him—and he'd never know which it was going to be? I think anybody who cannot control her emotional state is out of hand, is a nut. I couldn't control it. And most of the time, I just didn't care.

But a lot of that separation would have happened anyway, perhaps at a different pace, and it is always difficult for a parent to understand and accept it.

Matthew began having interests of his own. From playing ice hockey and practicing tae kwon do, he began to play defensive end on the high-school football team. He is not only a great marksman but most of the reading he does on his own is gun magazines, to the point where he is an expert.

He also learned to drive a car and fly an airplane. For obvious reasons, the driving scared me more than the flying, but I couldn't exactly lecture Matthew on the dangers because I didn't want to spoil his initiative.

Once Matt had his driver's license, he bought a truck with money he had saved, but when he was graduated from high school we took his truck and bought him a Volvo because we had seen a survey saying it was the safest car in an accident. We still worry. Parents always do.

You worry about one stage of growing up, but then you see another stage that makes you happy. Matthew came through the problems after the wreck and settled down at school. Then toward the end of high school, he surprised us by picking up a guitar and learning to play. Matthew had always steered clear of music, for obvious reasons, because music was what the Mandrell Sisters did. Matthew Dudney had his own life, and more power to him. But I always felt he had an ear for it, and I was curious, not ambitious.

At Christmastime, we were doing a television special whose premise was that my bus broke down on the way home and I was stranded with Nathaniel and my instruments. When we brought the bus back home, Matthew was helping me unload some stuff and he picked up the mandolin and he said, "Show me something." I plucked the introduction to "Christmastime's A-Coming," and in only five minutes, Matthew played it back for me. I was amazed.

We had never forced music on the kids. Jaime had taken piano lessons for all of six months. I should have said, "You want it, I'll buy it, you will stick with it," but I didn't do it, like my parents would have done. Now when Matthew expressed interest in wanting to learn to pick, I requested that Lonny Hayes give him private lessons once in a while. I was impressed how quickly Matt picked it up. Later, when he went off to college in Abilene, I played a benefit down there and we did "Dueling Banjos," with me on banjo and him on guitar.

Matt says he doesn't want a career in performing, and he insists he does not have a good singing voice, so I guess that answers that. But if he does choose anything in music, perhaps in the business end, at least he'll know something about what it takes to coax music out of an instrument.

I'm sure he doesn't want to challenge his mother and his aunts. Music is tough. It's hard for me to wish that kind of a career on my children, although I wouldn't trade my life for anything. Times are different now. We didn't have that much, and we did what we could. My children will have options that we didn't have. Still, I have to be careful not to discourage them. I've learned that kids need to dream.

My point is, you really have to want it. There has to be a certain kind of desperation, a drive, to make it in show business. Sometimes it works. You look at Kirk Douglas and Michael Douglas. Nat King Cole and Natalie Cole. Carl Reiner and Rob Reiner. I tell my kids, "There's no higher moment of elation than in show business, but there's nothing lower, either."

Jaime has some growing to do yet. She is the reader and the student in the family, often tucked away in her room with a book. But she is also active in school activities like cheerleading. We didn't realize how seriously she took it until we wanted her to go on a family vacation to Hawaii, and she didn't want to miss some games at school. Finally, Louise brought it to our attention that Jaime had other interests now, and we worked out a compromise. But it's hard for a parent sometimes to let go, to realize your child has another life.

Fortunately, Nathan is still young. I love having him with me on the road, seeing him bounce up fresh and happy every morning. And I still have somebody to play with. When Nathan was three, I brought him along to Ralph Emery's show, *Nashville Now*. Ralph knows that Nathan loves the puppet Shotgun Red, who appears on the show, so out of the blue, Ralph called Nathan out and introduced him to Red. Nathan was so natural on the show, just chatting away with Red. He couldn't have cared less about me and Ralph. They gave me the videotape, and I'll always treasure it.

We have to guard against him being spoiled. I don't want to turn him into a professional son, so to speak, and we have to make sure he doesn't get his head turned by all the fans. Everywhere I play, particularly at the music halls during the warmer months, the fans congregate near the bus, bringing us fresh corn on the cob and fresh fruit, even though they know I'm too busy to come out and thank each one. If they happen to see Jill and Nathan going for a walk, it's their way of being nice to me by chatting with Nathan. It's like having a huge extended family all over the country, but I want to make sure he remains Nathaniel Dudney. He's going to have to make his own grades in school, make his own friends, find his own career. I want him to stay his own man. Fortunately, there are signs that he will.

When Nathan and I are home, we go out in the woods and we play war. Just to show you how I've mellowed, sometimes I even allow him to be an Army man instead of a Navy man. It's the only subject I allow him to argue with me. I've done hundreds of shows for the Army, but let's face it, I love the Navy even more because I was a Navy wife.

I hate to admit it, but I try to brainwash the poor little kid. We have built this elaborate playground set in the woods below the house. When Nathan gets on the swing, he asks for an Army takeoff, I sort of push him easy, but if he asks for a Navy takeoff, I go through the whole clearance procedure Ken showed him: finger in air, thumbs up, elaborate signals. Then I take hold of the swing and push it as high as it will go. I say, "That's a Navy top-gun takeoff." I know it's sneaky, but that's the way it goes in the old service rivalry game.

This is one macho kid. Nathan absolutely adores his brother, and he knew Matthew was a football player in high school. At college, Matthew went out for cheerleading, which requires the same strength and agility and spirit, but Nathan has never seen male college cheerleaders. He just associates them with girls. When we told him, "Nathaniel, Bubba is a cheerleader at college," he just wrinkled his nose, he was so horrified. We tried to explain to him, but he said when he got to college, "I'm going to be a football player and I'm gonna wear a helmet, and nobody's gonna know who I am." He is so macho, so tough. I wonder where he gets it.

68

MY TURN TO FLY

I HAD A NEW CHILD, a new house, and a reborn career. I was ready for some new thrills. I had followed Ken's two hundred and seventeen landings on a Navy aircraft carrier, and now I wanted one of my own.

It seemed kind of backward, wanting to land on a carrier, because I was still afraid to drive a car in public. I had resumed driving on my own land but I just wasn't comfortable out on the highway, knowing my life could be jeopardized by something beyond my control.

But there I was, pestering somebody for a ride onto an aircraft carrier. Well, it made sense to me. I wasn't exactly naive about service flying. Back when we were doing the television show, when I was totally fearless, I had requested a flight through some of my military contacts, and was put in touch with one of the great pilots in the Air Force, Colonel D. L. Smith of the Thunderbirds, the famous precision flying team.

I'll never forget our first meeting. Boss (as the Thunderbirds always call their leader) Smith staged a briefing with a lot of press people, and then he said, "All right, everybody, just me and Mandrell." When we were alone, he said, "Everybody's gone, forget what I just told them, this is the way it is." And he told me things like, "The red knob on your ejection seat, you don't hit it until I tell you." A real straight guy. He was in charge, my life was in his hands, and that was fine with me. We raced around the sky, doing intricate high-speed stuff, and Col. Smith became one of my heroes of all time.

(About three months after Boss took me up for a flight, a bird flew into his engine and then the ejection seat didn't work—the kind of coincidences that are supposed to never happen. But they did, and Boss Smith was killed.

To this day, when I see a cumulus cloud formation, I think of Boss Smith playing in those clouds with me sitting right behind him.

When he died, we did a benefit show for his widow, because service benefits aren't all that great. The Air Force Academy choir appeared on the show and its leaders agreed to donate the fee to Mrs. Smith. The wonderful A.F.T.R.A. union insisted on collecting a percentage for union dues, but Marty Krofft, bless his heart, made up the difference.)

I had loved the mixture of speed and control, living on the edge. Now, even though I was terrified of the amateur drivers out on the highway, I sought a flight with the Navy flying team, the Blue Angels. They assigned me to Lieutenant Commander Curt Watson, who had been a great football player at the University of Tennessee.

He scheduled the flight for May 30, 1986, but we met on May 8 at Pensacola, Florida, during the filming of a Bob Hope television show. I got to talking with Commander Watson, and he told me his sister is a Navy pilot. I thought that was great until I heard that women pilots are not supposed to get into combat. I thought that was ridiculous, because who is better at fighting than women? It's like my lawyer, Alan Siegel, telling me there are more women than men in law school. I said, "That makes sense to me, because we're so good at arguing."

The first time I met Curt Watson, I told him I would love to actually sample precision flying during our scheduled flight. He looked at me kind of poker-faced and let it pass. Then I confided in him that my ultimate goal was to take off from a catapult on an aircraft carrier and to land on a carrier the way Ken had done.

I said I had been offered a chance to land on a carrier in a cargo plane, but I wanted the real thing, taking the wire in a fighter. He didn't think there was much chance, but he suggested I take the Navy pilots' emergency training, so I could tell the authorities that if, God forbid, something should happen, I would know how to survive during an ejection.

They started me off in the pressure chamber to learn how to recognize hypoxia, which is disorientation from lack of oxygen to the brain. We went from there to a simulated ejection seat, showing me where to put my hands and my head. Then they took me outside and hung me on a parachute and showed me how to unhook it. Then they put me in this enormous indoor pool, where you hook yourself into a parachute and you're pulled into the water, facedown, and you've got to turn yourself over and unhook yourself before you're pulled to the other end of the pool. I only had seven or eight feet left when I did it, and I was worried that I didn't do well, but the guy in the pool said, "We had a guy take eleven times yesterday. Don't worry about it."

Then I trained in the Dilbert Dunker, which gives you the experience of escaping from a cockpit, strapped in, upside down, underwater. I had loved everything else, but I will admit I had a moment of panic that I was going to die. I could see the Navy diver right outside the cockpit, and first I thought, "They wouldn't let me die," and then I thought, "No, you survived that awful crash and now you're going to drown in a Dilbert Dunker." But I unhitched everything, and got out, and I felt proud and macho.

I felt even better when Ken returned to the carrier after being with Matthew on his sixteenth birthday. Matthew had always wanted to drive a car for the first time to his solo flight in an airplane. I knew everything was all right when I saw Ken holding up the end of Matthew's tie, which had been snipped off in the traditional ceremony following his first solo. Then I went out and did the Bob Hope show that night. Not a bad day's work for the family.

Three weeks later, Curt Watson met me in Knoxville, Tennessee, and took me up in the A-4 and performed some of their great maneuvers. Ken had told me, "Barbara, if he asks you if you want to try it yourself, you say, 'Yes, sir!' " I remembered that, and he walked me through it. Finally he said, "Okay, you've got it." He let me take the stick and do a couple of aileron rolls and a loop. I loved the twists and turns, flying upside down, sharp angles, watching the earth getting smaller and suddenly getting bigger again.

Curt had another thrill saved up for me. When I had asked if it would be possible for us to fly in formation with his teammates, the way he does in air shows all over the world, he had given me a kind of noncommittal answer. After we had been up for a few minutes, all of a sudden, another Blue Angel A-4 showed up alongside, seemingly just a few feet from our wing. Curt had apparently arranged for his teammate to "happen" to be up for a little solo work at the same time we were. The boys don't normally do precision work with guests, because of the weight differences and the informality of it, but this was not precision flying. This was just a friendly meeting in the sky, if you see what I mean.

We flew alongside each other for a few minutes, enough to get the feel of just how closely those jets work. Oh, I loved being up there. I looked around for the recruiting slip, so I could enlist in the Navy, but nobody offered me one. I would have volunteered to be a passenger with Curt every day, but I didn't think I should ask.

Of course, now I was really hooked. But when I inquired about flying a jet onto a carrier, I was told there was just enough danger involved that the Pentagon would not want to take a chance with somebody in the public eye. If something happened, it would be bad publicity.

It's funny how these things work out. Two years later, I was performing at the Greek Theater in Hollywood in 1988 and was visited by my dear friend Gene Miller, now working as a singer in California. Gene was with his wife, Susan, and casually mentioned that her father was Rear Admiral Richard C. Macke, who was at the time the commander of Carrier Group Two.

"Susan," I asked, "could I please have a talk with your daddy?"

She called ahead for me, and I asked, "Did he say a flat no already?" She said, "No, he sounds interested."

When we finally talked, I told Admiral Macke that I had already trained with the ejection seat, the parachute, water survival, plus I had flown with Curt Watson of the Blue Angels and

Colonel D. L. Smith of the Thunderbirds. I had even been a Navy wife. I had done it all except take off and land on a carrier—my ultimate goal.

He was so nice to me. Here was this admiral in charge of the fleet, but finally he said, "I've got to check with my boss." Everybody has a boss. When he got back to me, he said it was possible. At first he said they didn't want publicity, but then they asked if I would be willing to do a press conference, with a Navy photographer. Not only would I do that, but I volunteered to bring my entire show on board to entertain the sailors.

On the day of my flight, December 14, 1988, we arrived in Norfolk, Virginia, by bus. I reported for my preflight exam. They have female pilots, but the medical people still had to scurry around and say, "Hey, guys, don't come in here right now, there's a woman being examined." When I passed that, they fitted me for a flight suit and the tight G-suit that goes under it. It was really snug, from a female Navy pilot who must be tiny.

Admiral Macke did not entrust me to any other pilot in his fleet, but he insisted on flying me himself. I was totally in awe of this man. I see how some people feel they have difficulty talking to me, because I am a so-called celebrity, but imagine how I felt talking to him. He's an admiral, in charge of aircraft carriers, he's a pilot, and he still flies. I said, "My word, you're everything that I want to be."

We sat at his desk for a while as he took out diagrams and drawings of the plane and began to explain it to me. I noticed the beautiful model of the F-18, which he later sent to me as a gift, right off his desk. Admiral Macke also told me that he had never flown a passenger in the F-18 before, and he wanted to prepare me. He told me what I would see in the cockpit, and he gave me a checklist and said he wanted me to participate.

When I left his office, Ken and JoAnn were still there, which made me worry because I wanted them to be on the carrier when I landed. But right after I kissed 'em and hugged 'em, they were put on a small prop plane for the short ride to the carrier. Then Admiral Macke and I got on the F-18 and he taxied out and checked out his instruments. I was supposed to adjust my oxygen mask and head set and sun visor and I couldn't close it with one hand with flight gloves.

He was ready, and he had clearance for takeoff, but I said,

"Uh, Admiral Macke, I can't get my oxygen mask back on, and I'm trying." I could think of all the sailor-hours I was taking, fumbling with my mask, but he was relaxed about it, saying, "Just let me know when you've got it." It seemed like an eternity until I got it, but I did, and he just turned it around and off we went, so bad and wonderful, the sun shining, but high gray seas, like in the war movies, and these gray carriers.

When we got up high, it hardly felt like we were going fast, just this real floating feeling, but we were actually going about 520 mph, heading for the carrier, the U.S.S. *Coral Sea*. That was our target.

All of a sudden, he said, "Look out the starboard side," and I saw an F-14, much bigger than the F-18, and then I saw another one on the other side. We flew in formation for a little bit. They came up and flew in formation along our wing. We zoomed down toward the deck of the carrier, not much bigger than a football field, and we did one wave-off, where the deck crew signals you to keep flying. Because the seas were high, the back of the ship was doing almost a figure-eight formation, fishtailing around, and we weren't lined up right, so he got a wave-off, which bothered him, but it happens to everybody.

We circled around and did one touch-and-go, where your wheels touch the deck but you blast off again while you still have enough power. Then we came around, and he asked me to talk to the ship, saying, "I have the ball," and all the other language they use, and they waved us in. For somebody who was still afraid to drive on the Tennessee highways, I felt a real sense of security as this great pilot aimed the plane toward the deck. I knew it would work, and it did. The nose felt very stiff, no shock absorbers, and they call it a controlled crash on that narrow space, but I felt the wire catch underneath and jerk us to a stop.

While we were landing, I could see this huge crew, average age nineteen, handling something like eleven planes on and off in forty-five seconds per plane. Land, taxi, take off. Leave it to the performer, but I was having trouble with the microphone on my helmet, so they shut down one engine and sent an electrician to crawl up to the cockpit to adjust the microphone, and I was very happy to see the electrician was a woman. There are a lot of them on deck, and I doubt they had time to engineer a woman just for me, not with all that other activity going on.

We taxied around, and they gave us a signal, and boom, we

were gone, shot out of there, from zero to a hundred and seventy miles in three seconds, something like that. The plane does all the work, and then the pilot takes over. Like a bullet, the most forceful thrust. We made four cat-shots and five arrested landings, and then it was over.

We climbed down from the F-18 after that final trap, and I must admit I felt sad because it was over. Ken joined me and gave me a hug, and then he said, "They don't do this for everybody," and I could hear them piping me on board, blowing their little naval whistles, whoo-ee, whoo-ee. We were greeted by the captain of the U.S.S. *Coral Sea,* Captain Ed Allen, who said that he had been on the U.S.S. *Independence* with Ken many years earlier.

I enjoyed meeting all the other pilots, these guys who fly off those decks nearly every day. They told me it never gets old and they said sometimes they can't believe they get paid for it. They all knew about my crash, and one of them said he heard I still wouldn't drive a car. I said, "Yes, it's true," but I would fly with these guys anytime.

One thing I realized from being on that carrier was how very few people in the Navy ever get to fly. The enlisted man who interviewed me for Navy television kept saying how much he'd love to fly in one of those things, and I kept thinking to myself, "Barbara, you are a lucky stiff." Then he added, "But you deserve it." I didn't know if I deserved it, but I knew I had just had one of the great moments in my life.

During the ceremony, I was standing in my G-suit with Ken standing right beside me. I told him how much I respected him for being able to do what I had just seen Admiral Macke do. It took so much training, so much knowledge, so much skill. I felt so good just standing there in that flight suit, feeling pretty macho, the tight G-suit underneath, the zippers, the famous mark on my nose that used to turn me on so much when Ken had it, all those years before.

Then I remembered a conversation I had with Ken when I was a Navy bride. Because I loved everything about the Navy, I used to pester Ken with questions about everything he did. One day I had asked, "Try to describe to me what it's like being shot off the carrier."

Ken had told me, "If it would last about three seconds longer, I might be willing to give up sex."

Now I had finally been shot off an aircraft carrier. In the

middle of our welcoming ceremony, I whispered to him, "You know what, Ken? I'm ready to give it up now."

That night, we slept in the captain's quarters, these fantastic accommodations reserved for visiting dignitaries. I could see Ken looking around, checking it out, knowing that he had given up this life so I could have my career.

"This could have been mine," he said softly. "I could have done this."

"I know," I said. "I'm very grateful for what you did."

I tried not to show how much I was affected by what he said. The way he was going, he might have been captain of a carrier like this. I don't know that I could have given this up for him. He must love me a lot.

When we were ready for bed, Ken started to get amorous. Remembering what he used to tell me when we were first married, I said, "Now, Ken, you know I'm a Navy pilot and my life depends on being sharp. I can't do this. I have to get my sleep." I had waited twenty-one years to drop that line on him.

69

FOUR-OH

JUST AS MY BIOLOGICAL clock sent me signals to have our third child before it was too late, my birth certificate started sending me messages, too. I looked up and I was turning forty. Four-oh.

Yeah, ha-ha, I told my audiences. I had always wanted to be forty. In bust measurement, not years.

Forty? I hated it. Somebody said, "Wait till you hit fifty," but I hate forty enough as it is. I hate to get back to that stupid wreck again, but it seemed that I was just thirty-six and one year later I was forty. We were at Aspen when the terrible event took place, and Louise made a beautiful big birthday cake, and she gave me a gorgeous pair of earrings, very expensive, pure Louise. I said, "Louise, that's beautiful, but don't expect me to do this much when you turn forty."

She and Irlene and Momma were so sweet, telling me how good I looked, when my daughter, my beautiful wants-to-be-a-model twelve-year-old daughter, said, "Well, you know, you are getting wrinkled." I told them, "You know, if I look in the mirror and I don't smile, it doesn't look as if I have wrinkles, but if I smile, it looks like the Grand Canyon." For the rest of that evening, whenever somebody made a joke, Louise and I would go, "Ha-ha-ha," and we wouldn't smile.

You know, youth is so important in this country. Unwrinkled faces, skinny girls, it's the way things are supposed to be, it's pounded into our heads. Some women are most beautiful as they mature, with wrinkles, but you're always being reminded.

Even onstage. My fans like to give me gifts during my show, and I'm honored, but the other day a woman handed me a T-shirt with something printed on it. I read it out loud to the audience: "Forty? I Demand a Recount." That ticked me off, and I kept thinking about it for the rest of the show.

It was too late to lie about my age. Since I had started off as the eleven-year-old Sweetheart of Steel in the summer of 1960, it would be hard to come around now and say, "Ooops, we made a mistake, I was only seven."

Besides, it's an honor to turn forty. There were a few months there when I didn't think I'd make it. I'm all for surviving.

One thing happened before I reached forty. The old Barbara Mandrell returned to the stage. Since my comeback in February of 1986, I had been getting by, singing my greatest hits. I had avoided playing the Las Vegas night clubs because I remembered the sprightly young woman who used to bounce around there.

But Bally's kept persisting, so finally I said yes, under one condition: "I'm not going to use the orchestra. I'm not going to do any big deal, just my concert show."

To be perfectly honest, I was doing it for money. It wasn't that we were poor, but I felt responsibility to a lot of people, so I decided to come out to Las Vegas and do my "concert show."

We drew people, they were appreciative, but I was downright ashamed of myself. It was as if I were two people. One would go out onstage and sing. The other would stand back and say, "Who is this? This is not Barbara Mandrell." Professionally, I was a critic, and that critic was saying, "Borrrr-ring." That was the turning point. That is when I started getting all the adrenaline pumping for becoming the old Barbara, at least as a performer.

In January of 1988, I had a tremendous mental healing. Boom, just like you see in the cartoons—the flash of lightning, the light bulb going on. I said, "We are going to have a new show next fall, with props and production numbers, like the old Barbara Mandrell."

Starting in August, I put a new show together, beginning with me pushing a jukebox across the stage—it was the one-hundredth anniversary of the jukebox, and I was just your basic blonde stagehand. I carried four sets of four different costumes, with every show including one change onstage, going from a tuxedo to another outfit underneath it, while I was standing behind a prop, singing at the same time.

We brought back my old "Lady Is a Champ" routine, a Fifties number with me strutting around in a miniskirt singing the old Aretha Franklin song "School Days." We put stairs back in, so I could climb up to jam with the house orchestra. We put in stained-glass windows so I could do a gospel medley. Oh, yeah!

We took all the lights and props in a truck on the road with us, and I started doing that show every night in theaters and hotels and auditoriums. When I ran off the stage, huffing and puffing and tired, I'd say, "I'm proud because *they* really liked it." Then I felt I had really earned my money, and more importantly, that they had given me an hour and a half of their time. That is a compliment, too.

I was living up to the challenge Tom Collins once made during a recording session: "Barbara, would you want this to be the last song you ever recorded?" Well, I could live with my shows in the fall of 1988. Each one of them could have been my last, and I would have been satisfied. And that got me to thinking.

My father had told me not to let that accident beat me. He told me to make a comeback, to prove I could get back to where I was. In the fall of 1988, "she" was back. I was back. It was as if the two people merged, the younger Barbara and the older Barbara.

I had done it. I could prance around onstage in miniskirts and give praise to God and my doctors and the marvels of costumes and makeup. But now there was nothing more to prove.

I hope some of my colleagues take this the right way, but I never wanted to be running around the stage forever. Maybe it's the wrinkles or losing a step or developing a new scratch in the voice, but I don't think some women look great trying to perform after they reach a certain age.

Just when I think I'm ready to pack it in, though, there is a new season. In 1989–90, we put in sensational new lights and props, and I started doing a couple of old ballads, "The Very Thought of You" and "The Nearness of You," with the Do-Rites providing a very classy pop-jazz accompaniment.

One friend of mine from New York says my cigarette-flavored voice would sound great doing old ballads in a night club at one o'clock in the morning. Some people have suggested I could go in a new direction, performing more pop songs, more standards, either in high-class concert halls and summer stock or in clubs, but I don't think that's me.

I've thought about acting. I did one television movie, *Burning Rage,* back in 1984, which by some twist of fate was shown right after the wreck. I played a geologist from Washington, D.C., who is sent to a small town where a fire is raging in an abandoned coal mine right under the town. My character falls in love with the local fish and game agent, played by Tom Wopat from *Dukes of Hazzard.*

I had never really acted before, and I had forgotten something that actresses have to do: Kiss. I love kissing, but only with my husband. Now, in front of a couple of dozen actors, actresses, camera people, technicians, directors, you name it, I had to kiss a handsome man who happened not to be Ken.

My reaction was natural for a novice. I started giggling. Every time poor Tom put his face next to mine, I would giggle like an eleven-year-old. We wasted a lot of film of me going, "Tee-hee-hee." When Gil Cates, the director, called a break to give me a chance to get my act together, I called Tom Wopat into the back room and said, "Tom, could you come here? I need to do something." He said, "What?" and I planted a real one on him, and we walked back in the other room, and everything was fine. I had to get beyond it.

I learned a few things from making that film. Gil Cates is a great director, but there were a couple of times when I didn't exactly agree with my directions, and because I was new to acting, I just did it the way I was told. When I finally got to see the film, I realized I had been right, just little things, but it taught me that the next time I would not let anything go. I thought I did a good job acting, but the accident put my acting career on hold for a while.

Recently I've been thinking of it again, but I have never found the right feature film. Scripts have been submitted to me over the years but most of them were full of profanity or sex or violence. There are a few movies that make me think, "I wish I could have been in that." One of them was *Seems Like Old Times,* with Goldie Hawn. I could never have done it as beautifully as she did it, but her character loved animals, and I would have enjoyed that so much. I swear I'm not a prude, but the only thing that would be acceptable to me would be something I would want my children to see.

I know that if a couple of guys are fighting, one of them is not likely to say, "Oh, golly, gee whiz, darn, you make me so mad." I know that. When there's a purpose for a character to do something, sure, I understand, and that's acceptable. But not when the makers of a film have chosen to "embellish" a script. That offends me. But I'll find the right role someday, I hope.

Not many people know that a couple of big-time Broadway producers tried to get me for *Annie Get Your Gun.* I love Broadway shows, and I love to visit New York, but I live in Tennessee. I keep hearing from the Broadway people but I just don't want to commit myself to being away from Nashville, to give up sitting on my porch, to give up playing with Nathan in the woods. I really am a country girl.

My experience with our television show told me that the next time around I want to be resurrected as a producer. I've always said I was an officer, not an enlisted man. Momma says it's been that way since she went to her first parent-teacher conference in first grade and the teacher said I would definitely grow up to be in charge of something. Well, what about a television program, or a major network or film studio?

The only thing wrong with that is that most television is based in Los Angeles, and I'm a Nashville girl. Or at least that's what I said when my children were younger. Who knows?

Maybe I'm looking forward to staying home, doing nothing when I feel like it, cooking supper when I feel like it, being there when the older children need me, playing with Nathan.

"You'd go wacko at home," says George, the man helping me write my book. "Ask anybody who's ever been on the road— ball players, performers, politicians, writers. You think you want to have a normal life, whatever that is, but after a few weeks your body starts to twitch, and you feel like you should be heading where the action is."

My girlfriend Minnie Pearl says, "Once you've gotten used to it, you can't give it up." She's a few years older than me, and she's still performing, but on the other hand, she chooses her spots, and she finds time to play a mean game of tennis and relax at the club and do other things around Nashville. Sarah Ophelia Colley Cannon knows how to live. Maybe I'll be as smart as Minnie.

Right now, I am so busy making records and commercials and giving shows that I resent it. I don't have time to go for lunch with my girlfriends, or get together with my sisters and their husbands, and I don't like it.

Sometimes I find myself asking, "Why don't we tell people when we feel love for them?" The reason is, I'm too busy on the telephone with a business deal. Then I get off the phone and try to make up for it by telling people I love them, and maybe they're busy by now.

Maybe it's time for me to help Ken instead of the other way around. He recently started a business building log homes. He could use a wife at home. He's been there for me, both in my career and in my recovery from the accident, and maybe it's time I was there for him.

I always said Ken deserved an award for doing what he did for me. He finally got one. I gave it to him in public.

Every year, the Patricia Neal Award is given to a few people who overcome physical obstacles, the way that great actress fought back from a stroke. A couple of years ago, I was honored at the same ceremony as Jim Brady, President Reagan's press secretary, who was shot during the assassination attempt in 1981 and has fought back from serious head injuries.

When I was called up to the podium, I realized I was proud to be a symbol of overcoming serious obstacles, and I wanted to show that people can do amazing things, but I was overcome with this feeling that nobody can recover on her own. We all need help. And there was somebody else who deserved this award.

Without thinking about it in advance, I said: "I accept this award for my husband, Ken," and I gave it to him.

I told people that Ken deserved that award for helping me

through my crisis. It takes quite a man to do what he did—not leaving my side, babying me, nursing me, putting up with my abuse when I treated him like dirt. I've apologized to him a thousand times for the way I acted, particularly during those early weeks when I was out of it.

"Please forgive me," I have said. "I have no memory of doing it, but I'm sorry."

Displayed prominently on Ken's desk at home is a set of porcelain roses—the Patricia Neal Award. It's got my name on it, but it belongs to Ken.

One thing I have learned from my injury: I hope I die before he does. I never leaned on him before, but now I cannot imagine life without him.

On the other hand, I depend on Ken so much that I resent it. It's just the way I am. I have always taken pride in my independence, but now I have been through a time when I could not have lived without him.

We fight more than we used to, and when we fight, I get truly mad at him because he is tougher than he used to be. He's gotten more like me. It would have been better if I had gotten more like him.

Nowadays, when we get into an argument, Ken will say, "Well, you're still not yourself."

Aaaagh. That just makes me furious. It's almost the same thing as saying, "You're some nut who just happens to be visiting this house."

My point is, "Don't blame it on my head getting hurt. This is the way I am now and that is the way I was then. Don't use the accident as an excuse. Let's stick to the nitty-gritty of what we're fighting about, but don't blame it on my brain."

It's not just Ken who does it, either. My father, the man who gave me my career, has said: "You'd have to be as close as I am, but her personality today is not what it was before the accident. Before, she was easier to convince, and I think she trusted people's ability or their word more than she does now. Nowadays, if she thinks it's this way, then that's the best way, period."

It's true, my memory is not as good as it used to be. But I think that flaw is sometimes used against me when we're having a difference of opinion. I know they're being protective, but I want that to end. They do it out of love, but I don't like it. I'm enough "me," if you will, that it upsets me and angers me when they think my brain ain't all there.

It's a fact of life that I changed rapidly in a couple of years. Maybe I became more set in my ways—which made me exactly like Irby Mandrell. I was always going to be like Daddy. I just got there sooner than I might have expected.

The old Barbara used to be more impulsive, more spontaneous, more optimistic. That was her and this is me. And that's okay. It's okay that I depend on Ken because that's the way I am now. She didn't—but I do.

It's true. I'm different. But the way I put it to my family is: You loved me before, I would hope and pray you will love and accept me the way I am now.

EPILOGUE

THERE WERE STILL A few frontiers.

Like reading. Ken gave me a giant-print Bible, and I was able to focus on that for a few minutes at a time. Then Bobbe Joy gave me a novel while we were shooting a Bob Hope special in the Bahamas. It was a real good book but I only made it through four or five chapters and then I quit. One time in Las Vegas, Mike Jones, my steel man, gave me a novel by two Navy pilots and I read it in two days and was sorry it was over.

That told me I could focus on the printed word again. I began to listen to people who had been telling me to tell my story. There isn't a word in this book that I didn't speak and read and edit, over and over again. You know me by now. I am a perfectionist.

The other frontier was driving. Nathaniel is going to be small for a long time yet, and I wanted to drive him to school, take him places, but idiotic drivers still petrified me. At Christmastime in 1988, we were going shopping and somebody pulled out in front of Ken and I started screaming. I couldn't help myself. Ken said, "Barbara, you're upsetting the children," but that's how I felt.

My Dad's right, although he's not a psychologist. He said, "Even though you have no memory of the wreck, there's got to be something there."

I wasn't going to let it beat me forever. Sometime early in 1989, I needed to drop down to Ric and Irlene's house, just off our property. I'd been up and down our private road, but not on the main highway by myself. This time I made sure Nathan was all right with Kathy, and I just turned the key in the car and drove down to Irlene's. It was stupid because my license had lapsed, and I probably wasn't insured, but it was only for a few seconds, and I had done it.

At Easter week, Ken's brother Don and his wife, Joan, were in town, and we were driving around, and I decided to drop off and apply for my license. There's no road test, no big deal, you just show your old license and get a new one. It was not a great time for me to practice my driving, so while Ken was at the wheel, I picked up the car phone and called Daddy and Momma.

"Guess what I just did!" I announced to Daddy.

"You just got your driver's license," he said.

How did he know? I had given him no hint. But he always knows.

I started practicing by myself, a minute or two at a time, just dropping down to Irlene's house. Then one morning I had an appointment at Tom Collins's office, down near Music Row. I said I would drive by myself.

"If anything happens, if you get scared, call me and I'll come get you," Ken said.

But I negotiated the interstates, and when I got to Tom's office, I called Ken and he asked how it went.

"To tell you the truth," I said, "it's like everybody's out there to get me."

I am much more aware and defensive than I used to be. It's true. Everybody *is* out to get you. They don't know those are lethal weapons, those automobiles. One day, a van pulled onto the highway, right in my path, on a two-lane road. I had to go to the left but there was a semi coming alongside me, so I had to squeeze back into my lane fast. When I got to Tom's office, I was sobbing. But I kept going. Now I come home in rush hour, and I'm fine. I've got my independence again. No telling what I'll do next.